Russia's Rogue Masters

Konstantin Savitskii, *Waiting for the Verdict* (1895), oil on canvas. The State Tretyakov Gallery, Moscow, Russia. Photo © Fine Art Images/ Bridgeman Images. This room in the Moscow court building was used for routine criminal trials. Note the sparse decor, the large portrait of the tsar behind the judges' table, and the evidence table in the center with the obligatory carafe of water. The jurors are out, with the court bailiff waiting to let them back in. The prosecutor is standing in the center of the room looking at the defense lawyer, who is seated at the podium, the two locking glances as if continuing their contest. The two defendants are sitting next to the podium behind a cast-iron grille, guarded by two gendarmes. Some of the spectators are in the foreground, the two women most likely being a defendant's family members.

Russia's Rogue Masters

ELITE CRIMINAL TRIALS IN THE AGE OF REFORM, 1866–1884

Sergei Antonov

Yale UNIVERSITY PRESS

New Haven & London

Published with assistance from the Kingsley Trust Association
Publication Fund established by the Scroll and Key Society of Yale College
and with assistance from the foundation established in memory of
Philip Hamilton McMillan of the Class of 1894, Yale College.

Yale University Press books may be purchased in quantity for educational, business,
or promotional use. For information, please e-mail sales.press@yale.edu (U.S. office)
or sales@yaleup.co.uk (U.K. office).

Set in Adobe Garamond Premier Pro type by IDS Infotech Ltd.
Printed in the United States of America.

Library of Congress Control Number: 2025947412
ISBN 978-0-300-25317-7 (hardcover)

A catalogue record for this book is available from the British Library.

Authorized Representative in the EU: Easy Access System Europe, Mustamäe tee 50,
10621 Tallinn, Estonia, gpsr.requests@easproject.com.

10 9 8 7 6 5 4 3 2 1

MIX
Paper
FSC
FSC® C183721

To Katya and the little ones

Contents

Introduction

Sergei Witte, renowned statesman and architect of Russia's capitalist modernization in the late nineteenth century, was also a convicted criminal. In 1876, early in his long career, he was sentenced to four months' arrest as one of the railroad executives responsible for the horrific Tiligul train crash near Odessa. More than 350 people were killed or injured because a portion of the track was disassembled for repairs during a blinding snowstorm. While Witte himself had no authority over repair crews, he had failed to ensure that the train had enough brakemen, that the repairmen used signal petards, and that the engineer maintained a safe speed. Poor safety procedures were endemic on hastily constructed Victorian-era railroads, and even the tsar's own train would derail in 1888. Negligence by nineteenth-century corporate directors or executives tended not to be punished severely, when at all. But the public outcry after the Tiligul crash forced the tsar's ministers to make an example out of Witte and his immediate superior, Admiral Nikolai Chikhachev. To show that these elite individuals were fully subject to the law, the government ironically had to tinker with legal procedures after the state prosecutor (one of whose deputies was Witte's brother Boris) refused to try it before a jury in Odessa. Instead, the case went to nearby Kamenets-Podolsky (Kam'yanets'-Podil's'kyi), where juries had not yet been introduced and a conviction was more assured. Much later, Witte remembered the period of 1875–1876 in Russia for its "spirit of hatred toward persons who stood out from among mediocrities because of their station in life or material prosperity," adding that "this ... sentiment [now] governs socialists and anarchists ... but at that time [it] ruled the entire educated liberal stratum."[1]

Witte exaggerated only slightly. Legal scandal became endemic in late imperial Russia following the landmark court reform of 1864, which introduced public, oral, and adversarial criminal trials with juries and professional lawyers.[2] Highly publicized criminal trials were a signature feature of post-reform Russia every bit as much as the great realist novel, wars in Central Asia and the Balkans, railroads, or revolutionary terrorism. Scandalous and spectacular cases were exceptionally frequent in the 1870s, after which the wave of landmark cases slowed down and their main models (such as the murder trial, the provincial trial, the forgery trial, the political trial, and so on) had been established. To be sure, routine criminal cases were rarely discussed or even reported.[3] But a small number of trials attracted extraordinary attention from the press, top attorneys, and courtroom spectators. Poor individuals occasionally found themselves in this spotlight, but Russia's legal Olympus was populated almost exclusively by defendants who were wealthy or socially prominent.[4] These included such colorful characters as the aristocratic forger Mother Superior Mitrofania, the banker and child tormentor Stanislav Kronenberg, the millionaire arsonist Stepan Ovsiannikov, and the French-born accused poisoner Margarita Jujean, along with dozens of other accused murderers, swindlers, and forgers.[5] The few cases in this set with lower-class defendants were presented to the public using images and vocabulary otherwise reserved for elites. Any digression into popular jargon during the trial was liable to be met with laughter by the attending public. Even the jury trial itself was originally conceived as an elite institution with property and literacy requirements; in practice, peasant participation turned out to be considerable in rural areas, but even there about one-third of all jurors were not peasants.[6]

Taken together, prominent criminal trials in late imperial Russia amount to a vigorous, though highly selective, campaign of public shaming of the rich and powerful administered by the reformed judiciary and by the press. The stories told in the courtroom and the events they purported to describe focused on the upper classes, explicitly and sharply scrutinized their fundamental qualities, and questioned their fitness to control their dependents, whether many or few. The trials publicly articulated and discussed many of the "questions" that agitated late imperial society, initiating the debate four decades before the upsurge of public culture at the turn of the century. The range of issues covered was impressively thorough, from abuses inside a patriarchal family and honor violence to political sedition and misconduct by newly emergent large-scale corporate business, to name just a few.

The very idea of criminal justice presupposes that at least occasionally members of the ruling class are called to account for their transgressions, since otherwise the law would "legitimize nothing, contribute nothing to any class's hegemony," as E. P. Thompson observed. But the mass of Russia's laborers and peasants could not be impressed with the majesty and fairness of the law other than perhaps indirectly through word of mouth or through occasionally reading or listening to a newspaper account. Trials were constructed and conducted as elite political and social events inscribed into Russia's already-existing elite culture of public or semipublic discourse. Almost all the defendants, and also jurors, witnesses, and victims, not to mention the lawyers and judges, were from wealthy or at least educated or propertied classes. So were the spectators. In sum, Russia's legal drama was directed primarily at its propertied groups and sought to reassert control over wayward members, to discipline and reeducate, and ultimately even to reconstruct them, guiding the new ruling class through the period of transition known as the Great Reforms.[7]

GOVERNMENT AND POWER

In addition to creating a new court system, Tsar Alexander II (1855–1881) and his officials emancipated the serfs in 1861, established local self-government in 1864 and 1870, and introduced universal military conscription in 1874, among other, less well-known changes.[8] The reforms were conceived as a comprehensive project of social engineering that would alter many fundamental principles of Russian life.[9] Still, the reformers sought to balance the interests of various groups, in particular those of elites.[10] Buying a village with enserfed peasants was no longer the coveted pinnacle of success for the nobility, and the reforms created more opportunities for the upper classes than they took away.[11] These included relaxed press censorship and greater access to foreign travel and to higher education and thus to the professions.[12] Also beneficial was the liberalization of economic conditions, vastly improved infrastructure with a railroad network, and improved access to bank credit. Nobles and merchants with means could start their own companies, invest in the new stock market, or bid for government contracts, and those not so wealthy could become white-collar clerks and managers.[13] While Russia's antiquated social division into legally delineated estates persisted, it was now far less important than wealth in determining social status and opportunities.[14] By the 1860s the empire possessed a propertied class proportionately small compared to the mass of its rural population but still significant, with approximately three million to five million members (out of the total population of sixty million).[15] In short, the recent characterization of late imperial Russia as an "anti-capitalist utopia" falls very far short of the mark.[16]

With new social and economic opportunities came new risks. Similar to other European and Eurocentric societies of that era, Russian elites feared that their wealth and cultural capital were ephemeral and transient, and that with increased freedoms society was losing self-control and succumbing to passion and greed.[17] Former serfs, servants, and laborers were losing attachment to their masters and allegedly developing criminal emotions and appetites. A respectable upbringing and education were not reliable either. Pavel Miliukov's famous invective against the "stupidity or treason" of the imperial family on the eve of the February Revolution of 1917 addressed high politics, but it can be applied to the entire post-emancipation upper class, whose members repeatedly succumbed to destructive emotion and greed. Newspapers reported that a university student who was guaranteed a lucrative career had become a vicious murderer. A titled nobleman of ancient lineage turned out to be a petty thief. And dozens of well-to-do men and women joined Sergei Nechaev's revolutionary conspiracy seemingly out of boredom. New times demanded new institutions, and after the reform, in 1874, journalist Nikolai Demert wondered nervously what would have happened if "everyone had gotten into the risky, dishonest stock market game under the cover of the [pre-reform] estate-based justice." A much more thorough history of these modern anxieties exists for Victorian England. Russian courts before and after the reforms negotiated and muddled through the same unsettling narratives of violence, profit, and power.[18]

Russia's particular path to capitalist modernity, though, was shaped by the traumatic legacy of serfdom and by the massive material and moral dispossession of the landed gentry who had for centuries buttressed the imperial state. The tsar and his advisers were aware that most provincial nobles opposed the emancipation, and they were concerned about noble discontent or even resistance to the reforms.[19] In the top echelons of the government there were likewise many conservative officials who opposed the reforms and on numerous occasions came close to sabotaging them. But this "aristocratic opposition," as Igor Khristoforov has called this group, also illustrates the fact that government and power in Russia changed considerably in the mid-nineteenth century.[20] Conventional wisdom has it that state power in late imperial Russia was uniquely personalized because the emperor was legally an unlimited ruler until 1905 and his exclusive control of ministerial appointments persisted until 1917. In reality, however, nineteenth-century tsars gradually surrendered much of their effective authority to a bureaucracy growing in numbers, confidence, and technical proficiency. Vladimir Shkerin's book on the freethinking though harmless Petrashevsky circle shows how even Alexander II's authoritarian father, Nicholas I, was unable by the 1840s to direct his top officials effectively.[21] As Ekaterina Pravilova has pointed out, both Nicholas I and Alexander II were all too aware that they had very little control over the ruble's exchange rate and thus Russia's financial health.[22] Contrary to the myth that the imperial government propped up the serf-owning nobility through cheap loans, the state relied on the interest payments from these loans to maintain its financial stability.[23] The tsar thus had to be concerned not so much about old-fashioned aristocratic conspiracies as about technocratic experts making him irrelevant, something that eventually would in fact happen under Nicholas II. The power that the last three tsars did retain, aside from the fragile symbolic and ideological capital of the monarchy, was through the fact that Russia had no prime minister until 1905 and the government was divided into autonomous agencies and ministries that could not easily coordinate policy. In the 1860s and 1870s top officials depended on the tsar as mediator and facilitator, but also on each other and on public opinion, heavily influenced by such figures as the nationalist publisher and journalist Mikhail Katkov (1818–1887). The emperor, in turn, was functioning as essentially another powerful politician, and personally he increasingly felt himself isolated and vulnerable.[24]

Not surprisingly, nineteenth-century tsars looked for ways to bypass the ministerial bureaucracy. Nicholas I's early solution was to create the Third Section, a higher political police force that was originally designed as a separate mini government performing a broad range of functions.[25] But by the 1860s its agents and officers were busy suppressing political dissent and had long turned into just another technocratic agency. Moreover, the Third Section could arrest suspects but could not try cases, much less do so in public, and so was of limited utility for containing large-scale elite misconduct. Alexander II therefore resorted to rebuilding the existing court system into an autonomous parallel hierarchy of power that could be used to check both the ministerial bureaucracy and discontented elites more generally. Before 1864, judges were subordinate to the minister of justice and thus integrated into the ministerial system.[26] On the local level, the courts were built into the provincial and district administration in several different ways, even though governors were prohibited from participating in trials directly. Pre-reform law was an indispensable element of governance and social control, but it was not intended to have political power or to make any public impact, even though, as Richard Wortman has shown, the ideology of the rule of law had by the 1860s accumulated considerable cultural and political capital.[27] The meaning of the reform of 1864 was to institutionalize that capital. The new courts, therefore, were an integral component of the Great Reforms that did not so much limit the autocracy as prop up the new post-emancipation regime as its ultimate line of defense while Russia's political and social foundations underwent deep changes.

By contrast, traditional narratives treat the reformed legal system as strongly at odds with Russia's authoritarian political system and with its persistent rural culture.[28] The reform tends to be presented as "a major concession to public opinion" by the tsar, who regretted it almost immediately.[29] Public trials and more generally elements of the rule of law in 1864–1917 thus appear either as "a glorious but tragic episode" of Russian history or as yet another example of a courageous but ultimately doomed effort to introduce a more humane political regime in Russia.[30] Neither of these views is completely off the mark. There were certainly many aspects of post-1864 justice that were unique in Russian history, and one would most certainly prefer to be on trial in that system than in any other. Many lawyers and judges defied the tsar's officials in defense of individual rights and human dignity, as their peers elsewhere also did.[31] But this opposition must be viewed as inherent in the very organization of the law as an autonomous social field. A field, as introduced by Pierre Bourdieu, is "an entire social universe . . ., which is in practice relatively independent of external determinations and pressures." The juridical field is composed of multiple actors and competing hierarchies of expertise and jurisdiction, and it defines itself in relation to the other elements within "the broader field of power," such as "administration" or "social or economic pressure groups."[32] It is therefore understandable that the tsar, many of his officials, and many other influential Russians were suspicious of and even hostile to the law's power and autonomy; but they were also hostile to many other social actors and forces—and indeed to each other. In short, the reformed court system often clashed with other actors and institutions, but it nonetheless also reflected the internal logic of the imperial regime that emerged during the Great Reforms.

It is one thing to recognize, as some earlier studies of late imperial Russia also do, that the post-reform judiciary was in some meaningful ways an autonomous social and political actor. From this it does not automatically follow that the courts had any tangible impact upon post-reform Russia's development, and the high-profile trials especially may at first sight appear as not much more than a form of entertainment for the idle rich. But a close look at the trial records, press discussions, and official documentation that has survived in the archives guides my argument that post-reform criminal justice had the power to do two very significant things. One was to publicly prosecute, scrutinize, and convict powerful persons on grounds that were clear or at least plausible to a neutral observer. What appears in some scholarship to be the rather uncertain and beleaguered authority of the post-reform judiciary was in reality a tangible power to ruin bodies and families through hard labor, prison, and penal exile.[33] There were clear limits to this power. Russia was the only major state at the time to have no capital punishment for ordinary crimes. Nor could the jury try such persons as the tsar's famous kleptomaniac nephew Grand Duke Nikolai Konstantinovich or the governor of Riazan province Nikolai Boldarev who killed a peasant in 1872, while dozens of other highest-ranking officials were tried in secret by a special tribunal of the Senate.[34] But there was an even longer list of aristocrats and plutocrats, and of officials ranking beneath ministers and governors, who were fully exposed to public justice. A number of leading jurists, such as the liberal Anatolii Koni or the conservative Nikolai Muraviev, built their careers through precisely such prosecutions. Trials could not eliminate abuses, of course, and they did not produce actual equality before the law, but Russian officialdom and the upper classes in the post-reform era were more accountable to the law than ever before or since.

The second significant impact of the public trial had to do with the trial procedure itself. After all, important people could be punished in other more reliable ways, and this was neither the first nor the last time Russia's elites underwent a form of forceful lustration. The bloodiest and most devastating episode would occur only a few decades later, during the Civil War. But the post-emancipation period was unique in Russian history in being conducted through public adversarial trials in which the defendants had a decent chance of acquittal. Post-reform trials were also unique in their emphasis on reconstructing and reeducating society, on correcting the public rather than simply suppressing transgressions and punishing transgressors. Trial publicity was a central element of the reformed justice system, and the courtroom became a sphere of strongly—though not absolutely—protected speech, which was disseminated through newspaper transcripts and discussed in shorter essays and editorials.[35] The courts therefore created an effective lens for viewing Russian life that had never existed before and that would not exist again until after 1991, if then. The public attending or reading about a trial could learn about the private life of an upper-middle-class family addicted to morphine, about the workings of Nechaev's short-lived but deadly radical circle, or about the posh officers of the imperial guard behaving like silly schoolboys. When was violence legitimate?

What were the limits of the authority of male patriarchs and of upper-class women? What were the commendable, or legitimate, or suspect but still permissible ways to acquire wealth, and what kinds of persons were legitimate participants in the marketplace? A public trial was a unique venue for public discussion, and dissection, of these issues with the examples of real people's lives laid bare. The cases explored here are exceptionally rich and detailed, and they unveil uncomfortable truths about elite families, concerns about the patriarch figure in a patriarchal society, concerns about wealth in the age of developing capitalism, and what people sometimes did to respond to these concerns—whether it was to embezzle from one's employer or kill a moneylender. We can of course debate to what extent many of these trial narratives were "true" stories; but it is reasonably clear that they were not fictional, nor entirely manufactured for effect, as in the later show trials of the Stalin era.

I therefore regard the operations of the post-reform public trials as a particularly sophisticated variety of the control and surveillance technologies discussed by Michel Foucault and commonly known as the "disciplinary" or panoptic "gaze."[36] Modern surveillance practices began to appear in the sixteenth and the seventeenth century and were first theorized by Jeremy and Samuel Bentham in the late eighteenth.[37] Most commonly associated with reformed penitentiaries, schools, barracks, and hospitals, new technologies of power sought to control a far greater range of actions and thoughts of a far greater number of human subjects. In Russia, disciplinary practices and mentalities likewise emerged in the eighteenth century and continued to develop in the first half of the nineteenth, even though autonomous and empowered professional communities were only beginning to form. Both officials and the experts they employed worked to improve their knowledge of Russian society and to use that knowledge to rebuild and improve their charges. Law was a crucial element in the rise of the "disciplinary society," but other historians have focused on the practices of punishment and the emergence of the modern prison, thus presenting an incomplete account. Foucault himself argued that the disciplinary practices controlled by professional experts superseded the authority of the law and lawyers in many settings. This is mostly correct with respect to the vast quasi-legal administrative field in Eurocentric states that grew continuously from the medieval era and exponentially in the twentieth century. But the period of roughly 1850 to 1950 was one of the exceptional visibility and social impact of the experts' purported antithesis—the adversarial criminal trial, which questioned and often mocked medical, forensic, and other experts. As a surveillance mechanism, trials targeted not only the persons most immediately subjected to them—defendants, witnesses, and victims—but also Russia's elite society more generally, the spectators and readers who consumed the trials.[38]

The public gaze of a criminal trial is different from other, better-known panoptic settings. Unlike, say, prisons or hospitals, the courts found their power not only in their structure and procedures but also in the content of the trial narratives, the stories of crime, criminals, and victims that were explicitly performed in the courtroom. The tales of crime themselves are, therefore, part of "the very stuff of rule," to borrow Ernest Zitser's expression.[39] But compared to other panoptical settings, in a trial the dissection of individuals and of an entire society is at the same time more random and more selective. Defendants and witnesses, though not chosen as such to be examples to their society, were presented by lawyers as being certain social types, which were essentially put on trial by proxy. Many other social activities remained outside this dissecting spotlight, for instance "routine" crimes committed by peasants and laborers or minor offenses and disputes adjudicated by local courts, which often brought up completely different issues.[40] The trials' mechanics were also peculiar, since the participants were represented by lawyers and in general were better able to dissimulate and evade, and to resist the panoptic gaze, to a greater extent than inmates or patients. The publicity of a criminal trial was also unusual because ultimately the viewer was not a prison warden or a physician but potentially the entire society, which thereby examined and dissected itself with the help of lawyers, journalists, and scholars. The lawyers and the judges, powerful though they were, could not fully and decisively impose their optics upon the jury for fear of losing the case. The panoptic gaze of the public courtroom was therefore not a uniform projection of power but rather a pulsating exchange, a negotiation of information, symbols, and emotions.[41] Moreover, it was not only society and elites that were subjected to the panoptic gaze but the juridical field itself. Thus yet another distinguishing feature of great trials is this introspective or self-referential quality, questioning the law's integrity and validity. I owe this idea to Jeremy Bentham, who argued that the judge conducting a trial is simultaneously being judged by "the court of public opinion."[42] In Russia, courts were judged by hypercritical cultural and intellectual elites observing, commenting on, and reading about the trials, as well as by top officials who attended the most important ones.

While some participants and spectators were routinely excited and even elated about courtroom dramas, it is important to remember that a criminal trial in any setting is not an impartial inquiry or an intellectual exercise but a complex and typically grim ritual not unlike what the McCarthy-era sociologist

Harold Garfinkel called a "status degradation ceremony." It may eventually clear defendants but must first strip them of their personal autonomy, individual character, and civic capacity. As Linda Ross Meyer has observed, a trial is a "wrenching, difficult, humiliating, and sometimes traumatic experience," it is "expensive, exhausting, and embarrassing." In the Russian setting, Sandra Dahlke has noted that the new post-reform courts "did not promise more protection and legal security" but rather created considerable anxiety in elite groups who were now exposed to massive negative publicity, sometimes for ostensibly trivial reasons like a routine property dispute.[43] While many lawyers sought to protect their clients' rights, playing dirty was endemic in the post-reform courtroom, even by people typically seen as champions of legality, such as prosecutor and judge Anatolii Koni or top defense lawyers Fedor Plevako, Vladimir Spasovich, and Aleksandr Lokhvitskii. In short, making the law more powerful and more effective did not automatically mean it was more rational, more evidence-based, or more humane.

THE HISTORY OF TRIALS

This book is primarily about the criminal trial, a central and even quintessential element of criminal justice. We can envision a world without prisons, lawyers, or written law, but some procedure for applying society's norms to specific factual situations is indispensable, although the forms and rules of such procedures have varied widely. The version that is familiar to today's readers is a public verbal contest between prosecuting and defense attorneys seeking to win over a jury, all under the supervision of a judge who may take a passive (in common-law systems) or active (in civil-law systems) role. This contest is reported by journalists and discussed by the wider public, sometimes far outside the locality in which the trial takes place. In imperial Russia this model was introduced by the reform of 1864, drawing all of its essential elements from the postrevolutionary French experience. But as David Bentley has pointed out, even though nineteenth-century trials may look superficially familiar to those of today, many of their principles and practices were quite different. Moreover, in Western Europe such trials at the time were a novelty as well. John H. Langbein and other historians of European law have shown that this model of criminal trial is not intrinsic to any "Western" model of legality but had emerged in the first half of the nineteenth century when the conduct of trials was taken over by professional lawyers, while judges, juries, and indeed defendants became passive observers. In Continental legal systems before the French Revolution the trial was essentially a bureaucratic inquiry closed to the public and based on written records. After 1791 it was replaced in France by a procedure adopted from the English model with juries and publicity, although some elements of the old inquisitorial procedure remained.[44]

The golden age of the criminal trial lasted for about a century and petered out after the Second World War (in Russia, ending abruptly already in 1917), so that today criminal justice in Eurocentric states is largely administered through plea negotiation, administrative mechanisms, and bench trials.[45] Most major legal systems today have either abandoned jury trials completely (Germany, Italy) or almost completely (France, post-Soviet Russia); or they have greatly restricted their use (England, the United States). Even in the United States today, traditional jury trials make up less than 1 percent of all criminal cases. They do, however, continue to attract the public's attention and to be regarded as an essential political right.

A close reading of a single "great" trial is an established and productive genre of historical writing. Works in the genre show that a single trial, such as that of John Brown in 1859 or of Alfred Dreyfus in 1894, can reflect and at the same time direct and reshape political, social, and cultural currents of its age.[46] This genre works best, however, in a legal setting that is already well explored. It is less productive in the case of Russia, where a comprehensive legal history does not yet exist, even for a short historical period.[47] The famous trial of the anarchist Vera Zasulich in 1878 in St. Petersburg is a good example.[48] Having shot a tsarist official in a crowded room, she was acquitted by the jury; thus, some say, inaugurating the age of political terrorism that would later claim the life of Alexander II himself.[49] Historians have correctly regarded it as a watershed in the history of the Russian radical movement and, misleadingly, as "the most important judiciary event in the history of Imperial Russia."[50] Court practice in post-reform Russia, even only its topmost layer, shows that elite young women who hurt people allegedly in the heat of passion or for generally nonmaterialistic reasons were typically acquitted. Indeed, it would have been much more significant for the history of Russian law and society had Zasulich actually been convicted.[51] Moreover, looking at her trial from a comparative perspective shows that the question of jury nullification, that is, acquittal of clearly guilty defendants, has been vexing and politically charged in other major jurisdictions with jury trials.[52] It is therefore essential to look at individual cases not only in their political and social context—which most case histories do—but also in the legal-cultural context of other trials that presented similar factual situations or took place in the same historical period.

The crime of Vera Zasulich was politically motivated. She had belonged to underground circles for years and shot General Fedor Trepov ostensibly to avenge his illegal order to flog a political prisoner. Taking a political case before a jury was exceptional in late imperial Russia, the only other example being the murder trial of the anarchist Sergei Nechaev in 1873.[53] But the post-reform era is still remembered for its great political trials, including the first public political trial of Nechaev's followers in 1871, the 1877 trial of the participants in Russia's first open political demonstration on Kazan Square in St. Petersburg, the "Trial of the Fifty" revolutionaries the same year, and the gargantuan "Trial of the 193" participants in the "Going to the People" movement from October 1877 to February 1878. These were followed by a large series of trials that lasted until 1890 targeting persons affiliated with the People's Will and revolutionary terrorism. While such cases as the two trials of the Nechaev circle or that of Vera Zasulich must be included in a general history of Russian criminal justice, most political trials were only partially connected to Russia's regular justice system: they were conducted by specialized tribunals without juries, albeit with regular defense attorneys, and their decisions were reviewed only by the Senate.[54] It is therefore puzzling that many authors of key accounts of post-reform Russia claimed that political trials were the standard by which its legal developments should be evaluated, even when they recognized, as Samuel Kucherov and Richard Pipes did, that nonpolitical trials also existed.[55] This reasoning is akin to reviewing videos of train crashes to learn how to drive a car.

An important corrective to the scholarly obsession with Vera Zasulich and political justice are the two major studies of post-reform criminal trials, which look at nonpolitical cases and link them to intellectual and cultural developments. Louise McReynolds's rich history of murder in late imperial Russia connects legal and journalistic debates with popular culture, such as detective fiction, showing how evolving attitudes to criminality and criminal responsibility contributed to middle-class phobias and fantasies associated with the fin-de-siècle.[56] Girish N. Bhat's earlier history of the criminal jury trial finds its "broader animating concerns" in Russia's traditional peasant culture, which, he argues, created a peculiar dynamic of "consensual jurisprudence" and heightened attention to moral, rather than purely legal, issues.[57] By contrast, I present the jury trial as a place of power in its own right, one that created and transformed meanings in addition to reflecting larger societal concerns. Difficult though it is to know what "really" happened in each particular case, I attempt to recover the vision of a post-emancipation Russia constructed through courtroom narratives of elite transgressions. This vision merged stories about wealth, kinship, gender, and authority. Greed and profit seeking, in particular, have never before been examined as a major source of criminal behavior in Russia, of crucial importance in violent as well as in property crimes. Finally, my book gives its due to the period of the late 1860s and especially the 1870s, when the largest, most spectacular, and most trendsetting trials occurred. This incredibly rich and important period in the history of Russian law, when public trials took root and matured, has been almost completely skipped over in earlier work on the legal reform.

Existing work on Russian law follows closely what Tracy Dennison has called the "peasant myth," that is, the notion that Russia's national essence was embodied in the peasant class, while the educated and propertied elites were alien transgressors.[58] It is common to argue that Russian peasant jurors were more likely to acquit defendants because their religious values inclined them toward mercy, or that they simply had no regard for the idea of formal legality. Historian Jörg Baberowski emphasizes peasant ignorance and contempt for the law, arguing that peasant jurors "understood nothing, and yet were to decide everything."[59] My book is in a sense a corrective to that stereotype. While peasants were indeed a majority, though not an overwhelming one, on the juries in the provinces, they hardly ever participated in the prominent trials discussed in this book, in which the jurors were officials, merchants, and other middle-class men.[60] The fact of these jury compositions makes it even more important to determine how middle-class values and practices in late imperial Russia engaged with the juridical field.[61] It is reasonable to say given that Russia's population consisted mostly of peasant farmers, their cultural values must have influenced trial practice, except that we are not sure to this day what these values were and how they varied in chronological, geographic, and socioeconomic terms. For example, Stefan Kirmse's study of post-reform district court practice among Volga and Crimea Tatars has shown that peasant juries were actually tougher than middle-class ones of the large cities.[62] Moreover, religiosity is not confined to the peasantry or to Russia.[63] Other legal systems, most important that of nineteenth-century France, perceived high acquittal rates to be a problem, correctly attributing them to particular legal rules.[64] In Russia, acquittals were caused primarily by poor performance of prosecutors and by the failings of Russian penal laws that, similar to French ones, sometimes imposed heavy penalties for trivial offenses.

THEORIES OF TRIAL

In contrast to innumerable non-Russianist histories of individual trials set in diverse locations, there are remarkably few theoretical studies of the criminal trial as a cultural and social practice. The most influential work by Robert P. Burns argues against the "received view" of the Anglo-American jury trial as a mechanistic process of determining the facts so that the legal norms can be applied.[65] As Marianne Constable has observed, Burns's "trial is a complicated practice, and not a simple two-sided fight between good and evil, innocence and guilt, truth and falsity."[66] Rather, it is a "consciously structured hybrid of languages and performances."[67] The jury does not simply evaluate the probability of events but, in one commentator's words, scrutinizes "the motives and virtues of the players and the competing values at stake in the litigation. The jury's Solomonic judgment, tacit and complex, weaves together judgments of morality, legality, credibility, probability, plausibility, and politics, and it expresses the jury's own sense of community identity." Burns's theory is grounded in the thought of the Russian literary scholar Mikhail Bakhtin (1895–1975), from whom Burns borrows the idea of dialogism or polyphony. Bakhtin famously explains dialogism as "a plurality of independent and unmerged voices and consciousnesses, a genuine polyphony of fully valid voices."[68] Burns's view of the criminal trial as a competition of two autonomous narratives or explanations of the facts is especially applicable to the adversarial model of the trial that emerged during the nineteenth century. By contrast, the "established" view of the trial, which Bakhtin would have called "monologic," asks only whether the prosecution's case had been proven.

To legal scholars, such as Martha Umphrey, Bakhtin's theory "helps to bridge the divide between 'law' and 'society' in ways recognizable to sociolegal scholars." To Umphrey, trial is a "liminal legal space" mediating between "formal legal rules and the unofficial world of norms, customs, common sense, and social codes"; it is therefore at once a space where conflicts are fought and one where solutions are negotiated. To combine the Bakhtin-inspired theory of the trial with Bourdieu's notion of the social field, the trial is a key space in which the juridical field is constructed, defined, fought over, and negotiated. We should not, however, imagine this process as two fully formed autonomous structures meeting in the courtroom. While legal codes and other authoritative texts derive their force from their relative autonomy and freedom from unauthorized interpretation, their meaning and their effect depend upon the "unofficial [normative] world," as Umphrey discusses.[69]

In larger trials with multiple defendants and attorneys and numerous victims and witnesses, such as most of the trials discussed in this book, there were many more than two competing voices or narratives. Even the jury's verdict did not decisively declare one of them as prevailing, especially since the questions to the jury and the resultant verdicts themselves were often polyphonous or outright confusing. Larger trials tended to be so complex as to create a messy and barely manageable environment or, to use another of Bakhtin's concepts, chronotope, despite all the efforts of judicial officials to organize and delineate. To give just one example in this otherwise theoretical discussion, at the scandalous and messy forgery trial of the Miasnikov brothers in 1872 "it was difficult to distinguish defenders and prosecutors: their roles became completely mixed." The key witness became a "two-edged weapon" harming both sides of the case.[70]

The multiplicity of voices and narratives produced during the trial was not neutral: it reflected, produced, and rearranged power and inequality. It is therefore helpful to keep in mind when discussing great criminal trials Bakhtin's concept of the carnival, by which he meant social rituals and cultural products characterized by the joyful, often violent, and always irreverent inversion of official values and power structures.[71] Nineteenth-century judicial proceedings were typically more orderly than early modern Shrovetide celebrations and other ritual festivities. But the rush of well-dressed crowds jousting for a place in the courtroom and the spectators queuing in the hallways or even on the streets created something of a carnivalesque atmosphere. Political trials are particularly notable for their ritual inversion of official values, as when revolutionaries used the occasion to publicly declare their beliefs. Even ordinary "great" trials had strong carnivalesque features: they verbalized, described, and detailed prohibited and obscene behaviors, making them acceptable or at least speakable. Trials recalled, represented, and enacted what was prohibited, making it real, although usually not good. Trials suspended social distances and boundaries, and they brought forth despicable individuals and exposed hidden behaviors and private information: financial secrets, greed and viciousness of wealthy and self-confident persons, illicit sex, and the hidden violence of domestic life. Trials, in effect, fought and mediated the worst terrors of the nineteenth-century middle classes who attended and administered the great trials, much the way Freud's psychoanalysis began to do in the 1880s.[72]

But as far as the defendants, witnesses, and most victims were concerned, trials above all humiliated elite men and women, connecting the judicial carnival to what sociologist Harold Garfinkel has called the "status degradation ceremony." The trial presented the accused as the opposite of peaceful citizens, placing them outside the "legitimate order," and as undergoing a "ritual destruction." Their unique personality was destroyed and turned into a new, criminal type, while their accusers claimed to represent the public and its values.[73] Although all Eurocentric legal systems, including Russia's, at least officially presumed defendants to be innocent until proven guilty, several writers have noted that the trial is "itself a punishment" and a form of ordeal that irreparably damages its object no matter the outcome.[74] The punitive or at least disciplinary character of the trial brings us back to Foucault's analysis of the modern disciplinary regime, which has little to say about the criminal trial per se, because he focused on the shift in modern penal regimes from imposing spectacular, public, and often gruesome punishments to the penitentiary system that attempted to rebuild the criminal's mind through nonviolent techniques, especially what Philip Gorsky has called "the technology of observation."[75] Foucault did realize that in the postrevolutionary era the spectacle of criminal justice moved from the public square into the courtroom, but he was uncomfortable with that observation (since discipline did not actually replace spectacle but only supplemented and enhanced it) and, as Katherine Fisher Taylor has noted, "discounted discipline as an appropriate object of study." Fisher Taylor also found that "it was not only the inquisitorial powers held by magistrates but the practice of discretionary judgment deployed by jurors that brought what Foucault called modern disciplinary power into the courtroom."[76] To this we must add the scrutiny of defendants, victims, witnesses, and defense lawyers by many other participants: journalists, other lawyers, legal scholars, the public, and even the distinguished observers occupying the seats of honor in Russian and other European courtrooms.[77]

The imperial Russian state used "great" public trials to scrutinize and discipline its elites. Whether the state foresaw it or not, the publicity and drama of the trials also opened the state as well as its elites to the scrutiny of the whole public of Russia. Now the trials themselves come under scholarly scrutiny, in order to take their place within an ever more coherent, accurate, and complete historiography of Russia.

SOURCES AND METHODS

This book is based on approximately fifty court cases tried between 1862, when the first modern public trial was held in the Russian Empire, and 1884, the year of the Skopin Municipal Bank case, whose scandalous existence spanned the entire reform period (see table 1). Prominent trials continued regularly until the end of imperial Russia, but they were exceptionally frequent in the immediate postreform years, in the late 1860s and 1870s. During this time many key patterns of courtroom narratives and tactics were developed, as were the archetypal cases, such as murder, bank crash, and forgery. These were elaborated and altered in the fin-de-siècle years, but discussing those changes in detail would require much additional space. Indeed, the very end of imperial Russia is already relatively well covered in existing literature, to the detriment of the formative years of the Great Reforms and their immediate aftermath. There are a number of important cases that are mentioned in the book but not covered in detail, mostly because they discuss the same themes and issues in less depth. I cover only trials in the ordinary criminal courts, almost always with juries, with the exception of some trials in the empire's borderlands, where the legal reform of 1864 was implemented later and typically did not introduce juries. I exclude ecclesiastical, military, and other specialized tribunals; I also exclude almost all political trials, with the exception of those few that took place in the regular courts. Examining Russia's political justice would require a much larger and therefore much less detailed book. Finally, I am omitting the lower courts of peasant townships and the justices of the peace that had jurisdiction over petty crime. Fascinating as they are, such cases did not reach the same public prominence, did not have as much at stake, and, in the case of peasant courts, are already covered in Jane Burbank's excellent monograph.[78]

Because of the novelty of the factual situations presented at landmark trials, and because Russian society was generally agitated in the post-emancipation years, the early criminal trials made a powerful imprint on Russia's cultural memory and especially on its educated and propertied elites. Legal scandals were reflected in a variety of cultural products, ranging from newspaper accounts to works of fiction, memoirs, and academic treatises. These were written by a range of authors, from journalist Katkov to litterateurs Dostoevsky, Chekhov, Staniukovich, and Saltykov-Shchedrin. It would be possible to write this book based solely on these sources, but it would lose much of its novelty and immediacy. Instead, I focus on the voices of the persons who actually participated in the trials, and therefore use secondary materials largely to provide supporting evidence. My main method in researching this book is therefore to conduct close readings of case proceedings, mostly from case transcripts. Post-reform trials in Russia were oral, which meant that no official transcripts were kept. But newspaper stenographers were invariably present at major trials. Their accounts were printed in newspapers and, for the largest and most important trials, published as separate books or pamphlets.

Last, but not least, I spent two years reviewing the inventories of the archival holdings of the tsarist Ministry of Justice (*fond* 1405 at the Russian State Historical Archive [RGIA]), as well as completing approximately a year in total of intensive archival research in St. Petersburg and Moscow. These materials are exceptionally rich and form an indispensable element of this study. Used by only a handful of scholars, the *fond* 1405 holdings in particular are essential for understanding government and society in late imperial Russia, including the era of the Great Reforms. Since the trials were oral, archival materials only occasionally provide information about what went on in the courtroom. Particularly helpful are the records of the Third Section, the tsar's secret political police, whose agents sometimes attended and reported on trials, as well as investigating and harassing some of the individuals featured in the book. But other archival collections provide essential information about what happened before and after the trial, including preliminary investigations and pretrial negotiations, appeals, and petitions for clemency. Given that the court building in St. Petersburg was burnt down in 1917, virtually all its records perished, including those of the preliminary investigations that tended to be especially voluminous. Moscow fared better, with some of the major investigations surviving all the wars and revolutions. Unnecessarily restrictive archival procedures at the Moscow municipal archive, however, mean that a researcher would need a lifetime to process even one case. Those snippets I did obtain were extremely informative.

This source base brings up the question how I "know" what "really" went on in the courtroom. Transcripts necessarily omitted some materials that newspaper editors thought to be less relevant but that could be invaluable to historians. Similarly, the total experience of attending the trial—light, temperature, sounds, people's gestures and personal appearance (and probably the smells)—is virtually altogether lost to us, aside from occasional printed references, though it would not be available to the readers at the time either, other than by analogy. It is even harder to piece together a "true" story of the facts behind each case, especially the prominent ones in which testimony was complex and unclear. Some of the convicted defendants were almost certainly guilty, but their trial was tainted by political motivations and manipulations, and one has to wonder whether contemporaries knew some obvious facts that are lost to us today.

There is no magic solution to this problem, but this book still needed to be written. One helpful strategy is to discard any preconceived notions about Russia, crime, or the law, especially ideological and political notions, as well as any monumental dichotomies like backward versus modern or conservative versus liberal. Instead I present a historical anthropology of Russian law and political and social power using what Jack Goody has called an "analytical grid" registering subtle gradations and distinctions.[79] Another helpful test is the fact that the trials were observed and then discussed by educated and often powerful people, who would likely have identified any glaring incongruities, abuses, and omissions. I do recognize that trials created their own version of Russia and of its people, much like the works of literature to which legal narratives are often compared.[80] My project is a reconstruction of this peculiar version of Russian reality, and thus it is twice or even thrice removed from actual persons and actions (taking into account that trial participants already worked with prepared

TABLE 1. MAJOR CRIMINAL TRIALS IN THE RUSSIAN EMPIRE, 1866–1884 (LISTED ALPHABETICALLY)

Short Title	Year	Charges
Arenberg	1870	Murder
Bezobrazov, Kovalchukova	1878	Murder
Castrati	1871	Illegal sect
Danilov	1867	Murder
Dmitrieva	1871	Theft, abortion
Gaevskii	1866	Embezzlement
Gartung	1877	Theft
Gorsky	1868	Murder
Gulak-Artemovskaia	1878	Forgery
Gusev Alley	1869	Murder
Ilarion (Mikhailov)	1873	Murder
Jacks of Hearts	1877	Fraud, forgery, theft, murder
Jaroszyński	1862	Attempt. political assassination
Jujean	1878	Murder by poison
Kachka	1880	Murder
Kairova	1876	Attempted murder
Kazan (Belskii, Khisamutdinov)	1873	Murder
Kazan square	1877	Political demonstration
Kharkov case	1866, 1872	Counterfeiting
Kolemin	1874	Illegal gambling
Kronenberg	1876	Torture
Kutais	1878	Blood libel
Kvitnitskii	1873	Assault
Landsberg	1879	Murder
Matov brothers	1868	Counterfeiting
Melnitskii and children	1881, 1883	Theft, accessories to theft
Miasnikov brothers	1872	Forgery of a testament
Mitrofania	1874	Fraud, forgery
Moscow Bank (Strousberg)	1876	Fraud, bribery, negligence
Musina-Pushkina	1873	Fraud
Nechaev Circle and Nechaev	1871 and 1873	Murder of a fellow radical

table continues on next page

TABLE 1. (*continued*)

Short Title	Year	Charges
Nepenin and Nepenina	1874	Murder
Nizhnii Novgorod Salt Case	1869	Embezzlement
Ovsiannikov	1875	Arson, insurance fraud
Protopopov	1867	Assault
Rogozhskoe Cemetery	1867	Robbery
Sedkova et al.	1875	Forgery of a testament
Skopin mun. bank (Rykov)	1884	Fraud
Sohn (Zon) (suitcase)	1870	Murder
Son'ka the Golden Hand	1880	Fraud, theft
Tiflis (Andreevskaia)	1876	Murder
Trial of 50	1877	Sedition
Trial of 193	1877–1878	Sedition
Umetskaia and parents	1868	Arson
Volokhova	1867	Murder
Witte (Tiligul crash)	1876	Negligence
Yukhantsev	1879	Embezzlement
Zasulich	1878	Attempted murder

narratives of the preliminary investigation). But I stop short of complete agnosticism and when appropriate weigh in on the credibility or cogency of particular stories or arguments without labeling them as unequivocally true or false.

ARGUMENTS AND ORGANIZATION

The main argument of this book is that criminal trials reconstructed by the reform of 1864 had the effective power to scrutinize Russian elite classes and to punish their wayward members. In the process of doing so the trials produced detailed narratives that publicly articulated and debated some of the most vexing questions raised by the Great Reforms.

The four chapters of part I examine the fundamental principles of Russian criminal law, arguing that the courts' power did not emerge overnight by the reformers' fiat but had to be configured, asserted, and negotiated. Chapter 1 examines the cornerstone principle of judicial autonomy that was defined in interactions with the other principal sources of legal authority in Russia, such as the emperor with his close advisers, and the police officers and agents subordinate to the large and powerful Ministry of the Interior. Chapter 2 argues that another fundamental principle—that of legal publicity—needed to be imagined, constructed, and negotiated. Chapter 3 dissects the multistage ritual of the adversarial jury trial, noting how each stage provided opportunities to create multiple narratives and meanings. In a similar vein, Russia's penal code, which is discussed in chapter 4, combined several ideologies and motivations from several distinct historical periods, most notably the Enlightenment-era classical criminology of Cesare Beccaria, Jeremy Bentham, and Paul von Feuerbach.

Parts II and III are centered on close readings of some of the major criminal cases of the post-reform era, seeking to uncover the vision of Russia and of its alleged ills, which were composed by the diverse participants. These chapters focus on the ubiquitous themes of violence, passion, greed, and deception.

The three chapters in part II focus on the cases of murder and other violent crime, asking how attempts to understand violence connected to such fundamental elements of Russian life as property, honor, and personal authority within the patriarchal family. Chapter 5 examines murder as a crime directed against the structures of property ownership, whether committed by elite persons against each other or by servants against their masters and employees. Chapter 6 examines honor-motivated violence in the setting of sexual relations or among state servitors, civil or military. Chapter 7 discusses trials that scrutinized the all-important physical power of male patriarchs over their relatives and dependents.

Finally, the three chapters in part III address the most numerous variety of the postreform legal scandal: namely, financial and other white-collar crimes. Fraud was exceptionally suitable for debating and connecting various fissures in the post-reform regime of social and political power, since it was not a capital crime and the victims were typically still alive. It was also a very diverse practice, ranging from individual forgers and swindlers to large banks that were in effect empire-wide Ponzi schemes before the term had been invented. Elite and well-connected forgers and embezzlers elicited sharp debates about Russia's past and present, and ultimately about the moral qualities and abilities of Russia's rulers. Chapter 8 discusses the legal construction of fraud and deceit in Russia through the trials of individual swindlers who had no official authority or control over the stolen assets. Chapter 9 addresses the crime of forgery, exploring the use of criminal law to contest formal wealth transfer and gender roles within Russia's elite circles. Chapter 10 discusses embezzlement of property by high-ranking merchants and financiers, concluding with a decades-long precocious and massive banking pyramid scheme concocted in a small provincial town.

PART ONE

The Juridical Field

Figure 1. The trial of the Moscow Commercial Loan Bank, from *Vsemirnaia illustratsia*, 1876, no. 26, p. 477. Top row (from left to right): spectators in the gallery; types of civil plaintiffs; evidence table with account books. Middle row: defendants Strousberg, Landau, and Polianskii; roll call of civil plaintiffs. Bottom row: the judges' podium; defense attorneys; journalists. Most participants in the trial are depicted, with the notable absence of the jurors. This one-page visual overview of the public court ritual closely resembles the iconostasis in an Orthodox church, which provides believers with a quick visual reference to the core Christian teachings. Within the drawing, the portraits behind the judges' table resemble icons. But the drawing also has a more chaotic and irreverent aspect, with one of the spectators leaning over the railing and the other using binoculars.

It is ironic that the first public trials in modern Russian history were held in military courts, institutions not generally known for robust protections for the accused. The first one took place on 2 August 1862, not in Russia proper but in Russian-ruled Warsaw. Ludwik Jaroszyński, a twenty-two-year-old apprentice tailor and radical activist, had shot and wounded the viceroy of the Kingdom of Poland, Grand Duke Konstantin Nikolaevich. The trial by a panel of military officers lasted almost twelve hours and predictably ended in a death sentence. Konstantin mentioned in his diary that he was satisfied with the experiment of admitting the public into the courtroom despite some "snags." These included the length of the session and the weak performance by the prosecutor, as contrasted with a masterful defense, as well as a weak legal foundation for the verdict.[1] The grand duke was proud of his innovation and felt piqued that the Russian public did not pay much attention: "I've always stood up strongly for publicity," he wrote in a letter. "I was the first to introduce it in practice, and bought my right to do so with my own blood."[2] Konstantin also headed the imperial navy, and together with the minister of war, Dmitrii Miliutin, was one of the leading liberal officials in the top tier of government pushing for legal innovations.

Konstantin's experiment was part of a transitional period lasting roughly ten years, when Russian lawyers and officials, and eventually the public, studied and discussed different ways of reconfiguring the legal system and more broadly what Pierre Bourdieu would later call the juridical field, which in addition to courts of law included other legal and quasi-legal institutions, and more generally the practice of engaging with the law.[3] The criminal justice system that emerged from these experiments centered on a system of administratively autonomous courts conducting public adversarial trials with oral procedure, the right to defense, and free evaluation of evidence by the fact finder. Ivan Butskovskii, the main author of the reform legislation, categorically considered these principles to be inseparable. In existing accounts of the reform they are presented as self-explanatory but today they require as much explanation as they did to Russians in the 1860s. As a leading historian of the reform, Aleksandr Korotkikh, observed, the reformers proposed what at the time was considered the most effective legal technology. But optimal policies and solutions do not get adopted automatically in any state or field. Ekaterina Pravilova recently discussed the intense political resistance in nineteenth-century Russia to the latest financial technologies, such as a convertible currency or an independent central bank. Similarly, it was not clear or predetermined that the Russian political system would succeed in introducing such an ideologically and emotionally charged juridical regime. Many influential officials and initially the emperor himself favored a far more limited solution.[4] But even after Alexander II did approve the final, more thoroughgoing option with juries and life tenure for judges, the practical meaning of its main elements was neither simple nor self-evident.

Each of the fundamental principles of the 1864 reform discussed in the following three chapters—judicial autonomy, legal publicity, and the adversarial trial—involved the careful balancing, negotiating, and reconstructing of institutions and relationships. Similarly, the Penal Code of 1845, which remained in force until the Bolshevik takeover, and which is discussed in chapter 4, was a composite of several legal ideologies, some quite recent and some centuries old. Although Russian lawyers only rarely argued points of law in front of juries, it of course mattered enormously with what crime a defendant was charged and how that crime was punished. All of that depended on evaluating and categorizing human actions and characters. This is what Russian lawyers learned in universities and this was the method they brought with them into the courtroom.

CHAPTER 1

Judicial Autonomy

One of the most remarkable criminal affairs of the transitional period was dubbed in newspapers and in official correspondence the "Kharkov banknote [counterfeiting] case" (*delo khar'kovskikh serii*). It began in June 1865 when gendarme officers followed a trail of forged paper rubles to about a dozen landowners, merchants, and military officers who ran a distribution network in the nearby towns of Lugansk, Bakhmut, and Izium. Eventually the police found engraving and glazing mechanisms manufactured in Berlin and Leipzig, disguised as threshing machines and hidden in a barn on the estate of the Bakhmut Marshal of the Nobility, Pavel Gavrilov. Also arrested were the Marshal of the Nobility from nearby Izium (whose brother was the local police chief) and Lieutenant-Colonel Aleksandr Beklemishev, along with about a dozen other nobles and merchants.[1]

The investigation quickly ran into obstacles because counterfeiting was among the most severely punished offenses in the penal code, and local authorities were not happy with the prospect of having their neighbors and friends exiled to deadly hard labor in Siberia. One key defendant who talked was soon found hanged in his prison cell, another was poisoned, and in the meantime a local landowner named Savich, having exchanged his entire capital of fifteen thousand rubles for forged notes, shot himself in a fit of despair. The trial in Kharkov in 1866 was conducted under pre-reform rules with their far stricter standards of proof and went on appeal to the Senate and the Council of State in

St. Petersburg, ultimately leading to the conviction of only the defendants who had fully confessed and leaving the ringleaders "under suspicion," which meant that they went home but remained under threat of renewed prosecution. After the reformed Kharkov District Court opened in Kharkov a year later, witness bribery was uncovered, the case restarted, and the twenty-three-year-old assistant procurator Anatolii Koni secured his reputation as an implacable foe of established interests and unearned privileges. In 1872 a jury convicted Gavrilov and Beklemishev, but Koni himself had by then had to resign and leave Kharkov under pressure from local elites.[2] This would not, however, harm his long and illustrious legal career.

The eventual conviction of the Kharkov counterfeiters illustrates with particular clarity that the reform empowered the judiciary to resist political and social pressures, but also that it had to be constantly vigilant about its elevated political, social, and moral authority. Existing literature describes this empowerment as autonomy or even independence and regards it as a cornerstone of the post-1864 legal order and a crucial first step in implementing the ideology of the separation of powers in Russia. It is less clear, however, what this autonomy or its lack meant in practice, especially because every government institution is autonomous in some sense, and conversely every legal system, including the American one, is responsive to political and other extrinsic pressures. The old court system established in 1775 was much more autonomous than other historians have assumed, especially on the eve of the Great Reforms. Creating independent courts (*nezavisimyi sud*), continued to reconfigure power between the judiciary and other influential individuals and groups that had traditionally exercised formal or informal legal functions. This included the emperor with his ostensibly unlimited power and his ministers and other top officials, who had for centuries been involved in the administration of justice. In addition, the courts interacted with the powerful police apparatus, whose officials conducted the initial inquiry (*doznanie*) and assisted judicial investigators during pretrial procedures.

THE TSAR'S JUSTICE

The Russian emperor stood at the apex of the administrative and judicial hierarchy. Article 1 of the Fundamental Laws famously described him as the "autocratic and unlimited monarch." No legislation could be enacted without his approval, and he at least in theory could change even those few laws that did constrain his power. These were the laws of succession and the requirement that he belong to the Russian Orthodox Church.[3] Historians have argued that the tsar's personal power, his mistrust of lawyers and of the rule of law, and his political control of the "administrative hierarchy," especially provincial authorities, inhibited the development of autonomous legal institutions.[4] While following logically from the premise of his possessing "unlimited" political power, this conclusion has to be qualified as a practical matter.

While officially unlimited, the tsars' legal and quasi-legal powers both before and after the Great Reforms of the 1860s were divided among many formal and informal channels of communication and influence, including, for instance, the practice of issuing manifestos in the tsar's name and the practice of accepting petitions from private individuals, including those from convicted criminals requesting a pardon.[5] Ultimately, the tsar's personal authority and effectiveness required him to balance power among the various interest groups in the bureaucracy and in the landed aristocracy. As a practical matter, the tsar could not avoid soliciting advice from legal and other professionals, and he could not avoid acting through some official institutions and procedures most of the time. At least in some areas, such as responding to petitions, legal and quasi-legal officials took over completely, as Barbara Alpern Engel has shown.[6]

Perhaps the most visible but least common type of autocratic intervention was direct and informal meddling in legal matters. One well-publicized example is the 1878 case of Vera Zasulich, when Alexander II and his minister of justice, Konstantin von Pahlen, in vain solicited assurances from Koni, then the chairman of the St. Petersburg District Court, that she would be convicted. But while Pahlen had long conversations with Koni, the tsar made his wishes known very clearly but indirectly: he personally received Koni in the palace and talked to him, which indicated his favor and engagement with the case, but did not bring up Zasulich directly.[7] Another example of direct intervention was the 1870 murder of the Austro-Hungarian military attaché Prince Ludwig von Arenberg. The killers were caught and convicted, but Alexander II personally ordered that the penal code be revised promptly and penalties for murder raised. He did so, however, only upon recommendation from the minister of justice, and the legal change was not applied retroactively to von Arenberg's killers. The tsar could also facilitate a criminal prosecution, for instance, when a military officer was charged with a crime. The tsar in consultation with the minister of war would immediately discharge the accused officer from service to enable a civilian trial, as, for instance, in the 1879 Karl von Landsberg murder case or in a less famous 1874 case, when the police shut down a gambling den kept by one Kolemin, an officer in the imperial guard. The tsar made sure that he could be prosecuted by discharging him effective the day of the police raid. After the scandalous failure of the Moscow Commercial Loan Bank in 1875, the minister of justice complained to the tsar that the persons interested in the outcome were impeding the investigation, including the bank's board chairman Daniil Schumacher, who were spreading rumors and slandering legal officials. The tsar wrote: "The lawful procedure should be strictly followed without any partiality." The tsar could also order that a particularly egregious crime be tried by a military court that could impose the death penalty even on civilians, whereas civilian courts could not do so.[8] After 1881, military governors administering the most important regions of the empire also received this power, but they used it either for political crimes or for exceptional cases that threatened public order, such as aggravated multiple homicides and armed highway robbery.

Most of the tsar's legal functions were formalized and well established. The most formal and tangible judicial function was his duty to review and confirm the criminal sentences of nobles and several other privileged categories of criminals, who otherwise could not be deprived of their status, according to the provisions of Catherine II's 1785 Charter to the Nobility.[9] While the tsar almost invariably confirmed the sentence, in some notable cases he reduced the punishment. For instance, noblemen Gavrilov and Beklemishev from the Kharkov case were sentenced to hard labor as required by the law, which the tsar reduced to penal exile in Siberia, but he did so only upon the trial court's recommendation. Mother Mitrofania, the aristocratic nun convicted of forgery in 1874, was spared Siberian exile and spent the rest of her life in comfortable monasteries in European Russia and Ukraine, but her conviction was not overturned. In 1873 the military court sentenced Staff Captain Erast Kvitnitskii of the imperial guard to Siberian exile for striking another officer but recommended a full pardon; the tsar only agreed to a probation period as a private. After a few years Kvitnitskii was reinstated and eventually became a full general. Sergei Witte, as I noted in the Introduction, was convicted of criminal negligence though sentenced to arrest rather than prison.[10]

A related prerogative of the emperor was to reduce sentences or to pardon convicted criminals of all social ranks in response to their petitions. The archive of the Ministry of Justice shows that the petition procedure following a criminal conviction was not exercised arbitrarily but rather was institutionalized and regularized. Petitions would be forwarded to the ministry and studied by its lawyers, who then made a recommendation, which the tsar appears to have always followed. The tsar once again sometimes reduced the punishment but did not eliminate it entirely. For example, even a criminal allowed to return from

Siberian exile would still be prohibited from living in the two capital cities. In its effect and in its regularity, the petition process in late imperial Russia resembled the Victorian-era English procedure of commuting capital sentences by the Home Secretary upon recommendation of the court, with the Home Secretary thereby wielding very tangible judicial power.[11]

Although Alexander II frequently extended some form of clemency, he apparently never pardoned criminals duly convicted by a jury trial. He was not in any sense "soft" in cases involving high-ranking defendants who were found to be particularly morally questionable. Archives of the Ministry of Justice retain a series of extremely expressive petitions by the millionaire arsonist Stepan Ovsiannikov asking to be allowed to return from Siberia, without admitting his guilt or giving any reasons other than his old age. The Ministry of Justice reported to the tsar that "given the infamy which the Ovsiannikov case has incurred, a reversal or alteration of the Court's sentence, which took place despite the numerous means employed by Ovsiannikov to evade the law's sanction, could rather harmfully impact similar decisions throughout Russia, for which the decisions of the St. Petersburg District court always serve as models." Arson was punishable by hard labor, which was dished out to Ovsiannikov's two accomplices, and which he himself was spared because of his age, and so Alexander II rejected all his petitions. Even the intervention of the heir (the future Alexander III) in 1880 was opposed by the ministry and again rejected by the tsar. Only after coming to the throne in 1881, Alexander III finally allowed Ovsiannikov to return to European Russia.[12] Another high-publicity convict, the noblewoman Liudmila Gulak-Artemovskaia, repeatedly asked in vain to be spared going to Siberia because of poor health, citing the tsar's patronage of her alma mater, the elite Smolny Institute.[13] The mother of Karl von Landsberg, the imperial guard officer convicted of murder in 1879, petitioned in vain to ease his punishment.[14] In all these cases, the Ministry of Justice prepared a balanced assessment of the petitioner's situation pointing out the severity of the crime and any leniency already extended.

In sum, the tsar's personal and institutional involvement in the juridical field was tangible and significant but did not compromise the autonomy of the judiciary, especially given that pardoning criminals is a typical prerogative of heads of state.

THE JUDICIARY AND THE ADMINISTRATION

In addition to the emperor, there were two other centers of power that competed with the judiciary in Russia, especially before the reform of 1864. One was the "higher" police known as the Third Section, and the other was the

Ministry of the Interior, which controlled the regular police and much of the provincial administration. Before the doctrine of separation of powers appeared in the eighteenth century, judging had been for centuries seen as the substance of rule, the most important administrative activity and power of European rulers. For instance, the medieval and early modern English parliament was technically the highest court of justice in the realm, and the bulk of its work was judicial in character. Similarly, early modern Russian government chanceries (*prikazy*) were headed by a "judge" (*sudia*) distinct from bureaucratic clerks processing documents (*diaki*). At the same time, judicial powers in medieval and early modern Eurocentric regimes were divided among various offices and agencies according to the subject matter being judged, the importance of the case (by the severity of the offense or the amount being disputed), and the persons involved (military, clergy, peasants, and so on). One of the central mechanisms through which a modern Eurocentric state, including Russia, developed in the sixteenth and seventeenth centuries was the imposition of a uniform system of criminal justice, at least for the most important cases, such as murder, forgery, and treason. But legal pluralism has persisted in some form or other to this day, and it was certainly the norm before the twentieth century.[15] In reform-era Russia it was not clear how the judiciary's power would be defined in comparison to the two older and more privileged agencies.

A constant presence in the post-reform courtroom were the armed gendarmes who guarded defendants. The Corps of Gendarmes was the armed muscle of the Third Section, which investigated political crime and—at least before the 1860s—also a wide array of other matters, including high-profile nonpolitical crimes. Its power and at the same time its weakness was that it operated outside the regular governmental organization, since it was numerically small and subordinate only to the emperor. The anarchist Prince Petr Kropotkin, whose youth was spent in close proximity to the imperial court, described the Third Section as the most powerful institution in the empire, in practice more influential than the emperor because of its control of information and its power of surveillance over important individuals and even the tsar's person. Gendarme officers were also stationed in every provincial city and kept an eye on local officials. In 1866–1874 the director of the Third Section was Count Petr Shuvalov, sarcastically dubbed Peter IV because of his ambition and influence on the emperor.[16] In the aftermath of Karakozov's attempted regicide in 1866, Shuvalov cleverly exploited the tsar's understandable anxiety to aggrandize himself by promoting conservative ministerial appointments and exaggerating the revolutionary threat.

The Third Section kept Russia's judiciary under surveillance as it did other officials. Secret agents attended and reported from at least some of the major trials of the post-reform era. It appears that the surviving Third Section records are incomplete, and the scale of surveillance was probably greater. One particularly detailed report was from the 1872 forgery trial of the Miasnikov brothers, one of whom had been Shuvalov's aide (*adiutant*). This may explain their interest, but the report sounds as if it was routine practice. The agent reported on Prosecutor Koni and described the presentation of the political aspect of the case: the chief defense witness had earlier fought for the Paris Commune and was then extradited to Russia. But the agent also reported misconduct by the court bailiff, who allowed his acquaintances into the packed courtroom and turned others away, causing a disturbance in the public. While officially the investigations in most of the cases discussed in this book were conducted by the judiciary, the Third Section's agents sometimes reported to their director on the cases' basic factual circumstances, although they do not always appear to have been well informed. In the 1878 forgery case of Liudmila Gulak-Artemovskaia, the secret agent reported no helpful insights about her alleged victim, Nikolai Pastukhov, even though he was a millionaire and a leading industrialist who owned a landmark building on Nevsky Prospect. The agent did, however, report Gulak-Artemovskaia's alleged love affair with an influential member of the Council of State, Baron Nikolai Tornau. In the 1882 embezzlement case of Fedor Melnitskii, the chief treasurer of the Imperial Orphanage in Moscow, the Third Section very tangibly intervened in the official investigation when it arrested Melnitskii's daughter and imprisoned her for several months on suspicion that she was a revolutionary, merely because she had visited the same hotel where the terrorist Olga Liubatovich was known to have stayed.[17]

Although liberal lawyers and intellectuals feared and despised the Third Section, and despite occasional practical frictions, they could all form a situational alliance. This applied even to Koni, one of Russia's most critically minded judicial officials. In 1874 he wanted to suppress the abovementioned Kolemin gambling ring in St. Petersburg with its high-profile clientele. The famed head of St. Petersburg's detective police, Ivan Putilin, reported that the regular police would simply warn the criminals, and so Koni resorted to the law of 19 May 1871 that allowed him as the district procurator to enlist the gendarmes to conduct investigations. The raid was successful, and though the owner of the casino only had to pay a fine, a much greater punishment was that the government seized all the cash found at Kolemin's apartment.[18]

But the Third Section's exceptional position in the government was also a weakness: its members had extensive powers of supervision and surveillance but few areas of activity in which they had the final say.[19] In the 1860s the Third Section became more focused on suppressing political crime, especially after the Polish uprising of 1863, and while attempting to carve out for itself a distinct sphere of activity, it became another technocratic agency with a narrowly specialized function that could not be fundamentally changed despite all the ambition of its chief Petr Shuvalov, even though it appeared almighty to arrested revolutionaries. Its main staff was always small—only several thousand NCOs in the Corps of Gendarmes, several hundred gendarme officers, and a few dozen officials in the central office, though it did employ numerous secret agents and informants. For all its prerogatives the Third Section was not allowed to try cases itself, and so it could not supplant or undermine the courts.[20]

In addition to the central government in St. Petersburg, local centers of power also participated in the juridical field. The reform of 1864 corrected a major structural limitation of the earlier legal system, which was its integration into Russia's uniform provincial administration, headed by a governor. Governors were appointed personally by the emperor, but they were considered to be officials of the Ministry of the Interior. Pre-reform courts had been officially separate from the rest of the provincial administration and subordinate to the minister of justice in St. Petersburg since 1775.[21] But as a practical matter first-tier courts were tied into the district (*uezd*) and town structure, while second-tier courts were built into province-level administration, sharing the same buildings and the same bureaucratic culture. The mass of court secretaries, clerks, and lower-level judges did not stand out among other local civil servants (*chinovniki*). Only the highest court, the Senate, was visibly located outside the provincial system, with departments in St. Petersburg, Moscow, and Warsaw. Moreover, by the mid-nineteenth century at least the most important, province-level courts were staffed by trained lawyers whose careers depended on the Ministry of Justice, not on local authorities or local elites.[22]

A major breakthrough in the drafting of the 1864 reform statute therefore consisted in uncoupling the new court system from the provincial structure that had existed since the Muscovite era and was formalized by Catherine II's provincial statute of 1775 (see table 2). The reform proposal prepared in 1859 by the official and by that time hidebound imperial codification bureau, the Second Section, still tied the courts to the empire's administrative division and retained elected lower-level judgeships, which conservative officials hoped would secure the influence of landowning nobles in the new judiciary—something reformers were attempting to combat. But in 1861 the tsar moved the reform project to the State Chancellery, a more efficient agency that coordinated the

TABLE 2. CRIMINAL JUSTICE HIERARCHY BEFORE AND AFTER THE REFORM OF 1864 (SIMPLIFIED)

Pre-1864	After 1864
Emperor	
State Council	
Senate (St. Petersburg, Moscow, Warsaw Depts.)	Senate Criminal Cassation Department
— Provincial governor (approves sentences) Province-level courts (criminal/civil *palata,* commercial, conscience)	Judicial Chamber (*palata*) (Spb, Moscow, Kharkov, Kazan, Saratov, etc.) (ca. three to eight provinces)
— District (*uezd*)-level courts	District (*okruzhnoi*) Court (serves one or more *uezd*)

work of the Council of State, and the final draft created a completely different judicial structure. The first-tier district or circuit (*okruzhnye*) courts created by the reform of 1864 were to serve several of the county-sized administrative districts (*uezdy*), although in the more populated areas there was one court per district. The second tier, known as Judicial Chambers (*sudebnye palaty*), tied together the courts from several provinces and exercised crucial supervisory powers over lower-level judges, as well as reviewing all trial indictments. The largest and arguably most important judicial circuit (*okrug sudebnoi palaty*) was centered in Moscow, and in the early years of the reform it supervised roughly 40 percent of the caseload. Other initially formed circuits were in St. Petersburg, Kharkov, Kazan, and Saratov. The reform also completely reorganized the Senate as the highest appellate tier for the new courts, with the pre-reform appellate departments being gradually eliminated, and the two new departments for civil and criminal cases established to replace them. The State Council debated whether the reformed Senate would operate according to the new principles, with public proceedings and judges with life tenures, and at first conservatives were winning the argument, until the prominent jurist (and later Russia's conservative mastermind) Konstantin Pobedonostsev convinced the tsar to make the system consistent.[23]

The reform of 1864 took from the governors their most direct role in judicial matters. The 1775 provincial government statute stated somewhat paradoxically that a governor was "the master of his province" (*khozain*) but in the same sentence emphatically added that he was "not a judge."[24] While a governor was thus explicitly prohibited from trying cases, his most important legal function was to review and confirm criminal sentences (other than petty offenses). If he disagreed with the ruling, or if the defendant was from privileged classes, or if the defendant or the provincial procurator appealed, the case was moved for review in the Senate, which would have no qualms about ignoring a governor's opinion. The governor's review power therefore served as an additional protection for defendants and not a way for governors to subordinate or subvert the legal process. Governors also had an important quasi-judicial authority to expel from their province individuals deemed to be a public threat, even if they were not prosecuted in a court of law, but it was not a power they could easily abuse, as the process required considerable deliberation and negotiation.[25] The security laws of 1881 that followed the assassination of Alexander II extended this power with respect to military governors who ruled the most important provinces of the empire, and who now had the authority to essentially suspend the rule of law if security conditions demanded it. But having such authority did not mean actually exercising it, and it is impossible to agree with scholars who argue that the laws of 1881 spelled the doom of the independent judiciary in Russia.[26] Before 1881 an administrative expulsion would require a justification from the local authorities and be subject to complaint, while after 1881 the security law was primarily used to suppress revolutionary activity and had no bearing on the nonpolitical crime that is the focus of this book.

PRELIMINARY INVESTIGATION

The strongest institutional challenge to the post-reform judiciary was not the monarchy or high officials but the routine grassroots power of the police apparatus, which as in other Eurocentric states had important judicial and quasi-judicial functions, including responding to complaints about crime and conducting preliminary investigations.[27] The ideology of the separation of government powers that developed in Europe during the Enlightenment prescribed judicial and police authorities to be clearly demarcated and independent of each other.[28] That is, judges were not supposed to make arrests or be involved in the daily maintenance of public order, while the police and local governors were not supposed to try cases. In reality, though, the boundary between the police and the courts was as indeterminate in imperial Russia as it is in today's Eurocentric states. The police and various administrative tribunals in many countries have extensive judicial powers, especially to try small crime and so-called administrative cases (under what used to be called police law). The conduct of police during preliminary investigations also has an enormous impact on the outcome of a case. Conversely, legal officials often claim the power of supervision over police activities, as, for example, in the extensive law of search and seizure in today's United States, or in the Russian procuracy, whose officials oversee the observance of legality in all the branches and agencies of the government. In imperial Russia, the overlap was also considerable, which the post-reform press noted immediately after the reform of 1864.[29]

Stereotypical imperial-era policemen were authoritarian, crude, and also ignorant, weak, and corrupt, embodying what Sandra Dahlke has called "Old Russia"—that is, what she poses as an alternative premodern way of conducting government through nonpublic informal relationships and negotiations. Memoirist Ekaterina Kozlinina, who spent many years as a court clerk and reporter in Moscow, presents a more nuanced picture of pre-reform detectives as not particularly mindful of suspects' rights but effective in a crude and often cruel way. Historians of Russia tend to include the police or "the administration" in the same power nexus as the monarchy (or "the autocracy"), on the apparent presumption that the tsar fully controlled his police.[30] In reality, however, the police had an institutional culture and motives of its own, both in terms of daily corruption and in terms of bureaucratization, which neither the tsar nor his top advisers could effectively control. Even before the Great Reforms, the police, in particular the specialized detectives in larger cities, were becoming more professionalized and turning into essentially technical experts, much like all the other branches and agencies of the imperial government.

After the reform of 1864 the police still conducted preliminary investigations: it sought out and arrested suspects, located witnesses, and secured evidence. But legal officials—judicial investigators and procurators—now questioned suspects and witnesses, decided which evidence would be presented to the jury, and prepared the case for trial. Moreover, according to the 1864 rules of procedure, all pretrial testimony had to be repeated and verified before the jury and be open to cross-examination, limiting the police's ability to tamper with evidence. Pretrial records and trial transcripts reveal both close cooperation and mutual dependence between police and judicial authorities, but also a persistent tension, in line with Bourdieu's observation that the juridical field is constituted by internal and external conflicts over expertise and jurisdiction. One major source of tension was the fact that preliminary investigations were conducted without many of the procedural safeguards that became available during the trial itself, such as publicity or legal counsel, and thus compared unfavorably with courtroom proceedings. To borrow the language of sociologist Harold Garfinkel, police proceedings were in effect an alternative "ritual of degradation" that competed with the individual and social impact of the public trial.[31]

Pretrial procedures contrasted strongly with trials themselves, where testimony was given before the jury and was subject to cross-examination. There were no public pretrial hearings, and the accused did not have to be informed of the evidence against them or allowed counsel until shortly before the trial. Occasionally newspapers published information about important investigations, including the nature of the crime, the names of suspects, and whether they had been arrested or had confessed. As in Victorian England, this type of pretrial publicity was mostly a liability for defendants rather than a protection.[32] In contrast to the trial itself, which typically lasted only a day, pretrial investigations lasted many months or even longer, given that post-reform legal officials were very overworked.[33] Post-1864 legal procedure is typically described as adversarial, meaning that both the prosecution and the defense were supposed to have equal opportunity to present arguments and to question witnesses. It is more accurate, however, to describe post-reform criminal procedure—as well as French procedure on which it was based—as mixed, combining adversarial principles with inquisitorial ones.[34] The latter meant that the judges' role was to establish the truth rather than merely preside over a judicial contest, and judges as well as prosecutors were required to disclose and consider any exculpatory evidence and to ensure that the defendant's interests were protected. While the trial itself was largely adversarial, with defense counsel and the defendant's right to confront witnesses, the pretrial investigation was firmly inquisitorial, and defendants had limited ability to plan their defense, especially if they were under arrest.[35] If they were free on pretrial bail, they were of course able to consult a lawyer but they could not get one to assist during interrogations or to formally negotiate with the state on their behalf.[36] It must be noted that the model system of criminal justice in the nineteenth century, that of England, also looked very different from our current notion of a fair trial: while English trials in the period from roughly 1750 to 1850 did involve a public confrontation between the prosecutor and the accused, the defendants there also had very little opportunity to prepare their defense, rarely had counsel, would have been incarcerated in squalid jails, been denied access to depositions and the names of prosecution witnesses, or not even been adequately informed about the charges against them, which could be changed in the last moment.[37]

The judicial ritual commenced when the suspect was first questioned or detained by the police. There were several distinct patterns of how individuals crossed the boundary between freedom and incarceration: a complex and deeply traumatic experience. One relatively rare alternative was to surrender voluntarily or be detained on the spot of the crime. When a violent crime was committed in an urban setting, the perpetrator often had no realistic chance of escaping or had no intention of doing so. One famous example is the case of Vera Zasulich, who shot the police chief of St. Petersburg in a crowded reception room and neither fled nor resisted arrest. A very similar but nonpolitical case (discussed in chapters 6 and 7) was the Nepenin married couple, who in 1873 fatally stabbed the wife's former lover and were tackled by the servants and friends of the victim. Other famous examples were the 1875 case of Anastasiia Kairova, who attempted to slash her rival's throat while she was asleep, and the 1879 case of Praskovia Kachka, who shot her boyfriend. Neither woman made any attempt to flee or resist.[38]

In other murder cases the perpetrator, whether rich or poor, attempted to flee to some safe location. A young Tatar man, Tazetdin Khisamutdinov, who killed his elderly employer in Kazan in 1873, was caught outside the city while walking to his village. That same year, an eighteen-year-old peasant, Ivan Mikhailov, killed an elderly monk in St. Petersburg and fled to his brother's home at the Okulovka station on the Moscow-Petersburg railroad, where a police detective found him drunk and hiding in a stack of firewood. In 1879, an imperial guard officer, Karl von Landsberg, slashed the throat of an elderly moneylender and fled by railroad to his family estate in Lithuania. He was followed by police detectives, who waited to arrest him until he returned to St. Petersburg a few days later. Another aristocratic murderer, Grigorii Bezobrazov, fled from Kharkov to St. Peterburg and was caught after a complex investigation. Finally, some suspects neither fled nor confessed but attempted to prove their innocence when confronted by police or investigators. Sometimes this happened in murder cases that were based on indirect evidence, as in cases as diverse as that of Aleksei Danilov in 1867 or Margarita Jujean in 1878. But this was almost always the scenario in major cases of white-collar crime, such as fraud and forgery, which tended to be complex and required investigators to determine whether illegal activity had in fact taken place. A particularly vivid example comes from the unique prison diary of Fedor Melnitskii, head treasurer of the Imperial Orphanage in Moscow, arrested for embezzlement in 1881. Fedor came to the police complaining that he lost a large sum of money when he fainted on the street. In his diary he described how he was at first allowed to leave the police building but before he was out of sight, a soldier chased him down and asked him to return. He was then told that the police needed to get his testimony and that he was only a witness, but several hours later, after the police notified Melnitskii's supervisor, he was told that he was now a suspect and arrested for good.[39]

Compared to the twentieth century, there are not many first-person descriptions of arrest experiences from the post-reform era. Aside from the Melnitskii diary, these descriptions mostly come from political prisoners, although their accounts generally conform in their external circumstances. Almost all political prisoners had engaged with the regular police system at the early stage of their incarceration and occasionally were kept in regular prisons for long periods of time. The difference in the revolutionaries' experience was no doubt in its psychological aspects, rather than physical ones: most had been long prepared mentally for their eventual arrest. Most had evaded police for years, and typically they were aware of police surveillance before the arrest, which would typically still come unexpectedly on the street or if they stumbled into a compromised location. Even with political suspects, however, the police tended to wait to be sure they had the right person, which does not seem to have been the practice in Germany, for instance, judging from Lev Deutch's memoirs.[40] Even in murder prosecutions the police occasionally waited to make the arrest, especially if a high-status suspect was involved.[41]

Memoirs show that even for experienced underground activists the arrest came as a severe mental and emotional shock. Other than sometimes attempting to flee or to fight their way out, most would immediately attempt to discard any incriminating evidence and if possible to argue that the police had arrested the wrong person. But nonpolitical prisoners, even wealthy and influential ones and even those who had every reason to expect a police search, often failed to destroy crucial incriminating papers, including, for example, the noblewomen Mother Mitrofania (1874) and Liudmila Gulak-Artemovskaia (1877), who failed to get rid of damning handwriting samples. Sometimes the police were able to seize entire stashes of papers in a sudden raid. This, for example, happened in the massive 1875 case of the Moscow Commercial Loan Bank (the so-called Strousberg Affair), which began when the police seized and sealed off the bank's office building and all its documents.

Once the initial interview with the police or the judicial investigator was over and the prisoners were finally allowed to rest, they would typically have an introspective experience or mentally review their entire life. Some recall having nightmares and visions of shrinking walls or nasty barracks full of rough people. For nonpolitical prisoners from the upper classes, the outlook was not as grim, especially if they had been arrested for a nonviolent crime and were placed under house arrest or set free on bail. Melnitskii was not so lucky: in his prison diary he wrote that neither on the day of his arrest nor in the subsequent days did he have anything to eat or to drink, he felt "heavy headed, had a dull feeling, an ache in all the limbs," but, in his fighting words, "not for a moment had I the thought to deprive myself of life."[42]

Incarceration conditions in late imperial Russia varied considerably. Prisoners from the privileged classes, including political prisoners who were almost exclusively of non-proletarian origins, were treated exponentially better than ordinary peasants and laborers, unless the police wanted to torment them on purpose. The famous populist Yekaterina Breshko-Breshkovskaia, who unsuccessfully posed as a peasant and was arrested for that reason, was not allowed to wash or change clothes for months and was kept in local prisons in several Ukrainian towns, full of lice and without clean water, until she revealed her real name. She noted that new, non-privileged prisoners were invariably subjected to beatings and extortion by fellow inmates.[43]

By contrast, upper-class inmates were kept in clean, dry, and well-lit cells, could have bedding, decent food, and reading matter, and sometimes were even allowed to move around within the prison building. Most would still start out deprived not only of their freedom but of all personal possessions and normal clothing; they would reacquire them gradually with the help of friends and relatives in what appears as a symbolic act of personal rebirth in the new conditions. The terrorist Mikhail Frolenko was initially taken to a local police station when arrested in St. Petersburg in 1881, allowed to keep his clothes, and only turned into a real prisoner at the Third Section headquarters, where he was given cigarettes and what he said was a warm and comfortable prison coat. Another terrorist, Nikolai Morozov, was arrested in 1875 when attempting to enter Russia with forged papers, and he was able to ingest an incriminating letter; he also kept his revolver for many hours until finally searched at the police station. He never thought to ask for a receipt for the money and personal property taken from him at the border, and it was stolen; but in other cases prisoners were given their property back.[44]

Privileged nonpolitical prisoners were treated even better and allowed not only their own clothing and bedding but also their own furniture and sometimes even a servant. The most lenient conditions I have seen were provided to Mother Mitrofania (Rosen), arrested for forgery in St. Petersburg in 1873. She was at first kept under house arrest in the hotel Moskva. Procurator Koni allowed her to go to church with a police officer and even to go on a pilgrimage. During the trial Mitrofania praised Koni for his humane treatment. Her subordinate nun claimed that Koni "knew how to ennoble the very act of arrest, he assigned secret police officers in plain clothes who were on duty in the corridor day and night." After Mitrofania was moved to Moscow, the conditions were stricter but still luxurious by any standards. She complained that her quarters insulted her feminine sensibility, but it turned out that she occupied a comfortable room at a police station with two windows, rugs on the floor, and her own bedding and furniture, and that she had a young novice to serve her. She was allowed to take walks in the garden that belonged to the police doctor and was also invited to take a carriage ride in Petrovsky Park with police officers, which she considered a mockery that would expose her to public curiosity.[45] Because Mitrofania was illegally communicating with supporters standing under her windows on the street, the bottom panes in the windows of her room had to be whited out.[46]

Other examples of privileged prisoners include the millionaire sectarian Mikhail Solodovnikov, who was allowed food from outside and walks, but no writing, and his servant, a Latvian who did not know any Russian. As for Melnitskii, on the day of his arrest he was forced to strip to his underwear and deprived of his money, watch, pencil, and even his toothpick. In a few days the police took his fur coat as well. He was taken to a room at the police station with a wooden floor and two beds with small pillows. He was not permitted to turn off the light. One of the beds was broken, and the entire room was "disgustingly dirty," with large black cockroaches, bedbugs, and fleas. When he put on his spectacles, he could see that the room was "literally covered in large grey insects." In the morning he was offered the disgusting prison tea but on that same day he was allowed to send a note home, and his children brought him clean bedding and food, and eventually another warm coat, while the lower-class prisoners washed the floor and the window in his cell and shook out the mattress. While walking to the court building for questioning he was able to stop by a bakery. Subsequently he was moved from one police station to another, and everywhere he had a clean and heated room with a bed and his own food.[47]

An important purpose of incarcerating suspects was to prevent them from communicating with the outside world, but both political and ordinary prisoners were able to do so on a regular basis. The anarchist Prince Kropotkin recalled that even in the Third Section headquarters there was an official who sympathized with the radicals and carried messages.[48] For nonpolitical prisoners the process was even easier. In the Kharkov counterfeiting case two of the defendants were paid by the wealthy ringleaders to take the blame, and while in prison they enjoyed large amounts of vodka, good food, and gambling. But the most notorious example was

Mother Mitrofania, who was able to send and receive numerous notes and even entire packets of documents, some of which were intercepted. She provided her friends with detailed instructions on how to hide notes in fried fish, kasha, and pies, and passed the notes with nuns, servants, and even policemen, with one note hidden in a ball of yarn that she sent as a gift to another nun. In one message she referred to the "fools" who were guarding her.[49] Similarly, Melnitskii was caught corresponding with his children, using his teenage daughter, who was not searched by the guards. Some of his intercepted messages were also sent through his servant, a former detective, Baistrukov. Even the accused killer of an entire family, a young home tutor named Gorskii, was able to write letters to his family from his specially guarded prison cell, according to a secret-police investigation.[50]

In addition to the physical isolation, prisoners had to contend with questioning by police and legal officials. This included taking a photograph and, in Melnitskii's case, walking with police officers on the streets of Moscow along the route where he claimed to have lost the orphanage's money, the entire time followed by crowds of spectators. The default interrogation methods of imperial-era police were clearly designed for unsophisticated prisoners, employing very basic psychological manipulation—for instance, lying that other defendants had confessed, affecting sympathy, or threatening severe punishment. Melnitskii was visited for hours at a time by a nonuniformed police agent, known just as Yurka (diminutive for Yurii), who would ask him about his life and urge him to confess to stealing the money. These visits lasted for several days, and at one point Yurka even promised to arrange for his release and make it look as if the money had been found accidentally. Melnitskii then wrote in his diary, "The best detectives from St. Petersburg are here, and the Trustee Seliverstov promises a 10,000 ruble reward." Political prisoners who were initially questioned by regular policemen reported similar crude tactics. When persuasion did not work, another tactic was to threaten to arrest someone close to the prisoner or simply summon the person for questioning. This method was applied to political and nonpolitical prisoners, and it worked on many radical activists and even on Vera Figner, one of the last prominent members of the People' Will to be arrested in 1883.[51] It did not work on Melnitskii, however, even though the police claimed that they had arrested his children, who were suspected of hiding the money stolen by their father: Melnitskii never admitted to any wrongdoing.

Nonpolitical prisoners occasionally complained about police and judicial investigators. Mother Mitrofania, who was perhaps the most solicitously treated prisoner in imperial Russia, was also the biggest complainer, claiming during her trial that she had been threatened and blackmailed by officials. The investigator said, in her words, "The court and the jurors will never believe anything I say because everything around me is fraud and forgery; my witnesses are bogus and my account books are forged. He was almost saying I'll go to hard labor." The judge responded: "You publicly recount such tortures, which, I believe, are not conceivable in this age in Russia, not only toward a person of your rank and station, but even toward the darkest peasant. And you took no measures to stop illegal actions or at least to counteract them to some extent?"[52]

Conversely, post-reform trial records show that police corruption directly affected criminal investigations, in particular when officers assisted an accused criminal. Returning to the Mitrofania case, when the nun was placed under arrest at the Sushchevskaia police station in Moscow, the authorities had to conduct a special search for a police officer who was not bribable, finding Major Zharinov to be of "high moral qualities," and two policeman Ignatiev and Filippov, who were "unbribable" and assigned to guard Mitrofania's room. Mitrofania also had connections to Moscow police: for instance, her attorney, Colonel Vrubel (Wrubel), had friends among police officers, according to a confidential memo from the Moscow district procurator to the minister of justice. Another police officer, and a witness for Mitrofania, Loviagin, had introduced her to one of her alleged victims, the merchant Medyntseva, while one Petr Globo-Mikhalenko, who was soon to become an important judicial investigator specializing in complex investigations—including that of the Moscow Commercial Loan Bank and of the criminal group called the Jacks of Hearts Club—acted as an unofficial go-between in negotiations between Mitrofania and Medyntseva's son (Globo-Mikhalenko's friend).[53] Loviagin continued his police service and in 1877 featured in another major fraud scandal, that of General Gartung, who engaged him unofficially to keep order as he negotiated with his alleged victims. When police officers who were actually on duty showed up, they forced Loviagin to leave. The case of the Jacks of Hearts noted that a local police officer, quarter overseer Schwind, helped some of the defendants find their victims and take loans secured by nonexistent merchandise.[54] In some situations, judicial authorities in St. Petersburg had no confidence in local legal staff: in the massive customs fraud investigation in Taganrog in 1885, the minister sent special investigators from the district of Odessa.[55]

DETECTIVES AND SECRET AGENTS

Another way in which the post-reform trial clashed with administration and police was that the police relied on paid secret agents and informants of varying virtue and reliability. Agents solved cases by gaining the suspect's trust and then betraying it, so the entire practice contrasted sharply with the principle of public oral testimony prevalent in the courtroom. In 1869 a legal journalist called the use of informants "the darkest" side of Russian pretrial procedure, claiming that they were "primarily" recruited from the criminal world and giving several examples of agents who acted as provocateurs. His proposed solution was to place detectives under direct control of judicial authorities rather than the police. Had this solution been adopted, however, critics would no doubt have claimed that secret informants were now corrupting the judiciary. Moreover, it is difficult to imagine that investigators in the more important cities did not already have their own network of detectives. The entire business of criminal investigations had been moving toward professionalization for some time. The usual example of this dynamic is the career of the head of the St. Petersburg detective police Ivan Putilin, who by the turn of the century had become a celebrity and published stories about some of his cases. But the profession of a police spy is as old as the organized state itself, and in imperial Russia there were professional private criminal detectives from the 1840s at the latest.[56]

In most cases discussed in this book secret agents and detectives were only briefly mentioned in trial accounts, usually as part of the indictment rather than in courtroom debates. In a fascinating murder trial that took place in Kazan in 1873, the police received a lead about the location of the suspect, a twenty-one-year-old Tatar man, from an informant whose identity and exact report were not revealed at the trial. One of the defense lawyers criticized this secrecy but was sharply rebuked by the prosecutor, arguing that the informant's identity did not add anything to the case and that the use of informants should not be attacked, since "if society understood the necessity of assisting the police and the judiciary in searching for suspects and in general in uncovering the truth in criminal cases, then naturally the police would not have any secrets, but . . . most [people] conceal the truth . . . either out of apathy or due to the inability to find their personal interest in the large common one, or due to the desire to not bother oneself and the lack of experience with the new courts." If the police publicized the names of their agents, they would be unable to use their services in the future.[57]

Despite this secrecy, however, some discussions of police informants are found in post-reform criminal trials. Some of these agents were either hired privately or at least semiprivately. In the Kharkov counterfeiting case mentioned above, a local official named Valerian Vittan aspired to be appointed as a judicial investigator and spent his personal money on an entire network of spies to solve crimes. One such spy, named Boris, was the first to discover that a local gentry landowner, Gavrilov, manufactured counterfeit money on his estate. Vittan then became so caught up in his investigation that he joined the counterfeiting ring himself and ended up on trial. In 1866 a former army officer of Polish origin, Wenceslaus Kossow, hired private detectives to track down two swindlers who had robbed his mother on a sea voyage to Lubeck. The agents followed them to Naples, Rome, Florence, Bremen, and finally to Ems, where the pair were arrested in 1867 and extradited to Russia. During the search Kossow himself may have impersonated a police agent to gain local authorities' cooperation. Another example is mentioned in Fedor Melnitskii's prison diary from 1882: in Moscow there allegedly was a police major who owned property and could afford to hire "rogues" to investigate cases for him. This officer allegedly said that "ten people will lie but the eleventh will help him, and sometimes, when he is lucky, he will get a decoration, and then perhaps a promotion."[58]

A standard example of open tension between the values of the public trial and the use of paid informants that made such a trial possible was the 1872 forgery case of the millionaire brothers Aleksandr and Ivan Miasnikov, in which either the police or (less likely) the civil plaintiff sent undercover agents to a remote provincial location to befriend one of the Miasnikovs' former employees and ply him with drink to elicit incriminating testimony. Anatolii Koni, the prosecutor, for all his liberal reputation, vigorously argued that there was nothing wrong with such tactics. The defense attorney, Konstantin Arseniev, disagreed, arguing that he fully acknowledged the necessity of detective police but maintaining that police "agents must act through honest means, and they do not have the right to provoke someone to speak and to systematically intoxicate him." Arseniev sought to question four police agents but could not get them to appear at the trial.[59]

Even more open in discussing secret agents was the Melnitskii case, primarily because it attracted many bounty hunters seeking the money allegedly lost by Fedor Melnitskii and the ten-thousand-ruble reward offered by the Imperial Orphanage. In his prison diary Melnitskii noted with a touch of pride that he was up against "the best detectives in Moscow and Petersburg." Two agents even testified at the trial, but they were not the best ones and seem to have actually impeded the investigation. They were not professional detectives but employees at the shop of Melnitskii's associate, who were bribed by the police to inform on their master, although the police had also engaged other agents. The trial account noted that these witnesses' "types and testimony are very characteristic." One of them, Cherepkov, was "a short stocky ruddy fellow about twenty-five or twenty-six, with mousy quick eyes, curly hair, small mustache and short sideburns. Dressed in a worn coat (*pidzhak*), a 'Little Russian' (*malorossiiskaia*) shirt, and tall 'Russian' boots. Speaks in a strained voice, always gesturing with his left hand." During a break in the trial Cherepkov pulled out his notes and began "rubbing his forehead and slowly rocking back and forth," apparently memorizing his testimony. The second witness, Krylov, was a "skinny, short blond man, with large grey eyes, stiff hair and a thin little beard. Dressed in a jacket, a 'Little Russian' shirt and untucked trousers." An officer of the detective police, an ethnic Greek named Nicholas, also testified during the trial. Nicholas explained that the police used "many occasional detective agents, they are paid between 5 and 5,000 rubles." He also said that Cherepkov and Krylov "lied a lot" and that he only paid them to prevent them from interfering with the investigation rather than for their actual services. He added, "To achieve our objectives, we use all kinds of means and sometimes we have to accept the services of persons in whom we have very little trust." Nicholas would not reveal which agent actually cracked the case.[60]

The appearance of informants as prosecution witnesses caused a minor scandal in the courtroom, and one of the lawyers mockingly asked Cherepkov how he justified his employer's trust by serving as an informant against him, causing laughter in the audience.[61] At the end of the trial, the prominent defense lawyer Vladimir Gerard, who represented a minor participant in the case, inveighed:

> The citizens' moral sensibility looks askance on a denunciation and one would think that the law cannot force one's conscience to permit to do what goes against this sensibility . . . woe to such a country where every citizen must see in his neighbor, in his friend, today a traitor and tomorrow a snitch! This would be the highest form of social corruption. Public opinion is even more indignant at a denunciation because, first, snitches are very rarely persons completely unknown to the criminal, but for the most part his friends, and second, because [informing] goes side by side with blood money, *Blutgeld* . . . every honest person is disgusted by snitching . . . having once tasted the pleasures of snitching, [the agents] then become scoundrels (speaks with particular excitement) I have been practicing law for 15 years and am constantly resenting this. When they crack a case—this is great, now drive them out and do not bring them to the trial, a place of oathtaking and trust (*prisiaga i doverie*).[62]

It appears that even respectable police detectives could overstate the significance of secret agents, however. A good example is the 1873 murder of an elderly monk, Illarion, in St. Petersburg by a former servant. The celebrated police sleuth

Ivan Putilin in his memoirs presents this case as a feat of detective work. In reality, the monk's former servant, Ivan Mikhailov, came under suspicion immediately, and the detectives learned about his likely location from his friend who worked at the nearby train station. The old-fashioned method of investigating crimes by questioning suspects and witnesses rather than gathering forensic evidence still remained highly relevant, because catching suspects and gathering sufficient evidence against them were different challenges. While under the new rules of procedure a defendant's confession was not as important as before, gathering incriminating statements that could provide further leads was still essential.[63]

The new courts operated alongside other institutions that were longer established, better funded, and had greater political and social capital. In addition to the monarchy and the person of the monarch, these included various government agencies and officials, especially the Third Section and the Ministry of the Interior with its policemen and provincial administrations, to say nothing of the various agencies that supervised their own tribunals (such as military and ecclesiastical courts). Most of these exercised legal or quasi-legal functions, all of which had to be readjusted in the course of the reform. The courts' autonomy thus was a practical as well as ideological issue. Although some agencies, such as the police and the Third Section, have been presented as antitheses to the courts of law, their cooperation was still indispensable if the criminal justice system was to function. Even the emperor and the monarchy as an institution, often seen as the antipode of the rule of law, operated within strictly defined bounds and supported the new courts more often than they attempted to subvert them.

CHAPTER 2

Public Justice

The experiment with public military trials that began in Warsaw in 1862 continued in Russia proper in 1865, that is, after the reform statutes of 1864 had been issued but before the reformed courts were inaugurated in May 1866. In April 1865, four men were tried in Novgorod for the murder of Aulic Counselor Leutenfeld's widow, although only spectators "in uniform" were admitted into the courtroom. Then, on May 29, a soldier and two peasants stood trial in Moscow for robbing and killing a tavernkeeper, his wife, and their three daughters. An "enormous" crowd of spectators flooded the former hotel used as a makeshift courtroom and incidentally named Evropa. Lacking a tradition of public trials, both the spectators and the participants seem to have relied on the closest equivalent and treated the proceedings as a theatrical performance, reacting with loud applause to the lawyer's speeches and to tearful appeals for mercy by the kneeling defendants. All three defendants were represented by the same attorney, a law graduate (*kandidat prav*) named Zorin, who fought hard to distinguish the extent of his clients' culpability, to secure for them a chance to speak freely in their defense, and perhaps to save at least some of them from the firing squad.[1]

By then, criminal trials had also become public in the other major European and Eurocentric legal systems. Publicity came to be viewed as an indispensable element of the rule of law. The foundational figures of modern criminal justice from Voltaire and Montesquieu to Beccaria and Bentham all strongly argued, beginning in the mid-eighteenth century, that justice had to be public and transparent, limiting government abuses. Judges to this day quote Bentham's words "Publicity is the very soul of justice . . . and the surest of all guards against improbity," while, as one modern scholar has noted, secret trials are viewed as "presumptively unfair."[2] In Russia this sentiment was known and influential, but before the reform of 1864 criminal trials followed the Continental inquisitorial model of written nonpublic proceedings. As soon as political issues could be discussed in print after 1856, however, prestigious "thick" journals targeting elite readers began to promote the idea that Russian legal institutions should, and soon would, become open to the public. Lawyers arguing the cause of reform in print and to their superiors in the government maintained that publicity was inseparable from the judiciary's independence and from having oral and adversarial trials, all of which were to become foundational elements of the post-1864 legal order.

In addition to the early experiments in the military courts, the old pre-reform courts were also made public by the law of 11 October 1865.[3] While the old courts soon closed down in the central provinces, they continued to function in the outlying areas of the empire, sometimes for decades.[4] Typically historians view the local (*zemstvo*) self-government and the press as the most important institutions of Russian civil society before 1905, but the public trial was another important, distinct, element, since it had a very tangible power to punish with prison and hard labor.

Although ordinary trials would officially remain public after 1917 as well, the late imperial period was the only time in Russian history when the public could do more than simply attend criminal trials but could also follow and discuss the proceedings largely unhindered by censorship. Courtroom publicity was especially important because most other types of public justice had by then largely disappeared in Russia: corporal punishment was abolished as a judicial sentence in 1863, and public executions were carried out only in exceptional cases.[5] But as this chapter argues, in the mid-1860s it was not immediately clear or predetermined who would be included in public legality, and where, when, and how that public would participate in the legal sphere. All these practices had to be negotiated and constructed.[6] The nineteenth century was also the golden age of the right to privacy for the respectable classes, who enjoyed unparalleled freedom from state intrusion into their family and economic affairs. But as Bentham observed, publicity and privacy were not a dichotomy but a continuum depending on "the number of the persons to whom knowledge is considered as communicated."[7]

This balance between private and public was affected not only by legal institutions and procedures but also by new communication technologies that spread during the mid-century, including railway networks, the telegraph, and photography, as well as mass-circulation print media.[8] Essential for these innovations was a large class of educated property owners who could participate in public trials and benefit from its lessons.

Even though great criminal trials by definition had a sensationalist and entertainment appeal, this attraction produced, and was implicated in, a wealth of political and social meanings. As Bentham and more recently Foucault have taught us, watching a public event always involves categorizing and evaluating. Simply allowing particular individuals to observe a judicial ritual was a political act, allowing them to know and giving them a certain power, and yet in turn also making them vulnerable to the participants' and the fellow spectators' panoptic gaze. This was especially so in late imperial Russia, when the courtroom public at landmark trials included the most powerful individuals in the empire. Bentham's quip about judges being exposed to the court of public opinion applied particularly forcefully in the Russian case. The courts were scrutinized by the elite, whose power and status were thereby elevated, though the elite itself was under scrutiny while scrutinizing itself. In sum, the variety of public justice created in post-reform Russia tended to raise the stakes for everyone involved, instead of creating larger public spaces or dissipating social pressure in some other way.

CONSTRUCTING THE PUBLIC

The failure of the Moscow Commercial Loan Bank in 1875 was Russia's first major public corporate scandal, which ruined thousands of people, both rich and not so rich. The bank's managers and directors as well as the German "railway king" Henry Bethel Strousberg were indicted for bribery and fraud when the trial opened on May 29 of the following year. Although a special commission had collected paperwork from about six hundred victims, on the day of the trial another two thousand showed up in the court building, creating such disorder that it took hours simply to write down and check their names.[9] This crowd struck observers as demure and poorly dressed, perhaps intentionally to emphasize their losses, and clearly contrasted with what had by then already emerged as a typical courtroom public that was well dressed and eager or downright festive. The impact of what was in effect a public demonstration was so powerful that the defense lawyers contrived to have the trial postponed. In the interim the poorer victims were compensated and did not appear at the second trial later that year.

The Moscow "bank case" demonstrates how trial publicity could take different forms and produce different effects, depending on who was included and at what stage of the proceedings. The introduction of public trials in Russia during the Great Reforms is taken in existing scholarship as a self-explanatory and necessary step, since most of us today have the notion of a spacious courtroom with spectators in rows of seats. In reality, legal publicity is not simple or clear even today: for instance, in the twenty-first century, is a trial that is not broadcast online truly public? In the nineteenth century, creating public justice was similarly not just a matter of opening the doors of the courtroom. Rather, the public had to be imagined and constructed or, in the case of England, which already had a form of courtroom publicity, reimagined and reconstructed. Public proceedings had existed in some form in various parts of the world, including Europe, long before the nineteenth century. But in Western Europe, trial publicity was suppressed by the influence of Roman law, which was "discovered" in medieval Italy and had been adopted in much of Europe by the mid-sixteenth century. Under the influence of Roman and canon law, the major Continental legal systems, such as those in France and the German states, used inquisitorial trial procedure, which was closed to the public, in contrast to punishments and executions, which, as the readers of Foucault know, were public and often gruesome. Even in England, where common-law courts were open to the public, the meaning and the practice of publicity was very different from today's understanding: as Bentham noted, getting into an English courtroom was one thing; hearing anything was a different matter. Moreover, many important legal matters in England were tried in equity and ecclesiastical courts, which used inquisitorial procedure and were as secretive as their Continental counterparts.[10]

Influential arguments for public justice as a fundamental principle that boosted or even created political legitimacy are generally traced to eighteenth-century reformers, whose ideas underpin Eurocentric criminal justice to this day.[11] Beccaria's influential 1764 treatise *On Crimes and Punishments* argued that "secrecy" is "tyranny's strongest shield" and proposed that "verdicts and proof of guilt should be published," because public opinion was "perhaps the only cement holding society together."[12] Beccaria did not, however, envision making the entire legal process public. Bentham, Beccaria's avid follower, discussed legal publicity in much more detail and argued strongly in its favor. One reason was that publicity discourages witnesses from lying and prevents mistakes, while at the same time does not add "to the mass of delay, vexation, and expense." While agreeing that publicity may prevent some witnesses from testifying at all, Bentham argued that this was on balance a small price to pay for all the benefits it offered. The second argument in favor of publicity was that it makes judges accountable to public opinion, and thus "it keeps the judge himself, while trying, under trial," at the same time protecting the reputation of an honest judge. Moreover, publicity encourages judges to give reasons for their decisions and thus will reveal the good and the bad aspects of legal norms. The third reason was that publicity operated as a "school . . . of morality," in which "men imbibe . . . the love of justice." Publicity was not an absolute right, however, and Bentham would extend publicity only to "all observations of which evidence is the subject," not to every aspect of criminal proceedings. Moreover, since Bentham conceived publicity and privacy not as a dichotomy but as a continuum, he offered nine exceptions when the judges should be able to close a trial to the public, including trials that agitate public order, protecting the participants, and preserving individual and family reputations, public decency, or state secrets.[13]

As I discuss in chapter 4, Bentham's works and his arguments for transparent justice were familiar to Russian jurists and legal officials. Imperial Russia has a reputation for authoritarianism, and indeed its government continued to prohibit many forms of public association and had neither political parties nor a free press long after these practices became common in Western Europe. But this does not mean that the Russian vision of the political and social order had no place for public life or civil society. What Alexander Martin has called the "imperial social project" of Catherine II sought to build a prosperous middle class inhabiting civic spaces with venues for public activities. Even Nicholas I's authoritarian regime encouraged or at least did not hinder many forms of civil society, as Susan Smith-Peter has shown in her book on provincial society and Nicholas's policies of "small reforms."[14] Still, there is some doubt as to whether by the mid-nineteenth century Russia had a "public" that could imbibe the lessons of criminal justice as Bentham contended. Most scholars argue that the courtroom became a unique space for public speech in post-reform Russia, and that public justice was a completely unprecedented practice.[15] Russians at the time said similar things, such as one trial observer in 1872 who wrote: "In Russia there are no other questions than those of criminal justice in which public opinion can have any role."[16] While a culture of public speaking and rhetoric had existed in Russia prior to the Great Reforms and enjoyed considerable prestige, it only became a mass practice in the 1860s with the introduction of public trials, relaxation of censorship, and the appearance of the local *zemstvo* self-government.[17]

Some forms of public life had existed in Russia for centuries, as they had elsewhere: this included church services, parades and processions, fairs and marketplaces, or popular celebrations. In the late seventeenth and early eighteenth centuries these were joined by Peter's famous *assamblei,* balls, official celebrations, academic events, and theater performances.[18] But the nineteenth-century version of public life envisioned events with social and political impact, some of which, like mass elections or public political debates, would not appear in Russia until the twentieth century. More in line with the general Eurocentric trend were the Russian "small reforms," including the establishment of various local societies, literary life, public libraries, schools, even firefighter companies.[19]

As for legal publicity, it is often emphasized that pre-reform Russian trials, like trials in other inquisitorial systems, were closed to the public. Even newspapers were not allowed to publish the details of actual court cases; however, this prohibition only appeared in 1817.[20] But this secrecy was not absolute. Even though defendants did not have the right to personally appear before the judges, the latter had the discretion to personally interview them. In Moscow, arguably the most important judicial center in late imperial Russia (since it served a much larger area than St. Petersburg did), one of the wings in the court building was set aside for the "provisional prison" (*vremennaia tiurma*), which held criminal defendants summoned by judges during trials, so that they would not have to be transported every day from the regular Butyrskaia prison on the outskirts of the city.[21] Although pre-reform trials were not public, a court building was a busy place, especially in larger cities, where it would house several first- and second-tier courts. On the second (provincial) and the third (Senate) tier of the court hierarchy defendants also had the right to employ a representative to review the case and make any comments in defense of their clients, which also made the case less "secret." Even though pre-reform attorneys were not required to be admitted to the bar (which did not yet exist) or to have a legal or any other formal education, the more upscale lawyers in larger cities did have legal training and experience. Long before the reform some government agencies, especially those administering the so-called state peasants, had already begun to experiment with public procedures at the lowest levels, most likely for the same reasons of expedience and efficiency that motivated early English courts to be public. Moreover, even though pre-reform trials could not be reported, newspapers published large amounts of legal and quasi-legal information, including notices about bankruptcies, properties being listed for sale or sold off for debt, as well as individuals being limited in their legal rights (for example, adult children not permitted to borrow in their parents' name).

Finally, there were two key aspects of criminal justice that became public long before the Great Reforms. One was punishment, which had typically been administered in public since the early modern period. Even though corporal punishment as a criminal sentence was abolished in 1863, a few public executions took place in the late imperial period, mostly of mass murderers and those radical activists who used violence. The second aspect was publication of legislation, which for Bentham was as important as public trials for making justice transparent. While earlier tsars published many of their laws and decrees, the landmark Complete Collection of the Laws of the Russian Empire covering 1649 to 1825 appeared in 1830, while the Digest of the Laws that included only legislation still in force, as well as numerous new provisions, was published in 1833 and went into effect as of 1835. Tsars and administrative agencies continued to frequently issue secret decrees and orders with the force of law, but these do not seem to have applied to the basic nonpolitical crime discussed in this book. In short: pre-reform publicity was limited, but it was not unheard of and developed gradually rather than as a forceful and artificial imposition from above.

The earliest projects for legal reform that appeared in the 1850s already called for extending legal publicity. An important 1857 article by the leading professor of criminal law, Sergei Barshev, argued on the basis of the teachings of German jurist Carl Mittermeier (1787–1867) that public proceedings were not a threat to Russia's existing regime and were superior to the existing secret procedure. Barshev noted the common objection at the time that because most judges in Russia were elected rather than appointed, public exposure would influence their fairness. He proposed a transitional period, during which public access would be limited to persons with special tickets and supplemented by the publication of case details in local newspapers.[22] In response, Konstantin Yanevich-Yanevskii, a lawyer working for the tsar's liberal brother Grand Duke Konstantin, argued that oral and public procedure enabling judges to freely evaluate evidence was not at all alien, because various courts were already using it to some extent, including military, commercial, so-called verbal, and rural police courts, though all of these were either specialized or used for very petty matters.[23]

The first complete draft of the judicial reform in 1859 proposed limited publicity, preserving the basics of the existing court system. Defendants and their relatives and friends would be permitted to attend the reading of the case extract by the court secretary to the judges—the closest pre-reform courts came to a trial. The proposal would also admit "other unrelated persons" in the courtroom, but it did not include trial by jury. Also unchanged would be the pre-reform practice whereby judges did not render their decision right away after hearing the case but issued it at some later point, so that pre-reform trials were typically split into three separate episodes (four if we also count the initial reading of the case extract by the defendant). The legal officials commenting on the proposal, including even those who would soon be among the most important reformers, such as Sergei Zarudny, almost uniformly agreed that Russia was not ready for jury trials. They were also split on the matter of publicity. A Second Section (codification) official, Yegor Brevern, argued that publicity by itself did not guarantee a fair trial, and that in France criminal justice had allegedly worked well under the secret procedure before the Revolution and then sank into terror after the revolutionaries made the courts public. Brevern argued that publicity did not consist of admitting into the courtroom anyone curious about the case or with nothing better to do: it was enough to admit lawyers, local "houseowners," deputies from the local community, relatives and friends, and journalists. An important Senate lawyer, Mikhail Goltgoer, argued (as if quoting Bentham) that this limited publicity was not sufficient and that the defendant's relatives and friends could not replace the "general publicity" that would introduce "the control of public opinion." Senator Butskovskii, who would soon write the final version of the criminal procedure reform, agreed. Also following Bentham's arguments, Butskovskii argued that publicity is "the most reliable control over any public activity and the only durable bridle for keeping public actors within the bounds of legality." Butskovskii argued that compromising or taking away any one element of the reform would make it meaningless. For example, taking away the jury would make judges too powerful and uncontrollable. Taking away oral proceedings would make publicity meaningless and also destroy the adversarial principle, that is, the contest between the prosecution and defense, "which is what normally attracts an audience." This comment, incidentally, suggests that Butskovskii wanted a public that would include not only the persons directly interested in a case but also those who would attend out of curiosity. Butskovskii's arguments would win the day, as the top officials with access to the tsar were persuaded that the reform would not work in a truncated form.[24] The fact that the tsar's advisers did want the reform to actually work is, incidentally, another indication that it was intended to serve as an effective check on other agencies and on the bureaucracy, not as a concession either to the landed nobility or to public opinion.

The final version of the statute, issued on 20 November 1864, did not introduce any official restrictions on who would compose the public: neither idle spectators nor any of the underprivileged categories would be excluded—neither women, nor peasants, nor any religious or ethnic groups. This should be contrasted with considerable restrictions on admission to the bar, especially limiting it for "non-Christians" in 1889, and with the tsar's 1876 prohibition on the licensing of women to practice law. Nor were there any temporary restrictions on public access as a transitional measure. It is also clear, however, that the lawyers who devised the new judiciary did not believe in social equality any more than Russian society as a whole did at that time. The journalist Mikhail Katkov, who would later become a vicious enemy of the new judiciary but initially supported the reform, was already worried as early as 1865, before juries had actually appeared in Russia, about allowing "a crowd from the street to rule the courtroom and feel itself at home."[25] The jury itself was not as inclusive as it might appear, as Aleksandr Afanasiev pointed out.[26] While provincial juries would include large numbers of peasants (between half and two-thirds of the jurors), the reform required jurors to be literate, as well as to possess a certain minimum amount of property, so as to exclude the vast mass of Russia's peasants and laborers. Given this lack of official restrictions on spectators contrasted with elitist restrictions on direct participation in the judicial process, the meaning of legal publicity in post-reform Russia would have to be constructed and negotiated in practice.

From the time the new courts opened in 1866, it became clear that attendance at a trial would in practice be a privilege reserved for the administrative, professional, and cultural elite. In high-profile trials priority admission went to local officials and other individuals of high rank, and then preference was given to members of the privileged or respectable society. For example, at the Kovalchukova and Bezobrazov murder trial in Kharkov in 1878, only two hundred seats were available in the courtroom, which were divided in the following way: 133 went to judicial officials, ten to military judges, ten to local university faculty, twenty to university students, and twenty-seven to the rest of the public. The 10 percent quota given to university students seems to be deliberate.[27] While students, especially those of the law, clearly attended prominent trials, it does not seem to be the case that the public was "composed mostly of students."[28] At the first criminal trial in St. Petersburg that attracted strong public attention—the censorship case against author and publisher Aleksei Suvorin—most seats in the courtroom went to "prominent men of letters and editors."[29]

The very top layer of Russia's elite, such as ministers, governors, and members of the imperial family, did not attend trials as a matter of course, but they did show up for the most prominent ones. The "suitcase murder" trial in St. Petersburg on 24 March 1870 attracted the tsar's brothers Konstantin and Nikolai, four other members of the imperial family, and many of the highest officials: ministers, generals, State Council members, and senators.[30] The 1872 trial of the millionaire Miasnikov brothers was attended by the tsar's brothers Nikolai and Mikhail and by his cousin Prince Petr Oldenburgskii (famous as the trustee of the Imperial School of Jurisprudence), which was not reported in the press but noted in a secret memo from the Third Section agent observing the trial. The dignitaries stayed only long enough to hear the speeches of Prosecutor Koni and the best known among the attorneys, Aleksandr Lokhvitskii; they refused a lunch prepared for them by court officials and promised to return after lunch but did not.[31] The 1873 trial of Erast Kvitnitskii, an officer of the imperial guard accused of assaulting another officer, attracted Grand Dukes Konstantin and Nikolai Nikolaevich.[32] The trial of Vera Zasulich was observed by the ministers of war, finance, and foreign affairs, but apparently no grand dukes.[33] A more typical list of notables from the trial of Fedor Melnitskii's family in Moscow in 1883 included two generals, Yegorov and Barmin, Moscow's highest judicial official, Procurator Goncharov, and Moscow's civil governor Perfiliev.[34]

The lower-class and even most of the middle-class members of the public were excluded whenever space was scarce, even though they seem to have been greatly interested in attending. At the first Melnitskii trial, in 1882, the crowd outside the courtroom was so large that the police had to spend more than an hour clearing the "simple" people out of the building, and even after that was done, "a mass of respectable public still remained" who could not get in. During the second Melnitskii trial, "only a relatively small, select, cultured (*intelligentnaia*) part [of the public] was given seats in the courtroom."[35] The journalist Mikhail Gradovskii recalled about the Zasulich trial that there was not a single nihilist or student in the courtroom, and students and "simple folk" were not allowed farther than the opposite sidewalk of the street, and on the nearby Liteiny Prospect a large crowd of young people had assembled.[36] Such de facto exclusivity seems to have caused some tension from the very beginning of the new courts: even the opening celebrations were staged as high-status events, and an important ethnographer and local activist, Aleksandr Gatsiskii, criticized those held in Nizhnii Novgorod in 1869 for being accessible only to privileged persons with special tickets, while an entire crowd was waiting outside and could only look into the building after the ceremony. He reported people in the crowd saying "Must be the gents (*gospoda*) amusing themselves." Gatsiskii concluded that "one can unwittingly decide that while our justice is equal for all, the opening of the court in Nizhnii [Novgorod] is [equally accessible] for everyone who has tickets."[37] The opening of the Moscow bank trial described above seems to have struck observers precisely for the fact that the less privileged individuals were very numerous but could not simply be excluded from the courtroom, because they had come as victims and civil plaintiffs. Perhaps because so many lower-status people had been affected by the bank's failure, the case seems to have attracted broader public interest: the legal historian Aleksandr Gradovskii reported that even his delivery man (*raznoschik*) knew about the course of the trial.[38]

While "simple" people were typically excluded from important trials, there were no such restrictions regarding women, and countless observers noted that ladies (*damy*) were highly prominent among the courtroom public, especially at trials with high-status women defendants, such as the poisoning trial of Marguerite Jujean in 1878 or the second Melnitskii trial in 1883, which was attended by "numerous dressed-up ladies."[39] In France, women's prominence at public trials created discomfort, apparently because women "from all classes and walks of life" were "apt to dominate the audiences" and were not turned away even by "sordid details of a case," although society expected them to be more sensitive.[40] In France women attendees wore black, but in Russia they wore ordinary or even formal outfits.

BEYOND THE COURTROOM

In addition to persons physically attending the trial, the public included those who read about it in journals and newspapers. To Bentham, the right to be present at the trial necessarily included the right to take notes about the proceedings, and once that was allowed, it was inconceivable to prohibit their publication in print media.[41] In eighteenth-century England cheap pamphlets about criminal trials were produced en masse and are to this day an important source for historians about trials not otherwise reported.[42] In the post-Napoleonic period, accounts of notable trials became a staple of Western European journalism, both respectable and sensationalist.[43] The Russian Empire experimented with reporting judicial decisions in the early nineteenth century, but, as already noted, Russian censorship law after 1817 prohibited publication of legal cases. When the legal reform began to be discussed in the late 1850s, however, the assumption seems to have been that while many crucial features like jury trials and life tenure for judges could not be taken for granted, the new court system would definitely permit press accounts of the proceedings. Some authors in Russia and (earlier) in Western Europe even thought that publicity provided by the press would be fully sufficient.[44]

While from the beginning of the reform in Russia it was clear that the press would be included in the reformed juridical sphere, its role was not predetermined.

The conservative populist journalist Mikhail Katkov argued in 1865 that publicity did not mean allowing everyone into the courtroom but rather was the same as "*glasnost*," literally translated as "vocality," which at the time meant largely a greater freedom of the press. Katkov then argued that the objectives of publicity would be met even with a small public at a trial as long as the press could record and publish the proceedings.[45] As it happened, public trials in Russia were reported in the press from the start, and until the end of imperial Russia the autonomous juridical field worked closely with the autonomous journalistic and literary field. Some journalists even suggested that the press was more powerful than the law, and during a trial the judiciary had to convince the press about the validity of the outcome in order to be fully legitimate.[46]

The judiciary was solicitous of the media, especially during a particularly important trial. During the bank trial in Moscow in 1876, there was a special dedicated telegraph line to St. Petersburg and special accommodations for journalists in the court building, including a special room in the court building, individual seats, and special mail-pickup service.[47] At the Melnitskii trial in 1882 journalists were the first to be allowed into a courtroom literally besieged by crowds.[48] It seems that much of the reputation of Evgenii Rink, a Moscow judge known for skillfully staging important trials, lay in his relationships with journalists, who would receive tips about which trials promised to be newsworthy; conversely, Rink had no qualms about expelling from the courtroom those journalists who displeased him.[49] During the 1884 trial of the Skopin Municipal Bank pyramid, the journalists were given privileged seats just behind the judges, though these seats were close to the windows and subject to icy drafts.[50] Anatolii Koni was another jurist who carefully cultivated his media image and considered public opinion in his courtroom speeches, with one particularly blatant example being the case of the Miasnikov brothers.[51] The influential liberal monthly *Vestnik Evropy* criticized Koni for rhetorically removing this case from the trial of the public conscience, that is, the jury, to the trial of public opinion with its lower standards of proof and in effect transforming "organized justice into a lynching."[52]

The introduction of enhanced publicity in Russian life coincided with the period when publication became not simply an accepted part of Eurocentric legal culture but an essential practice that transformed the trial from a local affair to a national and even international event, in which courtroom ritual was a central phase but not the only one. The press helped create the notion that there was a wider public that may not have been attending the trial physically but was still affected by the outcome. In the United States, the trial of abolitionist John

Brown in 1859 was such an event, since it was widely reported and as a result had extraordinary political fallout.[53] In other countries, including Russia, this change resulted from a series of trials, but in Russia the peculiarity was that when legal publicity finally appeared it was from the start the modern variety. Mass-circulation press emerged in Russia gradually during the first half of the nineteenth century with such publications as the *Northern Bee* (*Severnaia pchela*) and the *Russian Veteran* (*Russkii invalid*). The process extended exponentially during the Great Reforms, with news from the courtroom becoming a stable source of publishable material for all the major newspapers. Higher-status periodicals like *Golos* and *Moskovskie vedomosti* provided quality analysis and detailed transcripts, and specialized publications like *Sudebnyi vestnik* provided more in-depth information with more reporting from the provinces, from the lower courts, and about civil-law cases.[54] At the other end of the spectrum were the less reputable publications that focused on lurid sensationalism and frequently printed rumors and allegations.[55]

Press accounts were of two major types: transcripts and various editorial materials. A transcript was typically published in several issues of a newspaper and included a reprinting of the act of indictment and a reproduction of the most important episodes from witness examination to the lawyers' and prosecutors' speeches. Usually these were presented as verbatim transcriptions, although today it is impossible to check whether this was really so. Judging from the length of most trials, only parts of the proceedings were reproduced, including the lawyers' speeches. To this day such newspaper transcripts are our most important sources for most trials and even for some of those considered to be great or prominent. The reason is that post-reform trials were oral, and the court clerk only recorded the minutes of the trial (*protokol*) which did not reproduce the substance of anything said in court; at best it summarized a lawyer's procedural objection and the judges' response. There was no central register and no official legal transcription in late imperial Russia. For important cases, newspapers or perhaps a wealthy participant would hire stenographers.[56]

Occasionally trial transcripts were accompanied by a brief editorial commentary or described the atmosphere of the trial, the appearance and behavior of participants, or such information as the jurors' names (usually only their social ranks were published).[57] In addition, a few trial transcripts were published separately. Some of these were very famous cases like the Moscow bank trial or the case of the Jacks of Hearts, but others were less known, such as the fascinating Kazan murder case of 1873. The most important lawyers' speeches were also excerpted and published in separate volumes throughout the late imperial period.

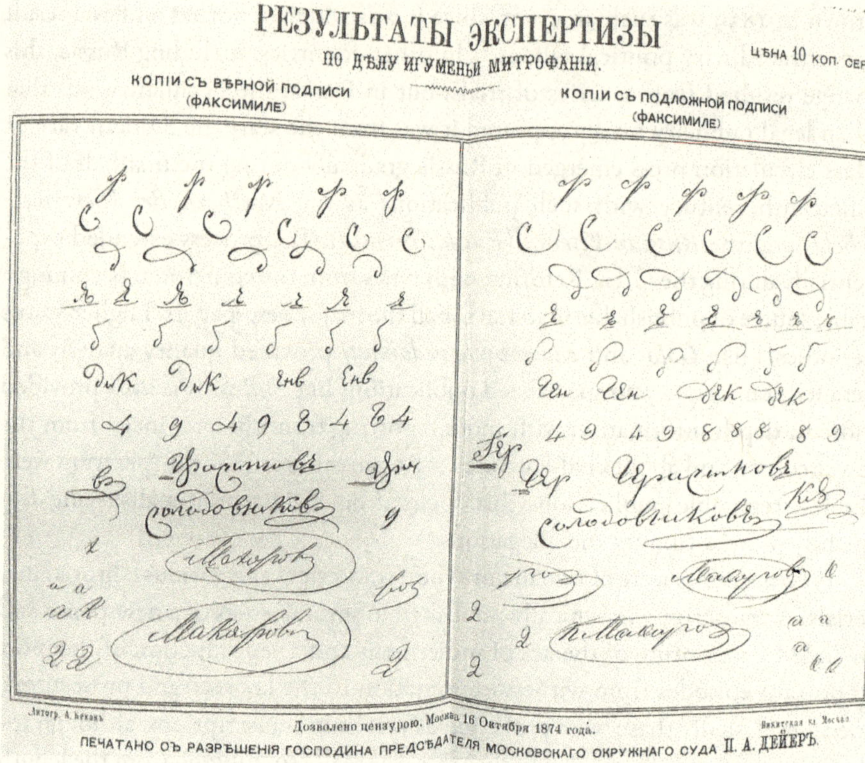

Figure 2. Handwriting analysis in the case of Hegumenia Mitrofania, 1874, lithographed and sold as a separate leaflet. RGIA, 1405.70.126, l. 275. Left side: genuine writing; right side: allegedly forged writing. Solodovnikov's signature is especially prominent.

The result of such selective transmission of legal materials is that we have a great deal of surviving information slanted toward celebrity cases that makes a systematic study of ordinary post-reform legal practice impossible, as opposed to the pre-reform courts that used written procedure.[58]

In addition to transcripts, the second type of legal publication was a newspaper editorial or feuilleton that usually appeared during the trial or shortly afterward. Editorials reported on the issues that were surprising, striking, or important for the public. They connected the facts of a case to larger moral or social problems. Very often the editorial was nothing less than a trial in miniature: it summarized the main arguments of the two sides, critiqued the performances of the lawyers, judges, and juries, and offered their own judgment. As one journalist noted, there was a sense that the resolution of a case did not fully end in the courtroom but continued "in the environment of public opinion." He even argued that such an examination is qualitatively different from the literal trial, because it is less partisan and the press can "weigh [the facts] without any relation to the desired result, i.e., with complete objectivity."[59] Such mini-trials seem to be prepared by lawyers or at least persons knowledgeable in the law: while pointing out the participants' errors and misjudgments, they also offered arguments and interpretations of their own, which are often themselves quite questionable.[60] Scrutiny by the press could even begin before the actual trial: for instance, the forgery trial of Mother Mitrofania was preceded by civil litigation, and the lawyer for her opponents, Fedor Plevako, published attacks against her.[61] The archives have preserved a sample of a leaflet with Mitrofania's handwriting sample, which was sold for ten kopeks, before and during her trial, so that buyers could draw their own conclusions (see figure 2).[62] She also had active and well-placed defenders, however, who published pamphlets and articles on her behalf. In short, in the most celebrated cases at least, Russian press accounts quite literally functioned as the parallel court of public opinion envisioned by Bentham.

Press accounts developed one other distinguishing element of a "great" (*gromkii, zamechatelnyi, bol'shoi*) criminal trial: its claim to speak beyond its particular facts and to discuss social and other issues of common interest. The public was therefore understood as also including persons not involved in the case and maybe not even aware of it, even all of Russia in an abstract sense. In the Yukhantsev bank embezzlement trial of 1879, the prosecutor referred not just to the bank's shareholders as the main victims but also to the "reading Rus" and even to foreign capitalists and investors who were underwriting the bank, and whose trust affected Russia's foreign credit rating. The Mutual Land Credit Society, nearly ruined by its chief cashier, was the largest bank in Russia, its shares guaranteed by mortgaged landed estates and sold in Europe through the Rothschilds.[63] In sum, trials and press accounts tended to operate in tandem, with the press distilling and emphasizing statements of general impact from the raw mass of a trial transcript.

THE SPACE OF PUBLIC JUSTICE

Public trials that began in military courts in Moscow on 29 May 1865 continued through the summer, and in late August there was another murder case. The journalist Katkov described what happened as "chaos," although this was long before he began to attack the new judiciary, and so he explicitly refused to blame anyone in particular, least of all the public. The trouble was that the "space was not adapted for public trial, [and] neither the public nor even the defendant had their own particular locations. The defendant moved back and forth and sometimes was completely surrounded by the public. In general, soon after the trial had begun the public became mixed with the participants. And when it happened it was difficult to restore order."[64] It was clear that introducing public trials was not a simple matter of finding a suitable hall and letting people in. It was necessary to rethink the basic ways the post-reform juridical field would deploy and organize physical space to exercise its future political and social power. Buildings and spaces, public or private, determined what procedures and rituals they could support and the kinds of people who would be able to participate. Bentham wrote that providing a small room for the trial was just as effective in limiting publicity as issuing a law.[65] One of the Russian lawyers commenting on the 1859 reform draft, Egor Brevern, even argued against courtroom publicity on the grounds that the existing courtrooms could not actually accommodate many members of the public.[66] Given the Russian government's penny-pinching proclivities, post-1864 courts could have easily inherited the old buildings—which would indeed happen in many smaller provincial towns—but as it turned out, the major physical spaces of the new judiciary were reconstructed in line with the general European trend to turn previously utilitarian buildings, halls, and courtyards into instruments of rule and symbols of power.[67] In European capitals, legal institutions had for centuries occupied spacious and even majestic buildings, typically larger and more expensive than their Russian counterparts, although not accessible to the public to a greater extent than the new Russian courts. In England, the common-law and equity courts had for centuries been housed in portions of Westminster Hall and in 1882 moved to a grand new building. But London's criminal court, the Old Bailey, was rebuilt in 1774 and then again on a grand scale only in 1902–1907, with public hangings taking place just outside it until 1868.[68] In other European capitals, various versions of a "palace of justice" were constructed. The best-known one was in Paris, a magnificent medieval building rebuilt in the neoclassical style in 1783–1786, restyled during the Revolution, and then rebuilt again by 1871 just before suffering heavy damage during the Commune.[69]

Pre-reform Russian courts and other official buildings were designed like their earlier Western European counterparts to serve utilitarian goals but also to send certain symbolic and emotional messages. Each province and district had a building dedicated to government offices, which were literally called "places of presence" (*prisutstvennye mesta*), meaning that state officials were required to conduct business there in person.[70] Government buildings were bustling with activity, which spilled over into neighboring urban spaces: for example, in the seventeenth century the Moscow courts were located in the Kremlin next to Ivanovskaia Square, where the main cathedrals are located, and once the courts were moved to Resurrection Square just outside the Kremlin in the eighteenth century, legal negotiations and discussions took place in the taverns across from the courts.[71] After Catherine II's administrative reorganization of 1775, the courts shared a building with many other agencies, such as the police and the Treasury, and all had rather small rooms. Although most business was conducted in the secretaries' offices (*kantseliarii*) that were open to visitors, the actual courtroom, known as the "presence" (*prisutstvie*), was open only to visitors summoned by the judges. Its key object was the Mirror of Justice (*zertsalo*), and the room was conceptualized as a sanctuary of justice modeled on the secretive ancient temple rather than, for example, a Christian church or the Roman basilica with its large and open public spaces.[72] Once the old courts were opened to the public in October 1865, the chambers could hold only a small number of spectators, most of whom had to try to hear the proceedings from the hallway.

St. Petersburg was the site of the imperial government and of the first post-reform public court, opened on 14 April 1866. It was ironic that in a city full of official buildings it was difficult to find a proper one for the courts. The minister of justice Zamiatin considered the Synod building, which was sensible since it was located next to the Senate, Russia's highest court; and the Engineers' (Mikhailovsky) Castle, the site of the 1801 assassination of Tsar Paul, which was spacious, well located, and underutilized. But in the end he chose what the jurist Grigory Dzhanshiev described as the "ridiculous" building of the Old Arsenal on Liteiny Prospect.[73] Dzhanshiev suggested that this was done in order to minimize hostility from the two rival and more powerful agencies—the Third Section and the Ministry of the Interior (whose building was heavily damaged by a fire in 1862). But the Old Arsenal was a landmark building constructed in 1771, and it certainly looked reasonably impressive in a city full of grand palaces. It had three stories, six stone staircases, and more than three hundred rooms. None of these was large enough to hold public trials of the kind envisioned by the reformers, so two large additions were rapidly constructed. The first floor housed prisoners and service personnel, and the other two floors each had a very large (196-foot-long) "reception hall" with a trial chamber on each end, one sixty-three by thirty-eight feet and the other forty-five by thirty-seven feet. The larger chamber had more seating, with an added upper gallery.

Figure 3. St. Petersburg District Court (the Old Arsenal), early twentieth-century postcard. Note the cabs and motorcars waiting outside and the large old cannon on the opposite side of Liteinyi Avenue.

There are not many surviving illustrations of the courtrooms or the building itself, but the 1869 engraving of the high-publicity Gusev Alley murder trial gives an idea of the size of the courtroom (figure 4). It gives the impression of a purposely public space and looks comparable to an Old Bailey courtroom in London, but it is not a huge public hall, thus illustrating the particular type of publicity created by the reform. Exceptionally large trials, however, used the large reception hall. The courtroom in the picture is elegantly finished with window curtains, stucco moldings, small columns all around (*kolonki*), large chandeliers, and a portrait of Alexander II. The chambers on the third floor were identical except that their ceilings were lower. The building had heat and gaslight, and court officials and clerks had "comfortable" offices.

Moscow was the second city to acquire a new court, and its judicial district was much larger than St. Petersburg's, with about four times as many trials. It was therefore fortunate to be able to take over the Senate building in the Kremlin. The Moscow departments of the Senate wound their business down after

Figure 4. The Gusev Alley murder trial in St. Petersburg District Court, 1869, from *Vsemirnaia illustratsia,* 1869, no. 5, p. 85. The defendants are seated on the right (note their plain clothing and the closed side doors of their pew), with their lawyers sitting in front of them and the gendarme guards off to the side. The jurors are on the left. The judges are around the semicircular table, together with the highest-ranking spectators. Note the large painting of the tsar in the corner. The podium and the table for material evidence are in the center. The front two rows of spectators are facing the judges; to the left is a table for reporters and stenographers. The prosecutor is entering the courtroom.

the reform and closed in 1871, and Russia's highest court would be the Senate Cassation Departments in St. Petersburg. Although the Moscow Senate building was constructed by Matvei Kazakov in 1776–1787 for the express purpose of housing government offices, it suffered from the great fire of 1812 and was not properly repaired. Its largest hall, the Round (Catherinian) Hall, was used as a flour warehouse and a military archive, to the ire of the architects who repaired and reconstructed the building in 1866–1867. After reconstruction the Round Hall was used as a large atrium for the public who came to attend trials, with booths for obtaining information about cases, paying court fees, and making copies of official documents. The hall was lavishly decorated, with a large rotunda imitating the Pantheon and a colonnade in the Corinthian style

Figure 5. The Senate building in the Moscow Kremlin. From Nikolai Naidenov, *Moskva: Vidy nekotorykh gorodskikh mestnostei, khramov, primechatel'nykh zdanii i drugikh sooruzhenii* (Moscow, 1884), p. 34.

all around. It also carried prominent symbolic meaning, since it retained its original decorations celebrating Catherine II's achievements, including a bas-relief commemorating her legislative activity, inscribed, "she receives not tribute but laws" (*ne dan,' a zakony priemlet*). The hall also included a statue of Catherine, to which another one of Alexander II was added in 1884, as well as smaller reliefs of other Russian rulers. On some occasions this hall was also used for trials, especially for that of the managers and board members of the Moscow Commercial Loan Bank in 1876 (the bank case mentioned earlier). The article describing the renovations patriotically claimed that the Round Hall compared favorably with similar buildings in Paris, London, Brussels, and Vienna, even though it did not have the historical significance or the art collection of the Parisian Palais de Justice. The article also complained that the Senate building did not match the general style of the Kremlin and that its finish was flimsy,

Figure 6. The Catherinian (Round) Hall in the Moscow Senate Building, present day.

cheaply made in plaster rather than in marble. If not for that, "the Round Hall would be among the greatest landmarks in Europe."[74]

In addition to making the new court buildings as large and impressive as possible (given the judiciary's endemic lack of finances), their internal spatial arrangements were designed to reflect the new practices of publicity, the new attention to disciplinary technologies, and the new hierarchies of the juridical field. Typically we imagine nineteenth-century law as more cognizant of individual liberties compared to the preceding age of absolutism. But the post-1815 "new regime" also created new constraints and structures, which seem less jarring to us today perhaps because they have become so deeply engrained in modern culture and society.[75] The trial's external furnishings reflected the judiciary's symbolic and ideological messages. For example, eighteenth-century English criminal justice involved active socialization in and outside the courtroom. Local trials were held in familiar places of socialization: town halls, churches, even theaters. While the spectators were physically separated from others in the English courtroom, the participants in the trial filled up the rest of the space fairly evenly, and in a rectangular room the judge would sit at the longer side. Outside, local elites staged balls, dinners, and processions to celebrate assize court sessions. In France the judge and the prosecutor were physically as well as symbolically elevated and clearly distinguished from everyone else in the courtroom; however, the public were permitted a greater range of expression than in England.[76] In pre-reform Russia, there were no balls or celebrations, and the legal space—aside from the sacristy of the *prisutstvie*—was not formally bounded or regulated, including the offices and hallways in the court buildings and sometimes also adjacent taverns, chapels, and other spaces.

Nineteenth-century legal regimes, including Russia's after 1864, reorganized their physical spaces to provide for public participation but sought to make it passive, orderly, and controlled. Only some areas were accessible to the public, such as the courtrooms, lobbies, corridors, stairs, and courtyards. Other areas remained nonpublic and indeed became far more numerous, including the judges' chambers, the jury and witness rooms, and the prisoner holding areas. All these categories of participants were prevented from interacting with each other and shielded from the public gaze unless they were in the courtroom. In the 1878 trial of Gulak-Artemovskaia, the defense filed an appeal claiming that Koni, then chairman of the St. Petersburg District Court, had had a conversation with the jurors in the jury room, even though all he did was come in briefly to announce his decision to break off the session due to the late hour.[77] The court building in St. Petersburg was designed with special internal staircases for defendants to be brought up from the holding area on the first floor directly to the courtrooms above. There were also separate conference rooms for judges, as well as for jurors and for witnesses, with the latter prevented from communicating with each other or with the public even in civil cases.[78]

The public courtroom was and is not a single space like a ballroom but rather resembles a theater, being carved up into sections, including the judges' bench with the prosecutor's podium in front of it; with the jurors' seats on one side and the prisoners' dock on the other facing the jurors, and the lawyers' seats in front of the dock. The public faces the bench, sometimes with special areas for journalists and stenographers as well as special seats for witnesses. All these participants are allowed to interact, if at all, "only under the controlled conditions of the courtroom."[79] In nineteenth-century England distinguished guests or friends of the judge could sit with him on the bench.[80] In Russia, dignitaries would be provided chairs behind the bench, facing the public, as if symbolically sending the message that the power of the state was behind the judges. The Russian courtroom as depicted in the abovementioned 1869 illustration (figure 4) appears regimented and theater-like, with the geometrical center empty as if it were a stage.[81] The opposing sides are on the edges of the picture, with the attorneys sitting in front of their clients and the prosecutor still entering the courtroom. The main tension or opposition in the courtroom is between the public and the bench with the row of dignitaries behind it. Perhaps the artist wanted to suggest a confrontation between the public and the state, except that, as we know, the public was composed of persons completely beholden to the regime. By contrast, the English courtroom was depicted without any empty spaces, with the geometrical center occupied by the large podiums of the opposing sides.[82]

Although the new court buildings constructed throughout Europe after the mid-nineteenth century were large and impressive, they did not create a truly mass public experience, coming nowhere near a ball or a palace celebration, or even a major church service. From the beginning, courtrooms did not have sufficient space for the public during any of the most prominent trials. This was not unique to Russia. In a major 1859 murder trial in Paris, the courtroom held only 250 spectators, or about a third of its counterpart in St. Petersburg or Moscow.[83] English courts were routinely packed, with standing room only.[84] A post-reform courtroom in Russia held two hundred spectators in Kharkov in 1878, as noted above, and about seven hundred at a major trial in Moscow, with extra spaces created for the purpose and every square foot taken up by chairs. In the latter case (of the Melnitskii children's trial in 1883) the trial account estimated that ten times as many people tried to get into the building.[85] An obvious alternative would be to use the nearby large hall of the Moscow Noble Assembly, which could hold more than two thousand people and had excellent acoustics. It would later be used for Soviet show trials in the 1920s and 1930s. Moving a major trial to a different building would, however, clearly create a logistical nightmare.

For those spectators who managed to get a seat in the courtroom, attending a trial was not a physically pleasant experience, even though the new court buildings had water closets, heat, and gaslight. Most observers were astonished at the patience and perseverance of men and women who stayed in their seats for many hours. Trials usually began around 10 or 11 a.m. and often lasted long past midnight. As in England, this meant that defense arguments would take place at the end of the trial, when all the participants were exhausted. Everyone felt severe discomfort from overheating and lack of fresh air. The acoustics seem to have been not ideal either, and on several occasions the public and even the stenographers could not hear some of the defendants or witnesses as, for example, happened repeatedly at the Miasnikov brothers' forgery trial in 1872. On that occasion, the judges could apparently still hear everything, although one might wonder about the jury.[86] Even a civil trial involving an important litigant could get so crowded that people sitting next to each other had a hard time communicating and "could barely keep [their] seat."[87]

In sum, observing post-reform criminal trials was an ordeal of its own: first, it meant getting a seat in the courtroom, which required energy and often personal connections. Second, individuals had to submit to the spatial discipline of the courtroom and in effect be confined to the seating area for long periods of time. Finally, spectators had to withstand the severe physical discomfort of a crowded, overheated, and unventilated room without easy access to toilets. And on top of all this, the public negotiating these obstacles was itself being scrutinized by lawyers and journalists. But as we will see next, none of this turned spectators into mere passive observers or negated the fact that the juridical field depended on the attention and approval of the elite crowd watching its activities.

THE PUBLIC ON TRIAL

Many accounts of late imperial Russia describe the outburst of jubilation in the St. Petersburg courtroom when terrorist Vera Zasulich was acquitted by the jury in 1877. Men and women cried, shouted, and applauded. Even the elderly Chancellor Gorchakov was seen shouting with joy.[88] Such reaction stemmed in part from the fact that the political context of the case had been carefully suppressed by the government as it prepared for the trial and so the public mainly saw a sympathetic woman defendant, and in part because Zasulich's victim, General Fedor Trepov, was not well liked, and so the trial was also a move in the game of elite power politics. But it is also important to note that nearly every prominent trial of the post-reform era included one or more episodes of this kind. Not simply the ovations during or at the conclusion of the trial but any movement or sounds among the spectators tended to be noted, indicating not only that the court was under the engaged and active scrutiny of the upper-class spectators but also that the public itself was watched and judged by officials, lawyers, and journalists. It was of course not a priori clear what role the public would play during the proceedings. After all, the trial jury in its original form in medieval England *was* the fact finder, the public, and the witnesses combined.[89]

The existing model of public behavior that most closely approximated the courtroom, namely theater, not only allowed but heavily depended on the feedback of and interaction between performers and the public.[90] The modern criminal trial was meant to do more than project and defend order and authority.[91] It was meant to educate and admonish the spectators. But the concern often voiced in Russia and elsewhere was that justice was being turned into a form of entertainment. Russian court goers tended to act as if they were in a theater, using opera glasses, socializing among themselves, and becoming emotionally excited. One journalist even suggested that the analogy went beyond superficial behavior and that the public who attended the Miasnikov brothers' forgery trial in 1872 came with the expectation of an attractive and familiar, though false, literary narrative coming to life, in that case, that of the new courts daring to prosecute a millionaire, and of "the surprising persistence with which the aggrieved heir had for more than ten years pursued the truth and came out of the court as someone he must be in the name of justice—the owner of a huge property."[92]

A crowd of spectators was the most important outward defining feature of a great trial. As soon as public trials in Russia began in 1865, at first in the old previously secretive courts, large numbers of people wanted to attend. In Moscow, there were several cases that attracted wide attention, even though there were no juries yet and the court would not issue a verdict until days later.[93] The same happened in the very first few trials in the newly opened Moscow District Court in the summer of 1866, even though they were essentially test runs and prosecuted vagrancy and petty theft. The trial of five vagrants on 8 July 1866 "attracted such numbers of the public, that the courtroom could barely hold [them]. Tickets were issued from ten in the morning, and by eleven it was impossible to find a single ticket."[94] The first "prominent" (*gromkoe*) jury trial in Moscow, in early 1867, prosecuted the robbery of Moscow's Old Believer compound at the Rogozhskaia *sloboda*. The large courtroom was "cracking" (*treshchala*) from the crowds.[95] I have not seen any references to large crowds at the first jury trials in St. Petersburg, in August 1866, which were the test cases of petty theft, but the censorship violation trial of the authors Pypin and Zhukovskii that same year attracted numerous spectators.[96] Even long after the public trial stopped being a novelty, important cases attracted large numbers of would-be spectators. For example, the Melnitskii embezzlement trial in 1883 attracted a crowd that quite literally took over the court building as soon as it opened at 9 a.m.; police spent hours restoring order.[97]

The crowd was not limited to the courtroom itself. The people who did not get in at first would often not lose hope and wait around to learn the result or perhaps to get a seat later. In the 1872 Miasnikov trial in Petersburg, the crowd stood on the stairs of the building and at the iron gate that protected the entrance to the courtroom itself the entire time of the trial.[98] Eleven years later at the Melnitskii embezzlement trial in Moscow people wandered around the corridors outside the courtroom, sat in the large Round Hall, and waited for days in vain hopes of gaining admission.[99] Those spectators who had gained a seat

Figure 7. Admission ticket to the Moscow Commercial Loan Bank trial at the Moscow District Court, 2 October 1876. RGIA 1367.9.20, l. 39. The text reads: "Ticket to enter the court session of the Moscow District Court, 2 October 1876." Note the stamp in the corner.

tried to stay until the end so as not to lose it by the time the verdict was announced, even staying during the monotonous reading of documentary evidence.[100] But occasionally the public's interest waned during long and jargon-filled trials. The Moscow bank trial of 1876 was one of the most important events in the history of Russian law because of its tangible effects on Russia's finances and in part because of the brazen misbehavior of the bank's managers and directors. The crowds grew bored, however, and stopped coming after a few days.

Once inside the courtroom members of the public were officially not allowed to disrupt the trial by applauding, laughing, or shouting, but all these reactions were routinely reported in the published transcripts. Sometimes the more reserved reactions were noted as well. Observers and participants in the trials clearly thought that the public's emotions indicated how the case was progressing. Some trial accounts note how lawyers and prosecutors played up to the spectators rather than trying to win their case. The most prominent trials were distinguished by, among other things, outsized emotional outbursts that would completely overwhelm the public—which was no doubt completely exhausted by sitting motionless all day in a stuffy room—resulting in everyone getting expelled from the courtroom. Even simple clapping could get the public expelled, as happened in the Pal'm embezzlement case in 1873, when the public applauded Vladimir Spasovich's defense speech.[101] At the 1879 trial of Russia's grandest embezzler, bank cashier Konstantin Yukhantsev, his attorney Zhukovskii criticized the bank from which Yukhantsev stole as having enabled the embezzlement through its negligence and denied that the bank embodied an important public interest. The spectators shouted "Bravo! Bravo!" in response, and Chairman Koni threatened not only to clear the courtroom but to arrest any particularly rowdy individuals: "The court is not a theater," he admonished, and "if the public cannot conduct itself [appropriately] towards the administration of justice, it will bear the consequences of its behavior."[102] Occasionally the public reaction was more vigorous. Like the Zasulich case, the landmark forgery trial of Mother Mitrofania ended in thunderous applause, which came in response to the speech by Fedor Plevako, Russia's leading defense attorney, who represented some of the alleged victims. The judge rang the bell and then ordered the public to be expelled, which caused additional commotion. The session was interrupted and the public cleared out, except for the witnesses and the lawyers. The noise then moved to the corridors outside the courtroom and was so loud that it was difficult to listen to the next speech, by another prominent lawyer, Mikhail Gromnitskii.[103] Later the public was allowed back inside. In the second Melnitskii trial, in 1883, the verdict caused "thunderous applause and shouts [of] 'Bravo, thank you!' which continued for over ten minutes, so that the chairman of the court had the public expelled in the name of order."[104]

In other situations observers noted a reaction from the public without explaining how it was expressed; presumably it was by people talking to each other and through facial expressions. During the second Melnitskii trial the defendant's daughter Elena Bleze started to sob and could not speak, causing the "extreme sympathy of the public" and in general "regarding all of them one could hear almost only pity." When the father was brought in to testify, his "longsuffering glance at his children . . . caused sympathy in the majority of the public." When Bleze had another sobbing fit, the chairman stopped the trial for thirty minutes and the foreman ran up and poured her some water, all of which "had a very favorable impression upon the public." At the same time, when Bleze's fiancé, Mel'nitskii's son, did not object to a sexually charged slur from the prosecutor, this made a disheartening (*udruchaiushchee*) impression.[105]

The most common, and least risky, reaction was laughter, which indicates what kinds of statements or behaviors clashed with the "magic circle" of the trial.[106] On a few occasions spectators laughed in response to simple and even simplistic wit.[107] But there were also several repeated patterns of behavior that evoked laughter. One was an illiterate or semiliterate testimony by a defendant or witness. A mere mention of illiteracy could make people laugh, as could testimony of an uneducated person read verbatim, as, for example, that of a seamstress

Bogatyreva at the Melnitskii trial, which "induced strong laughter."[108] In the 1872 Miasnikov forgery trial, a defense lawyer very openly mocked the main prosecution witness, who was a semi-educated drunk turning against his benefactors. He knew how to read but mostly consumed popular novels that formed his entire intellectual outlook. In an important letter he wrote that he had never ruined anyone's life by poison, and so the lawyers during the trial understandably began to wonder what he meant by that. It turned out that he had merely copied the phrase from a novel, and the public reacted with laughter. Another witness, allegedly an innkeeper (though actually his brother summoned by mistake), could not repeat the name of a police or private detective who made the arrest in his presence, saying that he "did not know his letters (*chelovek negramotnyi*)," again provoking laughter.[109]

Any sexual innuendos were also likely to evoke laughter. In the Miasnikov trial, a key witness named Shevelev mentioned that an important participant who had signed a contested will routinely engaged in relations with women much older than him, which Shevelev considered "more or less indecent," causing laughter and "movement" in the courtroom. The same witness made people laugh by making fun of himself being imprisoned in the Peter and Paul Fortress and thus invulnerable to corruption, saying, "I am hermetically sealed." Also hilarious was Shevelev's put-down of one of Russia's very top lawyers, Aleksandr Lokhvitskii: "You talk so much that I cannot get my thoughts together." Later Lokhvitskii tried to retaliate by mocking Shevelev's claim that on the day of Karakozov's failed attempt on the tsar on 4 April 1866 he was among the jubilant crowd in the Palace Square, even though he was a radical who would later fight in the Paris Commune.[110] A commentator discussing the Miasnikov trial in the press mocked Lokhvitskii's tendency to joke and laugh, claiming that even though he apparently knew his way around this complicated case, he harmed his client by his excessive wit: "Listening to his comic speeches, every single person laughed: the defendants (not every one though), and attorneys, and jurors, and the public, and finally the very incomparable comic-orator himself. Even the judges smiled (in a very restrained way of course)."[111]

In addition to occasional jokes about lawyers, the spectators laughed at the police informants when they took the stand in the Melnitskii case. Unpleasantly but not surprisingly, the public also laughed at Jewish defendants or witnesses. In the forgery trial of Liudmila Gulak-Artemovskaia, the story (also repeated by Koni) was that she had earlier swindled a Jewish merchant desperate to use her connections to get a profitable business deal. He kept giving her stacks of cash, and she kept urging him to give more, until "he gave everything and left cursing Petersburg, and business, and the salons where business is conducted (laughter)."[112] In the Mitrofania case, one of the defendants was a converted Jewish dentist named Trachtenberg, who claimed that he himself had suffered a loss when one of his debtors turned out to be a nun and thus was legally prohibited from entering into financial transactions. Mitrofania's lawyer Shaikevich (very prominent and himself Jewish) wondered whether "being Russian Orthodox, [he had to] know that monasticism has degrees," to which Trachtenberg responded: "I did not know. . . . It's a hassle (*kuter'ma*) and nothing else (laughter)."[113]

In addition to the expelling of the public for misconduct, occasionally publicity was limited for considerations of privacy. Throughout the late imperial period even an important case could be tried entirely behind closed doors and never be reported. The nonpublic jury trial of one of Moscow's leading attorneys, Saltykov, who had for years embezzled from his clients and even staged his own suicide, has been discussed elsewhere.[114] In great public trials, portions of testimony were occasionally presented behind closed doors: for example, information about an illegal abortion by a young noblewoman and the illicit relationship that caused it.[115] Questionable material could also be conveyed to the jury but not be read out loud. At the 1878 poison murder trial of Margarita Jujean, the court would not read the witness description of a sexual encounter between her and the seventeen-year-old victim.[116] In Yukhantsev's embezzlement trial, his family relationships were discussed as a possible motivation for his behavior, and Chairman Koni warned that some expressions in the couple's letters would be "awkward" to the "ladies" among the public, who were welcome to leave the courtroom (they did not).[117] In the Melnitskii children's trial in 1883, Melnitskii's daughter Valentina asked the court not to read out her shopping list and if necessary show it only to the jurors.[118]

The final moment for emotional reactions and connections came with the announcement of the verdict. The defendants' and the spectators' reactions were often contrasted. Unlike the public in the courtroom, the forgery defendant Liudmila Gulak-Artemovskaia calmly turned to her nemesis, the writer Petr Polevoi, and asked him in a sarcastic tone: "Are you pleased?"[119] Mother Mitrofania was completely indifferent to the jury verdict, but "some witnesses and a few of the ladies present in the courtroom engaged in something like an ovation for the convicted: they came up to her expressing regrets and kissed her hands."[120] After the trial of Fedor Melnitskii's children, "Many ladies from the public hugged Bleze [his daughter-in-law] and Varvara Melnitskaia, men gratefully shook hands with the jurors and attorneys, and some old man, a justice of the peace, came up to Lev Melnitskii [Fedor's brother] and loudly proclaimed: 'I am happy to have you acquitted, colleague, since you have endured falsehoods (*napraslinu*) for so long' and embraced him. At this time three boys aged twelve to fourteen ran into the courtroom in tears, Melnitskys' and Bleze's brothers (one dressed as a military cadet) and hung on to the acquitted. The scene was extremely touching and the public cried."[121]

Publicity was a key element of the new Russian courts. Officially the courts were open to persons of any status, but in practice attendance at the most important trials was limited to elite spectators. All others could only read about them in newspaper—if they knew how. One can suppose that such selective publicity put additional pressure on the juridical field, which was constantly under the quasi-formal scrutiny of the elites whose members were on trial. The power dynamic in late imperial Russia would likely have been very different if a broader spectrum of the respectable or even the lower-middle classes, especially the townspeople (*meshchane*), had been incorporated more actively into the legal process. But the power of observation worked in both directions: not only were the courts under constant scrutiny, the public itself was being judged and observed. The fact that the public attending trials generally adapted easily to the new institution suggests that the fears of greater political participation so prevalent in nineteenth-century Russia were seriously misplaced.

CHAPTER 3

The Adversarial Trial

A notable subgenre of the post-reform courtroom drama was the provincial trial, a case from outside the two capital cities that attracted rapt attention from the central press and the services of Russia's leading defense attorneys.[1] The first prominent instance took place in January 1871 in the town of Riazan, 120 miles southeast of Moscow. The thirty-year-old noblewoman Vera Dmitrieva and the former military commander (*voinskii nachalnik*) of Riazan province, Colonel Nikolai Kostrubo-Karitskii, were accused of stealing some interest-bearing bonds from Vera's uncle, as well as performing an abortion.[2] Also on trial were two doctors and the elderly wife of a civil servant who had assisted with the operation, making the case an imperial-era version of the Stalinist "doctors' plot." Dmitrieva was defended by Aleksandr Urusov, Karitskii by Fedor Plevako, and one of the doctors, Dusing, by Vladimir Spasovich. All three advocates were already highly visible in the legal profession. Facing a veritable invasion of lawyers, journalists, and spectators from the two capitals, the judges were extra careful and engaged in lengthy discussions with the lawyers on small procedural questions throughout the trial. Aside from that, the trial was as contentious as trials could get in late imperial Russia.[3] No longer in love, the two primary defendants and their lawyers viciously attacked each other, to the point of sidelining the prosecutor's efforts. While it was Dmitrieva who stole the bonds and was caught trying to sell them under a false name, everyone seemed to have believed that Karitskii was the "instigator" (*vorotila*) of the case.

In the legal community the trial even raised the question of whether defense attorneys could ethically attack each other's clients to defend their own.[4] The jury's acquittal of the clearly guilty defendants was striking and unexpected, though understandable in retrospect, as young noblewomen were the one category of criminal defendants that tended to benefit from juries' sympathies.[5]

The judicial reform of 1864 introduced adversarial trial procedure, widely seen as a drastic improvement over the old inquisitorial system. First developed in England and France during the first half of the nineteenth century, the modern adversarial trial involved not simply a public confrontation between the prosecution and the defense but above all a complex courtroom ritual handled and directed largely by professional lawyers from both sides, even though in the Russian and other Continental legal systems judges retained an active role.[6] Contemporary observers and modern scholars alike have described Russian post-reform trials as more streamlined and efficient than the old ones, but this was only partially true. All serious cases before 1864 had to go through at least three complete reviews at the district, province, and Senate levels, and eliminating this multitiered system was one of the most important issues on the reformers' agenda in the late 1850s.[7] The reform of 1864 retained only one trial stage in the district court, and appeals were allowed only for procedural reasons.[8] But while the legal process overall was streamlined, the trial itself became exponentially more complex, with more than twenty mandatory separate steps (see table 3), not counting the preliminary investigation and the appeals.[9] In this respect the trial ritual that emerged in Russia and elsewhere during the middle fifty years of the nineteenth century strongly resembles the process of factory production that spread throughout Europe and United States during the same historical period.[10]

Another level of complexity was added by the requirement that all material facts established during the preliminary investigation, which usually lasted for months, had to be recounted and verified in the courtroom during a short period of time (even very complex trials usually lasted only a few days). A different type of challenge stemmed from the introduction of the trial by jury, which like its French counterpart was required to be judged on the jurors' "inner conviction" rather than any formal standard of proof.[11] This meant that the more important trials consisted of an extremely complex mixture of narratives about the participants' background, character, and actions. The largest and more complex cases contained multiple conflicting narratives or what lawyers call "theories" offered by prosecutors, defendants, victims, or witnesses, which frequently differed not only from one another but also from the evidence from the pretrial

TABLE 3. POST-1864 TRIAL PROCEDURE

1. Preliminaries	Take seats Bring defendant Verify defendant Ask defendant and lawyer if they challenge any jurors Select jury Explain to jurors their rights and responsibilities Indictment read by secretary Plea
2. Trial testimony (*sudebnoe sledstvie*)	Question defendant Question victim Question witnesses
3. Trial statements	Speech by prosecutor Speech by civil plaintiff's (victim's) lawyer Speech by defense lawyer Additional statements/responses in the same order
4. Concluding procedures	Formulate questions Summation by the judge Instruction of the jury Jury deliberations Verdict announced Arguments re: sentencing Judges withdraw to deliberate Judges return and announce sentence (can be postponed for one day for complex cases); announce day and time for formal sentencing (must be within two weeks—art. 792 [826])

investigation, which could change during the course of the trial, and which could not completely prevail over competing narratives. In this way trials were polyphonic, to use Bakhtin's terminology, and sometimes indeed cacophonic. While all jury trials had to follow the same rules of procedure whether they had one defendant or fifty, the most important trials discussed in this book joined multiple and often completely unrelated factual episodes, as in the Dmitrieva case, where charges of fraud and abortion were litigated at the same time and the province's former military commander shared the defendants' bench with the town's leading physicians.

The adversarial nature of the new procedure may or may not have been more streamlined or less open to corruption than the old procedure, depending on which aspect of it you examine or which example you hold up to scrutiny, but what the classic high-publicity trial model that emerged in the early 1870s definitely did do was invoke and debate sensitive social and cultural issues with political overtones. These ranged from Russian national identity and sexual practices in a bourgeois family to capitalist acquisitiveness and political loyalty. These issues could not be discussed openly or with the same frankness in any other public venue before 1905.

SETTING THE STAGE

The trial began after the public took their seats in the courtroom, with all the difficulties described in the preceding chapter, and were joined by the judges, the prosecutor, the lawyers and the prospective jurors. Only after everyone else was in place were the defendants brought in. If they had been in prison, they would wear a prisoner's robe and be guarded by two gendarmes, but if they were out on bail they would be "invited to stand trial" (*stat' na sud*): wear their own clothing and not have guards.[12] This arrangement benefited wealthier defendants who could afford bail or find relatives and friends to provide it, as well as those who committed nonviolent crimes and were more likely to remain free before the trial. But the entire arrangement of the first minutes of the trial was clearly slanted against the defendants, who had to walk into a full room with hundreds of prying stares aimed their way, to be examined and judged before any words had even been spoken.

Observers assessed not only the defendants but sometimes also the victims if they were present in the courtroom, noting their age, gender, physical health, attractiveness, clothing, and demeanor (whether insolent, depressed, sullen, frightened, or neutral), and their interactions with each other and the public. People at that time firmly believed that "facial features told character and could be deciphered."[13] Most "great" trials involved serious crimes and were based on indirect evidence, thus inviting and even requiring an evaluation of one's moral character. The first look at the defendant as conveyed by newspaper reporters typically foreshadowed the verdict. Thus, Daria Sokolova, who was convicted of murder in 1869 (the "Gusev Alley case"), is described as wearing a "sheepskin coat (*tulup*), with an old dirty kerchief on her head. Her face is pale, she seems emaciated . . . she is blond; her face is unremarkable but does not lack concentration and energy." Her codefendants who were acquitted are described as "neatly dressed . . . respectable . . . calm . . . appear to be fairly developed mentally (*razvitymi*)"[14] Another convicted murderer, the merchant Vasilii Mazurin, had a "worn, pale-yellow face framed by thin sideburns . . . his dark, cloudy eyes looked bleary; his weak voice trembled."[15] Another observer noted that Mazurin had a blush on his cheeks; "his eyes shone with a feverish gleam; the accused's entire figure expresses suffering both physical and moral; his voice is fitful and trembling—everything in him shows that he suffers from consumption in its final phase."[16] Mother Mitrofania was described as unattractive and not conforming to a stereotypical aristocratic appearance.[17] By contrast, the peasant Mavra Volokhova who in 1867 was acquitted of dismembering her husband and hiding the pieces in a lavatory, was described as modest, respectable, intelligent, and "filled with a sincere religious sentiment," giving the impression that whether or not she committed the crime, "hard labor is not created for the likes of her."[18] The fraud trial of the Melnitskii children in 1883 began with a "surprised whisper in the courtroom at the sight of such young and mostly attractive defendants."[19]

After the defendants entered the courtroom, the list of jurors was presented to the prosecution, then to the civil plaintiff, and then to the defense. Out of the pool of thirty men selected by lot from a larger list, the prosecutor and the civil plaintiffs together could remove six jurors, and all the defendants together could remove six or more, up to twelve, if the prosecution did not fully exercise its right. Jurors had to be between twenty-five and seventy, able to read, and meet property qualifications.[20] Unlike the Anglo-American common-law jury trial that requires unanimity to convict, Russian and French trials required only seven votes out of twelve.

The next stage after jury selection was for the chairman of the court to ascertain the name of the defendant and for the court secretary to read the indictment (*obvinitelnyi akt*), a document that was the basis for bringing the defendants to trial, and that had previously been approved by the procurator of the judicial circuit (*sudebnaia palata*) in which the district court was located. Similar to the opening statement in a modern American court, the indictment was required to describe the event or action that constituted the crime, provide the name and social station (*zvanie*) of the accused, explain the evidence against the accused, and state which laws the action in question had violated.[21] It is noteworthy that all the indictments I have reviewed listed only the article numbers of the penal code and did not explain what these crimes were, so that observers who did not have a copy of the code handy would not necessarily know what exactly was at stake during the trial, especially in complex proceedings that involved many different laws and, in cases of white collar crime, for which there were many applicable provisions.

At the end of the reading, the defendants were asked to enter a plea. While most trial accounts noted only how the defendant pleaded, a defendant could use this stage as an opportunity to make an impression on the jury before being subject to questioning. In the oversized 1877 trial of the alleged criminal group dubbed the Jacks of Hearts, one important defendant, Sultan-Shakh, simulated insanity: he talked to himself, then shouted, threw his hat down, and opened up his prison robe. The judges ordered him to be excluded from the trial, at which point he suddenly came to his senses and asked to stay but was escorted out of the courtroom anyway.[22] In more ordinary situations, everyone in the courtroom watched the defendants' demeanor, and trial reports sometimes provided a second description including the defendants' voice and manner of speech. In the Melnitskii children's trial, an observer related that Boris Melnitskii had a "soft trembling voice" and spoke "slowly and deliberately," and his friend Dorvoidt spoke in a "thick loud voice," whereas Boris's fiancée, Elena Bleze, could say only "Yes, I am guilty" and broke down in sobs that prevented her from saying anything else, which induced extreme sympathy in the public. To the description of Boris's fourteen-year-old sister the observer added that she was a young girl "but physically developed past childhood." This case was an outlier, and the pleading continued for several hours, with most defendants giving a detailed response, turning this stage into a mini-trial (or a pretrial). The observer noted that "these doubtlessly sincere explanations outlined very clearly the character (*lichnost*) of each of them."[23]

The rule of thumb in pre-1864 Russian courts was that confessing was a very bad idea for a defendant because the rules of evidence would then require judges to convict. In post-reform procedure, ironically, confession accompanied by a show of remorse often had the opposite effect. Thus, the dynamic in post-reform procedure was split: many prominent criminal defendants maintained their innocence to the end, and indeed a large part of the courtroom spectacle consisted in the fact that the guilt or innocence of the defendant was not clear a priori. But confessions were also common in cases involving violence as well as in ones involving fraud and forgery. The two most notable criminal defendants of 1879, the murderer Landsberg and the embezzler Yukhantsev, both confessed.[24] In

Figure 8. The defendants in the Melnitsky children's trial, December 1883. Keltsev, *Delo*, after p. 106. Tense-faced Vera Getmanchuk, also accused of participating in political conspiracy and considered to be the most intriguing of the group, is at the top. Elena Bleze and Varvara Melnitskaia, who successfully courted the public's sympathy, are in the middle. Boris Melnitsky and Albert Dorvoidt, the main defendants, are at the bottom.

1864 a young Polish nobleman, Schomberg-Kollontai, was caught in Baku with a stash of counterfeit rubles and gave the names of all his contacts to the police, who seized "an entire cargo of forged notes and an entire nest of villains abroad."[25] In post-reform Russia, as well as in France, it was still possible to acquit a defendant who pleaded guilty, and so any confession at this stage attracted intense interest. After a guilty plea the judge was required to question the defendant about all the circumstances of the crime to ensure that the confession was true and voluntary, and so at this point yet another factual narrative of the crime would emerge. In the 1872 forgery trial of the Miasnikov brothers, the key prosecution witness, Karaganov, was also one of the defendants who pleaded guilty and was questioned by Chairman Keikuatov; since Karaganov was not very coherent, the judge—clearly prejudiced against the main defendants—in effect constructed his testimony for him, filling the large gaps. For example, Karaganov wanted to say that he had forged a signature but did not know for what purposes it would be used, and the judge had to work hard to get him to say that he at least "suspected" why he was being asked to sign a blank sheet of paper with someone else's name.[26]

If the defendants pleaded guilty, this did not end the trial, but the proceedings would move directly to the statements by the prosecutor and defense lawyers. If, however, anyone participating in the trial—the judge, the jury, the prosecutor or the lawyers—requested it, the court would still examine all the investigation materials and question the witnesses. In some cases, a sincere confession by defendants could earn them an acquittal, especially if they had spent considerable time in preliminary confinement and the crime was not murder or otherwise exceptionally serious. For this reason, courtroom arguments about a confession could take a turn that would be surprising today, when we normally expect a prosecutor to uphold the value of a confession and the defense to argue for its falsity or its having been given under coercion. For instance, in the landmark embezzlement trial of Konstantin Yukhantsev in 1879, this former bank cashier gave a full confession, but the prosecutor worked hard to minimize its value, trying to sketch out a difference between a false and a true confession based on details of the testimony and timing. Yukhantsev gave "nothing more than an arithmetical confession. There were five million [rubles], there are two and a half left, and he admits that he took [the rest]. But we know this even without him. But of a sincere and complete confession there is not even a trace, and Yukhantsev, hiding the truth, was only true to himself until the last minute." Chairman Koni was also nervous that Yukhantsev could be acquitted and likewise tried to minimize his confession, suggesting that his intimate history of family troubles was irrelevant and inappropriate: "You [the jurors] have the main right to assess how appropriate for a fair presentation of the case it was to 'bring to life' during the trial that family life, which, according to the defendant's own letter to his brother, had to 'fall silent among them' and to depict himself as a plaything of destiny between his moral values and his wife which were equally alien to him." By contrast, Yukhantsev's star lawyer, Vladimir Zhukovskii, ironically argued not only that a confession was the best evidence in the world but also that it had two "precious qualities": it "open[ed] up the inner world of the defendant" and showed his respect for justice and for the law, urging the jury to support Yukhantsev's attempt to give up his past antisocial instincts. Zhukovskii urged the jury to treat the confession as "an act of respect towards the court."[27]

TESTIMONY AND CROSS-EXAMINATION

The most important stage of the modern adversarial trial is the examination of witnesses and other evidence in the public courtroom.[28] Lawyers and prosecutors seek to bolster their own case and to identify inconsistencies and omissions in their opponents' case. This process did not exist in earlier Russian or other Continental inquisitorial trials, which consisted of the reading of the case extract by the court secretary to the judges.[29] The judges could and often did question witnesses or defendants in person but were not obligated to do so. The reform statute of 1864, however, required that all evidence and testimony obtained during the preliminary investigation be "verified" (*provereny*) during the trial. In large and complex cases that took years to prepare, some witnesses were dead or missing, and their earlier statements could be read during the trial instead. Judges, jurors, prosecutors, lawyers for the defendants and for the victims (civil plaintiffs), and finally defendants could all question witnesses. In Russian courts, as in the other Continental systems, the jurors and especially judges often took a more active part, whereas in common-law courts they are usually passive. The participation of multiple questioners was one of the reasons that witness examination in Russia (or France) was more chaotic and polyphonic than the common-law trials that Robert P. Burns participated in and theorized about.[30]

The overall tone and direction of witness examinations varied: certain trials were more bitter and confrontational than others; in some trials prosecutors or lawyers were clearly negligent or intentionally acted against their side's interest.[31] But in my review of all the most important trials from the post-reform era

I find no pattern of any joint search for consensus, or for truth, or for reconciliation that Girish Bhat has argued was a key characteristic of post-reform jurisprudence.[32] The larger trials tended to form coherent sets of opposing witnesses offering drastically contradictory testimony. Very often one set consisted of family members and close friends of the defendant, emphasizing the enduring importance of family ties in post-emancipation Russia. In the inheritance fraud trial of General Leonid Gartung in 1877, his codefendant, Olga Sanftleben, summoned her sisters-in-law and several other people who fully supported her theory of the case, as opposed to her late husband's grown children, who were trying to get her convicted. In the Gulak-Artemovskaia forgery case (1878), one set of witnesses were her business associates (the fact that she had no close family no doubt played against her), while her late lover's brothers were civil plaintiffs and testified against her.[33] Similarly, Mother Mitrofania was supported by a large cast of nuns, priests, and monastic novices involved in her philanthropic empire, who were clearly coached and who most likely manufactured evidence on her behalf.[34] In a typical trial description, one indication of the direction in which the case was going was when one set of witnesses would be criticized for being exceedingly biased toward the defendant, while defense lawyers would not succeed in making a similarly strong claim about prosecution witnesses who were in fact equally if not more biased.[35] In larger and more complicated trials, however, witness groups could be mixed up and confused. In the Miasnikov brothers' forgery trial, in 1872, the nobleman Shevelev, a revolutionary, a swindler, and a bit of a litterateur, was said to be a "double-edged witness" because of his political "unreliability": while he crushed the civil plaintiff's case, he benefited his own side best by speaking as little as possible."[36]

While Russian trials never devolved into a chaotic screaming match, witnesses routinely snapped at, mocked, or argued with the other side's lawyers or even the judge. In the Miasnikov trial, the abovementioned witness Shevelev mocked one of Russia's best-known defense lawyers and a professor of law, Aleksandr Lokhvitskii, and even rebuked him for suggesting that Shevelev spent his time in taverns: "Why do you necessarily stress going to the taverns; do you consider me a drunkard (*traktirnyi gospodin*)? You can say anything about a man but why do you have to abuse (*tretirovat'*) him?" Another witness in the same case, the defendants' aunt, Beliaeva, was asked the same set of questions twice, by Prosecutor Koni and by Lokhvitskii, and asked the latter: "Haven't you heard what I've just said?" She was then attacked by the chairman, Prince Keikuatov ("Why did you consider yourself to be in such high position . . . that [her late husband's business partner] would not even dare to talk to you?"), followed by Koni, and followed by Lokhvitskii again. Beliaeva's high-powered lawyer, Arseniev, objected to the way these three were questioning her, to which Chairman Keikuatov responded that they could ask questions in any way designed to identify a contradiction, as long as these were not designed to induce self-incrimination.[37]

It was more difficult and generally inadvisable for defendants to talk back or project anything other than a modest, even meek image. In a later forgery case, Liudmila Gulak-Artemovskaia said she was insulted by the prosecutor's question whether the man in question had proposed to her tête-à-tête or in the presence of witnesses. Chairman Koni, who was clearly prejudiced against her, replied that she could refuse to respond to a question but she did not have the right to criticize it. Gulak-Artemovskaia said that she did so involuntarily, to which Koni instructed her not to do it "even involuntarily." Much of the trial revolved around Gulak-Artemovskaia's bitter feud with the writer and publisher Petr Polevoi, who acted as the main prosecution witness and allowed himself unspecified offensive expressions such that even Chairman Koni reprimanded him. At one point Gulak-Artemovskaia shouted, "Akh, what am I hearing! They slander me! I cannot hear this. I am going to leave so I don't have to hear lies!" Koni said that she could respond to him later, but she still left the courtroom, though she soon came back.[38] It was far more effective for women defendants to conform to the gender standards of their age: in the 1882 Melnitskii children's trial, Melnitskii's daughter-in-law Elena Bleze sobbed on numerous occasions, and during her last speech she tried to say something but only fell back on her chair with "muffled sobs." Melnitskii himself "wept bitterly" for several minutes and sat down on the chair brought to him on the judge's order.[39] Vera Zasulich, the infamous revolutionary terrorist put on trial in 1878 for wounding the St. Petersburg police chief, created a favorable impression with her modest appearance and conduct throughout the trial, which cut against the stereotype of ill-mannered radical activists.[40] By contrast, another famous radical, Sergei Nechaev, extradited from Switzerland and tried for murder in 1873, refused to stand trial and was taken out of the courtroom, with the trial proceeding in his absence, with predictable results.[41]

Also favored were those witnesses who were more eloquent and better educated. The abovementioned Shevelev had been arrested in different countries for his radical activities, as well as ordinary crimes like embezzlement and impersonating a government official, but he was the most educated witness in the Miasnikov case, and his testimony clearly won the day: even prosecutor Koni conceded (inexplicably) that it stood out for its "extremely consistent and attractive, even refined narration."[42] Especially privileged were those victims who participated in the case as "civil plaintiffs" and had their own lawyers—which of course meant that such individuals tended to be moneyed and educated.[43] Having their own lawyers magnified their impact exponentially, as Mother Mitrofania's lawyer lamented when he appealed her case.[44]

Witnesses who for any reason were less eloquent, or simply more forgetful, were considerably worse off. The questioning typically started with the judge offering the witness the opportunity to explain everything she knew about the case, and many persons found it difficult to make a coherent statement in a crowded courtroom. In the Miasnikov case, one key witness, Karaganov, asked the court if he could just read his pretrial statement (he was not permitted to). In that case there were other lower-middle class witnesses who had the same problem, and the common solution was to request the judge to ask them specific questions, as, for instance, the impecunious noblewoman Antonina Makhaeva did during that same trial.[45]

EVIDENCE AND PROOF (RUMORS, HEARSAY, CHARACTER)

One of the most important innovations of the 1864 reform that contributed to the complex and polyphonic character of the trial in Russia was that the new procedure omitted any formal standards of proof, that is, any rules that the judges or juries would be obligated to follow when deciding on guilt or innocence. As in postrevolutionary France, jurors in Russia were specifically required to rely solely on their "inner conviction" (*vnutrennee ubezhdenie*) and were thus entitled to acquit defendants who had confessed their guilt or whose guilt was overwhelmingly clear.[46] This was a significant departure from the pre-reform system of formal proofs first developed in Western Europe in the late medieval period and intended to reduce judicial discretion and arbitrariness by setting clear guidelines for evidence required to convict.[47] Under this earlier system, any of the so-called perfect proofs were sufficient for conviction. These included a confession, testimony by two witnesses, documentary evidence, and expert testimony. Circumstantial evidence was considered imperfect proof, and conviction was only possible with several such items of evidence. Contrary to a common misconception, formal proofs thus did not rule out the use of circumstantial evidence: the presence of formal proofs meant only that the judges were required to convict, but they could also convict with sufficient circumstantial evidence.[48] Also contrary to the common myth, the system of formal proofs sought not an absolute certainty but rather to maximize the probability of arriving at the correct result.[49] Pre-1864 judges were anything but judicial automatons, since the formal rules of procedure operated solely through their discretion, in that all types of proofs whether perfect or imperfect had to be categorized and evaluated.[50] That said, in actual practice before 1864, higher-tier courts that reviewed the initial conviction tended to overrule cases where the formal proofs were not present.[51]

In post-reform Russia, there was no way to impose formal rules or limitations on the jurors without also defeating the point of having a jury.[52] Nor was there a reliable practical, informal way to ensure jury behavior. Given that juries were introduced in Russia quickly and in a fully developed form, Russia did not experience the prolonged struggle between judges and jurors that unfolded in early modern England, where judges could bully or even punish jurors who would not cooperate and demand them to reconsider their verdict.[53] Despite this history, nineteenth-century English juries routinely resisted and frustrated judges by refusing to follow their lead. Similarly, French jurists and officials at this same period were extremely concerned about jury acquittals and enacted a series of measures to reduce them.[54]

Russia's 1864 reform greatly relaxed the rules of evidence. Again following the French model, rumors and hearsay were all permitted to be introduced into the trial, excluding only rumors "with indeterminate origins."[55] One of Anatolii Koni's first trials in St. Petersburg as a young prosecutor, the forgery case of the Miasnikov brothers in 1872, was almost entirely based on rumors that were clearly started by the man who would have benefited from their conviction. This may be the most egregious known example, but many other trials admitted evidence that would have been excluded as hearsay in an Anglo-American court, though not in a Continental European one. One of the few limitations on the evidence that could be presented during the trial concerned what lawyers today call "trial by ambush," that is, the use of surprise witnesses. Such tactics are frowned upon but even in the United States today are not completely ruled out. In late imperial Russia the rules of procedure required the prosecution and the defendant to provide the names of all witnesses before the trial. But surprises still occurred, since the witnesses' mental condition and intelligence did not have to be disclosed. The abovementioned Karaganov shocked the courtroom because no one had any idea that he would wave his arms, mumble, and say nonsensical phrases, many of which only the judge could hear. Nor could it be assured that the right witness actually showed up: in the same Miasnikov case, it turned out in the middle of the trial that the man who had heard Karaganov's confession did not show up himself but sent his far less intelligent brother.[56]

In short, the extensive discretion that the reformers gave to the jury and a lax law of evidence meant that both lawyers and prosecutors were able to make wide-ranging and sometimes extravagant arguments about defendants' or witnesses' background and character, although the presiding judge could stop a lawyer from dwelling on irrelevant details.

Evidence offered at any criminal trial falls into two categories: evidence about the criminal act itself and so-called character evidence, that is, information not about the facts of the case but about the defendant's previous conduct, most importantly any prior offences and convictions.[57] Typically the defendant argued either that he had led a good life and so was not likely to commit the crime, or if his guilt was clear, that his previous misfortunes were to blame for the offense rather than a willful breaking of the law. Conversely, the prosecutor would seek to show that the defendant demonstrated a pattern of illegal and immoral behavior and was therefore inclined toward crime or, alternately, that the defendant had had a happy and prosperous life, and his offense could not have resulted from an adverse social or family environment.

Today character evidence is heavily used in criminal proceedings, but the major legal systems have developed rules to ensure that the defendant is not in effect being tried over and over again for earlier offenses. Beginning in the early nineteenth century, England and the United States gradually developed the rule that the prosecution could not introduce evidence of bad character, including prior criminal history, unless defendants themselves first claimed to be of good moral character.[58] But then, as well as now, an accused criminal's defense is hardly ever viable without character evidence and character witnesses. This was also true in the nineteenth century. In mid-Victorian England, "in capital cases character evidence was often of critical importance. Without it an accused would generally have little hope of mercy at the hands of either jury or judge." The lack of character witnesses was interpreted as evidence of bad character.[59] In postrevolutionary France, character evidence was used very broadly, so that often "the trials were of personalities as much as they were of crimes." After French juries were allowed to recommend leniency in sentencing (in an attempt to reduce acquittals) in 1832, character became even more important.[60] During the second half of the nineteenth century Western European academics and reformers began to argue for giving more recognition to the medical, psychological, and sociological underpinnings of criminal behavior.[61] Arguments using positivist theories about crime began to appear routinely in the courtroom. Judges and other legal practitioners did not, however, give up the fundamental, though rebuttable, assumption of Eurocentric criminal justice that crime is an intentional moral act committed by a fully autonomous individual.[62]

The Russian jury trial after 1864 similarly exposed a "powerfully moral temper," as Girish N. Bhat has observed. There is no evidence, though, that this moral temper was stronger in the Russian legal system than in other major systems. Moreover, it is an overstatement to claim, as Bhat does, that in post-reform courts a "finding of guilt or innocence before a jury was generally as dependent upon incriminating or vindicating 'moral' facts (the accused's personality, reputation, psychological and social background, material circumstances, and manifestation of remorse or repentance) as upon comparably compelling 'legal' facts (physical evidence, the defendant's own confession, expert testimony)."[63] Rather, character evidence was used to bolster, rather than replace, what Bhat calls "legal facts." It predominated only in cases when other types of evidence were not available or not in favor of the party making the argument. In either situation, character evidence appeared in cases that were complex and ambiguous, and when multiple narratives and sources of information emerged during the trial. While this was not a clear-line rule, evidence of good character or of past misfortunes tended to help young, educated, and female defendants and be largely irrelevant for everyone else.

In fifty or so major trials of the post-reform era only about a dozen did not rely on character evidence at all. These were mostly from the first years of the new courts, roughly from 1867 to 1872, involving mostly but not exclusively male defendants who committed both violent and white-collar crimes. Otherwise, character evidence was important, often extremely so, but it never sidelined the factual narrative of the crime itself. Chronologically, character evidence was used from the beginning of the new courts. What appears to have been the very first murder conviction by a jury in Russia, in November 1866, involved a retired junior official at the Foreign Ministry, Evgenii Rebinder, who had for years cohabited with his young sister-in-law and eventually in a fit of jealousy sliced her throat as she slept.[64] The jury was clearly shocked by such behavior from a respectable civil servant and asked for the details of Rebinder's life, which, it turned out, "was full of cruelty and violence, a long sequence of immoral and criminal acts."[65] Character was even more important in the trial of the civil servant Nikolai Protopopov in 1867 for striking his superior. But while the trial scrutinized Protopopov's life and emotional state, it did not ignore the factual circumstances of the incident.[66] In the abovementioned 1871 trial of Dmitrieva and Kostrubo-Karitskii, Vera Dmitrieva's past life, her early failed marriage, and her affair with Karitskii were brought up but not dissected or really discussed, and Karitskii's life and character were skipped over entirely. Similarly, in the Miasnikov brothers' forgery trial in 1872 the opposing sides scrutinized the morals and prior lives of the main witnesses but did not bring up any insights about the brothers themselves. In the massive forgery trial of Mother Mitrofania in 1874, the prosecution and the lawyer for one of the victims made scathing remarks about the aristocratic nun, but there was no real debate about her life or moral character, as the case almost exclusively focused on the complex details of her financial operations. In the even more massive trial of the managers and board members of the Moscow Commercial Loan Bank in 1876 there was some discussion of the defendants' character, but it was very much in the shadow of their financial operations. In the forgery and fraud trial of General Leonid Gartung and the merchant's widow Olga Sanftleben in 1877, some details about each defendant's life were brought up but in a very limited way—with good reason, since Gartung was Alexander Pushkin's son-in-law, and Olga's checkered past was only likely to elicit the jury's sympathy.

But as the 1870s unfolded, some of the other most memorable trials in Russian history debated and scrutinized the minute details of the participants' lives, whether defendants, witnesses, or victims. These were exceptional cases, and they fell into two broad categories. One set involved ambivalent factual narratives, which could not be evaluated and interpreted without introducing character evidence. Such were the 1876 trial of the banker Stanisław Kronenberg for tormenting his young daughter, the 1878 forgery trial of the noblewoman Liudmila Gulak-Artemovskaia, and the 1878 poisoning trial of Margarita Jujean. These cases are discussed in detail in subsequent chapters, but in all of them neither prosecution nor defense could build a solid argument without providing detailed information about the moral character and activities of everyone involved. Kronenberg's activities were clear, but their legal interpretation was not at all; and in the other two cases there was no direct proof of either side's position, so each had to draw upon any information possible.

The second variety of cases were those in which the defendant's guilt was beyond doubt, because of a confession or some other circumstances. The only feasible strategy available to defense lawyers in such cases was to argue that their client deserved a finding of extenuating circumstances, or perhaps even an acquittal. One of the first such cases was the 1870 trial of Aleksandra Avdeeva among several other defendants for murdering her client von Sohn and shipping his body out of St. Petersburg in a suitcase. In 1874 the nobleman and judge Nikolai Nepenin and his wife, Evgenia, were tried for stabbing Evgenia's former lover, Petr Chikhachev. Other trials for murder or attempted murder were of Anastasia Kairova and Ekaterina Kornilova, both in 1876, of Grigorii Bezobrazov and Maria Kovalchukova in 1878, of Vera Zasulich also in 1878, and of Praskovia Kachka in 1880. All these women were acquitted by juries, even though most of their codefendants, if any, were convicted. Male defendants typically had worse luck; for example, the bank cashier Konstantin Yukhantsev and the murderer Karl von Landsberg both confessed and were convicted in 1879 without a finding of leniency. In both cases lawyers and prosecutors alike scrutinized the defendants' entire prior lives. Trials with large numbers of defendants involved long discussions attempting to distinguish the guilt of each of them, necessitating heavy use of character evidence, and the results varied, although once again young women tended to be acquitted. This includes the 1875 forgery trial of Sofia Sedkova and others, the 1877 trial of the forty-eight defendants known as the Jacks of Hearts, and the fraud and embezzlement trials of Fedor Melnitskii and his children in 1882 and 1883.

As far as we can tell without being privy to jury deliberations, character evidence, either positive or negative, was central to the outcome of all these cases, but this does not mean that the facts of the case were not also important. To the contrary, they were scrutinized in as much detail as the defendants' prior lives. The division between legal and moral facts, while clear in many cases, is not at all clear in others. For instance, while murder usually takes place in the space of minutes or only slightly longer counting any preparation, other types of crime took many years to unfold, and thus the crime itself could not be practically separated from the defendant's past behavior and moral portrait. This especially applies to most cases of white-collar crime that were so prominent in post-emancipation Russia.

EXPERT TESTIMONY

Many criminal trials involve testimony by persons who have no information about the case but are experts in a particular area of knowledge that is necessary for interpreting the available factual or character evidence.[67] The best-known variety of expert witnesses come from the medical and natural sciences, such as physicians, pathologists, psychiatrists, and chemists. The type of experts who were most widely used in the nineteenth century, but were also the most controversial, were handwriting analysts. Indispensable in white-collar-crime trials, handwriting analysts were also used in trials for violent crime that involved disputes about documentary evidence. Finally, financial and accounting experts were also indispensable in white-collar-crime trials, but not often discussed or publicized. Elisa Becker's excellent study of late imperial forensic medicine, as well as my own earlier work on handwriting expertise, find that both types of experts were an integral part of legal procedure both before and after the reform of 1864 and that both types of expertise underwent considerable change in the 1860s.[68] While Becker focused on the longer-term trends and debates among legal scholars and judicial officials, here I adopt a micro perspective based on individual trials. While confirming Becker's conclusion that post-reform medical experts were questioned and challenged in the post-reform juridical field, I also want to emphasize that forensic experts were far from being aloof and impartial sages. They were drawn deeply into courtroom dynamics and into one or more of the conflicting narratives or theories of the case. Perhaps because of this unclear status of forensic experts, I found few examples when their opinions clearly carried the decisive weight in a case's outcome.

Modern medical experts appeared in the eighteenth century and continued to develop in the nineteenth. Their legal status was closely connected with the overall structure of the judiciary and of trial procedure. Becker has pointed out that in pre-reform courts testimony by "medical officials" had the status of a perfect proof (along with confession, sworn testimony of two witnesses, and documentary evidence), as long as it followed the legal rules for forensic medical examination, "contain[ing] a clear and positive attestation about the subject of testimony and not contradict[ing] the verified circumstances of the case."[69] If these conditions were met, and the defendant did not successfully contest this testimony, it was sufficient for conviction. By contrast, after the reform of 1864 experts were required to present their opinions in public and to be subject to cross-examination. But, in my view, the fact that medical experts had to present and defend their views in public does not mean that their position in the courtroom had become weaker. Publicity in the 1860s and 1870s was generally viewed as a source of power by all categories of actors, from high-level officials to radical activists. Particularly fascinating is the pioneering 1869 call by Leonid Vladimirov for the elevation of medical experts in the new courts as "scientific judges" who would be "immune from external challenge or evaluation and [carry] obligatory weight in legal decision-making."[70] Such further fragmentation of judicial power would not contradict the logic of the 1864 reform, and it would illustrate Foucault's argument about the emergence of "administrative alternatives" to the classic courtroom ritual.[71] But at least in the most prominent post-reform trials experts could not claim such exalted authority, because the factual circumstances were too complex, with other types of evidence or arguments being more weighty, and because the experts could not agree with each other.

The most famous early jury trial in which medical testimony was important was the trial of Nikolai Protopopov, who had struck his superior and was acquitted. The medical experts argued that he had acted in a state of frenzy induced by being mistreated and repeatedly passed over for promotion. As I discuss later, however, the case also presented the theme of honor-induced violence, which tended to be treated leniently by the courts. Even the pre-reform court acquitted the nobleman Kicheev in Moscow in 1866 on grounds of insanity after he deliberately shot another nobleman for insulting his sister.[72] Another prominent early case was the trial of Dmitrieva and Kostrubo-Karitskii, in which two of the defendants were doctors charged with assisting in an abortion. In the Miasnikov brothers' forgery case, the key prosecution witness and one of the defendants, Karaganov, acted deranged during the trial, but the two physicians who testified on his condition could not say anything helpful: the police physician Dr. Depp, who had had Karaganov under observation before the trial, was not trained in psychiatry, whereas the psychiatrist called as an expert had not seen Karaganov until the day of the trial. The two doctors simply continued to refer to each other in a circular and rather ludicrous way.[73] As one observer noted, the result of this was that "nobody believed" either the medical or the handwriting experts.[74] In the famous Kronenberg child-abuse trial, several physicians testified about scabs, wounds, and bruises on the banker's small daughter but once again could not come up with anything definitive, while Russia's first woman doctor, Nadezhda Suslova, testified that she had treated the girl for onanism and took Kronenberg's side, which could not have boosted her professional authority. Finally, in the 1879 trial of the French woman Margarite Jujean for poisoning seventeen-year-old Nikolai Poznanskii with morphine, several distinguished physicians examined the youth's preserved body parts. Aside from the conclusion that he had indeed died from morphine poisoning, however, they could not explain how morphine had entered his body. In sum, for all their professional status medical experts were unable to stand out as definitive authorities in the most prominent trials due to multiple conflicting factual narratives and complicated evidence, as well as procedural limitations and, at least in some cases, extraneous pressures.

An even more ubiquitous variety of forensic experts were handwriting analysts who attempted to identify forged documents or signatures in an age when handwriting was a carefully cultivated skill conveying multiple levels of information. Handwriting disputes could emerge in any type of case but were unavoidable in cases of white-collar crime, such as forgery, fraud, and embezzlement. Documents were accepted by pre-reform courts as perfect proof, but only if they were acknowledged by the party against whom they were submitted. Pre-reform rules for handwriting analysis were the same for civil and criminal cases.

The court appointed between three and nine experts selected from secretaries of local government agencies (*prisutstvennykh mest*), teachers of calligraphy, or other persons who were competent and not challenged by the litigants. It was still up to the court to interpret the experts' findings.[75] The important change that occurred in actual practice shortly before the reform of 1864 was that the custom of using panels of dozens or even hundreds of civil servants was replaced by panels of only a few calligraphy teachers. Post-reform rules of procedure provided for handwriting analysis but no longer listed any detailed requirements. In practice, post-reform courts continued to use small panels of calligraphy teachers. Compared to medical experts, handwriting analysts were even more open to questioning, doubt, and even ridicule by lawyers and prosecutors. Experts' opinions tended to be cryptic and contradictory. The Miasnikov brothers' forgery trial in 1872 was typical in using handwriting analysis, even though the participants thought that it was not as reliable as chemical or medical analysis.[76]

Clear triumphs of handwriting experts in the post-reform courtroom were rare. In the 1867 trial of the student Danilov for killing a moneylender, handwriting experts were able to identify the calligraphy style peculiar to the high school (*gimnazia*) that Danilov happened to have attended.[77] Such knowledge was clearly helpful in trials of elite offenders who shared a very small educational system. The 1874 forgery trial of Mother Mitrofania rested heavily on handwriting analysis. Indeed, this was perhaps the only case I have reviewed that can be fundamentally reduced to a contest between Mitrofania's calligraphy skills and those of the experts. Mitrofania's hobbies were calligraphy and painting, and she even engaged in icon painting. Samples of Mitrofania's handwriting on the disputed documents were sold as leaflets during the trial (see figure 2) and attached to the published transcript of the case. During the trial, one of the experts even demonstrated on a slate board his reconstruction of how Mitrofania forged the signatures on her victims' debt documents.[78] Before the trial, when her documents were found to have been forged, she was able to produce new documents (no doubt manufactured by her supporters) that did not contain the inconsistencies identified by the experts. She also seems to have contrived to have a supporter appointed as one of the experts, who steadfastly came up with opinions in her favor. One of the commentators on the trial thought that Mitrofania ultimately failed in her schemes because she relied too heavily on her handwriting and calligraphy skills, producing forgeries that were far more refined than the angular and awkward signatures of the elderly merchants that she allegedly defrauded.[79] But even during this trial handwriting expertise was challenged: Mitrofania's lawyer, Shaikevich, argued that this was "indeed a very shaky proof" because handwriting "experts tend to couch their statements in a scientific form even though the subject by its very nature does not allow for any scientific foundations." In England, Shaikevich continued, handwriting evidence is almost never allowed except as testimony from a witness who personally recognized a particular person's handwriting.[80] Shaikevich was correct that this was the traditional rule in English law, but precisely during the second half of the nineteenth century handwriting analysis was becoming more acceptable than handwriting recognition.[81] In another forgery trial in 1878, that of Liudmila Gulak-Artemovskaia, the prosecutor, Prince Urusov, mocked handwriting experts even as he relied on their findings: he said that the merchant whose signature the defendant had allegedly forged had intentionally avoided giving out samples of his handwriting because it could be easily forged, in which situation the handwriting experts would find "some resemblance" to his real handwriting and the court would make him liable.[82]

Another important but little-known type of expert testimony was offered by financial specialists, who were indispensable in any fraud case but especially so in large-scale trials for bank failure or corporate embezzlement. Trial records contain very little information about what these experts did or said, most likely because laypersons had a difficult time understanding the details. For example, the landmark 1884 case of the Skopin Municipal Bank (also known as the Rykov case) was observed by the young Anton Chekhov, who wrote a witty and highly readable account but explicitly noted that he tuned out any finance-related testimony, which, ironically, seems to have taken up most of the trial.[83] This and many other similar cases, such as the Moscow bank case, the Yukhantsev embezzlement trial, and the arson and insurance-fraud case of Stepan Ovsiannikov, involved an in-depth reconstruction of many years' worth of financial operations involving millions of rubles, which can be described as forensic accounting. Ovsiannikov's trial also employed a group of professional architects who were allotted between four hundred and five hundred rubles to build a detailed model of a destroyed mill, using original blueprints and on-site measurements conducted by the "best" members of the Academy of the Arts.[84]

In sum, professional experts became even more indispensable in the post-reform period, coming from a variety of disciplines and their testimony sometimes being probably the most important element of a trial. But they never came to dominate the proceedings so as to determine the outcome or be more than one set of participants among many. Experts never amounted to being "scientific judges."

TRIAL ADVOCACY: TACTICS AND RHETORIC

Defense attorneys are to this day the best remembered participants in pre-1917 Russian legal culture, with numerous collections of courtroom speeches published before the revolution, some appearing in the Soviet era, and many more republished after 1991.[85] Thanks mostly to Samuel Kucherov's book, post-1864 lawyers have been seen as liberal professional experts steadfastly fighting to protect the reform and the rule of law against tsarist bureaucrats.[86] This picture is a bit one-sided, as we shall see, but it is accurate to say that professional lawyers were central to creating the modern adversarial trial both in Russia and elsewhere.[87] Previous thinking about legal representation was similar in pre-Victorian England and in the Continental systems employing inquisitorial procedure: lawyers were appropriate and helpful in civil cases, but in criminal trials they only obscured truth and helped criminals escape punishment.[88] In England criminal defendants began to enjoy the assistance of counsel only in the seventeenth century, and then only in trials of crimes against the state, and only when the trial involved questions of law.[89] Early modern English judges often prosecuted cases and provided legal advice for both sides in a criminal trial, a practice that did not fully disappear until the end of the nineteenth century.[90] The right to counsel in England appeared only in 1836, when individuals initiating criminal prosecutions began to themselves employ professional lawyers, unbalancing a system that was already stacked against defendants, but this law of course did not benefit all defendants equally, just as it does not today. In France the right to counsel was built into the postrevolutionary legal system. In pre-1864 Russia, the government refused to allow an autonomous bar, fearing its potential disloyalty. Russians were, however, allowed to hire representatives (*poverennye*) to submit court papers in civil trials (which, after all, consisted solely of an exchange of written statements by the parties), as well as to assist their clients in the second (provincial) and third (Senate) stages of criminal proceedings. Lawyers could review the case extract and add written comments and arguments, and with the court's permission could also offer oral arguments. Lawyers could not participate in the first, district-level stage of a pre-reform trial, which was not outcome determinative but was the only opportunity to shape the case record that would be reviewed by the higher-status judges on the province and Senate levels. Nor could pre-reform lawyers or defendants question witnesses or argue with the person prosecuting the case, there being no prosecutors in pre-reform law.[91] Given that pre-reform procedure was not public, the lawyer's personal network of information was essential for simply knowing when the case was moved to the higher-up court and when the documents became available for review. But this system did work for those defendants who were wealthier and especially those charged with nonviolent crimes, who could afford to be free on bail or under house arrest.

In the 1850s and 1860s the right to counsel in Russia was debated like all other aspects of the court reform, but it was by far the least controversial issue. Even the initial restrictive version of the reform allowed counsel at all levels, although lawyers would only read their written memos to the judges. To this the minister of justice added the option to present oral arguments by both prosecutor and the defendant or the defense lawyer.[92] As already mentioned, the initial 1859 draft of the reform was only an incremental improvement over the old procedure. But the 1864 reform that introduced a fully adversarial trial with juries allowed defendants to engage either a sworn attorney registered with the local court or any other person not banned by law from serving as a legal representative. Defendants could also request that the court appoint a sworn attorney to defend them. In England and the United States this right did not fully appear for another century.[93] The rationale for suddenly changing the long-standing policy in the 1860s was only in part to protect the defendants. More important, members of the judiciary were looking for any ways to make trials more efficient. They concluded that the insufficient presence of counsel was a major obstacle, adding work to the court personnel and prolonging the proceedings.[94] The legal profession, therefore, was elevated in status to help the judges rather than to fight them.

Post-reform lawyers were a diverse group. In the top layer were several hundred sworn attorneys (*prisiazhnye poverennye*), equivalent to English barristers in terms of their prestige but without their monopoly on legal representation. Very few legal representatives from the other, lower layers of the profession ever participated in prominent trials, and most of those were assistant sworn attorneys. Unlicensed legal advice continued to be available due to the small number of top-tier lawyers.[95] In the Miasnikov brothers' testament-forgery case, the alleged victim who had acquired Miasnikov's claim from a legitimate heir had engaged a variety of unlicensed lawyers and brokers, who filed lawsuits and petitions in every possible court and government agency, including a complaint to the tsar personally, and seem to have only damaged their client's case by making it appear disreputable.[96] While women acted as legal representatives both before and after the reform, the tsar's decree of 1876 prohibited them from officially joining the bar, although they apparently continued to occasionally appear in the lower-level courts of the justices of the peace.[97]

From surviving case records one can see that the skill set of top attorneys was twofold. First, at the trial stage—which is the focus of this book—attorneys

Figure 9. *St. Petersburg Types: A Conference with a "Lawyer,"* drawing by N. S. Negadaev. *Vsemirnaia illustratia,* 1876, no. 7, p. 125. The elite perspective on lower-level legal practice as depicted in this upscale illustrated weekly. A semi-licit legal broker is consulting with his peasant clients in a drinking establishment. Note his outlandish and foreign clothing. The shady morality of this practice is emphasized by the figure of a small girl buying alcohol, prominently placed in the center of the picture.

were primarily dealing not with the "law" as such but with the facts of the crime, and legal issues rarely arose. This was not because of some unique defect of Russian procedure, as some literature argues.[98] Rather, the jury was there to find facts and not to interpret statutes and appellate decisions. If the indictment made a mistake in the legal categorization of the facts at stake, this was a matter for the appeal, not the jury, to decide. Lawyers and prosecutors did occasionally argue about statutory definitions of crimes, and it was the responsibility of the judge to explain to the jury in his final summation what legal rules were applicable in the case. But almost invariably jurists sought to exclude legal jargon from a jury trial.[99] The lawyer's first task when taking up a case was to familiarize himself with the facts, for which he had no more than seven days, even though some case files were exceedingly long. On some occasions, it is clear that lawyers found out about the facts only during the trial itself. The lawyer then had to determine for himself whether his client was guilty, which was an extremely important point, as we shall see in a moment. During the trial itself, the lawyer had to deploy superior memory, both long-term and short-term, superb verbal skills, and also superior psychological judgment. Attorneys and prosecutors were free to prepare their speeches in advance and memorize them, but as a rule they were not permitted to read a prepared speech. In the 1867 murder trial of merchant Vasilii Mazurin, his lawyer, Kicheev, read from his notebook and was reprimanded by the judge.[100] Speakers were, however, allowed to refer to notes. Moreover, defense lawyers had to have the mental strength to stand up to a legal system that was still very heavily biased against them: in a large trial they would have to oppose not only the prosecutors but also the judges, who were often hostile, as well as the attorneys for the victims (civil plaintiffs), who were typically wealthy and able to afford expensive counsel, and those for the other defendants, who could offer different arguments and sometimes attack each other.[101]

None of this means that lawyers did not need to be legal minds.[102] Both sides could appeal the case to the higher-up Judicial Chamber and then the Senate, and sometimes also the Council of State. An appeal, or, technically speaking, cassation, was allowed only on procedural grounds, alleging either that proper procedure was not followed or, alternately, that the law was applied incorrectly.[103] For this appellate practice the lawyer had not only to have a complete trial record but also to know all the relevant appellate decisions. In Russia (as well as in France), there was no formal doctrine of judicial precedent (stare decisis). The Senate was free to vacillate between different positions from case to case, to the considerable frustration of legal scholars who sought in vain to find patterns or consistency.[104] Much as in the U.S. Supreme Court, considerations of policy supplemented those of legal doctrine. But while Russian cassation lawyers could make policy arguments, they of course could not ignore issues of statutory interpretation and relevant Senate decisions, and they typically engaged in hairsplitting arguments on minute points of the law.

It would take a separate book to adequately analyze even the most important courtroom speeches in terms of their legal and rhetorical strategies. Here I suggest that there were certain aspects of the criminal trial that especially challenged lawyers' professional authority and legal skills. The first such moment was the lawyer's initial decision to take up a client or, alternately, being assigned by the court to represent one who could not afford a lawyer.[105] Through this mechanism it frequently happened that a young peasant who had committed a relatively minor offense would be represented without charge by a top lawyer, who would use this opportunity to gain additional publicity and attract paying clients. In the Kronenberg child-abuse case, the appointment of Vladimir Spasovich as his lawyer by the court was not accidental, given that the chairman of the St. Peterburg District Court, Likhachev, had extensive business dealings with Kronenberg's father and co-owned a leading newspaper (*Novoe Vremia*) that Kronenberg was underwriting.[106] When given the assignment, the lawyer would often have to consider how to defend a client who was clearly guilty or even had confessed to the crime; if the lawyer had a choice, he had to consider whether to take up the case at all. While the legal profession had certain formal and quasi-formal rules, most of these addressed conflicts of interest, financial accountability, and professional civility and competence; there were no explicit rules about which cases could or could not be accepted.[107] But informally it mattered enormously whether the lawyer had ever in his career argued the innocence of a defendant who was clearly guilty, especially if he twisted the facts and viciously attacked victims, witnesses, or other defendants. Even though it may not be apparent to a nonlawyer, an attorney in many settings to this day, including the United States, does not merely represent a client but also essentially stakes his reputation on, and vouches for, the veracity of the defendant's arguments, and not merely on their persuasiveness.[108] The post-reform Russian press even engaged in a debate about a lawyer's responsibility to refuse to take up disreputable clients.[109] While we do not have very many accounts about lawyers' informal interactions with their clients, courtroom speeches occasionally mentioned the lawyer's first meeting with the defendant, which allegedly convinced him of the client's innocence.[110] This first interview can be viewed as a mini-trial, or a pretrial, in which the defendant faced a potential ally who at that point was critically minded, given that his professional reputation rested on this interview.

In practice, most prominent lawyers were selective in accepting clients. For example, the eminently competent Konstantin Arseniev took up the defense of one of the millionaire Miasnikov brothers charged with forgery in 1872, and he was criticized by what was then a semireputable newspaper *Novoe Vremia* for letting his standards go: "How could this attorney who had a reputation for extreme fastidiousness not realize that such a case would cast a shadow on his reputation . . .?"[111] Today, however, Arseniev's decision suggests that the brothers were indeed innocent in this generally cryptic case. The case created an unusual rumor that sounds like a play by Nikolai Ostrovskii, that the Miasnikovs engaged "another unofficial attorney—a broker (*khodatai*) well known in Petersburg and with a very unseemly reputation—who is the main motor (*vorotila*) of the entire matter and whose skill . . . reached an extreme degree," and who was able to secure an impeccable lawyer for the Miasnikovs and to ensure that the civil plaintiffs were represented by an unsavory one (*Lokhvitskii*).[112]

Another well-known example of lawyers' selectivity was the case of Mother Mitrofania, in which all the top attorneys refused to defend her except for Samuil Shaikevich and Semion Shchelkan, and even their relations with the nun quickly deteriorated, as I discuss later. Another disreputable defendant, Fedor Melnitskii, the treasurer of the Imperial Orphanage in Moscow, was accused of a massive embezzlement in 1882. He engaged a top-notch attorney, Kurilov, but only because Fedor's brother Lev, himself a justice of the peace, had convinced Kurilov that Fedor was innocent. Kurilov was paid out of Fedor's loot, as it turned out, and later had to return the fee. Lev's own attorney, the even more prestigious and reputable Vladimir Gerard, argued that even though Lev had deceived Kurilov, "who would have taken up his brother's defense if he admitted that the brother was guilty? I respect our corporation too much to consider this possible."[113] In 1875, the millionaire arsonist Ovsiannikov paid five thousand rubles to the prominent lawyer Borovikovskii to write a brief legal petition, which created a press scandal. Borovikovskii decided that Judge Koni was his moral compass and asked whether he should return the fee. Koni said only after the trial, if Ovsiannikov had been convicted. The top criminal defense lawyers would not defend Ovsiannikov, but he engaged Pavel Potekhin, who was highly prominent but specialized in civil-law trials.

Three influential and extremely talented lawyers had a reputation for taking on ethically doubtful or outright shady cases: Aleksandr Lokhvitskii, Fedor Plevako, and Vladimir Spasovich.[114] One of these three invariably defended the most unsavory characters appearing in this book. In the Dmitrieva case, Plevako defended Colonel Karitskii. Spasovich specialized in disreputable male patriarchs (Dr. Dussing in this case). Lokhvitskii in the Miasnikov case represented the civil plaintiff who had no connection to the inheritance under dispute and had acquired his claim years before as a gift from one of the heirs (and was caught bribing witnesses).

Lawyers defending ethically challenging cases deployed several strategies, all risky. One was to acknowledge the defendant's guilt and to claim that the defense was only working to uncover the entire truth of the issue, in hopes that the jury would take the defendant's confession or circumstances into account and find him "deserving of leniency." In the 1872 embezzlement case of the minor litterateur Aleksandr Pal'm, his lawyer, Spasovich, argued that "given the defendant's difficult position the only service that is possible to provide him is the most severe, most merciless truth, with no falsehood, no embellishment, and the defense must present his act as it was, not any worse than it was, nor any better."[115] Spasovich went so far as to disavow Pal'm's claim that another nobleman,

Belli, was complicit in the crime. When defending a member of the aristocratic Schomberg-Kollontai family caught with a stash of counterfeit money, Spasovich said: "I have nothing to do, and you have no need to think, deliberate, and waver—you are only going to say two words—yes, guilty," and he then proceeded to argue that his client had been led astray by a mysterious Jewish counterfeiter based in England.[116] The lawyer for Mother Mitrofania, Shaikevich, admitted during the trial that "many of the prosecution's arguments appear extremely strong and almost incontrovertible," even though Mitrofania steadfastly denied any wrongdoing.[117] Shaikevich specialized in complex finance-related litigation, and this admission is noteworthy and in retrospect rather scandalous.[118] In the 1879 embezzling case of Konstantin Yukhantsev, his lawyer, Zhukovskii, argued that his client's confession actually made his task easier because he knew for sure that he was guilty and could build his defense more effectively and argue for leniency.[119]

Another strategy in a case with multiple defendants was for the lawyers to shift the blame onto each other's clients. The case of Dmitrieva and Kostrubo-Koritskii that brought up the question of whether this was ethical has already been mentioned. Even earlier, in the 1867 Nizhnii Novgorod salt-embezzlement case (tried without a jury), Lokhvitskii defended the most high-ranking embezzler, whose strategy was to claim that Russia's strategic salt reserves were stolen by his modest subordinate, Terskii. In other trials, there could be a presumption in favor of cooperation among the defendants. The strongest example is the 1874 case of the Nepenin couple who killed the wife's former lover; both spouses implored their lawyers to protect the other at all costs.[120] In the Mitrofania case there were three other defendants, and at first there was a sense that the lawyers would not attack each other's clients. But then Mitrofania's second attorney, Schelkan, less competent than Shaikevich, and no doubt hired because the case was too complex for one lawyer, attacked a minor defendant (Makarov), whose own very capable lawyer, Kharitonov, then began to attack Mitrofania, followed by the other equally good lawyers, making her position exponentially more difficult.[121] Aside from this, the main strategy of the lawyers for the secondary defendants in Mitrofania's case was to attract as little attention as possible, and they said very little throughout the trial, even though Keikuatov, Przhevalskii, and Kharitonov were among Russia's top attorneys.

Finally, lawyers frequently contrived to shift the blame onto the victim or to make other outrageous if not exactly novel arguments. The best-known case is the trial of the revolutionary Vera Zasulich, whose lawyer, Aleksandrov, with tacit encouragement from Chairman Koni, managed to shift the blame onto her victim, General Fedor Trepov.[122] In the equally famous Kronenberg case, Spasovich turned the trial of his banker client into that of his abused seven-year-old daughter, arguing that Kronenberg had merely tried to improve her behavior. In some of the most prominent trials, when one of the lawyers was facing what seemed like an impossible task, he would occasionally make statements that sounded desperate. In the Miasnikov trial the lawyer for the alleged victims, Lokhvitskii, acted as if he were unprepared for the trial. Addressing the fact that the case against the Miasnikovs was based almost entirely on rumors fabricated and circulated by Lokhvitskii's client, he claimed that rumors tend to be true: "From military and political events we know that undertakings that are very secret are still uncovered and the servants learn about them from very subtle hints." Lokhvitskii neglected to mention that almost all such rumors about planned military campaigns or new government policies turn out to be false.[123] In the 1878 forgery trial of Gulak-Artemovskaia, her lawyer, Zhukovskii, seems to have realized during the trial that his client was going to be convicted and spent most of his energy mocking the prosecutor, Prince Urusov. The proper strategy for Zhukovskii would have been to disrupt the prosecution's narrative fixated on his client's financial operations, but he instead argued that her actions were technically illegal but actually harmless. He made fun of Urusov's guesswork and even ironically but incompetently called his client "a Queen of Hearts" in reference to the recent and similarly overblown trial of the Jacks of Hearts.[124] Zhukovskii then more or less directly asked for jury nullification, most likely remembering the recent acquittal of Vera Zasulich, but unlike in cases where this strategy was successful, Zhukovskii seems to have presented this option to the jury too aggressively (the jurors knew full well that they were entitled to acquit).[125]

Prosecutors used dirty tactics as well, even Anatolii Koni, the best-known Russian jurist of the post-reform era, who served as a prosecutor, a trial judge, and later, under Alexander III, as the procurator of the Criminal Cassation Department of the Senate, that is, the highest-ranking criminal judge in Russia. Koni had considerable literary ability and a powerful reputation as a dispassionate and liberal champion of the rule of law, in which capacity he especially appealed to later readers accustomed to Soviet-era abuses of justice. A closer look at his conduct during actual trials shows him to be above all a political actor and strategist who was acutely aware of the post-reform configurations of power, of its potential, and of its limitations. Koni protected and helped many people, but he also harmed and attacked. Often it is not easy to tell what he was doing exactly, and even harder to determine why he was doing it. This ambiguity is particularly visible in his first high-profile trial as prosecutor in St. Petersburg, that of the Miasnikov brothers in 1872. He went far beyond the expected standard of diligence in prosecuting a case and deployed a wide array of nasty tactics while pursuing a very weak case based on rumors and the testimony of a mentally unstable alcoholic. Koni fought hard to suppress medical evidence and to postpone the introduction of damaging evidence, and he made preposterous or completely irrelevant arguments. He even claimed that bribing witnesses was not unethical because (he incorrectly believed) it was a routine practice in "England and America."[126] Even though Koni's task was further complicated by the antics of the alleged victim's lawyer, Lokhvitskii, he appears to have been concerned not so much about justice or even winning his case (though he did try hard to win) as about making himself look forceful and effective to the public (and possibly not damaging his social reputation by getting an important person convicted). Koni's viciousness came off as somewhat incompetent, but in other trials prosecutors seem to have not tried their hardest, for reasons that remain obscure.[127]

Both prosecutors and defense lawyers used several sets of strategies that were not corrupt per se but that aimed to divert the jury's attention from the facts of the case when these were unfavorable to the speaker. Most important, these strategies included excessive eloquence and literary polish, especially broad and vague statements about the case's alleged impact upon Russia's society and culture. Anna Schur has argued that top defense lawyers of the post-reform era routinely aspired in their speeches and publicist writings not merely to influence the jurors' emotions but also to take advantage of the elevated role of the literary sphere in Russian society. Lawyers aspired to be more than legal experts and hired professionals; in the absence of an opportunity for a political career, they sought to be regarded as intellectuals and cultural figures with certain moral and cultural capital. Schur concluded that this aspiration was not, however, accepted by Russia's intellectual elite and was frequently mocked both inside and outside the courtroom.[128] On my reading, though, the use of an elevated literary style in the courtroom was much more ambiguous, and it harmed the speaker and his case only in such situations when eloquence and wit were used openly to replace an evidence-based argument, rather than to strengthen a plausible position. Moreover, criticism or mockery of a lawyer's style or literary ambitions by journalists or other lawyers did not mean that the literary style failed as a trial strategy.

Those lawyers and prosecutors who aspired to literary polish often used literary references directly as a standard of contextualizing, evaluating, or comparing the facts of the case. In the Gulak-Artemovskaia trial, the prosecutor, Urusov, claimed (probably correctly): "If you read about this story in a work of literature, you would not believe it. . . . You would think that even if [her crimes] were possible, then hardly so here, and that such mores are perhaps brought by the novelist from a different society that is more corrupt than ours; that at least here in Petersburg this is unthinkable!"[129] The principal existing account of Mitrofania's trial referring to the nun's attempts to gain control over the assets of a wealthy but alcoholic woman exclaimed: "Surely this [story] is asking to be put in a novel. We would call it *Guardianship* (*Opeka*)."[130] In other cases the use of literary imagery was clearly too brief and complex to be readily comprehended by the jurors, but it looked impressive in a printed account, which may have been the objective. Thus, Anatolii Koni in his first important St. Petersburg trial, that of the Miasnikov brothers, mocked the top defense witness, Shevelev (who himself had quasi-literary aspirations) and made a confusing reference to Gogol's Chichikov from *Dead Souls:* "From [Shevelev's] theatrically-beautiful story the notes occasionally break through, which characterize that Russian type which is outlined with such genius by one of the greatest Russian writers, the type of the kidnapper of the governor's daughter and 'the man who had not played checkers for a long time.'"[131]

The Miasnikov trial, taking place in 1872, caused passing but intense critical commentary on the use of rhetoric in the courtroom. One journalist noted that Koni's task was "primarily artistic" and that his driving energy was "the power of his imagination." He presented his view of the case "superbly" and "drew such a lively and full picture of the entire alleged crime that it became as if unquestionable—but unquestionable in imagination only." While Koni also tried to use evidence as well, the journalist commented: "The completeness of the picture [he presents] does not replace the firmness and clarity of legal evidence and the confirmation of at least a few firm facts." The jurors were to be credited "for not succumbing to the power of mere psychological probability" and "turned out to have been more demanding as lawyers than . . . the prosecutor considered them to be."[132] By contrast, the defense lawyers, Arseniev and Yazykov, did not make any literary references or give particularly ornate speeches. Their arguments were presented simply and clearly, and yet Arseniev was criticized because his speech had shaky substance though "undisputable literary merits," and that "the very process of argumentation [would] interest anyone by the literary resourcefulness (*oborotlivost'*—with a negative connotation) of the defender." Arseniev's colleague, Yazykov, somewhat overstrained his powers of eloquence, rhetorically summoning deceased witnesses from the afterworld and stunning many observers, including Arseniev. But the journalist describing the trial also mocked Lokhvitskii, who represented the victims but acted like a clown despite his high professional reputation.[133]

While press criticism of excessively embellished courtroom oratory continued into the late imperial period, as Schur's book demonstrates, my reading of the top cases from the post-reform period suggests that by the late 1870s such embellishments became accepted as a given and no longer attracted much attention. In the 1878 trial of Gulak-Artemovskaia, her lawyer, Zhukovskii, in effect dedicated his speech to criticizing the prosecution's excessive use of rhetorical techniques and attacked the contrived way the case was put together with extensive use of circumstantial and questionable evidence. Zhukovskii mocked "the artistic sculpture created by the prosecutor who, having scooped up all the dirt from the bottom of the case, used that dirt to create a bust of Artemovskaia, thinking that this is sufficient for her conviction." Zhukovskii in vain argued that Gulak-Artemovskaia's fault was only to allow herself to be financially involved with practical but immoral men, and that "this gives the prosecutor the excuse to present her as a *rusalka* (a deadly female water spirit) who pulls underwater the witnesses for both prosecution and defense, her highly-ranked [anonymous business partners], and the entire building of the Cassation Senate. Circles are spreading in the water, and the prosecutor in the state of deep contemplation is amazed at the depth of the social ulcer."[134]

A related variety of rhetorical strategy was to claim—often plausibly enough—that the trial would have a powerful social or cultural impact extending far beyond its particular factual circumstances. A prosecutor could argue that acquitting a defendant would indicate to Russian society that the behavior in question is not effectively punishable by the courts and thus encourage destructive appetites and processes. The prosecution's case could be bolstered by showing how it was caused by some deeper, general trends in Russian life.[135] This tactic was particularly important when the alleged crime was committed by a respectable person. For example, in the 1873 Kazan murder trial of a mid-level civil servant with a large family, the prosecutor argued: "Each case has two sides: one superficial side is all in front of you; the other is the inner, behind-the-scenes side."[136] The existence of a hidden side of the defendant, Bel'skii, was supported by some evidence, but for the most part it would have had to be imagined by the jurors. In the Nepenin murder trial that same year, the defendant (who had openly knifed his romantic competitor) was "educated, well-developed [intellectually] (*razvitoi*), could adequately evaluate his actions, a man who had been a judge and taught others about respect for individuals and the law, about bridling one's urges."[137]

Defense lawyers, conversely, would urge jurors to look beyond the facts of the case that allegedly concealed the true causes of the crime, which tended to reduce or even nullify their client's culpability. Such tactics resulted in some spectacular and scandalous acquittals, such as that of the banker Kronenberg in 1876, but more typically generalized statements indicated a weak case and could result in a finding of extenuating circumstances at best. Thus, the same lawyer, Spasovich, who secured Kronenberg's acquittal used the same tactics to defend the embezzling bank cashier Pal'm, asking the jury in vain to look at the "actual truth of life and not merely [at] the abstract truth of the law."[138] Other scholars have noted that such statements sound rather odd coming from a leading officer of the law in the country, but considering that Pal'm's guilt had been fully exposed, Spasovich was left with little else to try.[139]

The first jury trials, in the late 1860s and early 1870s, tended to avoid generalized sociomoral claims. For example, in the 1867 trial of the student Danilov for murdering a moneylender, the transcript only discusses the facts of the case, and only an observer publishing the transcript mentioned Russia's "new spirit of avarice," though just briefly as his own opinion and not as a quote from the transcript. In the exceedingly scandalous Miasnikov brothers' trial in 1872, the prosecutor, Koni, and the victim's lawyer, Lokhvitskii, commented liberally on the personal habits, social status, and economic activities of several defendants and witnesses, but in a pointed fashion without generalizing about Russia as a whole or the spirit of the age. Even the trials of the millionaire arsonist Stepan Ovsiannikov and of Mother Mitrofania made numerous innuendoes but no direct attacks—with good reason, since, as I discuss later, it was not clear whether it was the old spirit or the new that had brought about these cases. The pattern changed beginning in the mid-1870s, when more drama, or rather melodrama, became acceptable in the courtroom and unduly moralistic and generalized claims were typically used to open and close prosecutors' and defense lawyers' speeches. The prosecutor Nikolai Muraviev, one of Russia's best courtroom speakers, was particularly known for melodramatic and moralistic imagery (the mere mention of a particular type of case "brings to the surface singular types of evil, precious because of their vitality, brought up from the murky waters of modern society").[140]

Defense lawyers' clients too had the opportunity to participate in the trial. Although the law permitted defendants to refuse to answer any questions, and, provided that their silence could not be interpreted as a sign of their guilt, defendants were permitted to make statements and to question witnesses. Today the common wisdom is that defendants should be heard from as little as possible and to subject themselves to cross-examination only in exceptional cases. In nineteenth-century common-law trials, especially before professional attorneys became ubiquitous, defendants were of necessity in charge of their own defense.[141] In pre-reform Russia, it seems that the notion that criminal cases were decided in the absence of the accused is largely a myth, in that important cases were not decided without questioning the defendant. After 1864, criminal defendants mostly relied on the skill of their attorneys, and they definitely did so in the high-profile cases, at most playing an auxiliary role. Mother Mitrofania's trial was one of the few prominent exceptions, no doubt contributing to her falling out with her lawyer, Shaikevich: she took a very active part in her defense and "with her sharp, bold questions and comments frequently caused discomfort even to the chairman, prosecutors, and defenders, who were all used to that kind of thing."[142] Mitrofania's St. Petersburg equivalent, the noblewoman Gulak-Artemovskaia, tried for forgery in 1878, likewise actively participated in her own defense.

Judges and even jurors frequently added their voices to the trial's polyphony. Russian judges were more proactive than English or American judges, in that they participated in questioning witnesses and defendants. But they were far less "inquisitorial" than French or German judges, in that they generally allowed the lawyers and prosecutors to run the proceedings and in most cases did not directly indicate their opinions of the case. That said, some judges were exceptionally active. In the Miasnikov case, the judge was Prince Keikuatov, who would soon leave the bench and become a prominent defense lawyer. During the trial he went far beyond his obligation to initiate the questioning of the defendants and witnesses, acting instead as essentially another prosecutor, perhaps to assist Koni's floundering efforts. In the trial of Mother Mitrofania, Chairman Deier was extremely active and again without exaggeration acted as an additional prosecutor, asking questions like "Do novice nuns in the monasteries exist to write *veksels* (debt obligations)?" (addressing a novice who acted as Mitrofania's go-between). To this Mitrofania responded correctly that this was not illegal: "I don't know, but they have full legal rights, they can own property, donate to monasteries, and issue *veksels*."[143] In the late 1870s and early 1880s the chairman of the Moscow District Court, Evgenii Rink, was known for manipulating trials by posing incisive questions and giving skillful summations, and apparently he was routinely able to achieve a particular outcome.[144] The memoirist Elizaveta Kozlinina wrote that in his summations to the jury, Rink "always presented a case skillfully as being not a separate episode from the life of the defendant, but always as a page from the life of this or that social milieu."[145] In the

TABLE 4. JURY COMPOSITION

Name	Year	Jury composition			
		Nobles, officials	Merchants	Townsmen	Peasants
Murder, other violence					
Rebinder[a]	1866	4	4	2	2
Volokhova[b]	1867	6	8 (5 wealthy)	0	0
Mazurin[c]	1867	3	5	0	4
Troitskaia[d]	1873	9	3	0	0
Kronenberg[e]	1876	3	9 (w/ meshc.)		
Landsberg[f]	1879	6	3	2	1
White-collar: Fraud, forgery, embezzlement					
Rogozhskoe[g]	1867	7	5 (+ 2 spare)	0	0
Dmitrieva[h]	1871	3	4	3	2
Miasnikov bros.[i]	1872	11	1	0	0
Mitrofania[j]	1874	1	7	0	4
Moscow Bank[k]	1876	2	6 (+ 2 alt.)	2	2
Jacks of Hearts[l]	1877	4	3	4	3
Gartung[m]	1877	2	9	1	2

a. SV, no. 93 (24 Nov. 1866).

b. Liutetskii, 243–244.

c. SV, no. 260 (29 Nov. 1867).

d. Veretennikov, *Delo o . . . Bel'skom,* 1. Included three university professors, two of them of the law, and three important provincial officials. Six juror votes were enough for acquittal.

e. SpbV, no. 24 (1876); SV, no. 19 (24 Jan. 1876).

f. SpbV, no. 183 (6 July 1879).

g. Liutetskii, 27. Included two university professors (Babst and Medvedev) and one senior official (Actual State Councilor Malinovskii).

h. *Protsess G-zhi Dmitrievoi,* 19. A schoolteacher is listed among officials, as is a chancery clerk.

i. OZ, no. 3 (1872): 77.

j. *Delo Mitrofanii,* II/2.

k. RGIA, f. 1405, op. 73, d. 2348, l. 143.

l. Golos, no. 40 (9 Feb. 1877).

m. *Delo Gartunga,* 2.

Note: Some sources include two alternate jurors, and some list only the empaneled jury.

Melnitskii case he directly told the jurors the ridiculous tale that one of the defendants, himself a former judge, who had helped to hide stolen property, was only helping to preserve it rather than conceal it.[146] Koni's behavior after he became chairman of the St. Petersburg District Court in 1877 fell along similar lines, especially in the celebrated trials of Vera Zasulich, Margarita Jujean, Liudmila Gulak-Artemovskaia, and Konstantin Yukhantsev. In the Yukhantsev case, for instance, Koni's summation was indistinguishable from a prosecution speech.[147]

The least active participants of a trial were jurors. The majority of the jurors in the Russian Empire were peasants, but from this it does not automatically follow that Russian jury trials were peasant or even lower-class institutions.[148] In reality, juries did not turn out to be as elite as perhaps originally intended by the reformers, but even in rural areas peasants made up only around two-thirds of the jurors.[149] In cities and even in small towns other groups predominated. In the prominent trials described in this book, most of which took place in Moscow and St. Petersburg, peasant jurors were extremely rare (see table 4). It is therefore not accurate to assume that the jury was a lower-class institution somehow pitched against the other trial participants: namely, the elite judges, the less elite but still respectable and often wealthy defense lawyers, and the rather refined and often exalted spectators. Rather, the jury fitted very well into the culture of a courtroom that was diverse but still shared the fundamental elite culture of education and "gentility."[150] Sometimes jury members were clearly handpicked or somehow contrived to get themselves selected. During the first few important trials in Moscow in early 1867, the jury foreman was the notable economics professor Ivan Babst. During the Kazan murder trial of 1873 the jury included three university professors, of whom two were law professors, which could not have been an accident either. Jurors occasionally asked questions that were important to the proceedings and indicated the direction of the case, even if they did not by themselves determine the outcome. In one particularly grisly murder case, of Evgenii Rebinder, most likely the first jury murder conviction in Russia, the jury inquired into his (nonexistent) education and (licentious) prior life. In the Mitrofania trial, the jury asked why if she needed money to support her charity works she did not simply call upon wealthy individuals to donate or even ask the authorities to provide for the orphans in her care.[151] The most active juror I have encountered was prominent journalist Vasilii Poletika, who managed to get on the jury in the famous forgery case of Gulak-Artemovskaia in 1878, and who essentially acted as another prosecutor.[152] But jurors could also be extremely solicitous, likewise indicating the likely verdict. In the Melnitskii case, after the young and attractive defendant Elena Bleze had a tearful breakdown the jury foreman, Levinson, ran to the table and poured her a glass of water. Chairman Rink stopped the trial for half an hour, which was unheard of in an ordinary trial and contrasts sharply with Chairman Koni's rude behavior in the case of Gulak-Artemovskaia. When a sympathetic woman defendant was acquitted, the jury and sometimes also the public could collect money to provide relief to the exonerated defendant.

Far from streamlining courtroom procedures, the reform of 1864 complicated them exponentially. A trial was broken into a multitude of separate steps that had to be followed precisely to avoid a successful appeal. Moreover, each step involved multiple participants and, typically, spectators, all with their own strategies and interests. The judge in charge of directing the proceedings could only do so to a limited extent. At the same time, post-reform trials became unique political and social rituals, distinct from other governmental procedures, and especially from the ubiquitous nonpublic bureaucratic tribunals and inquiries. A trial's power stemmed from its precise combination of rigidly following the rules of procedure and of the opportunities these rules provided for presenting the content of the case to the public and to the jury.

CHAPTER 4

Texts of Transgression

The source of substantive criminal law in late imperial Russia was the Penal Code of 1845 ("the Code" unless specified otherwise), which largely reproduced its predecessors, the Digest of Criminal Laws of 1835—Russia's first modern criminal code—and the draft code of 1813. While the rules of criminal procedure were replaced by the reform of 1864, the Code's categories and definitions of crimes and punishments remained in force until 1917 with only minor changes. Its role as one of Russia's fundamental governing instruments has not been sufficiently understood or appreciated, with most studies either grounding it in the transient political context of Nicholas I's reign or dismissing it as an archaic embarrassment, a "jumble of incoherent principles inherited from the past."[1] Laura Engelstein has argued that the Code's provisions on sexual crime were less up-to-date than those of the 1813 draft, although the European models used as the standard of comparison were themselves "far from clear or uniform."[2] Other historians presented particular elements of the Code as actually forward looking, although with different valences. Thus, Richard Pipes claimed that its state crime provisions were uniquely restrictive and became the ideological and administrative "fountainhead" of later totalitarianism.[3] Conversely, the most authoritative scholar of the Code, Igor Arkhipov, argued that the Code's nonpolitical provisions were "bourgeois" in nature and prepared the way for the reforms of the 1860s and 1870s, and eventually for the constitutional transformations of the early twentieth century. On the whole, though,

Arkhipov viewed the Code as balancing between modern and reactionary "feudal" principles. That is, the Code "reflected the interests of the absolute monarchy" by providing an effective legal machinery for suppressing any undesirable political activity; it "regularized" Russia's political system by providing a detailed legal framework for punishing official misconduct, as well as individual offenses against various administrative regulations; and it promoted economic growth by providing strong protections for private property and commerce.[4]

Aside from its oversimplified Marxist framework inherited from the Soviet era, Arkhipov's interpretation is not completely off the mark: the Russian bureaucrats who drafted and edited the Code did feud and bargain and divide into inchoate interest groups. Much like the procedural rules, the Code encapsulated a variety of interests and positions, which had to be balanced, accounted for, and evaluated both in the minds of the drafters and in the minds of the lawyers who used the Code in actual cases. But it is not credible to link the Code to specific economic structures or classes. Russia's growing bourgeoisie was interested in stable governance as much as Nicholas I, and noble serf owners benefited from secure property rights as much as Old Believer merchants in Moscow. Moreover, neither interest-based politics nor the legislative process in the mid-nineteenth century worked the same way they do today, or even the way they would work later under the last three tsars.

Both the Code and the earlier Digest of Criminal Laws of 1835 were fundamentally creations of Mikhail Speransky, who dominated the legislative sphere in the early years of Nicholas I's reign. Speransky of course operated within a restrictive political climate in the aftermath of the failed Decembrist uprising of 1825, but he was a complex individual imbued with liberalism inherited from the age of Enlightenment as well as nationalism, religious mysticism, and a sincere effort to discover and reinforce an authentic Russian legal tradition.[5] Speransky's great codification project, of which the Digest of 1835 was a part, succeeded, as Tatiana Borisova has shown, largely because he was able to tap into a newly formed consensus among Russian elites that a codified body of law was needed as a key ideological instrument of building a national identity and maintaining national cohesion.[6] A codified Russian national law would affirm Russia's rejection of the ideological principles of its defeated enemies, the French revolutionaries, as well as of Napoleon's enormously influential competing codification project, in much the same way that the famous triad of official nationality (Orthodoxy, Autocracy, and Nationality) was meant to fend off the revolutionary principles of Liberty, Equality, and Fraternity.[7]

Speransky's codification program came in three stages. The first was compiling all the legislation enacted in Russia since the Conciliar Code of 1649. This became known as the Complete Collection of the Laws. The second step was the Digest of the Laws of 1835 that came in fifteen volumes, the last of which contained the penal laws. The Digest purported to extract black-letter norms from those statutes and imperial decrees that were still active law at that time. In reality, though, the Digest was an entirely new product rather than a compilation of old laws. Anyone who checks its references can easily see that there is no connection to source material, although the label "digest" continues to bamboozle laypersons and specialists alike.[8] The Digest was an up-to-date code that provided good definitions of individual crimes, but its major defect was to omit a corresponding inventory of punishments, instead referring to the "existing" laws, which were generally either inadequate or nonexistent. The digest was meant, however, to be only the second stage in the three-step codification process, to be replaced by a brand-new penal code, which Speransky began to prepare shortly before his death, in 1839. The project was then taken over by his assistant Pavel Degai, an experienced lawyer who composed the first full draft of the new code but lacked political clout and was soon replaced by the tsar's trusted statesman Dmitrii Bludov. The final version was drafted by Bludov's aide, an important Polish lawyer named Romuald Hube, although it was based on existing materials originally prepared in the 1830s by Speransky and Degai for the Russian-ruled Congress Kingdom of Poland. Bludov was emphatic in his rejection of the French Revolution, but otherwise he was as much a product of the Age of Enlightenment as Speransky had been. Neither these personnel changes nor the tinkering to which the draft code was subjected during the review in the State Council touched upon its core values and assumptions.[9]

The Code was not so much a compromise as a composite or even a palimpsest of ideas about crime, criminals, and their victims.[10] Each set of ideas stemmed from a different historical age, was reinforced by different canonical legal or quasi-legal texts, and closely followed similar developments elsewhere in the Eurocentric world. This chapter argues that the Code's most important black-letter norms and its underlying jurisprudential ideas originated in the second half of the eighteenth century during the reign of Catherine II. Both earlier and later developments were also material, however, and each of the Code's twelve parts mixed ideas and legal traditions with different emphases. Thus, the first part, containing the basic definitions of crime and punishment, was derived from works by Montesquieu, Beccaria, Bentham, and Feuerbach, as well as Catherine II's *Instruction* (1767), which reproduced large amounts of the first two writers' texts. Parts 2 through 9 punished offenses against the state, religion, administration, and public order: everything from treason to blasphemy and smuggling. Here the animating concern was to create an effective state apparatus, grounded in (and inherited from) the pre-Petrine codes of 1497, 1550, 1589, and 1649, strengthened in the eighteenth century by the logic of German cameralism and *Polizeistaat,* and reinforced in the early nineteenth century by people like Fouchet, Vidoq, and Benckendorff.

Finally, parts 10 through 12 contained what we typically think of as the norms of criminal law and covered crimes against persons and private property. These were heavily shaped by the policies and ideas of post-Napoleonic Europe, although murder and theft had of course been punished long before then and, in particular, had been singled out for protection by Enlightenment-era thinkers. Overall, this was a typical arrangement for nineteenth-century codes that today is a bit outdated but still immediately comprehensible to anyone familiar with these sources.

The incorporation of Russia's legal past into active legislation in part deliberately followed a common post-1815 European trend. Speransky and other lawyers of that era were very much aware of German historical jurisprudence taught by Friedrich Carl von Savigny, under whom a group of Speransky's protégés had studied in Berlin.[11] Savigny and his followers argued that each nation possessed its own unique legal tradition that stemmed from its particular national character or "spirit," not from natural law or a fiat command of the sovereign. The jurist's task was to uncover and preserve his national tradition rather than rationalize and invent from scratch.[12] Under the influence of the historical school, the juridical field in nineteenth-century Russia was defined particularly strongly by common bonds of emotion and experience, even when formal institutional ties were less robust.[13]

Tribute to history and tradition formed an important rhetorical veneer in Russian law. For instance, the two leading professors of criminal law who trained the future authors of the judicial reform of 1864 and most of the defense lawyers mentioned in this book, the brothers Sergei and Yakov Barshev, emphatically praised the value of history and tradition in opposition to creative legislation of the revolutionary era. None of this, however, meant that the Code and other Nicholaevan-era statutes literally preserved or resurrected the outdated norms of, say, the 1649 Conciliar Code or of Peter I's Military Articles. Thus, Sergei Barshev's influential textbook initially denounced revolutionary-era creative lawmaking in the introduction but then focused entirely on formulating the principles of criminal law and did not include any material that was historical or peculiarly Russian. Yakov Barshev's influential lecture on the historical development of Russian criminal law named various historical materials but did not even attempt to show how the historical texts influenced each other or developed into Russia's current laws.[14] Actual legal norms fixed in the 1845 Code were of very recent provenance. Technically and conceptually Nicholaevan-era legislation was exponentially more complex and more logical than eighteenth-century law, amounting to a legal revolution. But despite this innovation in the content of individual legal norms, deeper conceptual and structural changes in law are typically quite slow and involve much backtracking.[15] While Thomas Kuhn's idea of a paradigm shift may apply to innovations in legal scholarship, it is not directly applicable in law as a field of practical activity.[16]

So for all of their energy and creativity, Speransky and other legislators were not engaged in anything like a free and conscious choice between competing sets of fundamental legal concepts beyond the superficial ideological veneer of more or less nationalistic narratives. Any new statute had to build upon the existing legal edifice of the early imperial, Eurocentric, cameralist, bureaucratic military-police-fiscal state strengthened and tempered by Enlightenment innovations and modified by the post-Napoleonic cultural and social consensus.

THE LEGAL ENLIGHTENMENT AND PENAL CALCULUS

Part 1 of the Code (also known as the General Part) set out the basic definitions and principles of Russian criminal law, as has been typical for modern criminal codes, ranging from Napoleon's penal code of 1810 to the U.S. Model Penal Code of 1962. The General Part did not define any particular offense, and it could not be applied directly to any actual case; thus it served as a rhetorical and political statement of the empire's criminal justice policy. But the General Part also had immense practical significance: it was incorporated by reference into numerous articles in the rest of the Code, as well as into judicial decisions, and, even more important, it provided a template for structuring all the provisions against specific crimes, from treason and blasphemy to theft and fraud.

The General Part was based on the writings of the foundational figures of classical criminology, Cesare Beccaria, Jeremy Bentham, and Paul Johann Anselm von Feuerbach, which were well known to the statesmen and legislators in imperial Russia and which exercised a profound but unrecognized influence on imperial Russian law and on statecraft more generally. Classical criminology assumed that it was possible to affect individual motivations and decisions through policy and proposed a new principle of criminal law known as the penal calculus, which would carefully differentiate and calibrate punishments for maximum psychological and social impact. In contrast to eighteenth-century laws that left the details of sentencing to the discretion of individual judges and had a very simple set of penalties for most crimes, nineteenth-century codes featured an elaborate ladder of punishments that in its Russian version consisted of thirty-seven steps, from reprimand to the death penalty (the latter being reserved for the gravest crimes against the state).[17] One of the reasons for designing these categories was to reduce corruption by court personnel, but judges still retained considerable discretion under the new regime: for instance, in late imperial Russia murder was generally punished under the Code by twelve to fifteen years of hard labor, which may not seem like a large degree of variability from a present-day perspective but was no doubt important to convicted persons.

My contention is that in order to function or even be proposed at all, this new calculus of punishment required an equivalent calculus of crime and of the criminal that would weigh the offender's external circumstances, as well as internal motivations and dispositions, in order to move the punishment up or down the ladder. It is often claimed that the classical criminology of the late eighteenth and early nineteenth centuries had not yet arrived at this angle of analysis, and that it adopted a black-box view of the criminal, who was presumed to act freely and rationally.[18] But while it is true that classical-school writers did not pay as much attention to criminals' emotional passions and physiological urges, as it became so fashionable to do later in the nineteenth century, the classicist project of calibrating pains and pleasures necessarily involved an inquiry into the criminal mind. While European and Eurocentric law, including Russia's, had always differentiated offenders, especially according to their social status, the new calculus of the criminal was exponentially more complex than the early modern version, and it presaged later positivist sociological criminology.[19]

The invention of the modern penal calculus is credited to Beccaria, who for the first time presented a detailed, eloquent, and coherent argument for a more humane and more rational system of criminal justice in a small treatise published in 1764 and translated into Russian in 1803.[20] Beccaria is most remembered today for his impassioned attack on torture and the death penalty, which were the mainstay of criminal justice in early modern Europe. Beccaria was not, however, a radical activist à la Voltaire, and he did not set out to weaken old-regime governments. Rather, as Foucault famously observed, the objective of Beccaria and other reformers was "not to punish less but to punish better."[21]

Thus, as Piers Beirne has shown, alongside his appeal to the humanistic values of Montesquieu and Voltaire, Beccaria offered a deterministic logic of social engineering that was based on the English and Scottish utilitarian and empiricist "science of man" developed by Bacon, Newton, Hutcheson, Hume, Locke, and Adam Smith. Central to these thinkers' view of human nature was the doctrine of associationism, which meant that human ideas and sensory experience connect and acquire meaning when they occur in close proximity.[22] Thus, in order for punishment to be effective as social policy, punishment must be prompt and, just as important, must closely match the offense both in character and in intensity. For instance, Beccaria proposed to punish violent crime with corporal punishment and theft with incarceration.[23]

But while Beccaria is very clear on how to punish crime, he is less so on what kinds of people commit it and why. Like much of his treatise, his underlying view of human nature is ambiguous. Like most Enlightenment thinkers, Beccaria maintains that humans are capable of rational choice and of mastering their evil desires and impulses. At the same time, he seems to agree with Locke that not all persons are equally rational. To Locke, only property owners are fully rational, while to Beccaria, "clear and simple" laws liberate people from the "slavish" fear of one another and enable "free men" to "ponder the sciences and interests of the nation [and] envision and aspire to great things."[24] Conversely, "slavish men are more debauched, more sybaritic and crueler," they are "content with the present moment and seek amid the din of depravity a distraction from the emptiness of their everyday lives." Bad laws reinforced the harmful emotions driving criminals and exacerbated the less savory aspects of each nation's character, whether these aspects were "idleness and stupidity" or tendencies to intrigue and betrayal, or, at best, fluctuations between freedom and slavery. Lack of education was also important, because "unsophisticated" people were unable to properly calculate the consequences of their actions unless the law provided a clear link between the crime and the punishment. However (per contra Locke?), bad laws that fail to protect the "weak and the poor" could subvert the upper classes as well, and "wealth" could "[feed] tyranny." Beccaria's penal calculus therefore would fully apply to nobility as much as to commoners. But counterbalancing this optimistic belief in the power of effective legislation, Beccaria also seems to believe that crime cannot be eradicated entirely, given that human activities are chaotic and "cannot be reduced to a geometric order devoid of irregularity and confusion." Some crimes, such as theft, result from "poverty and desperation." It is therefore a "fantasy" to believe that laws can prevent all "disturbances and disorders among the infinite and very opposite motive forces of pleasure and pain."[25]

In sum, Beccaria's calculus of the criminal mind is grounded in juggling the motives of profit and emotion so evident in existing societies, in addition to the effects of inadequate education and social conditions promoting idleness and poverty. Beccaria claimed that all these factors could be reduced or even eliminated through transparent and carefully adjusted laws that would eliminate the arbitrariness of the powerful, as well as the informational asymmetries causing crime.

Beccaria is barely mentioned if at all even in specialized literature on Russian law and government, in contrast, for instance, to recent work recognizing his monumental importance for the legal system of the early American republic. Yet Beccaria's ideas were just as fundamental for rebuilding Russian criminal justice in the late eighteenth and first half of the nineteenth century. Similar to Western European law, Russian law began to use formal judicial torture and execution quite liberally from the mid-seventeenth century. Corporal punishment and penal exile were used for lesser crimes. By the end of the century, however, the most grotesque forms already began to fall out of use.[26] The Military Statute of Peter the Great (1715) may seem like a counterexample because it provided for more severe punishments than previously and because it covered ordinary offenses such as theft in addition to specifically military ones. But it did not apply to persons who were not subject to military jurisdiction. Later in the eighteenth and early nineteenth centuries, in part no doubt due to Peter's overall mythologized stature in Russian life, the Military Statute came to be viewed as a key monument of Russian legal thought alongside the code of 1649 or Catherine II's *Instruction*, and Speransky's *Digest of the Laws* used all three of these texts as its ostensible sources to fabricate its historical provenance.[27]

In his treatise Beccaria mentions Peter's daughter, "the Empress Elizabeth of Muscovy," who "set the leaders of all peoples an outstanding precedent," but he does not find it necessary to explain her contribution to the history of criminology. Most educated Russians today do know that upon seizing the throne in 1742 Elizabeth suspended the death penalty. The reasons for this are not clear, aside from the abovementioned long-term trend of moderating punishment. Elizabeth's officials mostly opposed her decision, and the Lopukhin treason trial of 1743 tested her resolve (the defendants were tortured and mutilated but not executed). By mid-century and certainly by the time Catherine II seized power in 1762, Russia had a ruling elite that shared Enlightenment sensibilities beyond the immediate circle of the imperial court, including legal practitioners who were competent in major issues of criminal law and who lobbied higher authorities for its improvement in terms of fairness and predictability. The new empress immediately signaled her intention to govern better by prosecuting several nobles who murdered and abused their serfs, especially the infamous aristocratic serial killer Daria Saltykova. Catherine also retained the suspension of the death penalty for ordinary crimes, although she would allow executions in three exceptional cases: Lieutenant Mirovich's attempt to free the deposed emperor Ioann Antonovich (1764); the four ringleaders of the Moscow plague riot of 1771; and the six leaders of the Pugachev uprising in 1775.[28]

In 1767–1768 Catherine convened the Legislative Commission with delegates from all the estates of the realm except enserfed peasants for the purpose of preparing a new code of laws to replace that of 1649—neither the first nor the last effort to do so. To direct the commission's activities Catherine prepared a manual of policy and statecraft, known as the *Instruction* (*Nakaz*), which reproduced virtually verbatim the writings of Montesquieu, Beccaria, and the Encyclopedists. It is clear from Catherine's own notes and drafts that she carefully reviewed, annotated, and extracted her sources and rearranged them to suit her objectives. The *Instruction* is widely regarded as a manifesto of mainstream old-regime Enlightened absolutist governance, while in Russia it served as, in effect, an informal constitution at least until the 1820s.[29]

As is well known, Catherine was no more prepared to grant her subjects full political freedoms than her Western European counterparts. She toned down or removed most of Montesquieu's and Beccaria's more emotional language. At the same time, the *Instruction* repeated their key arguments, including the proposal for a penal system designed to deter crime through prompt, moderate, and "measured" punishment assigned in proportion to the offense and classified according to its object (that is, crimes against faith, against the state and the sovereign, against the public, and against private persons). Much like her sources, Catherine criticized the death penalty and torture. She did not add very much clarity to their ideas about the causes of crime, although her assumptions can be surmised from the *Instruction.* She attributed crime to "passions" that "plant [in the criminal] ideas to be evil," although the individual has the capacity to understand that it is "more useful to him not to be evil." The *Instruction* argues for equality before the law or at least good laws that would "prohibit the rich from abusing those who have less." Later, in 1774–1775, in the wake of the Pugachev uprising, Catherine even drafted a law that would have criminalized cruel treatment of serfs by their masters, although it was never enacted, and serfdom continued to flourish during her reign.[30] Laws enacted in 1762 and 1785 greatly extended noble privileges in Russia, among them rights of private property (including enserfed peasants) and exemption from corporal punishment.[31]

Catherine's *Instruction* was not intended to have any official legal force, and the legislative commission for which it was written was short lived and did not produce any laws. But this does not mean that the *Instruction* was an isolated or a stillborn intellectual exercise. Quite the contrary. To begin with, the *Instruction* was only the most representative example of the jurisprudential and legislative activities of the empress and her closest advisers. Catherine herself produced numerous draft laws, including several versions of a penal code and the so-called fundamental (*korennye*) laws that were akin to the United States and English Bills of Rights, but none of these was ever enacted. Much of this material elaborated upon the key principles of the criminal calculus, including the balance of aggravating and extenuating circumstances, calculating the responsibility of multiple participants in a crime, and the degree of individual culpability depending on premeditation, criminal intention, and criminal negligence.[32] But in addition to all the unrealized drafts and projects, the major principles of the *Instruction* and of its sources were incorporated into actual Russian legislation. Perhaps the most important piece of substantive criminal law under Catherine was the law on theft of 1781, which categorized different types of property crimes, such as theft, robbery, and fraud, according to their objects and degree of violence, and provided differentiated punishments. Also important was the law against dueling of 1787 that, following Beccaria's prescription, punished the culpable party with Siberian exile. Procedural protections introduced during Catherine's reign cannot be discussed here in detail, but they were groundbreaking for the time, they followed Beccaria's advice closely, and they show the legislator's inquiry into the defendants' mind-set and circumstances. For instance, the landmark law of 1775 for the first time successfully established a specialized regular court system in Russia, which included special "courts of conscience" to deal, among other matters, with crimes committed by minors who were punished noticeably less severely. The secret decrees of 1767 and 1774 required that criminal investigations comply with chapter 10 of the *Instruction* (reproducing Beccaria's text), dealing with legal procedure.[33] Subsequently these rules migrated into volume 15, part 2, of the Digest of the Laws of 1835, and thus imperial Russia's law of criminal procedure before the reform of 1864 followed Beccaria's principles on such issues as the rules of evidence, witnesses, confessions, and the presumption of innocence.[34] Finally, the decrees of 1763 and 1774 limited and then prohibited torture.[35]

Even more extensive, although virtually unknown, was the influence of the *Instruction* on legal practice. Our most importance source here is a brief but fascinating 1917 article by Mikhail Klochkov, which shows that a diverse and representative sample of courts and authorities in the late eighteenth century applied the *Instruction* directly as if it were active law. It is fair to conclude that with the introduction of the principles of the *Instruction* into Russian legal practice the significance of the code of 1649, officially still in force, and of Peter I's military law, not officially applicable to civilian cases but nonetheless applied occasionally from the mid-eighteenth century, migrated into the category of historical monuments important primarily as rhetorical and ideological sources of the national legal tradition.[36]

Until the codification project of Nicholas I and Mikhail Speransky in the early 1830s, the *Instruction* was regarded by Russian officialdom as being very near to binding. When Catherine's grandson came to the throne in 1801 as Alexander I, the *Instruction*'s privileged role in Russian lawmaking and statecraft was confirmed in the decree of 5 June 1801, which established another legislative commission and proclaimed that Catherine's *Instruction* "contains the choicest truths of their kind and can [therefore] shed a great light upon the Commission's exercises." A decree of 1804 stated that Catherine, "having considered many truths relating to legislation, which were discovered and proven by the observations of great statesmen, set them out in this superb creation [i.e., the *Instruction*]," which "for the most part denotes the foundations of the law" and is "a priceless fruit of her deep reflection into, and a mastery of, legislation."[37]

Neither Beccaria nor Catherine's *Instruction* provides very detailed discussions of the etiology of crime, different factors influencing criminals, or different categories of offenses or offenders. It was clear that new rules were needed to recalculate the system of criminal penalties, but it was not clear what these rules were going to be. But the two other founding figures of classical criminology, Bentham and Feuerbach, developed and systematized Beccaria's utilitarianism and provided detailed guidance that was carefully studied by Russian legislators and remains the basis of "Western" or Eurocentric criminal justice to this day. Bentham's *Introduction to the Principles of Morals and Legislation* (published in 1789) included a topography of the criminal act and of the criminal mind that closely resembles the rationale of the Russian draft penal code of 1813 and the codes of 1835 and 1845.[38]

Summarized briefly, Bentham's utilitarian theory holds that crime, like any other action, occurs because individuals seek to maximize pleasure and minimize pain. The business of criminal law is to punish those acts that disturb the happiness of society, which consists of "enjoyment of pleasures, security from pains" (*Introduction,* chapter VII, section I).[39] Every action that may be subject to punishment is evaluated according to six factors. The first four are "1.

The act itself. . . . 2. The circumstances in which it is done. 3. The intentionality that may have accompanied it. 4. The consciousness, unconsciousness, or false consciousness, that may have accompanied it" (VII/VI). The fifth factor is the motives that cause the act (VII/VII) by "influencing the will of a sensitive being" (X/III). Because a "motive is substantially nothing more than pleasure or pain, operating in a certain manner" (X/IX), motives are good if they produce pleasure and evil if they produce pain (X/XII). Chapter X contains a long list of possible motives that include displeasure, physical desire, pecuniary interest, love of power, and self-preservation, while earlier in the *Introduction* he lists fourteen types of pleasure and twelve types of pain (all with categories). Bentham also maintains that individuals experience pleasure and pain differently, and in chapter VI lists thirty-two different variables affecting human experience, which include biological, environmental, and social factors.

Finally, Bentham asserts that the sixth and perhaps most enigmatic factor in evaluating crime is one's "disposition" to suffer oneself "to be governed by such or such motive" (XI/I). He describes disposition as "a kind of fictitious entity, feigned for the convenience of discourse, in order to express what there is supposed to be *permanent* in a man's frame of mind." The evidence of such permanent characteristics is found not in some intrinsic moral qualities but in one's prior actions and is evaluated "according to the influence it has, either, 1. on its own happiness; or, 2. on the happiness of others" (XI/II). Bentham provides four rules for evaluating disposition, which balance, in different combinations, "the apparent mischievousness of the act," "the strength of the temptation being given," and "the degree of deliberation with which it is accompanied" (XI/XLII). In Bentham's calculus of crime it is therefore crucial to determine whether the person has done mischief in the past, of what kind and why, and whether he was likely to do it again (XI/VII and XI/XLIII). All this material is necessary for understanding the structure of any modern penal code, including the Russian ones, in which the definitions of specific types of offenses include a complex balancing of many aggravating and mitigating circumstances combining mental and emotional as well as social and other external factors.[40]

Bentham's *Introduction* was widely read in Russia (in French translation by his disciple Étienne Dumont), and he himself traveled there in 1786–1787 to visit his brother Samuel and to offer his services to the tsar's government; he corresponded with some of Russia's top officials and with Alexander I himself. Assessing the results of this engagement, imperial-era scholar Alexander Pypin argued that after a brief infatuation the tsar and educated society lost interest in Bentham's reform proposals because of the mystical ideology of the Holy Alliance of Austria,

Prussia, and Russia taking hold after 1814. Sponsored by such politicians as Metternich and Arakcheev, the new post-Napoleonic conservatism reduced the urgency of Bentham's call for a public, transparent, and rational legislative process. I cannot agree with Pypin's conclusion that Bentham's influence on Russian life was without any practical consequences.[41] To the contrary, it was pervasive and lasting. Russia's legislative process and its legal culture more generally did become considerably more transparent and public in the first half of the nineteenth century, with the State Council formed in 1810 as the official legislative body and staffed, in part, by former high officials who were able to critique and to vote on legislative drafts. The broader public was better informed as well, with the episodic publication of court decisions and of major legislative proposals such as the draft of the 1845 code. Finally, the entire enormous body of Russian law became accessible to the public as the result of Speransky's codification project.[42] But even more important, Speransky and other legal reformers read Bentham's work with great interest, and whether directly or through the study of other scholars and of other states' legislation, Bentham's insights ended up in the legislation that would govern Russia until 1917 and even beyond.[43]

Ludwig Feuerbach (1775–1833) too left a strong imprint on Russian law. A utilitarian like Bentham, he was not only an academic thinker but a practical reformer who prepared the immensely influential Bavarian penal code of 1813, as well as a practicing judge. Feuerbach is important for reconceptualizing European criminal law (as opposed to jurisprudence more generally) as a science. Today he is mostly remembered for his maxim "*nulla poena sine lege,*" meaning that one can only be punished for something that is explicitly prohibited by the law, one of the key principles of the modern idea of the rule of law. This principle appeared in the Russian Penal Code of 1845 in Articles 96 and 155. Feuerbach's other important idea still remembered today is that crime is a violation of someone's rights, which also made its way into Russian law as the very first article in the Code of 1845. In addition to studying the Bavarian code of 1813, Russian officials read Feuerbach's textbook, essentially a model penal code, first published in 1801 and translated into Russian in 1810–1811 (the third part, containing procedural rules, was published in 1827). This translation was a milestone in Russia's legal development because it appeared before any systematic account of existing Russian criminal law was available, and its anonymous translators provided detailed footnotes that matched Feuerbach's categories with existing Russian laws (mostly the code of 1649 and the laws of Peter I and Catherine II). Translators even had to coin a number of legal terms, in effect inventing much of Russia's modern legal idiom.[44]

In sum, by the time the project of codification picked up speed in post-Napoleonic Russia, there were several principles animating European statecraft. Criminal justice was a major instrument of state policy; it punished actions specifically listed in a document that was to be as clear and logical as possible, avoiding contradiction and duplication. These norms assumed humans to be rational beings to the extent that their choices could be influenced and manipulated by policy. To make that policy effective, legislators and judges had to carefully differentiate varieties of prohibited conduct and to take into account a complex set of circumstances that concerned the criminal's character, abilities, wealth and social status, mental and emotional states, and motivations.

FROM A GUNPOWDER EMPIRE TO A BOURGEOIS NATION

In addition to the calculus of crime and punishment, the Code was animated by two other logics or perspectives that are apparent in the General Part and even more so in the other eleven divisions that define specific crimes. One logic was concerned with protecting the state, its daily operations, its monopoly on violence, and its guardianship of the Orthodox faith. The second logic sought to protect private individuals' physical security and property rights. Both of these objectives are of course found in any other European or Eurocentric penal code. Possible Russian peculiarities include Russia's strong reliance on corporal punishment in the absence of the death penalty, since lashing was used to supplement the sentences of hard labor and penal exile; also unusual was the resulting dual ladder of punishment for exempt and nonexempt groups—the exempt groups including the nobles, clergy, and wealthier merchants, and the nonexempt groups including all the lower estates, such as peasants and the poorer townspeople.

The logic of state building first shows up in Articles 19 through 95 of the General Part, which contain the Code's ladder of punishments. The most significant of these were hard labor, lifelong penal settlement, temporary administrative exile, and incarceration of varying length and severity. The penal system envisioned in the Code was complex and extensive, necessitating numerous facilities to house inmates, a transportation network, and a system of surveillance and control over those convicts who were required to reside in particular locations or were prohibited from exercising certain rights, for example, from buying serf villages or entering government service. None of this was possible without powerful and reasonably efficient administrative agencies far superior to those Russia actually possessed in the early nineteenth century. Indeed, the very notion of a penal calculus is unthinkable without a system of gathering information about criminal defendants that is possible only in a highly centralized bureaucratic state. In other words, the logic that created the new system of criminal justice—more humane in some ways but also far more powerful and more intrusive than early modern systems—was inseparable from the rest of the European "new regime" that emerged in the wake of Napoleon's defeat.[45]

The focus on the state was even more clear in divisions 2 through 9 of the Code, which dealt with crimes against the Orthodox faith; political crimes like regicide, treason, and sedition; misconduct by state officials; and numerous violations of fiscal, health, mining, and other administrative regulations. Even though these provisions made up the bulk of the Code, they hardly ever came up in high-publicity trials, except for a handful of cases involving political crimes, counterfeiting, and official embezzlement. Discussion of them here is therefore abbreviated, but some understanding of the major principles is necessary. The state's interests were inscribed in the Code in three distinct layers. One was the set of laws against treason, sedition, and undermining the Orthodox faith. Relatively rare though such cases were, they were highly ideologized, attracted official and public attention, and almost always went to specialized tribunals.[46] The tsar's and his officials' choice to direct such cases as the pre-reform Petrashevsky affair of 1848 or the cases of the populists in the 1870s to this elevated layer of the justice system may or may not have been mistaken or avoidable, but there is no doubt that this choice was highly consequential. Russia's entire legal development is often—mistakenly—judged on the basis of this extremely narrow, specialized, and ideologized body of law that reflected neither the bulk of the Code's provisions nor the bulk of the courts' caseload.[47] Nor does it suggest an aberration on Russia's path of legal development from a Western trajectory; rather, the attention paid to political crime and protecting official ideology—the monarchy and the Orthodox faith in the Russian case—is very much in line with the logic of penal reform crystallized in Beccaria's treatise, which regarded sedition as the "greatest" and "most damaging" type of crime.[48]

The second layer of the laws protecting the state contained detailed provisions against bribery, embezzlement, and other malfeasance by government officials. It is often claimed that these laws did not make much of a dent, considering the pervasive corruption observed throughout the entire state apparatus in imperial Russia. Moreover, Ekaterina Pravilova has shown that the tsarist administration successfully resisted reformers' efforts to establish a specialized court for trying cases of official malfeasance. Instead, high-level officials were investigated and tried in the Senate, while the rest were tried by ordinary courts. Before indicting an official, it was necessary to get permission from the official's superiors, which, as a practical matter, would not be withheld in clear-cut and egregious cases.[49]

The third and largest layer of crimes against the state's interests protected its social and economic activities. Perhaps the oldest and most elevated variety was the law against counterfeiting, followed by smuggling and other attempts to defraud the government through government contracts, liquor buyouts, forestry, mining, fishing, and similar activities. Other laws protected public and individual interests as much as those of the government: building, fire safety, health, and railroad or navigation regulations, as well as laws regulating public morals (gambling, prostitution, public misconduct), educational establishments, and publication censorship. This body of law was already present in Russia in a rudimentary form in the seventeenth century but was greatly expanded under Peter and especially Catherine, whose police statute (*Ustav Blagochinia*) of 1782 closely resembled similar German police regulations. As Marc Raeff famously observed, Catherine's police legislation was influenced by German cameralism seeking a well-organized police state, where police officers represented not oppression but rather order and efficiency, generating prosperity. This body of law is seldom noticed, but it is important to remember that it became indispensable more than a century before the rise of the twentieth-century administrative disciplinary state. In the Russian case, these laws were scattered throughout the 1835 Digest of the Laws, brought together in the 1845 Code, and after the Judicial Reform of 1864 were once again separated into a separate code and during the time frame covered in this book were enforced by justices of the peace outside the regular court system.[50]

In contrast to the numerous laws protecting the state's interests, the bulk of the courts' caseload and virtually all high-publicity cases came from only three divisions, which protected private persons and property and were tucked away at the very end of the Code. Prohibitions against murder and theft are as old as law itself, but the codification drive that began in most European and Eurocentric states in the second half of the eighteenth century and continued in the nineteenth increased these laws' complexity and sophistication exponentially. Protecting individual rights from criminals was no longer simply an aspect of maintaining the state's monopoly on armed force but a government's major objective in its own right, whether in England, Prussia, or the Russian Empire. The topography of crimes against persons captured in this new legislation came from the same sources as the idea of the penal calculus itself, most importantly from Locke and other empiricist philosophers with their glorification of economic independence and property ownership. In a similar vein, the government of Catherine II sought to rebuild an upper- and middle-class society of noble landowners and urban traders and merchants, who were all freed from the requirements of government service and given various privileges. While we know very little about the cultures and practices of crime in the age of Catherine, it seems logical that the policy of creating a nonserving segment of the ruling elite would entail creating more robust laws for protecting their persons and property. It is telling that, in the Russian case, Catherine II's government never managed to codify the entirety of criminal law but produced a coherent set of rules punishing theft in 1781. The authority of the emancipated elite was especially boosted by the freedom from corporal punishment that divided Russia's criminal justice into two segments until 1863, when most of its forms were abolished. The list of exemptions was constantly extended, and after 1845 it was found not in the main body of the law but in an appendix. The impact of this division, huge as it was, did not mean that elite criminals were immune from punishment, since they could still be, for example, sentenced to hard labor for murder. Conversely, there was no system of laws or punishments that applied only to enserfed peasants. Even though serfdom was the mainstay of Russian society before 1861, it hardly features in the Code of 1845. The murder of one's master was punished more severely, but so were several other categories of victims mentioned in the relevant provision.[51]

The body of law that built upon Catherinian innovations and fully emerged after the codification of the 1830s and 1840s reflected the cultural and social consensus of the post-Napoleonic period. The fundamental premise of this consensus was that European middle and upper-middle classes would support their rulers under the restored status quo in exchange for two powerful benefits. One was the new concept of private property as a fundamental right separate from social, political, or cultural entitlements and interests.[52] The second benefit was the formalization and extension of patriarchy, that is, the increased empowerment of the adult sane male property owner who exercised extensive control over his dependents—family members, servants and employees, service subordinates, and, by extension, community members. Post-Napoleonic national conservative ideologies throughout Europe formed around these elements, and monarchs began to present themselves as patriarchal and frugal heads of family rather than glorious military leaders.[53] Specific consequences for criminal law meant that the state no longer practiced wholesale property seizures or reprisals against criminals' family members. Conversely, the state punished even small offenses against property and provided various enhanced protections to family members, to young, insane, or poor persons, to servants, to women, and to ethnic minorities.

The establishment of this post-1815 consensus is well documented for Western Europe, but it was equally important in Russia, where political participation appeared only in an extremely limited form in the 1860s, a large proportion of the population were treated as slaves in fact if not in law, and therefore the personal freedom of movement and occupation as well as the right of property ownership assumed a particularly exalted status.[54] In this larger context, the draft penal code of 1813 provided strong protections for private persons and property, which migrated with very little change into the Digest of 1835 and the Code of 1845. In contrast to the early modern concern with armed robbers and outlaws, the Code envisioned a society when criminals, victims, and the family members of either lived in close proximity. Parents and children, masters and servants, senior and junior servitors all operated in a tangled network of dependencies, both legal and informal, which were invariably revealed in a typical criminal proceeding and heavily influenced the outcome. The task of criminal justice was not simply to solve a crime but also to analyze and to balance multiple perspectives and influences.

TEXTS OF TRANSGRESSION IN THE REFORM ERA

The Code of 1845 remained in force until the end of imperial Russia with only minor changes. In the early 1860s there were proposals to create a new penal code to accompany the procedural reform in 1864. Instead, legislators chose to only slightly adjust existing laws to conform to the new procedures, missing a perfect opportunity to improve the penal code. The more important changes introduced in the 1870s and early 1880s included higher punishments for aggravated murder, laws against illegal societies, changes in death penalty law, punishments for minor criminals, and also removing petty burglary cases from jury courts to local ones, with a corresponding reduction in penalties. Russian lawyers generally realized that the Code of 1845 needed to be streamlined to eliminate redundancies and contradictions, and a commission was set up in 1870 for that purpose. The project was delayed, however, because judicial officials decided that the prison system and the penal regime in general had to be reformed first, which was accomplished in 1879.[55] The commission to revise the Code continued to work during the 1880s and 1890s, finally producing a full draft written for the most part by Russia's two leading criminal law professors, Nikolai Tagantsev and Ivan Foinitskii. The draft was approved by the State Council and signed by Nicholas II in 1903. Yet the tsar never actually gave his final go-ahead, and the code never went into effect other than in its provisions about the crimes against the state and several others. After 1917 the code of 1903 became the basis for the new Soviet penal law.

The draft code of 1903 was far better organized than its predecessor, but it did not alter the fundamental principles of Russian criminal justice, such as the structure of the penal calculus and the presumption that criminals act from free will. Positivism barely made an appearance in the draft.[56] This fact does not, however, indicate any inferiority or relative lack of progress on the part of Russia and its laws, since the "classical" views on crime and punishment derived from Beccaria, Bentham, and Feuerbach remain to this day at the core of Eurocentric penal systems. The competing positivist framework for understanding criminality appeared in the 1830s and 1840s and became especially influential in academic criminology. Positivist criminologists and sociologists focused on obtaining accurate information about the prevalence and the patterns of criminal activity and on drawing correlations between crime and socioeconomic conditions. As conventional wisdom has it, positivist criminologists were interested in learning about the person of criminals, their motivations and their psychological conditions, as opposed to the classical school's concern with studying criminal actions in order to assign appropriate punishments. But upon a closer look, classical criminologists and especially Bentham were also deeply interested in the criminal's person and motivations, which could explain why the classical framework has proven flexible enough to weather the challenges of positivism and modern industrial society.

As Zygmunt Bialkowski has observed, the leading jurists in post-reform Russia were reluctant to convert to positivist criminology and remained "eclectic" in their theoretical outlook. Cesare Lombroso was translated, but his teaching about born criminality did not win over Russian legal thinkers.[57] This is not to say that the new theoretical currents failed to leave their mark, but as in other Eurocentric systems they did not take over actual court practice, and their influence was ambiguous. The insanity defense had existed in Eurocentric legal systems for centuries but was defined rather narrowly. The Russian Penal Code of 1845 likewise excused criminals held to be insane, but it meant complete and permanent disability and not temporary fits or delusions. In the 1860s and 1870s this language was reinterpreted to allow for temporary affect. Several of the most celebrated criminal trials of the post-reform era employed complex psychological analysis to argue that the defendant charged with murder or attempted murder acted in a fit of passion and could not be held fully culpable. One of the earliest cases was the nobleman Kicheev, tried publicly but in a pre-reform court in 1866. A year later, a jury in St. Petersburg acquitted the civil servant Protopopov. In both of these cases, prominent physicians testified on the defendants' behalf, but one can easily surmise that the favorable outcome was due not to medical arguments but to social ones, the defendant's actions being interpreted from the perspective of defending the honor of an elite male.[58] Other prominent murder cases that implicated avarice rather than rage did not use forensic medicine, for instance those of Danilov and Landsberg in the case of noble defendants, or of young servants or employees committing multiple murders (discussed later), where one might think such an analysis could be appropriate. By contrast, psychiatric evaluation and arguments were strongly visible in several trials of young elite women accused of crimes of passion: Palem, Kairova, Kornilova, Nepenina, and Zasulich. In short, psychiatric analysis and argumentation continued to be a standard technique during criminal trials in the post-reform era, and its use was even expanded. It was not used universally, however.

In contrast to jury trials, other institutions and practices of criminal justice used positivist technologies, which were added to the old-regime practices of what Foucault has called the "custodial state" and Raeff has called, using German terminology, the "well-ordered police state" (*Polizeistaat*). Various government agencies gathered statistics, observed suspect population groups, carried out routine police work, investigated reported crimes, dispensed summary and noncustodial justice, practiced forensic medicine, and so on. Most of these tasks involved officials other than those of the Ministry of the Interior: from Foreign and War to Finance, Education, and the Holy Synod. Government agents were also increasingly assisted by private and semiprivate expert communities. None of these was supervised or reviewed by judges, lawyers, or juries, other than as an exceptional matter and with a strong and virtually insurmountable presumption in favor of the state. Some of these activities did not touch on the upper classes, like sex work or residence and passport regulations. But many did. Even the local courts dealing with petty crime were very active in fining or even arresting prominent men and women for uncivil behavior. As Barbara Alpern Engel has shown, administrative bodies oversaw family-law disputes that the regular courts could not engage.

Great trials were taking place in a larger disciplinary context; when looking at the disciplinary function of the courts, we need to remember that there were other bodies performing the same or similar functions. While policing prostitution may not have applied extensively to the upper classes, there were, for instance, noble trusteeship boards, which had existed since the eighteenth century and supervised a wide range of transgressive behaviors. Education officials were also relevant to policing elites. The Foreign Ministry policed Russians abroad. The Third Section policed potential subversion, and so on.

The Penal Code of 1845 incorporated several distinct ideologies and doctrines of crime and punishment that originated in different historical periods and emphasized different objectives of the legal system. These objectives ranged from the early modern goal of protecting the state against traitors and outlaws, to the Enlightenment-era search for a generally applicable mechanism of power to promote general social and moral development, and finally to the post-1815 emphasis on protecting the physical autonomy and property interests of private individuals. The specific definitions of crimes provided in the Code were only rarely debated during jury trials, mostly brought up when there was a glaring discrepancy between the facts of the case and the article invoked in the indictment. But it was of course of critical significance whether the defendant faced decades of hard labor in Siberia or a relatively comfortable noncustodial or semicustodial deportation. Even more fundamentally, every individual in the courtroom who had studied law at a Russian university—judges, attorneys, prosecutors, and some spectators as well—would have been familiar with the Code's categories and its overall logic. This logic was first clearly articulated in the writings of Beccaria, Bentham, and Feuerbach and was adopted in Russia much like in other European and Eurocentric states. It involved categorizing and evaluating the offender's (and sometimes the victim's) condition, actions, and state of mind in order to assign appropriate punishment. Much like the procedural law that enforced it, the Penal Code did not consist of bright-line either/or commandments but assumed a delicate process of balancing and negotiation. The chapters that follow discuss some of the most noteworthy examples of such balancing and negotiation that occurred in actual practice during post-reform trials.

PART TWO

Violence

Figure 10. The trial for the "suitcase murder" of Nikolai von Zon (Sohn) in St. Petersburg District Court on 30 March 1870. *Vsemirnaia illustratsia,* 1870, no. 68, p. 292. This is the smaller courtroom, originally intended for appellate cases. The defendants—four men and two women—are on the right. Their youth is emphasized. The prosecutor on the left is giving his speech, pointing at the defendants, and almost everyone in the room is looking in their direction. Of particular interest is the lively demeanor of the spectators, many of whom are women. One man in a uniform is directing his binoculars at the defendants, many others are chatting with one another. More reserved are the elite spectators, including several grand dukes, seated behind the two sides of the judges' table and behind the jury's bench. Note the two women stenographers sitting at the evidence table in the center. This was to ensure they could hear well (compare this to the reporters' station in figure 4).

Dostoevsky's biographers note that only days before the first installment of *Crime and Punishment* appeared in January 1866, the novel's plot was presaged when a reclusive moneylender named Popov and his housekeeper, Maria Nordman, were found cut down in their blood-soaked apartment in central Moscow.[1] The killer was caught on 31 March, Russian Orthodox Easter. The investigator reasoned that everyone in the city would have stepped outside at some point on the most important Christian holy day, and he engaged a boy shop clerk who remembered the suspect's face to walk the area of the city where he likely resided. While ostensibly pragmatic, government agents may also have been mindful of the Russian folk saying "God will mark the scoundrel" and likely hoped for some divine assistance. The boy did spot the suspect driving by in a cab and followed him home, where he was promptly arrested. Popov's suspected murderer was one of his clients, Aleksei Danilov, a twenty-year-old law student from Moscow University: attractive, smart, and self-assured, and—unlike Dostoevsky's fictional Raskolnikov—not at all penniless.

The crowd that came to see Danilov's trial in February the next year was unprecedented in the short history of Moscow's new courts.[2] Tried only four days after the same jury had acquitted a peasant woman, Mavra Volokhova, of murdering and dismembering her husband, Danilov's case was to be the first contested murder conviction by a jury in Russia.[3] The few earlier homicide cases were badly put together and resulted in an acquittal or otherwise the accused admitted guilt and did not even try to mount a defense. By contrast, Danilov's case immediately stood out, not only because of the gruesome facts of the crime and the respectable social standing of the accused and his victims but also because of Danilov's not-guilty plea and the absence of the direct evidence that would have been required in a pre-reform trial. The case was therefore bound to become a "standard for comparing the level of interest attracted by a case, the skill of the defense, and the virtues and deficiencies of the new court system."[4]

But as in every "great" trial there was more to the Danilov case than legal novelty or analogies to great works of fiction. Together with a set of other high-profile cases, it shaped the first publicly disseminated "true" portrait of a Russian culture of violence, a subject that is to this day poorly understood. While we by now realize that Russia was not as lawless or "backward" as historians

Figure 11. Aleksei Danilov. From *Dvoinoe ubiistvo,* 4. His hat is askew, creating a somewhat rakish impression.

previously thought, it is still an open question whether it was a relatively violent society compared to its nineteenth-century counterparts. Historians of crime and violence in Western Europe have argued for long-term decreasing rates of violence and violent crime, meaning primarily murder and deadly assault, the types of crime that were visible even before modern crime statistics appeared in the nineteenth century.[5] Other varieties of violence, such as domestic abuse, prizefighting, or urban brawling were also targeted by nineteenth-century reformers but are much more difficult to document.

Russia was of course heading for the massive conflagration of the early twentieth century, and historians have been tempted to look back into the nineteenth for rising rates of violent crime, a failing system of criminal justice, and a greater cultural tolerance for daily violence that supposedly stymied efforts to implant "Western" values of civility.[6] Much of this work is influenced by Émile Durkheim's concept of anomie, the notion that crime and lawlessness rise as traditional cultural ties weaken in the modern urban industrial social milieu.[7]

This interpretation appears to be supported by official statistics, which show that the number of convictions for murder and violent assault in the post-reform period grew slightly ahead of the rate of population growth.[8] Alternately, Boris Mironov reads these statistics as showing that crime grew under the "liberal" regimes of Alexander I and Alexander II but fell under the "conservative" ones of Nicholas I and Alexander III.[9] Unfortunately, existing studies do not connect conviction rates to investigative, reportative, and prosecutorial practices. These are admittedly extremely difficult to study even today when archival materials have become more accessible.[10] Russian history simply has not had the services of a legion of legal and social historians sifting through raw historical data in the 1970s, 1980s and 1990s, as its American and Western European counterparts did.[11] What I can do is offer a contextualized reading of the leading trials for violent crime, noting how they connected attacks on the victim's body with tangled issues of property ownership, kinship structures and hierarchies, gender roles, and elusive notions concerning elite self-control, emotions, and personal authority.

CHAPTER 5

Killing for Property

Russians killed for the same reasons as people do anywhere: greed, revenge, anger, fear, or (more likely) a mixture of motives that is impossible to untangle. But one important and hugely disconcerting scenario has evaded the attention of historians of Russian crime and criminal law: the intentional and calculated killing for material profit.[1] Cases such as Danilov's are clear examples of murder for profit, but even those that were ostensibly about other issues, such as sexual relationships or revenge, still involved financial interest and economic calculation. Private property was the best-protected and most tangible individual right in imperial Russia, and it became even more important after the financial liberalization of the 1860s.[2] Murder was the quickest, the riskiest, and the most illegitimate recipe for getting rich, and thus it most directly invaded and injured a social order based on civil interaction and voluntary exchange. The cases of murder for profit discussed in this chapter fall into two sets. One set, similar to Danilov's, involved violence among members of the respectable classes, while the second variety was the killing of elite persons by their servants and other dependents.[3] Each set of cases had its particular themes and dynamics. For instance, intra-elite violence connects to the literature on dueling and masculinity and youth violence, as well as domestic violence in imperial Russia.[4] Murder from below implicates the issues of social hierarchy, social control, and attempts to create a discipline-based society in Russia. It forced elites to confront the legacy of serfdom, which lasted in Russia long past the point when it had been undermined ideologically, and to confront the ambivalent effects of the 1861 emancipation.[5] The genteel social order, private life, and indeed daily existence was enabled by an army of domestic servants, tutors, and other dependents, but the idea that after emancipation this social order benefited from the superior qualities of hired labor, that a market relationship was superior to the old ties of serfdom, was brought into sharp question.[6]

But both types of attacks, from one's peers and from below, undermined the elementary notions of physical privacy and physical safety, the security of one's home; and the basic notions of trust, since privacy and safety were destroyed not by strangers invading one's home but by people the victims had trusted.

As in all great trials, victims of violent crimes were typically scrutinized at least as much as if not more than the accused. Because such cases rested heavily on the analysis of the mental state and intentions of perpetrators and their victims, the trial tended to expose and scrutinize the lives and mentalities of respectable middle-class property owners whose very identity rested heavily on privacy, concealment, and personal autonomy.

Murder for profit also undermined its own logic by bringing under suspicion the very notion of rational calculation and evaluation. The presumably ultimate irrational act of murder could be shown to be fully rational and profitable, carried out by educated and intelligent individuals who thought it through carefully and made an informed calculation. Even though today we may think about these cases as not actually thought through in a rational manner, at the very least the relationship between violence and rationality was extremely uncomfortable. It was not always easy to distinguish between anger and calculation.

In the late 1870s the cultural imaginary of calculated murder expanded to involve individuals who were not simply respectable or well-to-do but belonged to the high aristocracy. As in any other society, Russian aristocrats were occasionally accused of murder. Perhaps the two most famous legal cases from pre-1864 Russia were those of the serial killer Daria Saltykova (related to the imperial family), convicted in 1768, and the playwright-to-be Aleksandr Sukhovo-Kobylin, from an ancient Muscovite family, who was accused in 1850 of murdering his French mistress, Louise Simon-Dimanche, and eventually acquitted.[7] After the legal reform, however, the Russian public was forced to confront a large number of such cases.

THE BUSINESS OF MURDER

The murder of an old moneylender for which Aleksei Danilov stood trial on 14 February 1867, was not the first or the last time a well-to-do person was targeted by criminals. It was the nineteenth century's equivalent of robbing a bank, because most financial transactions, whether purchasing real estate or lending money, took place face-to-face among private individuals. This continued to be the case even after large banks and joint-stock companies rapidly multiplied in the 1860s. Individual capitalists could take certain precautions but were still vulnerable to criminals. Popov, Danilov's victim, was more vulnerable than most. Originally a military officer, he was new to Moscow: in 1865 he sold his landed estate in Finland in order to move to the city where he had been stationed in his younger years. Renting a small apartment in a quiet, middle-class residential neighborhood, he had neither the relatives nor the servants who were essential for physical safety in a respectable household. To make matters worse, Popov lived in seclusion and was hardly ever seen even by the building's yardman (*dvornik*, a role most easily translated as what New Yorkers call a "super"). His housekeeper, Maria Nordman, was in her forties: much younger, very energetic, and "economical." She seems to have provided the drive behind Popov's decision to get into moneylending as a retirement activity. Popov's family insisted on a more proper (*prilichnoe*) occupation of mortgage loans (a long-term investment attractive to people hoping to eventually inherit it). Nordman, however, talked him into pawnbroking, which promised a quicker stream of cash and was less dependent upon the legal system and social connections.[8] The only trouble with this plan was that Popov did not know much about jewelry, which people usually like to pawn, and so he had to be on his guard against fraud. After a few months, the business proved to be too much for Popov, and shortly before his murder he wrote in a letter that he wanted to get out, "so as not to risk [his] property."[9] Meanwhile, Popov paid a jeweler named Feller to make estimates for him. This meant that before visiting Popov and killing him, Danilov had to go to Feller's shop to show him the ring that he wanted to pawn, and that Feller's young shop clerk remembered Danilov's face and was able to identify him on the street on that Easter Day.

On the day of the trial, Danilov attracted attention by his respectable appearance, his manners, and his speech. On the surface, unlike the fictional Raskolnikov, he had no clear reason to commit murder. Given his future law degree, he could look forward to a comfortable and promising career in state service, in private legal practice, or in business. While not exceptionally sociable, Danilov was already taking commissions from an acquaintance, a noblewoman named Sokovnina, to sell or pawn property, including expensive jewelry, and had a banknote for five thousand rubles.[10]

Nor did he have any personal reasons to commit violent crime: there were no signs of any financial turmoil, any large debts, gambling, or involvement with women of easy virtue.[11] Danilov lived with his parents and his unmarried sister, was provided with free room and board, and for several years had been enjoying an extra income of up to seventy rubles per month from tutoring (equivalent to the salary of a white-collar clerk). The ethos of public service that we can see in memoirs by reform-era lawyers such as Anatolii Koni and Mikhail Gromnitskii should also have kept him from violent crime.

Because Danilov denied killing Popov, we do not have a first-hand account of his actions and motivations. The obvious one was getting his hands on Popov's property, which consisted of more than twenty thousand rubles. This would have allowed him to begin his career in comfort. Moreover, he was preparing to marry a woman from a "good" family (neither the fiancée, named Aliabieva, nor Sokovnina testified at the trial), and this cash would have been helpful.[12] The alternative is clearly illustrated by the case of a prominent Moscow lawyer, Aleksandr Saltykov, who started his career at approximately the same time and spent most of his money on luxury items and on setting up his married life, so that even his considerable earnings were not sufficient. Saltykov did not murder anyone, but he embezzled from his numerous clients, was eventually caught, and unsuccessfully faked his own suicide.[13] It is therefore plausible that Danilov committed murder to secure his status as a financially and socially autonomous middle-class property owner.

The trouble with any such plan was that Popov's assets, as Danilov knew very well, were kept not in cash but in bank deposit tickets (*bilety*), which circulated almost like cash but could not have been exchanged for cash as soon as the murder became known, and the list of compromised ticket numbers would have been sent out to all the banks in Russia. Apparently it was not impossible to still benefit from such a situation, but doing so was well beyond Danilov's abilities. Both the press accounts and Mikhail Gromnitskii, who prosecuted Danilov, thought that at least one more person was involved in the murder, and they took a hard look at Danilov's father; but they did not have any evidence to take their suspicions further.[14] After Danilov was convicted, the father bribed another convict to take the blame for the crime. While the ruse was quickly discovered, it is interesting that the father had no trouble arranging the transaction.[15] His work as a discipline inspector (*nadziratel'*) at an unspecified school would not have provided for the comfortable lifestyle that everyone agreed the family was enjoying. Also, after Danilov had been sentenced to ten years of hard labor, his parents and his sister followed him to Siberian exile and apparently died there, which suggests a closer involvement in the case.[16]

Having been caught purely by accident, Danilov himself failed to come up with a convincing story to explain the healed cuts on his hand that precisely

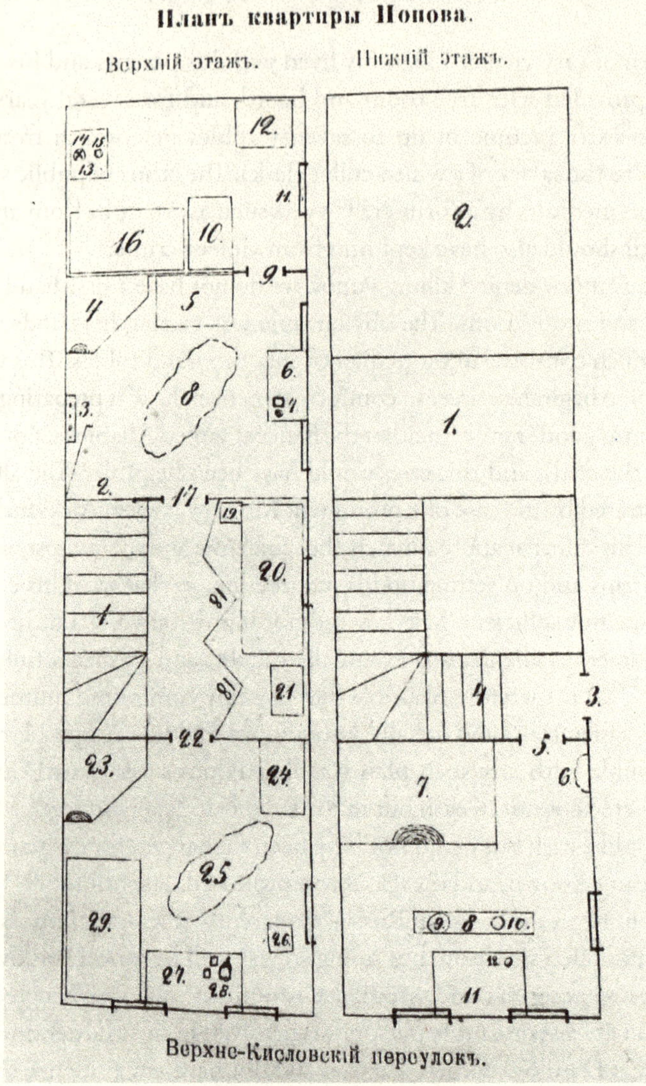

Figure 12. Floor plan of Popov's apartment in Verkhne-kislovskii Alley in Moscow. *Dvoinoe ubiistvo,* 40–41. Note the building's isolated situation and the precise marking of each object's location. Right: bottom floor. 1 and 2—storage; 3—entrance; 4—stairs to the second floor; 5—door to the kitchen; 7—fireplace. Left: top floor. 1—stairs; 3—coatrack; 4—fireplace; 5—cupboard; 6—table; 7—box with baking soda and cash; 8—Nordman's body; 9—door to Nordman's room; 10—wardrobe; 11—two glass jars on the windowsill; 12—table; 13—dresser; 14—samovar; 15—washing basin; 16—Nordman's bed; 17—door to Popov's room; 18—screens; 19—side table; 20—Popov's bed; 21—washing basin; 22—door to Popov's office; 23—fireplace; 24—dresser; 25—Popov's body; 26—chair on which Popov was killed; 27—desk; 28—beer bottle; 29—couch.

matched the blood stains left by the killer in the apartment (other than large amounts of blood, there were no signs of struggle in the apartment). Nor could he explain how he was able to get his hands on the banknote that he had previously pawned to Popov and shortly after the murder re-pawned to a different lender; his explanation was so awkward that it caused laughter among the public in the courtroom.[17] It seems that immediately following his arrest Danilov was quite despondent, once mentioning to the representative of Moscow University who oversaw the investigation that like the main character of Victor Hugo's *Les Misérables,* he was hoping for a kindly old bishop to appear and rescue him at the last moment.[18] But soon he became more optimistic. Because he gave a fake name to Popov when doing business with him, there was very little information that could have helped the police, had he not been identified by the shop clerk. Later he claimed that "it is considered dishonorable to reveal one's surname to a pawnbroker."[19] Other than his loan from Popov, Danilov appears to have had no links with him, and so the trial theory employed the narrative of the violent, modern, calculating, and yet careless acquisitiveness invading the existing genteel (though not necessarily gentle) world of face-to-face transactions and relationships based on acquaintance, trust, and reputation. Popov's casual habits and precautions could not withstand Danilov's skills and ambitions.

Danilov's case became something of a paradigm for the post-reform culture of violence among elite and middle-class groups. In 1879, at the height of the era of the legal scandal in Russia, an almost identical case took place in St. Petersburg, and the two murders are typically mentioned together.[20] The differences were significant, however, and illustrate the passage of time between the two cases. The St. Petersburg case began when a laborer painting the outside wall of an apartment building saw dead bodies through the windows. The police broke down the door and found retired Aulic Councilor Yegor Vlasov and his servant, Aleksandra Semenidova. Both victims had been stabbed expertly in the neck, the apartment was locked, and evidence found on the scene suggested the killer himself was wounded. Approximately fourteen thousand rubles in bank notes were stolen. Presumably by questioning the building's staff the police found out that the most recent visitor had been Karl von Landsberg, an officer in the ultra-prestigious Guard Sapper Batallion, only twenty-five years old and twice decorated for courage during the recent campaign under General von Kaufman against Khoqand. His family was well off and owned a landed estate in the Kovno (today's Kaunas) province in Lithuania.

Superficially similar to Danilov's, Landsberg's story was different in several essential elements. First, he came from an upper-class, aristocratic background, and his opportunities for financial prosperity were much greater, despite clichés about bankrupt nobility. During the trial there was much discussion about the lifestyle and the required expenditures of young men in Landsberg's situation. Unlike Danilov, Landsberg claimed that his crime was caused by the pressure to maintain a lavish lifestyle in the capital. This was very much in line with emerging positivist criminology, which explained crime by social and economic conditions. Before the war of 1877–1878 Landsberg had led a modest life, visiting with highly respectable families. But after the war he became involved with several dissolute noblemen and started to gamble, getting into debt. First he tried to break out of this vicious circle through marriage, securing preliminary consent from Maria Totleben, the daughter of the famous military engineer Count Eduard Totleben. This connection would have been extremely helpful to his career and finances, but Maria Totleben (or her family) changed her mind about the marriage. Using funds borrowed from his then friend, Vlasov, Landsberg also tried to play the stock market, ending up with even more debt. Landsberg's narrative thus suggested that his natural thriftiness was disrupted and destroyed by the violence of the two wars, by the rejection of his fiancée, and by the treachery of the stock market. But one could also see Landsberg's military experience getting him accustomed to the violent acquisition of status and possibly wealth. Aside from this added complexity, Landsberg's case was also different from Danilov's because his victim, Vlasov, was well aware of the benefit of establishing useful social connections, was anything but reclusive, and presented himself as Landsberg's friend. Ambitious to enter higher social circles, Vlasov offered him interest-free loans and apparently was even willing to forgive him his debts as a present for the proposed wedding. This story no doubt resonated with many elite men, so that Landsberg received the mildest sentence possible for premeditated murder, which was punishable by fifteen years to life at hard labor.[21]

Thus the criminals who most closely approximated Dostoevsky's fictional Raskolnikov were his complete opposite socially and came from well-off or even upper-class families. The third famous murderer of a moneylender was Grigorii Aleksandrovich Bezobrazov, forty-eight years old, grandson to the eighteenth-century strongman Fedor Orlov and uncle to infamous Aleksandr Mikhailovich Bezobrazov, who contributed to the outbreak of the Russo-Japanese War in 1904. On 10 December 1877, Grigorii Aleksandrovich arrived at a hotel in Kharkov (Kharkiv) and sent for the local doctor, Kovalchukov, because he felt ill. He then killed the good doctor with an axe because, as he explained later, he had read in a newspaper about the axe murder of a usurer. The doctor was far better known locally as a leading local capitalist and moneylender. Bezobrazov tried to make it look as if Kovalchukov was killed by one of his borrowers and left a note in a semi-Russian, semi-Ukrainian dialect: "Let this usurer die like a dog, he ruined me, let him stuff himself now, goddamned devil, let him have it hot in hell."[22] Bezobrazov then went to a barber, had his beard shaven off, and left town.

The police were able to find Bezobrazov in Petersburg, however, because they immediately suspected the doctor's young and estranged wife and started to look through her known acquaintances as a matter of routine. Kovalchukova was described as a "beautiful and crafty lady" (*krasivaia i lovkaia dama*), and it did not take long to uncover that she was having an affair with Bezobrazov, who was essentially an aristocratic gigolo, making some of his living from having resort-town affairs with visiting noblewomen in Yalta, in Crimea. As part of this bizarre pattern of mixing business with pleasure, Bezobrazov wanted to free Mrs. Kovalchukova (and her property) from her husband's control. Following the murder, he informed her by telegraph. After being arrested, Bezobrazov confessed and was sentenced to eleven years of hard labor in October 1878. Typically for post-reform criminal justice, Kovalchukov's wife was acquitted.

While the Bezobrazov trial mixed greed and calculation with illicit, or at least semi-illicit, sex, two other prominent murder cases were even more explicit about connecting murderous calculation with irrational forces or motives. Only two weeks after Danilov's conviction, on 27 February 1867, a woman merchant, Aleksandra Mazurina, the senior member of a fabulously wealthy commercial clan, finally found the missing key to a locked shop located in the bottom floor of her vast mansion on a fancy street in central Moscow.[23] The shop had been standing empty for months, after her thirty-six-year-old son, Vasilii, who had been trading there, was confined to the city debtors' prison only a few blocks away. It so happened that 27 February was Clean Monday, the first day of Lent, when Orthodox Christians wash their sins away and also physically clean their houses, which is presumably how Mazurina found the key. She immediately sent two servants into the shop to clean it out. In the back of the shop the servants stumbled upon an oilcloth covering a decomposed body, half of which was mummified and the other half "spreadable." The floor was covered by a "blackish mass," and there were dried blood stains on walls and cabinets. On the floor there was a razor blade modified to make its foldable handle stronger. The police officer called to the scene at once remembered that eight months earlier Vasilii Mazurin had been visited by the "free artist" Ilya Kalmykov, who had not been seen since. Kalmykov's main profession was not fine art but jewelry and financial operations involving jewelry. While the body's features were decomposed beyond recognition, Kalmykov's brother recognized his clothing, watch chain, and cufflinks. Vasilii Mazurin had been the only one with access to the shop, and he was brought from the nearby debtors' prison. He quickly confessed that Kalmykov did visit him the previous June with more than three thousand rubles in cash to be used to redeem the family's pawned jewelry, that he lured him to the empty shop, came up behind the unsuspecting artist, and sliced his throat with the razor.

Mazurin's trial in late November gathered the largest attendance yet in post-reform Moscow.[24] Although Mazurin had confessed to the crime and described it in great detail, observers were puzzled. The defendant was a gentle-tempered man of good character—that is, he led a modest life and did not drink or gamble. Moreover, at the time of his trial he was mortally ill with consumption. Although he personally was bankrupt and confined to the debtors' prison, financial ups-and-downs were as much a part of Moscow's business life as drinking tea, his family was fabulously wealthy, and killing someone for three thousand rubles seemed senseless when it would have been much easier to simply redeem the jewelry using Kalmykov's money and then sell it for a far higher amount. Equally senseless was the murder of a friend whom Mazurin's family had known for more than twenty years and had employed for various financial transactions ("being a wealthy man, he felt ashamed to pawn his property [in his own name] to the Board of Trustees").[25] And yet Mazurin had clearly calculated his actions, and he elaborated his cover-up operations even more. Unable to come up with a didactic lesson focused on Mazurin's character, the case revolved around the question of whether Mazurin intended to kill Kalmykov and had made preparations beforehand. All the evidence clearly showed that he had: he chose a day when none of his relatives or servants would be home, he lured the man into the empty shop with a false story of a document that was stored there, and prepared a special weapon. Afterward he went to great lengths to hide the traces of the crime, all the while forming the impression that there was no break in his daily routines: he visited a local court on behalf of his mother and the next day went to see Kalmykov's brother, wondering where his friend was. Mazurin had time to soak the shop floor in the so-called Zhdanov liquid used in late imperial Russia to fight strong odors, but he was supposedly unable to find a way to dispose of the body because a month later he was arrested for debt.[26] This last point is somewhat difficult to accept, given that Mazurin had enough privacy to commit the murder and hide it even from his servants and, moreover, that debt imprisonment at that time was highly permissive and Mazurin enjoyed regular home visits. It appears that his mother suspected something, at one point commenting on his depressed mood and offering him to unburden his soul. Not surprisingly, Mazurin's lawyer, Kicheev, did not have much of an argument. Apparently a hotshot among Moscow's old-fashioned merchants, he was ridiculed for attempting to read his speech from his notes but did make the best out of a bad situation, asking the jury to take into account Mazurin's confession, which freed from suspicion the numerous male servants in the household, who would otherwise have been arrested and questioned. Mazurin was sentenced to fifteen years of hard labor; given his illness, it is highly unlikely that he survived the trip to Siberia.

Finally, one of the most important and yet most strange murder cases in imperial Russia weighed against each other the opposing motives, or forces, of deliberate, controlled calculation and unstoppable, elemental violence. The Tiflis murder case of 1876 raised numerous questions about the reliability of witness testimony, police corruption, and the daily habits, privacy, and security of elite families, as well as the strong undercurrent of ethnic tensions on the eve of a major war.[27] The victim or assumed victim in this case was Nina Erastovna Andreevskaia, in her early twenties and the daughter of the personal doctor to M. S. Vorontsov, one of the most powerful men in nineteenth-century Russia. Erast Andreevskii was Vorontsov's "gray cardinal," enjoying huge influence and vast wealth in Odessa. His wife, mother to Andreevskaia, was born Princess Tumanova (Tumanian/Tumanishvili, of the old Georgian/Armenian aristocracy). Nina and her mother were visiting Tiflis (Tbilisi), dealing with property arrangements after Erast's death: Erast's children inherited huge estates in Georgia in addition to property back in Odessa. After a few days Nina disappeared from their villa without a trace. One evening she was sitting in a bedroom next to her mother; she stepped outside and never came back. Her outer clothing was soon found neatly folded at the bottom of the river landing next to their villa. Her body was found the next day floating downstream in the Kura River.

Suspicion fell on her brother-in-law, Prince Shervashidze, but he was nowhere near Tiflis and, it was shown, had no direct profit from her death. As part of the investigation the police arrested the caretaker of the villa, Prince Chkhotua, and his brother as well as three servants, who also did not have any possible motive for the murder. The investigator then decided to ignore motive, resulting in several witnesses claiming to have seen mysterious carriages driving through Tiflis. The investigator also attempted to shift the burden of proof to undermine Chkhotua's alibi, but there was no positive proof that he was involved in any way. In the end, the prosecutor's arguments were positively ludicrous.

There was one possible motive for the murder, though. Nina had come to Tiflis with her mother to inspect the vast forest preserve that she had inherited with her siblings. The property was divided: her brother had the villa, and she had the forest. She met with the caretakers and with the peasants who were working on the forest property. At this time she gave them some kind of speech that concerned the abolition of serfdom (Georgia had a very peculiar type of serfdom; it seems that the workers on the estate had no idea what was going on). Nina was described as an intellectually "well-developed" woman (*razvitaia*), dressed like a "nihilist," and was extremely wealthy. Rumors suggested that either she actually was a radical activist or Chkhotua was. If she was a nihilist or was generally believed to be, this alone could have provided a motive to her brother-in-law or any of the others with a stake in the property. She could have been killed to stop her from agitating among the peasants, or to prevent her from diminishing the value of property, or simply to take the property out of her hands.

It is, however, also possible that she simply drowned by accident. There was much discussion during the trial among forensic and landscape experts whether she drowned or was strangled and whether she could have floated down the stream and been found in that particular condition. Some evidence suggested that she was a competent and bold swimmer who had lived by the sea, while others claimed she was shy and cautious. All of this was confusing and impossible to verify (especially today), and most of it frankly sounds bogus. But the effect of making the argument that Nina was dragged to her death by the force of nature diverted the judges' (and the public's) attention away from the people suspected to benefit from Nina's death. Instead of presenting the case in terms of competing rational motives, which must have had something to do with her coming to Tiflis to take over her inheritance, any such motives were subsumed into alternative "natural" theories, whereby the prosecution blamed the local nobleman, Chkhotua, and defense blamed the unpredictable forces of nature, but both sides in effect equated the two.

Because the trial took place in Tiflis, there was no jury, which would probably have acquitted the prince. But the panel of judges convicted Chkhotua of murder and sent him to hard labor. According to memoirs by Nina's niece, a daughter to Yelena and Georgii Shervashidze, Chkhotua was eventually freed after the real killer confessed to the crime.[28] Such confessions happened occasionally in Russian practice; but it is also possible that the "real killer" was paid to confess, as in the Danilov case discussed above (which would not, of course, rule out Chkhotua's innocence). After his conviction, Chkhotua appealed to the Senate and hired Spasovich, one of Russia's best defense lawyers. In other cases, including those involving natural forces (for example, the landmark Ovsiannikov arson case in St. Petersburg in 1876), Spasovich argued for conviction based on very vague evidence.[29] Yet, in this case where evidence was of exactly the same vague variety, Spasovich had no trouble arguing the opposite, elaborating on the theory of a natural death, only hurting his own case by weakening the role of reason and calculation and thus at the same time weakening his best argument: that Chkhotua had no possible motive to commit the murder.[30]

Beginning with Danilov and ending with Landsberg, this series of cases of often exceptionally brutal murders committed by social elites, often with motives unclear or seemingly flimsy, established a cultural model that, while often deplored, came to be familiar, with similar cases after 1879 losing their shock value, instead becoming associated with these very prominent early cases as another of that type: a type that came to define some of the limits of what modern Russian reality could encompass. These cases connected deadly violence with greed, acquisitiveness, and lax financial discipline, but also with a sense of the deadly potential in outwardly respectable or even resplendent young alpha males. Not only was there an apparent pattern of unrestrained, amoral greed from these kinds of perpetrators, they also tended to be met with, if not sympathy, a laxness in response from jurors as much as from the judicial system.

MURDER FROM BELOW

While violent crimes committed by high-status men and women attracted rapt attention from the public, they were numerically very much an exception in the sea of violence within Russia's social underworld. Homicide or violent assault committed by peasants and laborers was still reported in newspapers, sometimes in considerable detail, but such cases became infamous household names only when the victims were either masters (or employers) or close family members, and the crime therefore represented a direct assault on Russia's fundamental social hierarchies. Violence committed by one's dependents in the privacy of a middle-class bourgeois home showed how the daily comforts and power of respectable property owners rested in the most immediate way on the goodwill of trusted servants and other domestics. This trust was easily violated out of greed or anger, revealing the potentially high cost of bourgeois privacy and personal freedom.

Few people could have been more aware of the tension between privacy and personal safety than the victim in the paradigmatic and consequential Russian home-invasion case from 1870.[31] Thirty-two-year-old Prince Louis Charles Marie d'Arenberg was the Austro-Hungarian military attaché in St. Petersburg and a younger brother to the president of the Suez Canal Company (figure 13). The year 1870 was of course an exceptionally sensitive one for European diplomatic affairs, and d'Arenberg was presumably concerned that his servants might be bribed to get into his papers. He came to Petersburg without any servants of his own and rented a large apartment on the ground floor of an aristocratic mansion on Bolshaia Millionnaia Street, next to the Winter Palace and across from the barracks of the Preobrazhenskii Guards. He hired several Russian servants, who always left the apartment for the night, except for one kitchen worker (*kukhonnyi muzhik*), who slept in the kitchen and presumably guarded the back entrance. He came highly recommended and replaced one Gurii Shishkov, who had ended up doing jail time for theft. Despite these precautions, the prince was remarkably careless and did not properly lock the front doors to the building and to the apartment: the building entrance door was unlocked when he was home, and the apartment door was unlocked when he was out.

The capital's high society was shocked when d'Arenberg was found strangled in his own bedroom. The killers had left behind a plate of butter that they must have been eating while lying in wait for the right moment to rob the prince. (They planned to do it when he stumbled home late at night but accidentally woke him up by knocking over some furniture in the dark.) Getting away with some items of relatively little value, the killers failed to open the prince's massive safe that contained his money and his secret diplomatic correspondence.

The tsar himself demanded an hourly report on the investigation, and the crime scene was crowded by various grand dukes, ministers, and legal officials, and of course the Austro-Hungarian ambassador. Given this pressure, the chief of the city's detectives (the famed Ivan Putilin), took only a few hours to locate Shishkov, d'Arenberg's former kitchen help, who quickly confessed and gave up his accomplice, a merchant's son named Petr Grebennikov, who was arrested the next day. Unlike Shishkov, Grebennikov was from a respectable middle-class family and at some point had even worked as a secretary to a legal investigator. Also notable are the killers' ages, twenty-seven and thirty-two, respectively, much more advanced than was common in these kinds of crimes. Because Shishkov knew Arenberg's daily routines, they were able to hide under the staircase until everyone had left for the day.

The trial that took place on 13 May 1870, a mere three weeks after the murder, has the distinction of being one of only two or three individual cases discussed in this book that single-handedly changed Russia's penal law, a process

Figure 13. Prince Louis Charles Marie d'Arenberg. *Vsemirnaia illustratsiia,* 1870 no. 72, p. 357.

that ordinarily took decades to accomplish. The tsar was so incensed at the brazen nature of the crime and the relatively mild punishment imposed by the court (fifteen years of hard labor for each killer) that on the day of the trial he convened a committee of lawyers to immediately toughen the punishment for aggravated murder to include the option of hard labor for life.[32] Of course, Russian tsars held enormous power and intervened in the operations of Russian law in a variety of ways, but they hardly ever directly ordered a specific change in statutory law. The only other time Alexander II did so appears to have been after the trial of Vera Zasulich in 1877, when cases involving attacks on imperial officials were transferred to a special division of the Senate. But that change was procedural and relatively minor. This, however, was a direct change in the penalty for a major crime, seemingly as an expression of the tsar's personal horror at this affront to the safety of even the highest officials.

The second prominent example of a lone-victim murder took place on 10 January 1873. Hieromonk Ilarion was knifed down in his comfortable cell in the Alexander Nevsky Monastery (Lavra) in St. Petersburg.[33] The monk was wealthy and reclusive, and the monastery servants did not bother checking on him until the next afternoon. Upturned property and blood stains everywhere indicated a violent struggle. It was clear that Ilarion fought hard for his life and very nearly escaped. Suspicion immediately fell on the eighteen-year-old peasant Ivan Mikhailov, who at one time had worked in the Lavra as a servant and then moved on to become a switchman on the railroad. Mikhailov attempted to evade pursuit but bungled the effort. In his memoirs the detective Ivan Putilin made his work look much more difficult and mysterious than it actually was. He claimed to have figured out that the killer had been hurt in the attack and ordered all the policemen and gendarmes to look for a suspicious man with a wound. The truth was prosaic and reflected not fancy deduction methods but the old-fashioned police strategy of searching for a suspect's contacts: they quickly located Mikhailov's acquaintance, who told them exactly where to look, and two days later the killer was caught hiding in a pile of firewood at the Okulovka train station on the Petersburg-Moscow railroad, where his brother was then living.

Mikhailov confessed to the murder, and the sole contested legal issue at his trial was whether he had planned the deed or—as he unconvincingly claimed—it was a sudden urge. The members of the jury did not believe that Mikhailov had any other reason to visit Ilarion, who did not like idle guests, or to choose a secretive, roundabout path to his cell at a time when everyone around him was away at a church service. They further wondered why he had carefully crept up behind the monk to attack him and then viciously cut him up, pulled out his beard, tormented him and spilled "rivers of blood," and then carefully plundered his possessions (taking only money and a gold watch and none of the flashy but less valuable trinkets that would easily have gotten him caught), burned his own bloody clothes and put on those he found in the monk's drawer; and when leaving the cell, he carefully locked the door behind him. Anatolii Koni, then a rising star of Russian judiciary, had no trouble persuading the jury to convict Mikhailov, who received thirteen years of hard labor, as opposed to a life sentence, only because he was under twenty-one.

Mikhailov's trial competed for coverage with two other landmark cases examined elsewhere in this book: the Kvitnitskii military-honor case and the political trial of the radical revolutionary Sergei Nechaev. While lacking the rich social context of these two cases, the murder of Ilarion appears nonetheless to have struck a sensitive cord among Russia's upper classes, since Mikhailov, much like d'Arenberg's killers, was a paradigmatic example of an uprooted peasant

Figure 14. Hylarion's murderer, the peasant Ivan Mikhailov from Novgorod province. RGIA, f. 1405, op. 71, d. 587, l. 52.

who went through a succession of jobs and was disorderly enough and demoralized enough to commit a gruesome crime in an effort to instantly improve his material circumstances. As we shall see further below, they are also examples of former servants returning to take advantage of their intimate knowledge of wealthy victims, betraying the trust of former employers.

Even more traumatic invasions of domestic safety were a series of what can be called family-butchery cases, when either entire families were cut down or a murder was perpetrated in the midst of a large family within the privacy of a home by persons enjoying the family's trust. In such cases the assault on the privacy and the protected status of a mid-nineteenth-century bourgeois home was greatly intensified: though living with other people was of course safer than living alone, it amplified the potential harm when danger did come. An early such murder with extraordinary social impact took place on 1 March 1868, in the town of Tambov, southeast of Moscow.[34] The coachman and the nanny who worked for a local merchant, Zhemarin, returned home and were suspicious that no one was answering the locked door.[35] The police came by at the same time as Zhemarin returned from his shop and walked through the house, finding his entire family either shot or bludgeoned to death, including his mother (sixty-seven years old), wife (thirty-two), and two sons (twelve and four), the yardman (thiry-seven), the cook (forty and about to give birth), and the maid (thirty-six). Zhemarin lifted the younger boy's body and carried him to the bed because he was still showing signs of life (he would die the next day). Nothing was stolen from the house, and on the floor there was an iron club made out of a hand scale (*bezmen*). Zhemarin said that he suspected a local high-school student, nineteen-year-old Witold Gorsky, an ethnically Polish Roman Catholic who was tutoring Zhemarin's elder son, Petya, in mathematics and was giving him a lesson when the merchant had gone out earlier in the day. Two witnesses, Gorsky's classmates, said that they had seen him with a loaded revolver. When Gorsky's parents' house was searched, his clothing—coat, boots, and pantaloons—showed extensive traces of blood that someone had tried and failed to wash off. The murder created massive aftershocks in Tambov, with a population of less than forty thousand. For days "huge crowds" gathered outside the site of the murder. At first denying his guilt, after six days Gorsky confessed. The story of his crime is remarkable, first, for the sophisticated way it was carried out, yet with such wildly unnecessary violence, and, second, for the puzzle of Gorsky's motives.

Gorsky claimed that he led a dissolute life and, needing money, he decided to rob Zhemarin. Having tutored Petya for a year and a half, he apparently learned from the boy that the merchant had large amounts of cash in the house. He related in detail that because it would have been difficult to rob the house with so many people around, he decided to kill them first—as if this was a reasonable conclusion. He had a special club made to order, claiming it was for gymnastic exercises. Then he stole a five-shot Colt revolver from his friend's brother, a doctor at the local hospital. On the day of the murder, Gorsky came to Zhemarin's house with a toy gun (*khlopushka*) and taught Zhemarin to shoot it, with the idea of getting the family used to the sound of gunshots. In the afternoon, after Zhemarin had had tea and left for his shop, Gorsky interrupted his lesson with Petya, took out his club, and hit the boy on the side of the head, killing him instantly. He dragged the body into the study and hit it several times more to be sure Petya was dead. He then went to the boy's grandmother and said that Petya had a nosebleed. He let her through the doorway, took out the revolver, and shot her in the back of the head. Next he went into the kitchen, called for the yardman to clean up the tea things, shot him too in the back of the head, and dragged both bodies out of sight. The cook saw this and tried to escape, but Gorsky shot her in the head, striking her cheek. Still, she managed to run out into the yard, but Gorsky caught up to her and killed her with his club, pulling her inside. A short while later, before Gorsky had a chance to rob the house, the mother came back from a visit to the local monastery with the younger son and the maid. They came into the house through the back door. Gorsky was waiting behind the stove, and as soon as the woman took off her coat he shot her in the back of the head with his last bullet. He then tried to shoot the maid, not realizing that he was out of bullets, grabbed a piece of firewood, smashed her skull, and also struck the child twice on the head. At that point, rather than robbing the house and making his escape, as he presumably would have done if robbery was indeed his motive, he instead went to the nearby fitter shop of the 71st Infantry Regiment, where he had one of the soldiers repair the revolver and reload it with bullets. He returned to Zhemarin's house and saw that the nanny and the coachman, who had just returned, were wondering where everyone was and why the door was locked. The nanny assumed that this was done because the cook was giving birth. Gorsky suggested that they go to the stables to warm up, but they refused, thus saving their lives. He then went home and fell asleep, having hidden the gun (so well that it could not be later found), and washed his clothing. Two hours later he was arrested.

Given Gorsky's Polish ethnicity, it is not surprising that many Russians saw a political connection, since only a few years before, in 1863, there was a massive uprising against Russian rule in Poland, and in 1867 the Polish nationalist Antoni Berezowski shot at Alexander II when he was visiting Paris. Indeed, the conservative commentator Mikhail Katkov's editorial decided this was a political case. A secret report from the local Third Section officer about a month after the murder claimed that public opinion in Tambov considered Gorsky's crime a "fruit of his upbringing at home as a Pole fanatically disfavoring the Russians, although he was born in Tambov; and of that lax and negligent supervision and misdirection that has recently distinguished Tambov's provincial *gimnazia* (elite high school), which society primarily blames on Inspector Neslukhovsky, a cunning and duplicitous Pole."[36] Neslukhovsky lost his job running this *gimnazia* after being blamed for recommending Gorsky to Zhemarin as a tutor despite his mediocre academic performance (he had had to repeat a year of school) and his having been caught for petty theft several times. But a proposal by Prince Petr Oldenburgsky (Peter von Oldenburg, in charge of women's education at the time) to ban Neslukhovsky from all subsequent employment in education, including Tambov's women's school, was turned down by Count Shuvalov, the chief of political police, because Neslukhovsky, "by origin from the western provinces and married to a Polish woman, has not revealed a single instance of sympathy for Polish propaganda or any fanaticism of a true Pole (*istogo poliaka*)."[37] More to the point, Neskukhovsky secured his reputation during the uprising of 1863, when he helped the government translate intercepted letters written by the rebels.[38] Prince Oldenburgsky replied that even though there were no facts against Neslukhovsky, he still had an impression of his disloyalty that was "formed by those small daily nuances of life that serve as faithful expressions of internal convictions that are skillfully and diligently concealed." To this Shuvalov replied that he thought the prince was right but he could not ban someone from service based on guesswork.[39]

The tsar ordered that Gorsky be court-martialed. As we have seen, this procedure was occasionally applied in cases of crimes deemed to be exceptionally dangerous, such as deadly home invasions. Alexander II considered court-martialing d'Arenberg's murderers but was persuaded against it. Military courts did not have juries and were considered to be tougher on violent criminals, but in other respects they had all the same protections as civilian courts, such as defense attorneys and the ability to question witnesses. The trial of Gorsky took place on 30 April in a special session of the Moscow military court that came to Tambov and was to sit in the local Noble Assembly. The main hall, which could fit two thousand people, was packed. The public were especially interested because Tambov at that time did not yet have public procedures in ordinary courts.

Gorsky remained calm throughout the proceedings and methodically narrated the entire story of his crime, not leaving out even the tiniest details. Mikhail Katkov's newspaper, *Moskovskie vedomosti,* sent its own stenographer to Tambov and published a complete transcript, which was an exception even for the most celebrated trials of that age. The court sentenced Gorsky to be hanged, and the tsar commuted the sentence to a lifetime of hard labor.[40] As Dostoevsky students and scholars know, sentence commutations in late imperial Russia were typically announced at the last moment after a mock execution, but Gorsky was clearly warned that the tsar had decided to spare his life. The crowd "rather loudly" expressed its dissatisfaction with the tsar's mercy. The gendarmes reported that the locals grumbled and called all the court-martial and public procedures "an empty comedy fit only to entertain children." The officer also noted that just two years previously three people were shot in Tambov for a very similar crime, though it had far fewer victims. If Gorsky had been a commoner, the gendarme officer claimed, he would not have been pardoned, but he was a nobleman and ethnically Polish, and so his "unprecedented outrage went unpunished."[41]

In addition to the way it handled the insinuations of political motives for Gorsky's crime, this case is interesting because it resulted in reprisals against

Gorsky's family, which were extremely rare in late imperial Russia and not applied to family members of the regicides and other exceptionally infamous criminals who were not themselves implicated in the crime. After Gorsky was sent to Siberia, Zhemarin petitioned the local government to expel his parents and siblings from the city.[42] Gorsky's parents, Ludwig and Angelika, his brother, Ludwig, sister, Wanda, and sister-in-law, Ludwiga Dalidovich, were exiled to the tiny town of Kologriv far to the northeast of Moscow. The father, already sick, died in exile, and the sister was freed from police supervision only in 1876, on the condition that she never enter Tambov province.[43] Gorsky's case made a strong impression on the public, and Dostoevsky scholars claim that it gave the first impetus to his future novel *The Possessed.* Clearly the implication of Polish nationalism as a motive captured the public imagination and worried officials at every level, but the evidence does not support it as a factor in the case. At the same time, Gorsky's stated motive—greed—also fails to convince, since the murders, especially the large number of them, are difficult to see as a real logistical necessity, and the elaborate planning and cool execution were all directed toward accomplishing the murders, with theft an apparently unthought-out whim that in fact got neglected when it came down to it. While it would take a novel to even begin to speculate on Gorsky's state of mind, the pattern that links this case to the others discussed in this section is the betrayal of trust by someone employed in the home in an act of violence against family sanctity itself.

This pattern is repeated in yet another infamous provincial murder, known as the Saratov murder case, which took place in the large provincial city on the Volga on 5 October 1871.[44] On that day, a sixteen-year-old student at the local women's high school (*gimnazia*) went to pick up her friend, Tatiana Chetverikova, who lived in the same apartment building and whose father was a well-to-do local merchant. Thinking that Tatiana had slept in and seeing that the door to the apartment was not locked, the girl walked in with her manservant, and inside the foyer they found the body of a woman cook. On the floor was Tatiana's five-year-old sister, still clinging to life and twitching her limbs (she died soon afterward). Behind the stove was the body of Tatiana's mother and next to her the body of Tatiana herself. All of them had been bludgeoned with a heavy blunt instrument, and the entire apartment was covered with blood and brain matter. Money and some jewelry were gone, as was the passport of the Chetverikovs' nineteen-year-old coachman, Andrei Poliakov. It did not take long for the gendarmes to telegraph his description and to arrest a suspicious youth on the train to Moscow, given that he was wearing his master's clothing and had on him more than a thousand rubles in cash. Poliakov quickly admitted to the crime, although he lost his calm and tried to set himself on fire and had to be put in a special padded cell.[45]

Unlike in the Gorsky case, there were no possible political motivations to distract observers, and unlike Gorsky, Poliakov struck the public by his attractive appearance—in an age that connected one's looks with one's character, this must have been particularly discomforting—and by the way he testified "in a quiet and peaceful voice with added hints of sadness." There had been no indication that Poliakov was capable of such violence or rage. Given his social status, he had a good life, and Chetverikov was pleasant to work for. The boy had worked for the family in the past and left because of an illness, then (like the other defendants discussed here) subsequently went to work for Chetverikov again, with the sole purpose of murdering and robbing the family. Like Gorsky, he prepared for the crime with striking care yet allowed himself to be caught through the utmost stupidity, although his escape plan was elaborate enough: to go to the market and hire as a servant—allegedly for his master—another man who looked similar. Poliakov then took the man to a random house, took his passport, allegedly to give it to the owner, and told him to go and fetch his belongings. Needless to say, when the man returned, Poliakov was nowhere to be found, and had his papers.

Poliakov took his time to plan the murder and apparently almost gave up several times. Perhaps the most heartbreaking part of the gruesome tragedy was that Poliakov, after killing Tatiana, her mother, and then the cook, led the little one, Sofia, home by her hand to have tea and killed her inside. Yet the court flatly rejected the defense lawyer's request to examine Poliakov's mental condition, which may have been helpful given his suicide attempt and the vast difference between his affect after the crime and the nature of the crime itself. One possibility that does not seem to have been explicitly discussed at the time was that Poliakov had pretensions to Tatiana's hand—though he was only a peasant, her father was a merchant and not impossibly socially removed, at least not in Poliakov's mind. His violence may have been a response to rejection, an interpretation bolstered by the fact of his having donned Tatiana's father's clothes in his attempted escape, as if trying on what it felt like to be a merchant patriarch.

Poliakov was given twenty years of hard labor instead of a life sentence because of his young age. Aside from his unsuccessful attempt to have Poliakov examined, the lawyer failed to say a single intelligent thing in his speech, only spouting such vague claims as "the unfortunate victims could have died by another's hand or from a fire."[46] The notoriousness of this trial, as of the others, was in the almost unimaginable assault against the very notions of safety or trust linked to the respectable middle-class home.

St. Petersburg's equivalent of the Gorsky and Poliakov cases was the infamous Gusev Alley murder case.[47] It took place nine months before the Gorsky murders, on 4 June 1867 (the trial was delayed until January 1869).[48] Its significance was not so much in that it was a test of the new court system, which by 1869 was reasonably well established, as in the subtle and complex bargaining that took place between the lawyers, the prosecution, the judge, and the jury.[49] The murder was discovered when the police broke into the suspiciously quiet apartment of retired Major Ashmarenkov and his common-law wife, townswoman (*meshchanka*) Grigorieva, finding them bludgeoned to death in their bed. Also dead was their woman servant, while their relative, a teenage schoolboy, who had been spending the night in their living room, was still alive under the couch covered with a bloody sheet; he would die a few days later from his injuries without regaining consciousness. Ashmarenkov's dog was also killed. The entire apartment was covered in blood stains, and behind the stove the police found a bloodied piece of firewood with bits of hair and two clothing irons, also covered in blood.

Ashmarenkov kept his money at home, and there are some indications in the record that he was engaged in moneylending, although in a much more circumspect way than the victims described elsewhere in this chapter. Much of his money was still intact in his bureau. Later, Ashmarenkov's heirs, cleaning out the apartment, found in the side compartment of the kitchen stove a packet with bonds for more than five thousand rubles and a bloodied piece of a woman's shirt. It became immediately clear that the murder was committed by insiders because the doors and the windows were locked and the bureau and the dresser had been carefully opened with a key. The killers did not touch expensive items in plain sight (bronze, ivory, porcelain, and silver knickknacks) but went straight for the compartments with cash and gold items. The police also thought that only someone hoping to come back to the apartment later would hide the packet of money inside the stove.

The building's *dvornik*, his wife, and a laundrywoman were immediately suspected, and some portions of their stories did not add up. But after the piece of the shirt was found in the stove, the police somehow—undoubtedly through an undercover agent—discovered that it belonged to Daria Sokolova, a thirty-five-year-old soldier's wife who lived in a village not far from Petersburg and in the past, ten or eleven years before, had been Ashmarenkov's servant. After leaving his family to care for her father and then getting married, Daria later continued to visit Ashmarenkov because she was friendly with his wife, Grigorieva, who sometimes allowed her to spend the night in the apartment when Daria came to the city to sell her farm's butter and could not make the evening train. The police made a sudden visit to her village, and in her house they found the rest of the shirt, as well as some items from Ashmarenkov's house, including jewelry and a gold watch.

Daria confessed almost immediately, explaining that she woke up in the middle of the night with a "sudden thought" to commit murder, afterward climbing out of the window and taking the first train out of the city. She soon retracted her confession, however, and claimed that the detective had bullied her into incriminating herself by promising that she would be set free if she confessed and by posing as an important official who had the power to do so (a "general," while in fact it was Chief Detective Ivan Putilin). Daria then unconvincingly maintained that she woke up to the sounds of murder and hid under the couch, although she still recognized that one of the two murderers was the building's *dvornik.* She mistakenly grabbed the bag prepared by the killers and fled the apartment.

Daria's story failed to add up, but the same could be said about the other defendants. It is difficult to believe that she could have committed four murders with very heavy objects, carefully and efficiently plundered the apartment, and quickly cleaned herself up without accomplices. The result was, as happened in many other cases with multiple defendants, that the courtroom battle was waged not so much between them and the prosecutor as largely among the defendants' lawyers, none of them belonging to the top tier of the bar. The second day of the trial went into the night, and the jurors only returned with the verdict at six o'clock in the morning after debating for two and a half hours and praying three times before pronouncing their decision. Surprisingly, all the defendants were acquitted of murder, but Daria Sokolova was found guilty of unlawfully appropriating the property of the victims. The lawyer insisted on adding that last point to the list of questions to the jury, no doubt hoping that it would make it easier for the jury to clear her of the murder charge and that she would get a light prison sentence for theft.

The judges, however, in effect nullified the jury's verdict and instead of penalizing Sokolova for theft, applied the article of the penal code that punished accessories to a crime, who were penalized only slightly less than actual participants. Under that article, Sokolova was given twelve years of hard labor, although according to the verdict her crime consisted solely in removing property from the scene of the murder, not in intentionally assisting the killers, which is what being an accessory is supposed to mean. Sokolova's lawyer understandably brought an appeal, but the Senate rejected his arguments, engaging in something that can only be described as verbal gymnastics and extending the definition of an accessory—usually someone intentionally taking the fruits of the crime from the principal—to include someone intentionally altering the scene of the crime and concealing its traces.[50]

Superficially, instances of people murdering for profit seem to be simple, even prosaic: the wealthy kill to become even wealthier, the rest kill to gain wealth. The rights of private property were threatened and even undermined, the masters were made to look vulnerable to attack by the lowliest of servants, of Turgenev's "Gerasims," to use Ilya Gerasimov's imagery.[51] But the cases that attracted attention and set the standard for post-reform Russia reached far beyond this vulgar cliché. Whether carried out by a peer or by a servant, lethal violence attacked the very foundations of post-Napoleonic bourgeois sociability, which rested on personal safety and personal autonomy. Ultimately, personal safety depended on the mutual vulnerability of social actors, and on their mutual trust that underpinned the networks of property ownership and sociability. In short, violent attacks on property rights threatened to unravel the other premises of social stability. On yet another, even deeper level, we see that a murderer's allegedly rational and profit-seeking calculation was ultimately based on emotions, and the reverse. In sum, the very idea that a well-organized nineteenth-century bourgeois society was reliably based on self-interest and rational evaluation, while emotions were safely contained within firmly controlled channels, was compromised.

CHAPTER 6

Striking for Honor

A major but subsequently forgotten murder trial in 1874 debated Russia's cultural models of violence in exceptionally rich detail. It involved the first widely publicized honor killing in modern Russia, roughly equivalent to the French Henriette Caillaux case of 1914.[1] The murder took place in November 1873, when Nikolai Nepenin, a thirty-six-year-old retired officer of the imperial general staff then serving as a justice of the peace in the remote Novorzhevsk district, and his twenty-seven-year-old wife, Evgenia, came to the St. Petersburg apartment of their old acquaintance, a retired civil servant, Petr Chikhachev (also serving as a justice of the peace). Before walking into the building, Nepenin handed his loaded revolver to Evgenia. A heated argument with Chikhachev led to a physical fight, and Nepenin—a devotee of weapons and martial exercises—expertly struck his opponent in the chest with a knife. The building's *dvornik* was nearby and ran into the apartment, having heard the commotion. He pulled Evgenia away, but not before she fired at Chikhachev twice, missing both times. Chikhachev died the next day from the knife wounds.[2]

Before killing Chikhachev, the couple had engaged in a veritable manhunt for about five months, after Evgenia had confessed to her husband her brief premarital affair with the older and unhappily married Chikhachev, a local nobleman whose family was much wealthier and had been established in the area since the sixteenth century. The lethal outcome of this story was unusual but not unique. Men and women in the nineteenth century attacked and even killed each other to avenge an insult, a sexual impropriety, or a broken promise—wrongs for which there was no official recourse. People do these things today as well, but nineteenth-century courts, juries, and the public regarded them far more seriously and even sympathetically. This chapter discusses several prominent trials for honor-motivated violence, dividing them into two categories. In the first set of cases, including that of the Nepenins, honor violations infringed on individuals' physical and especially sexual autonomy and integrity. The second set addressed more abstract damage to masculine reputation and social standing, in which any physical altercation was of only symbolic significance. Taken together, these cases show that the new courts in post-reform Russia reconstructed and reenacted the culture of honor-instigated violence among elites undergoing a massive transformation, and as in other fin-de-siècle societies, the condemnation of extrajudicial violence was highly contingent.

Nineteenth-century rules of honor have been described in the French context as an "invisible code," which was distinct from the codified formal law but equally impactful in the daily relations of the respectable classes. The informal code of honor was invisible, according to William Reddy, because "official ideology did not sanction it as an explicit value," and it was primarily articulated in the breach.[3] In the American context, Martha Merrill Umphrey's account of Henry K. Thaw's 1906 "trial of the century" with facts virtually identical to those of the Nepenins' case also counterposes the code of honor to formal law, although to her the social strictures of honor were much more explicit and tangible. She even applies Bakhtin's notion of the carnivalesque, that is, a temporary forceful inversion of established hierarchies (of the presumed primacy of written laws over unwritten ones).[4] My review of court cases about honor-inspired violence confirms that the rules of honor were of course not enunciated the same way formal laws were, but at the same time shows that the informal rules became quite visible during courtroom proceedings and vigorously competed with the default legal norms. Trial observers and participants summarized the norms and practices of honor and weighed them against legal rules, and eventually even wrote them down in published and widely disseminated trial accounts. Despite their ambiguous status, the rules of honor were central to conceptualizing the problems of gender roles, violence, and personal autonomy that underpinned the practices of criminal justice. Russia and many other countries had another, better-known set of informal laws, those of peasant farmers, who apparently punished certain types of offenses differently from the regular courts.[5] But the upper classes had their own equivalent of customary law, focusing on similar issues, for instance those of sexual propriety, also similarly open to interpretation and mythmaking, and ultimately similarly crucial for understanding the impact of state-made, official law, which custom purported to transgress or ignore.[6]

The "invisible" rules of nineteenth-century elites were of several varieties. For women, honor meant above all their own sexual and gender conformity, which were of course frequently challenged and redefined. Male honor meant courage and even ferocity, a man's readiness to spring up without notice to react with violence to avenge transgressions against himself or his dependents, in particular those committed by his peers or even superiors. In some celebrated cases, women were known to adopt a more forceful position and personally use violence to avenge insults to themselves or even to other persons—though such insults were generally related to physical or sexual autonomy.[7] For both men and women, honor also meant gentility, generosity, self-sacrifice, integrity, and fairness, especially toward one's social inferiors. Respectable life depended upon sensitivity to others' opinions and an ability and willingness to conceal certain failings on the part of oneself and one's friends and close relatives. Certain aspects of life had to remain nonpublic, and a dishonorable exposure was prone to provoke a violent retaliation. In the Russian context, the scenario of a passionate but premeditated violent outburst avenging a wrong is best remembered from the 1878 case of Vera Zasulich, who shot and wounded an important tsarist official and blazed the trail for subsequent populist terror. But this chapter argues that the Zasulich trial can be appropriately understood only in the larger context of post-reform legal practice, suggesting that the case cleverly deployed themes and tactics that were well known at the time, and that while the outcome was widely reported as unexpected, it was anything but surprising.

THE BODY, SEX, AND ANGER: SHOOTING THE TIES THAT BOUND

Post-emancipation Russia witnessed a number of high-profile trials of elite, generally young women who killed or injured to avenge an insult. The circumstances of the insult varied, usually involving romantic betrayal, but in every case the act to be avenged had in some way prevented the attacker—or in a few cases someone close to her—from enjoying the customarily accepted practice of gendered family and sexual life. In such trials, the facts of the attack itself were rarely in question. The inquiry focused instead on the character and prior actions of everyone involved, including the victim. Social, political, and economic circumstances were analyzed at length and often found to have negated or reduced the defendant's culpability for the crime. Such practice was very much in line with the contemporary fashion for positivist criminology, seeking the driving forces of crime in social and economic conditions. And yet, as we have seen, positivism did not directly contradict the earlier, Enlightenment-era theory of criminality, which presumed that the criminal acted voluntarily but which allowed for circumstances that could negate that presumption. The new positivist view accepted this idea and then elaborated further complexity onto it.

Evgenia Nepenina's personality and past history became the focus of her and her husband's trial, which opened in 1874 and attracted intense public attention. Although she came from poor provincial gentry, her sister worked as a music teacher at the elite Smolny Institute in Petersburg and was able to obtain a place there for Evgenia.[8] The institute provided young noblewomen with the polish and social connections that went a great deal toward ensuring a good marriage. Soon after her graduation Evgenia married Nepenin, a local nobleman and social activist who was well regarded for his honesty but was also resented for his nasty character and tendency to anger. But five years later Evgenia told her husband that soon after graduating from Smolny she was staying in her brother's house and that while she was visiting there Chikhachev had seduced and raped her.

Nepenin had harbored lingering doubts about his wife's innocence on their wedding day, but after about five years of living together his suspicions grew, and it appears that it was his daily psychological pressure that induced her to finally confess. Nepenin then claimed that he did not believe his wife's account, and the couple staged a face-to-face confrontation with Chikhachev, cornering him at a local tavern and forcing him to admit to a relationship with Nepenina and, according to one version of the story, to raping her. To her husband's reported amusement, Evgenia then told Chikhachev that the appropriate action for him was to kill himself, giving him five minutes to make the decision. Chikhachev—a lecherous but sociable man unfamiliar with the culture of violence and weapons—was shocked, but he succeeded in getting away from the tavern. He quickly left the province and managed to avoid the Nepenins for the next five months, while the couple wrote him three extremely abusive and threatening letters accusing him of dishonor and cowardice. Nepenin repeatedly challenged him to a duel, which Chikhachev refused, although he did make a half-hearted attempt to learn to shoot a gun with the help of his military brother-in-law, von Raaben. Still, Chikhachev had only ever fired fifteen to twenty shots in his life; a duel with Nepenin would be as sure a death for him as being murdered directly.

Nepenin's anger grew exponentially during the final month or two before the murder, and he also began to severely beat and abuse his wife. It appears to have been largely an accident, however, that Nepenin then needed to visit Petersburg to testify in a disciplinary proceeding against another judge, from Pskov. One may suppose that if not for this coincidence, Evgenia might have become his victim instead of Chikhachev. As it was, Nepenin could not resist the urge to drop by the house that belonged to Chikhachev's sister, although the police address clerk had told him that Chikhachev was not staying there but had gone to Moscow. Nepenin did not believe this and decided to check for himself. When, to the couple's surprise, Chikhachev was found at his sister's house and agreed to see them, Nepenin said that the reason for his visit was to repeat his challenge to a duel. When Chikhachev once again refused, Nepenin slapped or punched him so hard that he fell. It appears that at this point Nepenin took out his knife and stabbed Chikhachev in the chest. Several other people then ran into the room, including the *dvornik,* Chikhachev's brother-in-law, Popov, as well as von Raaben, who subdued the Nepenins.

While the murder was witnessed by several people and the trial did not debate any significant questions of fact, the Nepenins were defended by two of Petersburg's finest lawyers, Spasovich (representing the husband) and Vladimir Gerard (representing the wife). The trial became an in-depth examination of the lives, emotions, and characters of what the weekly *Nedelia* described as Russia's "average people" (*srednie liudi*). Everyone involved belonged to the old but not exceptionally wealthy provincial Russian nobility whose culture is known both from Russian fiction and from recent archival studies.[9] These people enjoyed a comfortable lifestyle even after they lost their serf villages in the emancipation and had many lifestyle options: they often pursued civil or military service careers but could also engage in social activism (like Chikhachev and Nepenin) and in commercial or intellectual pursuits. Most of these former residents of "gentry nests," to borrow Turgenev's phrase, did not end up like the persons in this case. But it was also obvious that the Nepenins, Chikhachev, and all their friends and relatives were indeed ordinary. Having affairs before or during marriage was not unheard of in that culture, for men or for women, even though Nepenin acted as if ideal Victorian morality was binding on him and everyone else. Challenges to a duel—and refusals to fight—also happened regularly.[10] Nepenin's rage and persistence were extreme but not unheard of, nor was the culture of concealment practiced by Evgenia and others. Finally, knifing someone in a fight was not unique either, though more expected in tavern brawls than in genteel living rooms.[11] At best we can say that Nepenin's exceptionally pugnacious personality brought all these challenges and complications to a particularly high boil.

What did honor mean to everyone involved? Nepenin was on a campaign to clean up local politics, specifically to improve transparency in government. The fact that his wife had concealed an important secret was an insult to his entire way of thinking. It appeared to him as though Evgenia and Chikhachev had been laughing at him. The more socially acceptable way to handle this situation would have been to challenge Chikhachev to a duel and perhaps beat him up if he refused; this should have happened during the first confrontation and ended the story. But one legal observer made a different claim: that Nepenin's actions reflected a clever calculation rather than or in addition to an irrational urge. While prone to sudden anger and rather misanthropic, Nepenin was above all a man of business (Chikhachev had at one point asked him for investment advice). One witness even suggested in a letter to Chikhachev, written long before the murder, that Nepenin was engaged in this manhunt for the sole purpose of getting rid of his wife.[12] The witness thought that Nepenin would force his wife to kill Chikhachev because she would be treated more leniently by the jury and likely be acquitted, but, Nepenin allegedly planned, if she were instead convicted, he would be rid of her and become free of a permanent insult to his sense of honor. Nepenin of course would never confirm this story, but it is striking that he gave his wife the gun but not the knife when they went to see Chikhachev.

From Chikhachev's perspective, honor meant above all preserving bourgeois proprieties, which included keeping secrets. It appears that he was unable or unwilling to keep entirely silent, however, and leaked information about his relations with Nepenin's wife to several of his friends and even to his own estranged wife. The Nepenins themselves also contributed to spreading the rumor by openly cornering him in a tavern in a busy commercial village. The second element of honor for Chikhachev was willingness to fight a duel. At one point he seriously contemplated doing so and even took the one shooting lesson from von Raaben. But it appears that self-interest and practicality triumphed on this point, too, as it was too apparent he could not hope to survive a fight with a former military officer who loved weapons. Finally, Chikhachev's relationships with and treatment of women was an important third component; the honorable way to behave was above all not to treat respectable women as if they were prostitutes, and vice versa. (Lechery alone was not considered dishonorable.) Here Chikhachev again failed completely. On the one hand, he treated prostitutes in a "knightly" way and even tended to take his fellow judges and court personnel to places where they would meet prostitutes. Conversely, he had treated young Evgenia as if she were a girl of easy virtue and not an innocent recent graduate of the most elite cloistered women's school in Russia, under the close attention of the imperial family. Even if she had made the first move and invited him into her room where she was lying in bed in her undershirt, Chikhachev was obligated to resist the temptation. While several men testifying during the trial and even the prosecutor said openly that anyone in Chikhachev's position would have taken advantage of the girl, this assumption of brainlessness and crudity in "any man" is interesting. Several people also noted that Chikhachev appears to have behaved as if he were sleeping with a prostitute and acted in a mechanistic way, using an unspecified but "utterly revolting method of precaution."

Nepenina's honor took the biggest assault not only over the several years of her post-Smolny life but even more so during the trial. Both defense lawyers presented her as a person of reduced intelligence, warped partly by the cloistered education of the Smolny Institute, but more so by her subaltern status within Smolny, expressed not in material discomforts but in reduced attention given to her by teachers and governesses. As Yulia Sofronova has observed, Smolny's customs in the 1860s maintained virtually intact the bygone culture of the early nineteenth century with its exaggerated sentimentality and somewhat freer sexual expression compared to the late Nicholaevan era.[13] The effect was allegedly that Evgenia was, first, completely ignorant of the dangers presented by lecherous older men; second, had a certain easiness of manners that caused her not to doubt the propriety of receiving visitors *en negligée;* and third, that her mind was filled with romantic nonsense drawn from light romantic fiction. This story is difficult to accept, especially, as one commentator noticed, since she would not have been taught at Smolny to undress in front of strange men. But Evgenia may have learned from her romantic novels or from her Smolny friends that aristocratic ladies received visitors in often outright risqué garments, and she was possibly imitating aristocratic culture, which she was allowed to taste at Smolny but not allowed to fully participate in. None of this is of course to discard the possibility that she simply wanted to seduce Chikhachev or to play at seducing him.

In addition to a defective upbringing, the legal observers of the weekly *Nedelia* thought that ultimate blame for the tragedy belonged to the double standard of Russia's gender roles. Women were brought up to be ignorant but sensuous, and they were constrained only by threats to their reputation and other such external superficial rules (as one writer put it, all Evgenia had was "the fear of publicity as a bridle, and sentimentality to sweeten things up"). Men, however, did not experience such restrictions and were free to indulge in romantic love before marriage, as long as they did not mix their respectable and their "outside" life and properly discarded their romantic partner as soon as a suitable marriage was arranged.[14]

Nepenina's acquittal can be explained in part by the fact that her gunshots had missed their target. Yet the model of women avenging their honor with violence and being subjected to a criminal trial continued in subsequent years, leading to some of the most iconic legal scandals in Russian history. One case involved Anastasia Kairova (1844–1888), who in her younger years had been a secretary at a leading Petersburg newspaper and cohabited with no less than Anatolii Koni's father, Fedor Koni, an important scholar, editor, playwright, and theater critic. Having become disappointed in her life in the capital, Kairova joined a theatrical troupe in faraway Orenburg, where she entered into a relationship with the theater owner, Vasilii Velikanov. In 1875 the theater became bankrupt, and the couple moved to Petersburg in hopes of using Kairova's connections to enter the capital's theatrical world. Very soon they were joined by Velikanov's wife, also an actress, who intended to win her husband back. Kairova at first agreed to surrender him, but on the night of 8 July she sneaked into the Velikanovs' suburban dacha and slashed her competitor's throat with a razor. Velikanova was not seriously injured, and Kairova did not attempt to flee. She was quickly arrested and spent almost a year in a mental hospital before going on trial for attempted murder. Given the nature of the case, Kairova faced a long sentence of hard labor, and, as Olga Makarova has argued, the trial could have severely damaged the ascendant career of Anatolii Koni. Makarova plausibly suggests that the trial was carefully prepared and even manipulated by Koni, by the influential newspaper editor Aleksei Suvorin, the defense lawyer Evgenii Utin, and the chairman of the St. Petersburg District Court, Vladimir Likhachev, all of whom were tied in a knot of personal and business relationships.[15] With the help of testimony about Kairova's family history of mental illness, she was acquitted, though apparently by the smallest margin (the jurors' votes split in half, resulting in acquittal). She went on to become one of Russia's leading journalists and covered the Russo-Ottoman War of 1877–1878 at considerable personal risk.

Another landmark trial with similar facts involved the nineteen-year-old noblewoman Praskovia Kachka, who led a bohemian life in Petersburg full of Marx and poetry but was abandoned by her student lover, whom she proceeded to shoot to death in 1879. Since there was nothing particularly adverse in her life circumstances, her defense by Fedor Plevako focused on her family's history of mental disease and alcoholism, making one of the most forceful connections between crime and heredity in the post-reform courtroom. But at the very end of his speech Plevako made the somewhat different argument that the jurors represented Russia, which was Kachka's only and true family, and urged them to accept her, thus turning a psychiatric argument into a social and emotional one. In the end, Kachka was not "acquitted," as some literature has maintained, but sentenced to confinement at a mental institution, which was of course a radically different and rather grim outcome compared to Kairova's case.[16]

The Kachka trial took place soon after the acquittal of Vera Zasulich for a shooting that looked superficially similar. This timing may account for the fact that the questions for the jury were worded in a way that prevented the possibility of Kachka being acquitted outright. As noted already, the Zasulich case is the one trial in late imperial Russia that is known to all students of Russian history, because of its role in the development of Russia's radical movement and for the way it allegedly undermined the achievements of the judicial reform of 1864. A twenty-nine-year-old anarchist and former follower of Sergei Nechaev, Zasulich was a political assassin who shot and wounded the St. Petersburg governor General Fedor Trepov. The exact reasoning of the men who gathered in the jury room to acquit her of attempted murder on 31 March 1878 will of course never be known, but the outcome itself was not at all surprising in its contemporary context. There were many trials for murder or attempted murder during the late 1860s and 1870s in which a sympathetic young woman seen to have acted out of passion to avenge her honor was acquitted, or at least not convicted of murder despite clear evidence that she in fact had done the deed: in addition to the cases of Nepenina, Kairova, and Kachka, other chapters in this book discuss those of Volokhova, Dmitrieva, and Jujean. While Zasulich would certainly have been convicted by a special tribunal for crimes against the state, the government insisted on treating her case as an ordinary attempted murder tried by a jury.[17] Since Sergei Nechaev had been convicted quickly and easily by a jury in 1873, and since Zasulich's actions were not in question, conviction was a reasonable expectation from the government's point of view. But Zasulich's defense attorney presented the case as that of honorable violence to avenge the illegal flogging of a political prisoner, Bogolepov, on General Trepov's orders. Even though this insult was not administered directly to Zasulich, and she was not acquainted with Bogolepov, the case succeeded in presenting Zasulich as victim to similar administrative heavy-handedness (due to her earlier involvement with Nechaev's group). Moreover, the case's focus on a flogging, that is, a physical violation of the body, likewise helped Zasulich, because it turned a dispute over abstract ideological and political doctrines into a one about a violation of Bogolepov's physical integrity, and from this perspective there was nothing particularly fantastical to a jury in her violent reaction.[18] After the shooting, the assumption among the Petersburg public was that Zasulich had had a romantic relationship with Trepov (which was not the case, but the jump to conclusions is revealing of how the public viewed the case very differently from the government and, as it happens, from the actual facts). Thus, Zasulich was acquitted even though her behavior was quasi-masculine in defending her own honor by defending that of another person. The stretch was that the other person was completely unrelated to her.

When the relationship between the avenger and the protected party was clear, the case would be clearer too. Consider briefly the 1877 case of a major-general's widow, Elena Aleksandrovich, who attempted to shoot a nobleman (a gentleman of the chamber of the imperial court) who inappropriately courted her seventeen-year-old daughter and tried to induce her to elope with him. Aleksandrovich actually challenged her daughter's failed suitor to a duel, apparently because she decided that she could not jeopardize her son's career in the military by allowing him to do so.[19] The jury in the town of Tula acquitted Aleksandrovich, even though the victim's renowned lawyer, Lokhvitskii, gave one of his most unethical and most ludicrous performances in viciously attacking the widow and her daughter.

OFFICERS AND GENTLEMEN

In addition to family-related disputes, another context where tensions between individual autonomy and corporate rules—and the power of rumor and social reputation—triggered violence was the vast and highly structured world of Russia's civil and military officialdom. The civilian bureaucracy in imperial Russia was divided into ministries that were ultimately responsible directly to the tsar and that engaged in vigorous interagency conflicts and rivalries. The larger ministries, like Interior or Finance, were themselves divided into departments that functioned like mini empires feuding with each other. The military too was divided into branches of service, into imperial guard versus regular troops, and into several hundred individual regiments with their own histories, traditions, and rivalries. The fragmented nature of the imperial bureaucracy is well known to historians, but as Kirill Soloviev has argued it should not be exaggerated.[20] Despite the rivalries, civil and military officers were united by their common loyalty to the tsar, by shared educational experiences, and by a common ethos of service (which of course had its variations but also important common principles). Given this context, it is not surprising that civil servants and officers alike were not especially eager to publicize their scandals, whether they involved physical altercations or promotion conflicts (or embezzlement, which I discuss later in the book). But in the early post-reform period this was exactly what happened. True civil servants rather than the fictional ones depicted by Gogol or Sukhovo-Kobylin featured in many of the earliest "great" criminal trials. These cases explicitly pitched the corporate interests of a service agency and the people running it against the personal honor and autonomy of their subordinates and families. The very meaning of interests—whose should prevail in a conflict, who had the right to personal interest—was under contestation as the Great Reforms vastly expanded and complicated bureaucracy in the name of greater individual participation within the state and society.

The first jury trial involving a conflict among civil servants indicted a junior official from St. Petersburg named Nikolai Protopopov; it was also one of the very first major jury trials in Russia in general, taking place on 22 March 1867. It is still remembered today for its role in the development of Russian legal and forensic psychiatry, and thus we understand what the case meant to medical and legal experts.[21] Here I look more closely at the incident that gave rise to the case and at what it may have meant to the persons involved.[22]

On 4 July 1866, Protopopov walked into the office of Count Koskul, a senior official but not his immediate supervisor, had a short verbal altercation and then struck him once or twice on the face, after which other bureaucrats ran in and pulled him away. Protopopov walked out on his own and was later arrested. He was thirty-nine years old and had served the tsar for twenty-three years; he was reported to be diligent, good tempered, and of "splendid" conduct. His place of service was the Department of Foreign Religious Confessions of the Ministry of the Interior, supervising the numerous non-Orthodox faiths throughout the vast Russian Empire.

Given his length of service and good record, Protopopov was promised the position of assistant section head (*pomoshchnik stolonachal'nika*), which, as often happens in the world of office intrigue, went instead to a young aristocrat, Count Komarovsky. Around the same time, an anonymous libelous pamphlet (*paskvil'* [pasquil]) about Protopopov circulated around the office, alleging unspecified misconduct for which other officials had recently been fired. Described as "perverse conduct" (*porochnoe povedenie*), it likely meant homosexual contacts, for which Russian officials were occasionally dismissed and imprisoned.[23] Protopopov was unmarried in middle age, and other types of allegation can be ruled out: financial misbehavior could get one fired but would not be called a *porok,* while drinking could be labeled *porok* but was unlikely to get one fired and would in any case have been made explicit, as it often was. The indictment claimed that Protopopov came to believe that Count Koskul was the pamphlet's author. The pamphlet itself was destroyed by the department head, Sievers; neither he nor Koskul attended the trial, and so they could not be asked whether the accusation had any influence on the decision not to promote Protopopov. But both Sievers and Koskul admitted that the pamphlet did exist. Also, Sievers apparently told Protopopov when promising him the promotion that he paid no attention to the libel. In addition to being incensed by the pamphlet, Protopopov was angered by Koskul's reaction to his visit: the count "expressed his utter contempt for him with a shout 'Whaaat?! (*chto-o*?!)'" and may have called him a scoundrel (*negodiai*).

A leading legal journalist, Aleksandr Liubavskii, who published a transcript of the case, argued that the "principles of service hierarchy and service subordination that are so important in a state" were at stake.[24] That much is true. Cases like this, however, were not exceptional before, during, or after the Great Reforms. Government officials and military officers were constantly punched, slapped, and insulted by their peers, superiors, subordinates, and unrelated private citizens. Count Koskul was fairly high up in the service hierarchy but not exceptionally important. Liubavskii himself did not see anything strange in the fact that Protopopov would have felt slighted and hit his superior; the journalist argued that it would have been stranger if Protopopov had punched someone completely unrelated to his service or if Koskul was actually his benefactor rather than an enemy.

Yet soon after the incident this prosaic office conflict was transformed into something else entirely, as Protopopov claimed insanity in one of the first such episodes in the history of post-reform Russian law. He obtained the services of one Dr. Chekhov, who gathered evidence from Protopopov's family, finding that his mother was hysterical with a mental disorder and one of his sisters was mentally disabled (*poloumnaia*), while Protopopov himself had insomnia, dizziness, and headaches following a recent bout of typhus. His other sister testified that on the day of the incident with Koskul her brother was in a strange state, so that she had to hide his uniform; but he donned some random pieces of clothing and went out anyway. No doubt coached by Dr. Chekhov, Protopopov testified during his trial that he actually intended to hit his supervisor, Sievers, who was out of the office on that day, and that he did not even know Koskul and had no animosity toward him; Koskul simply happened to be in Sievers's office at the wrong time.

Protopopov was exceptionally agitated on that day. Other doctors did not agree with Chekhov's conclusions, but since Protopopov was not examined on the day of his episode their testimony was not more influential than Chekhov's. One physician who was present during the first interrogation of Protopopov said that he appeared completely normal and completely aware of what he was doing. When another doctor was asked whether it was possible to incriminate Protopopov, he merely responded that this was a legal question and not a medical one. Finally, a Dr. Meidel testified that it was possible to understand that one's action is illegal but at the same time be in an affective fit.

Other witness testimony adds important nuance to the case, turning it in my view into something other than a medicalized narrative of a raving underground man or an instance of frustrated personal interest.[25] The two officials who were standing just outside the office where the attack took place testified that after Protopopov came out following the attack, he said, according to Secretary Moravin, that "such scoundrels must be thrashed" (*takikh podletsov sleduet bit'*), and the other official, Chelnokov, reported Protopopov saying, "Gentlemen, be my witnesses that I thrashed him." This sounds like an honor attack, and it would not be surprising if these two junior bureaucrats were standing there in the role of seconds to Protopopov, to witness how he had redeemed his honor. The entire story seems to come straight out of studies of the duel in Russia and its relation to the culture of honor, where a refusal to honor a promise resulted either directly in a challenge to a duel or in a violent physical attack, which could then have resulted in a challenge.

Finally, there appears to have been some collusion between the various participants in the case.[26] Like all important trials, this one involved complex negotiations among the many participants in the case that were closely observed by the jurors before they engaged in their own discussion. The prosecutor's speech was exceptionally short and lacking in content. He merely said that Protopopov admitted to striking Koskul and that he was clearly aware of his actions.

Protopopov's attorney was the extraordinarily talented Konstantin Khartulari, who argued that since Protopopov had been approved for promotion roughly twenty times in the past, something unusual must have happened, such as the ridiculous belief that Sievers believed the pamphlet and for this reason denied him the promised position, while in fact neither Sievers nor Koskul needed a pamphlet, or indeed any explanation, to deny Protopopov a promotion at any moment or to fire him altogether.[27] The chairman of the court at that point interrupted Khartulari, asserting that he was drawing inappropriate conclusions, but the effect of such interruptions in this and other cases seems to have been merely to draw the jurors' attention to what the lawyer had already succeeded in conveying. Khartulari in effect used the power of the chairman against the prosecution by making him, through his interruptions, add emphasis to all the most important points. Finally, the lawyer also discussed Protopopov's bad heredity, leading to his famous phrase, "Punishment is inconceivable where medical treatment is needed instead." The crowd started to applaud and was warned by the chairman. After Khartulari had discussed Protopopov's family, how much he cared for his mother and his sisters and how they would be ruined by his conviction, the prosecutor attempted to respond but instead actually helped him: "Of course, most family members upon the defendants' conviction are in a rather pathetic condition. But this circumstance must not have any influence for the court."[28]

In the end, Protopopov gave a cryptic last statement supporting the argument that this was above all an honor attack. He said that he had no feelings of honor toward Koskul because he had suffered this abuse for ten years and Koskul had been appointed barely three years previously and had no power over promotions. He said, "This is what I am guilty of: I am someone who has had a service position, worked diligently for twenty-three years and for the last ten years not getting any [additional] remuneration for the [extra tasks] I was assigned, so that ten years of service were lost for me, and suddenly I was hit on the head as if with a stick with this pamphlet, then I lost my mind and don't remember what I did. This is my fault and nothing else." Protopopov also said that he had been denied a promotion about twenty times but that this meant nothing to him because he lived not from his service "but from outside activities." In other words, he had an independent source of income and was not the pathetic petty Petersburg civil servant (*chinovnik*) described in Gogol's fiction; rather, he was a well-educated and genteel individual, given that he had been home schooled and knew foreign languages. But the difference in this last incident, Protopopov said, was that his "honor was insulted when they showed the pasquinade (*paskvil'*) to those persons who were my patrons and had a good opinion about me." Moreover, when Protopopov's uncle, the court surgeon Yenokhin, wanted to petition on his behalf, he was not believed, and his letter was not forwarded to appropriate persons, whereas the pasquil was (this, incidentally, supports the suggestion that Protopopov was accused of homosexual behavior, since a surgeon's testimony was important). The chairman then interrupted Protopopov: "You are claiming that Count Sievers showed the pasquil with the intention of publicizing it. You therefore accuse him of a dishonorable action. You are not allowed to say that." Protopopov responded: "Am I allowed to speak the truth?"[29]

The jury took half an hour to acquit him; the members of the public burst into applause and were expelled from the courtroom. Neither Protopopov nor anyone else involved in the case had any political ideas, and they did not intend to criticize the way the tsar's government operated. Yet many people seem to have interpreted the case as undermining the service hierarchy and subordination. The government appealed all the way to the Senate, in effect accusing the judges of gross incompetence in the way they conducted the case, but it lost the appeal, most likely because the judges, then busy establishing new courts and procedures, were also sensitive to interagency rivalries and challenges. The government still expelled Protopopov from the city, however, using its police powers.

The conflicts between individual honor and corporate solidarity and between violent rage and rational calculation (often difficult to distinguish) that were revealed in the Protopopov case were highlighted even more strongly in another case that began as a prosaic personal conflict yet became a cause celèbre of the imperial military on the eve of the landmark military reform of 1874. Just as the other cases discussed in this book revealed the inner workings of the bourgeois family or the modern capitalist market, the travails of Captain Erast Kvitnitskii exposed the most elite tsarist military officers as operating like a bunch of juveniles.[30]

The story began with Colonel Khlebnikov, who commanded a battery in the Horse Artillery Brigade of the imperial guards. Like the Sapper Battalion, the horse artillery was the crème de la crème among the tsar's elite soldiers, its officers requiring excellent horsemanship and the intelligence to operate guns and explosives, as well as the connections and the social skills to participate in the functions and rituals of the imperial court. On 26 November 1872, Khlebnikov returned from being presented to the tsar at the Winter Palace and took a carriage with his wife down Nevsky Avenue to pay a social visit to another officer, who lived on the corner of the Fontanka Embankment and Nevsky. That officer was not home, and Khlebnikov started to walk down the stairs to exit the building when another figure suddenly appeared on the staircase. It was Khlebnikov's former subordinate, Staff Captain Kvitnitskii, who had recently transferred to another battery of Guards Horse Artillery stationed in Warsaw. The reason for the move was his poor relations with fellow officers, with Khlebnikov being one of the leaders of the anti-Kvitnitskii movement. Matters became so aggravated that Kvitnitskii challenged his former commander to a duel, but

Khlebnikov refused to fight. Now Kvitnitskii again asked Khlebnikov whether he was willing to fight, and once again he refused. Kvitnitskii then bared his sword and struck him on the head with the flat part, and again on the arm, with which Khlebnikov tried to protect himself. The colonel ran outside shrieking for the police. Kvitnitskii followed him out and drove away in a cab to brigade headquarters, where he turned himself in. Khlebnikov went to his barracks and had a "hysterical fit" that lasted for about an hour, during which he lay on the couch, "shaking and banging his feet against the divan."[31] He was so traumatized that he could not leave his home for ten days.

Violent fights between officers were nothing extraordinary in any nineteenth-century military, yet the way the authorities chose to deal with this case was novel and in step with the prevailing reformist spirit of their moment. Instead of quietly firing or demoting Kvitnitskii, he was subjected to a public court-martial in Petersburg, which took place on 8 and 9 February 1873. Aside from the spirit of the age, this may have happened because the top brass could not agree on a single policy, creating a miniature Russian version of the future French Dreyfus case. The war minister, General Dmitrii Miliutin, wanted to punish Kvitnitskii in an exemplary fashion to protect military discipline. The aristocratic party dominating the guards and the grand dukes, however, sympathized with Kvitnitskii, who had graduated from the Page Corps, the most elite military school in Russia; his three brothers were or were going to be high-ranking officers, and his father had been a general who distinguished himself during the 1830–1831 Polish revolt. Tsar Nicholas I had a particular sympathy for those Polish officers who remained loyal to the Crown despite their nationality. Kvitnitskii himself had a medal for action against the Polish uprising of 1863–1864.

This impeccable pedigree ensured that Kvitnitskii had many supporters and would get a fair trial (aside from the fact that a court-martial was not an institution that tended to impose lenient penalties). In addition to the wealth of detail about the inner workings of the imperial army that closely resembles the quasi-fictional works of Aleksandr Kuprin from the early twentieth century, the trial of Kvitnitskii is a poignant narrative of a talented individual struggling against the mass of gilded mediocrity. Given that Kvitnitskii's actions were not in question, the trial, like so many other "great" trials, focused on the excruciating detail of daily lives, social relations, and motivations of Kvitnitskii and his fellow officers. In the process, the trial revealed the same tension between personal honor, emotion, and calculating material interest that is so noticeable in the cases discussed in the rest of this chapter.

The case could have focused on Kvitnitskii's emotions and mental state and have presented him as Protopopov was in his trial. For instance, Kvitnitskii in his testimony claimed that he was acting in a blind fit of anger and that he did not even intend to attack Khlebnikov and thought he was following another senior officer of his unit with whom he wanted to discuss his situation. When realizing that it was Khlebnikov, he was reported to have said something like "Ah, Colonel, it looks like fate brought us together."[32] Conversely, Khlebnikov suffered mostly psychological damage from the attack. None of this information about emotions and anger, however, had much bearing upon what happened during the trial.

The most important theme raised by the trial was instead the tension between the "community" (*obshchestvo*) of officers and the individual. While the Russian army was as hierarchical as any other, it was distinct from twentieth-century militaries in that it had relatively few officer ranks, and subordination was relaxed to an extent that would have astounded today's Russian officer. Aside from military exercises and parades, rank did not mean quite as much in daily social situations, at least until an officer reached a general's rank. Otherwise, a lowly subaltern (*praporshchik*) could easily socialize with captains, and captains could socialize with colonels. This was especially true in elite units of the imperial guard. Vaguely resembling officials in the gentry service corporations of early modern Russia, a unit's officers operated as a single body; they voted on admission of new members after carefully examining their character and credentials, and they operated special informal officers' courts to deal with interpersonal conflicts or offenses against their common sense of honor.[33] Theoretically this created a remarkable esprit de corps among the career officers. In practice, however, the Kvitnitskii case showed how this communal identity was easily highjacked by particular factions and how, in the case of the Guards Horse Artillery, new and not particularly qualified officers of low rank could make life extremely difficult for someone like Kvitnitskii. Interestingly enough, other officers in the battery also complained that peer pressure by junior comrades made their lives miserable, that many meetings that were supposed to make decisions for all the officers were secretive and selective, and Lieutenant Khitrovo even said openly during the pretrial investigation that he intended to transfer to another artillery unit, even the less prestigious Guards Foot Artillery.

What caused the informal confrontation between Kvitnitskii and some of his fellow officers that pathetically resembles a modern-day American high-school drama? The prosecutor who put together the indictment related the story of how Kvitnitskii, despite being a Page Corps graduate and a cavalry cadet (neither known for academic accomplishments) nonetheless graduated from the Artillery Academy and then successfully completed training at the General Staff Academy, which made him one of the few most highly educated young officers in the military. But when he came back to his original unit, the less accomplished of his fellow officers began to grumble that he did not know real service, that he should transfer to a staff position, that they would "mess up" (*portili*) his horses and inflict all types of nastiness (*gadosti*) on him. Kvitnitskii was very highly regarded by his superiors, however, including the overall commander of the Guards Artillery, Prince Masal'skii, and was at one point even appointed acting battery commander. Then at an exercise in January 1872 Khlebnikov confronted Kvitnitskii and said that he dressed so sloppily that he "besmirched the honor of the Guards Horse Artillery." Kvitnitskii allegedly had a hole in his pantaloons. Kvitnitskii immediately challenged him to a duel, but Khlebnikov said in his evidence that he had merely conveyed a message at the request of the officers' community and that "these words only concerned his clothing and not at all his honor."[34]

While their riding exercise was no doubt rigorous and not very clean, the various guards units competed with each other in their smart appearance, and the symbolic link between the torn and dirty pants of the most competent officer in the battery and the unit's corporate honor is suggestive. It later turned out that the other officers only told Khlebnikov to tell Kvitnitskii that his pants were torn and not to convey anything about besmirched honor. Kvitnitskii made a great deal out of this insult and soon became sick with a "nervous fever," taking leave to go abroad for treatment. The brigade commander, General Gubskii, took an anti-Kvitnitskii stance but still had to admit publicly that Khlebnikov's actions were "awkward and inappropriate" (*neudobnye i neumestnye*). But when Kvitnitskii came back to Petersburg from his treatment, Gubskii started to press him to leave the Guards Horse Artillery altogether, to which Kvitnitskii replied that he "did not consider it possible to obey the whims of those officers who were mostly young and by their education without any right to serve in the artillery at all and who were admitted only because of insufficient numbers of available officers." Despite Gubskii's opposition, Prince Masal'skii transferred Kvitnitskii to Warsaw, where he had originally begun his service before attending the General Staff Academy and where he was well liked. Khlebnikov and several other officers, however, composed and signed a critical pamphlet, a pasquil similar to that composed against Protopopov, and sent it to the Warsaw officers. At that point, Kvitnitskii and two other officers who agreed to serve as his seconds took a train back to Petersburg to seek a duel with Khlebnikov and other officers who had signed the pasquil. Kvitnitskii's friends visited these officers and conveyed the challenge. Khlebnikov refused to fight, and the other man, Captain Shatov, said that he had to ask the other officers' permission, to which the seconds responded that "in these kinds of affairs it is inappropriate to ask the entire group for advice because it will amount to disclosing the challenge." A challenge to a duel had to remain confidential to prevent official reprisals, since dueling was officially illegal. All this honor-driven violence was based on concealment and confidentiality, like most other aspects of elite and middle-class life relating to money and sex. A few days later, the incident already described took place.

This story was convincing and, it appears, true in its details, but Kvitnitskii's lawyer, Vladimir Gerard (whom we have already seen in the Nepenins' case that was tried at exactly the same time), had something shameful and unsavory to add to the narrative. One of Russia's most spectacular defense lawyers, he was the only civilian involved in the case. He came from the same Polish-Lithuanian-Belorussian aristocratic background as Kvitnitskii, with whom he was closely acquainted. Gerard's father was a guards officer, and his brother was the governor-general of Finland. Gerard had graduated from the exclusive Imperial School of Jurisprudence (which tended to produce future judges and procurators) and specialized in politically sensitive cases, which because of his connections he could do with less fear of reprisals than many of his colleagues. For instance, in 1881 he would defend Nikolai Kibalchich, who built the bombs used in the murder of Alexander II.

In his speech in Kvitnitskii's defense, Gerard first pointed out that the captain had in fact been harassed by a small group of five or so officers who presumed to act in everyone's name, and no matter how hard the investigators tried they could not come up with any reasonable explanation of what anyone in the battery could have had against Kvitnitskii. Gerard then made a grave accusation that demolished the honor of the officers who had campaigned against Kvitnitskii, alleging that the bullying was not the result of some immature personal emotional conflict as it was made out to be, nor the result of daily tension or of the well-known and commonly noted dislike of officers with general staff credentials (as the indictment alleged). Rather, it was the manifestation of a very calculated and very rational struggle for service promotions and preferences. Kvitnitskii was clearly groomed for a quick and stellar career; he was preparing to take over Khlebnikov's battery and to surpass him and his friends. Moreover, the officers of the Warsaw battery were far more capable academically and more serious about their studies, most likely because they were stationed close to the border with newly emergent Germany. They therefore had a much higher General Staff Academy attendance rate than the officers from Petersburg (who would have been busier with court events and partying), and academy graduates were given precedence in promotions. Kvitnitskii's tormentors made a shrewd calculation of the number and sequence of future promotions and decided that his career needed to be assassinated so that theirs could be saved. "Here," Gerard concluded, "one involuntarily supposes that the reason [for the conflict] is so bizarre and that it is immoral to such an extent that I do not dare to state it directly"; to confirm it one merely needed "to ask whether the [Warsaw] battery had the joint system of promotion with those in Petersburg and what could be the reason why the officers were so opposed to Kvitnitskii's transfer to Warsaw."[35] Gerard then noted that an important effect of the trial was to "expose the failings within our army." Kvitnitskii added an impassioned final word: "Because I loved military service with all of my soul, because I loved my branch of service, I was subjected to moral torment for four years. I was deprived of my health, almost deprived of my life and even of what is more dear to me than life—my honor. If the law allows a man the right to defend one's life, can it, I ask, deprive one of the right to defend his honor? I was placed in the position of a man who had only two options: either give up in shame or to defend myself. I chose the latter and ended up on trial."[36]

Kvitnitskii's sentence was that he be stripped of all his noble rights, ranks, and decorations and be exiled to reside in Siberia for the rest of his life (this sentence, though harsh, must not be confused with the sentence of hard labor in Siberia given to murderers). The court applied the article of the military code that punished harshly any attacks against one's superior, even though Khlebnikov was not actually Kvitnitskii's superior at the time of the attack. The law made a "huge distinction" between insulting one's superior and simply a senior officer. At the same time, everyone observing the trial was astounded that the court then petitioned the tsar (with the prosecutor's consent) to issue a complete pardon to Kvitnitskii, thus ensuring that the final decision would be a compromise between the two factions: the tsar would obviously reduce the sentence greatly but not actually pardon the officer. Predictably, Alexander II allowed Kvitnitskii to keep his status but demoted him to a private and ordered that he be sent somewhere offering a chance to fight his way back to favor. This was a punishment typically applied to participants in a deadly duel, or other similar misbehavior, immortalized by Dolokhov in Tolstoy's *War and Peace*. Kvitnitskii was sent to the ongoing campaign in Turkestan, where he served under his famous classmate General Skobelev and quickly restarted and actually accelerated his career, becoming a colonel in 1877 and ending his life in 1907 as a full general. He never came back to the artillery, however, and continued to serve in the cavalry, thus wasting all his specialized education and staff training. As for his tormentors, some of them were decorated during the war against the Ottoman Empire in 1877–1878, but they had utterly ruined their reputations and one by one left the military.

Part of the intention behind the detailed trial narratives that appeared in the press in the years during and immediately following the Great Reforms was no doubt didactic: to show that even elite individuals were not beyond the law's reach. But the result was ambiguous: the tsar's subjects saw that even the most elite individuals could be humiliated in public virtually overnight. Moreover, elites were shown to be not particularly nice or honorable—murdering, attacking, and otherwise tormenting people for no reason that could be clearly articulated. Furthermore, Russia's elites were made to confront the fact that their complacencies about privacy, security, and trust within the enclaves of bourgeois homes was misplaced and that their very trust in those domestic circles was also a point of weakness. Finally, Russia's elites, when they read newspaper accounts and attended the trials, were left with very compromised self-portraits, forced to think about the ways their emotions—their anger, fear, and envy—interacted with and were inseparable from base material interest. But just as trials for violent crime exposed the inner workings of a Russian modernizing mind, its greed, its rage, and its unbridled calculations, these trials also exposed the dark underworld of the bourgeois family and kinship ties.

CHAPTER 7

False Patriarchs

Few causes célèbres in late imperial Russia exposed the inner workings of a respectable middle-class family as publicly, as powerfully, and as controversially as the murder trial of the forty-year-old French governess, Marguerite Jujean, in St. Petersburg in November 1878. She was accused of poisoning her charge, seventeen-year-old Nikolai Poznanskii, the son of a colonel of the tsar's secret police. The only high-profile poisoning trial in late imperial Russia, it scrutinized the daily routines and relationships in the Poznanskii household, and its members' motivations, thoughts, and emotions. Attention veered away from the hapless Mademoiselle Jujean and instead focused on the weaknesses of Colonel Poznanskii and his negligent upbringing of Nikolai. Together with a series of other landmark cases of intrafamily violence, the travails of Marguerite Jujean challenged the power and exposed the failures of the nineteenth-century patriarchal family model that Russian propertied groups had by then adopted as eagerly as those in other countries in the post-Napoleonic world.[1]

A modern women's movement challenging the post-Napoleonic status quo appeared in Russia in the 1850s in elite intellectual and professional circles.[2] It coincided with a number of other "questions" appearing in Russian social and cultural politics that sought to protect and advance subordinated groups, such as peasants, industrial laborers, children, and ethnic and religious minorities.[3] While placing less emphasis on voting and other political rights for women, which were almost completely denied to the men of the Russian Empire as well,

Russian feminists shared their European counterparts' quest for the greater physical, emotional, and sexual autonomy of the individual, while they also emphasized the affective basis for marriage and family, challenging the persisting legal and social power of male patriarchs and "traditional" kinship structures.[4] These tensions are observable in many of the most prominent trials of the post-reform era. A closer look at these trials modifies our view of when and how these aspects of modernity took root in Russia. The existing view has it that the "modern" understanding and discussion of gender, family, and sex became a mass phenomenon with palpable effects in Russian society only at the end of the nineteenth century, and maybe even only after 1905, and that before then discussion was limited to extremely narrow circles of medical and legal professionals (a few hundred and likely just a few dozen persons).[5] But the narratives produced by the "great" trials modify this picture substantially, because they appeared much earlier, in the mid-1860s, and, moreover, fall into an in-between category of cultural and social phenomena that were distinct both from truly popular cultural artifacts and from specialized legal or medical publications, falling somewhere in between. This chapter does not attempt to offer a new full-scale history of sex and family in late imperial Russia but instead presents the trial of Jujean and several other equally scandalous and influential cases as evidence of a much earlier and more far-reaching discussion.

CREATING PATRIARCHY

The conflict in the mid-nineteenth century Russian family is commonly represented as pitching (Russian) tradition against ("Western") modernity. A crucial element of tradition was patriarchy: that is, the extensive, legally sanctioned authority of the male head of the family over his wife, children, dependent relations, and servants. In a broader way, the patriarch's authority was extended to his peasants, laborers, and civil or military service subordinates.[6] Needless to say, patriarchs and the people who challenged them also existed in other times and places. Our "modern" ideas of individual autonomy and romantic love are neither recent nor specifically European inventions.[7] Similar to the allegedly traditional Russian understandings of legality discussed earlier, some of the central elements of "traditional" Russian society were in fact recent inventions. To understand the last decades of pre-Soviet Russia we must first identify the contradictions and conflicts built into the kinship, gender, and social regime erected in Russia in the wake of the Napoleonic Wars and their aftershocks.

After 1815 tsar Alexander I granted constitutional liberties to his Polish and Finnish dependencies and to the restored French monarchy but not to his Russian subjects. Instead the state delegated its absolute authority through the male patriarch. The state demanded political loyalty along with subordination for men in state service in exchange for strong private property rights (including, before 1861, the reaffirmation of serfdom) and social power. Patriarchs officially controlled their dependents' physical movement and residence; "unemancipated" children could be jailed at a police station and "emancipated" ones could be sued for maintenance payments to their parents, and even after serfdom was gradually abolished, beginning in 1861, nobles retained considerable social and economic authority over their former enserfed peasants. For elite women, divorce was extremely difficult and expensive, and until the end of the imperial period they were excluded from civil service and from most professions and were active but marginalized in cultural production, journalism, and business.[8]

One key contradiction or limitation built into the post-Napoleonic reconstruction of "tradition" throughout Europe was that the male patriarch's authority was supposed to be ultimately based on affection and mutual respect.[9] He was expected to have cordial relations with his dependents, especially his wife, to respect her rights and to meet her material and emotional needs.[10] A crucial element of the system was that the wife was to be given her separate sphere at home that included certain physical spaces, certain types of social contacts, and power over the childre n and the servants, as well as, for example, the ability to access her husband's credit.[11] In the male world, earlier bonds of loyalty and character enforced by inner morality or community norms were to be replaced by relationships based on contract and economic interest enforced by the law. But at the same time, a man's family life was to be regrounded in emotional affection rather than economic planning or coercion.

In the Russian context, nineteenth-century gender and family roles were as clearly defined as in Western Europe, but, as noted in the previous chapter, there was more flexibility as to who would perform the roles of, for example, a property manager or an intellectual and moral authority. Moreover, separate spheres could be reimagined and redrawn in creative ways.[12] The Russian regime of private property allowed married women to retain full legal control over their property acquired before or during the marriage. Moreover, both noblewomen and women merchants routinely exercised this control: they did not simply own and dispose of property, such as rural estates or, for example, urban apartment buildings or even industrial enterprises, but also actively managed it. It is important to note that this rule was not a tradition stemming from "time immemorial" but was developed gradually in the eighteenth century and finalized only in the middle of the nineteenth, almost on the eve of the emancipation.[13] Similarly, minors could acquire property in their own name, for example, by gift or inheritance, or even purchase it with their guardian's approval. While minors could not themselves dispose of property, legal guardians were not permitted to squander it either. Finally, enserfed peasants often controlled property as a practical matter and in certain regions routinely amassed fortunes from trade and industry, and in 1848 they were allowed to purchase property in their own name, rather than in their master's.

The imperial Russian government, while enshrining patriarchy and private property at the expense of individual political participation and the rights of subordinate groups, still reserved for itself the authority to curb excesses of especially unruly patriarchs. Before emancipation, the serf-populated estates of particularly abusive masters could be taken over by the government and placed into trusteeship. Abused or neglected children could be sent to boarding schools or turned over to relatives, and abused wives routinely petitioned various government agencies—provincial governors and the Third Section, Russia's "higher" police—for separate residence permits. Minors were absolutely forbidden by law to engage in property transactions without their guardian's approval until they turned twenty-one, which provided an additional safety mechanism against predatory adults. As Barbara Alpern Engel argues, the "traditional" Russian state in many ways was far more solicitous of women than the "modern" regime that partially replaced it after the Great Reforms. Engel shows, for example, that post-reform courts sought to curtail the government's authority to grant marital separation.[14] Another example is women's ability to practice law or represent clients on official business, which was not legally restricted in the pre-reform era but was subsequently contested and finally circumscribed in 1876, when the government explicitly prohibited admission of women to the bar in response to several petitions and lawsuits, including by the court clerk and reporter Ekaterina Kozlinina.[15]

A key prerogative of a patriarch was to impose "domestic" corporal punishment on his children and enserfed servants (and informally in the case of hired servants), which did not officially extend to his wife, dependent elderly parents, or junior siblings. What constituted the abuse of parental authority was not clearly delineated in the Penal Code of 1845 (for example, inducing a dependent to commit suicide or a crime was penalized, but what constituted excessive punishment was not defined). Nonetheless, imperial law as a whole did gradually shrink the extent of legally permissible violence, after Catherine II, Paul's and Alexander I's laws freed nobles and other privileged groups from court-imposed corporal punishment, and Nicholas I abolished the use of the knout.[16] The Great Reforms of the 1860s abolished serf owners' previously extensive police authority, which had included minor whipping, and, in another major milestone, abolished the whip and the lash as court- or police-imposed punishment for non-privileged groups, as well as corporal punishment of schoolboys in the upper grades.[17] But the lash and other non-life-threatening beatings continued to be accepted as a private (*domashnee*) disciplinary measure.

The narratives presented during criminal trials reflected this polyphonous exchange among competing versions of modernity. These stories exposed to the public men who neglected, robbed, abused, hurt, or even killed their dependents and family members, exposing them not only to legal punishment but also to public scrutiny and empire-wide humiliation. As a legal observer from *Sanktpeterburgskie vedomosti* (one of Russia's most important newspapers) noted when discussing the case that begins the next section, he was "delighted because using the lash . . . finally began to bring the perpetrators on trial." The objective of the trial in his view was "to suppress the wild instincts of our citizens who are still in the process of becoming civilized."[18] The difficulty was that this was not a one-way triumphal advance of individual rights; the most progressive legal reformers viewed women and individual liberties with suspicion—and even when they did not, they still needed to earn their legal fees.

FATHERS AND DAUGHTERS

Perhaps the best-known violent "anti-patriarch" in post-reform Russia is Stanisław Leopold Kronenberg, son of the famous and fabulously wealthy Polish-Jewish banker and railroad tycoon.[19] On the eve of the 1863 uprising in Warsaw, Stanisław was prudently sent away to complete his education in Paris. Having then fought in the French army in 1870–1871, Kronenberg had a child with a highly ranked married woman and left the little girl, Maria, in the care of a rural pastor's family in Switzerland. A few years later he decided to adopt Maria and brought her to Russia along with his new mistress, Adeline Zhezing, when he came there to manage his family's banking, railway, and publishing interests. Although his father had been "one of the most important creditors" to the Polish rebels, there seem to have been no reprisals, and the family was able, for instance, to underwrite the most successful Russian newspaper of the period, Aleksei Suvorin's *Novoe Vremia*.

In 1875, Kronenberg, Zhezing, and Maria were spending their summer at a country dacha just outside St. Petersburg when their servants reported to the

Figure 15. Stanisław Kronenberg by Józef Łoskoczyński, from *Tygodnik Illustrowany,* 1894, vol. 9, no. 15, p. 236.

police on 25 July that the little girl was being cruelly beaten, that her clothing was soaked in blood, and that people would even gather outside the dacha gates when she screamed. For five days, the local police were not inclined to do anything, but they were finally spurred into action after the Third Section, Russia's secret political police, received an anonymous "agent's report," presumably from someone assigned to keep an eye on the politically suspect banker, perhaps the dacha's property manager, who initially suggested to the servants that they file a police report.[20]

Several days after the police opened the case Maria was subjected to a physical examination in the presence of two independent witnesses (*poniatye,* to this day a feature of Russian criminal procedure designed to reduce police misconduct), in this case two well-meaning lower-middle-class women who testified that when told to undress Maria they feared that the purpose was to inflict further beatings. Her body was so covered in black and blue bruises on her back, chest, and stomach that one of the *poniatye,* Balasheva, fainted (when she was asked during the trial whether she punished her own children with lashes, she responded in the negative, but she knew other people who did). Overall evidence against Kronenberg was strong: the testimony of two of his servants, the two independent witnesses, and three medical experts. Kronenberg himself admitted during the interrogation that he was beating Maria "without being aware of what he was doing." Material evidence included a blood-soaked shirt and a bunch of lashes that were far too thick for disciplining a small child and to observers during the trial resembled the *spitzruten* that in Russia's recent past were used when making soldiers run the gauntlet. The banker was charged under article 1489 of the penal code, which punished inflicters of "severe and life-threatening beatings or other tortures and torments" with prison or exile to Siberia, albeit not the hard labor reserved mostly for murderers. Kronenberg was not charged with exceeding his parental authority, because Russia's penal code did not have an applicable provision.

Because of the Third Section activity and because there was some information in the transcript that Kronenberg was "busy" with the Vistula railroad that summer, we cannot rule out that the objective of this prosecution was in part to harm or slow down his business activities or perhaps to stop his aggressive involvement in the Russian newspaper business that replicated his father's activities in the years before the 1863 uprising in Warsaw. It is also important to remember that the Kronenberg scandal took place precisely when the so-called Strousberg Affair (discussed in chapter 10) was at its height. That scandal involved Russia's first modern bank failure, when the bank in question was looted by its managers with the help of another Central European railroad tycoon, also born Jewish and baptized into Lutheranism, also well educated (he earned a doctorate at the Sorbonne), who was at exactly the same time busily establishing commercial and investment connections in Russia. The difference was that Strousberg was guilty only of white-collar crimes and that his background was English-German as opposed to Kronenberg's Polish and French ties. These cases must be viewed together as reflecting a like sentiment, seeking to cleanse Russian big business and financial structures of unwelcome foreign meddling.

The prosecutor did not play up the opposition between Russian and foreign national character, however, as was done in many other trials, including the Strousberg case. Nor were there even the slightest hints of anti-Semitism, although in other cases, including that against Strousberg and the earlier Mother

Mitrofania trial, there were very explicit and even graphic remarks of that nature. The issue of ethnicity and Russianness was, however, folded into the debate about social status and class.[21]

As noted earlier, the Russian government was not a monolith with a single will, and there are strong indications that other people attempted to redirect the trial. First, the jury panel just happened to consist of merchants and townsmen (*meshchane*), with only three educated individuals (the opposite would usually be the case in Petersburg), and thus would be presumed to be less likely to decide that lashing a child warranted lifelong exile in Siberia. Second, it is striking that Kronenberg was charged under an article that did not seem to fit his crime: while Maria was horrifically abused, it was debatable that her life was threatened, whereas another article of the Code (1482) covered lesser beatings and would have been more appropriate. The prosecutor could also have framed the questions to the jury to combine these two articles but chose not to do so. Finally, an important sign that Kronenberg had good friends among Russia's judiciary was the fact that he was given the services of the top criminal defense attorney in Petersburg, author of Russia's best treatise on criminal law and also Polish like Kronenberg. His name was Vladimir Spasovich (Włodzimierz Spasowicz). Officially he was appointed by the court and defended Kronenberg free of charge, which partially absolved him of the infamy that his colleague Aleksandr Lokhvitskii had aroused for defending unsavory causes. It could have been luck, of course—luck that peasants and laborers accused of beating someone in Petersburg also enjoyed on rare occasions. But the fact that, like Kronenberg, Spasovich was prominent in the moderate wing of the Polish national movement may have helped as well. An idealistic view of the legal profession would see Spasovich as merely doing his duty, but the reality in nineteenth-century Russia, as in the twenty-first century United States and in every other time and culture, was that securing a competent attorney required financial and social capital. As Danilov's murder case, discussed in chapter 5, showed, lawyers had no difficulty rejecting assignments they did not like by claiming to be sick or out of town on an urgent errand.

Still, despite the best efforts of the Kronenberg-controlled newspaper *Novoe Vremia,* the public's impression of him was not favorable. The more liberal daily newspaper, *Sanktpeterburgskie vedomosti,* conveyed an image of a man who was harmless and refined on the surface but vicious inside: "A young man . . . with regular facial features and a soft gaze not revealing his beastly nature . . . [who] conducts himself with dignity, is somewhat agitated, his voice shakes."[22] Given that Kronenberg was not able to explain why he treated his daughter so cruelly, other than that he lost his temper, Spasovich had to work hard to undo this unfavorable impression. In the event, Spasovich went above and beyond what almost every defense lawyer managed to accomplish in post-reform Russia. His defense strategy earned him much criticism, such that Dostoevsky wrote in his *Writer's Diary* that Spasovich was more on trial than Kronenberg.[23] It is to this day common to view the case through a liberal versus conservative lens, with the "liberal" lawyers and newspapers cheering against Kronenberg and "conservative" ones supporting him. But Spasovich, a moderate liberal himself, appears rather to have turned the prevailing models of family and power into a mash of "liberal" and "conservative" narratives in the service of getting Kronenberg out of his jam.

Spasovich's first strategy was to claim that the case was an invasion of a respectable family's private life and that at stake was the issue of parental rights and their limitations—which the prosecution was supposedly trying to impose. Spasovich therefore petitioned to hold the trial behind closed doors, which was almost without exception allowed only for cases involving frank discussions of sex. Here the prosecutor of course protested and said that the case did not allege anything about parental rights and that the fact that Maria was Kronenberg's daughter was irrelevant; it was strictly about torture. This strategy resembles that in the trial of Vera Zasulich two years later, in which the prosecution decided to ignore the obvious political motives of the crime and so doomed its own case. Here the prosecutor likewise unwittingly played into Spasovich's hands. While the court rejected the petition to close the trial, Spasovich needed only to plant an impression in the jurors' minds, and in that he succeeded.

His next strategy was the common and old one of putting the victim on trial. Spasovich went out of his way to turn Maria into a little monster. He argued that she was a deeply flawed child, that the beatings were not severe, and that her father had only Maria's best interests in his heart, so that his behavior—while excessive—was not criminal, given the challenges he was facing. "In the normal order of things, normal means are used," Spasovich argued. Here the means were not "normal," he admitted, but the circumstances were not normal either. Kronenberg's witnesses, including the girl's governess, claimed that Maria was a bright but "exceedingly spoiled and willful" child, who while living in a foster family in Switzerland had become accustomed to rough country ways and sinful habits. She always tried to spend time with servants despite being prohibited from doing so. The observer for *Sanktpeterburgskie vedomosti,* while not well disposed toward Kronenberg, played up to this image by describing how during the trial the girl acted confident and "extremely jaunty . . . not realizing what

Figure 16. Nadezhda Suslova, Russia's first woman medical doctor. Postcard by V. N. Lapin, early twentieth century.

role she was to play thanks to the mistakes of her own parents" and that she "entertained the public."[24] The observer writes of her being a "very likeable and pretty girl, well-built and holds herself at ease, converses only in French and answers questions quickly and without shyness."[25]

Aside from Maria's governess and tutors, Kronenberg was able to obtain the services of a far more important witness, Russia's first officially recognized woman doctor (surgeon and gynecologist), Nadezhda Suslova, to this day an iconic figure in Russia.[26] Dr. Suslova testified that she first treated the girl's mother, Adeline Zhezing, and then observed that Maria was "very clever but had one flaw, that she could not control her natural needs. Moreover, she had harmful habits that strongly affected her health: that is, she masturbated and that illness . . . afflicted her for several years; the girl herself later confessed to having this illness."[27]

At Kronenberg's request, Suslova then "treated" Maria for onanism. The newspaper reporter commented that "given the fresh, pink, and extremely attractive little face of the girl, it's difficult to believe that she is an onanist."[28] We are not told what methods Suslova proposed to treat masturbation, but Spasovich and the public assumed that the beatings were in part inflicted to deal with this "illness." The journalist from *Nedelia* soundly criticized this method:

> Not so long ago we happened to have attended a public lecture by Professor Leshaft, the subject of which was the physical disciplining of children. . . . Parents and educators subjecting children to any corporal punishment whatsoever inflict upon them great harm; if they also use lashes, if they beat children, then they are barbarians and criminals. By these means they undermine the young forces of a vulnerable, weak, and frail organism of a child; they wear them out. Moreover, by lashing they corrupt the children's souls as well as their bodies, they destroy their sense of shame, blunt their sensitivity, so that the punishment must become stronger and stronger; and what is most terrible—lashing instills in children the beginning of that terrible affliction, that devastating disease that is called masturbation. Lashing lays the foundation for masturbation, develops and supports this terrible illness.

The professor demonstrated his point using a skeleton.[29] None of the medical expert witnesses, including Suslova, was asked questions about masturbation, its harm, or its "treatment."

Other medical expert witnesses scrutinized all the various scars and bruises found on Maria's body, some of which went all the way back to her time in Switzerland and were of the wrong shape to result simply from a fall, as her former foster family claimed were their cause in their written testimony sent to the court. The witnesses could not agree on when, with what, and how strongly Maria had been beaten, and whether her injuries were "heavy" or "light." Doctors Landsberg and Gorskii concluded that Maria's injuries went beyond simple domestic discipline. If it had continued, it would have harmed the child's health. The scars suggested that she was beaten indiscriminately all over her body. The third expert, Cherbishevich, pointed out that Maria had scars on her face; one on her nose was so straight it could not have come from a fall as Kronenberg claimed but came rather from an instrument like a ruler, and there was a similar scar on her cheek. The two pro-Kronenberg experts, Florinskii and Kreminetskii, argued that Maria had suffered no permanent disfigurement and that she simply had thin skin that was prone to irritation, such that the slightest touch or squeeze produced bruising.

After the witnesses had been questioned, the prosecutor offered a nondescript speech, followed by Spasovich's. Spasovich argued that the indictment applied incorrect legal provisions. Questions of interpreting or applying specific provisions of the penal code hardly ever appeared at any of the trials discussed in this book, even the most complicated ones that went on for months, because the role of the jury as fact finder was very sharply defined in Russian courts. For example, lawyers were even prohibited in their speeches from mentioning the punishments assignable for various offenses. Any questions of law were to be left to professionals: to the prosecutors who put the indictment together and to the Senate proceedings if an appeal was later filed. Jurors were only supposed to focus on plain-language facts, such as "Did X intentionally strike Y? If yes, did she intend to kill her? If yes, did she fail to do so due to circumstances out of her control?" Yet in the Kronenberg case, Spasovich engaged in an unusually rich though highly questionable discussion of applicable law. He argued that the language of "torture and torment" (*istiazania i muchenia)* in Article 1489 referred to exceptional cruelty, a more intense and more prolonged degree of suffering compared to "common" (*obyknovennie*) beatings, even severe ones. Spasovich cited an 1872 Senate decision holding that "severe" injuries were ones that inflicted illness, a prolonged disorder in the body, or an inability to work for a certain period of time. Maria was beaten, Spasovich concluded, but (apparently despite her numerous scars) not subjected to "*istiazania i muchenia.*" Kronenberg should have been put on trial for inflicting minor bodily harm, for which the proper venue was the local justice of the peace court, not a full-blown jury trial.

Spasovich then returned to his initial claim that the case was merely an attempt to legally circumscribe the limits of parental authority. He claimed that since no one claimed that parents did not have the legal right to discipline their children, Kronenberg should be punished only for that part of the beatings that exceeded the limits of parental authority. He should not have been put on trial as if he had injured another, unrelated adult. Viewed that way, Kronenberg's marginal excessive cruelty did not fit the torture law in Article 1489. While Spasovich's speech at the time deeply impressed observers, and some contemporary scholars have accepted his arguments, upon more careful examination there is much that is questionable about his logic.[30] Why was Kronenberg to be judged only for the "marginal" cruelty that exceeded his authority? This notion could be taken to absurdity: for example, if you poison someone with arsenic, should you be judged only for administering the amount that exceeded the safe limit and, therefore, be acquitted because that marginal amount was not enough to poison? Moreover, the legally permitted amount of parental violence was of course not defined in Russian law (or apparently in any other nation's law at that time), but this did not mean that the written law, as opposed to custom and practice, permitted it; after all, there was no law against beating wives in Russia either, yet even Spasovich would (one hopes) not have tried to argue that this fact could be taken into account when judging a husband who beats his wife bloody.[31]

In addition to his legal arguments, Spasovich claimed that punishing Kronenberg threatened Russia's social order:

> This is exactly like a habit of lying; once it takes root, it grows more and more like that wild thorn that covers the field if it's not rooted out . . . to punish the father for punishing his child painfully but for a reason, is doing a bad service to the family, bad service to the state, because the state is only strong as long as it is based on a strong family. Bless the father that stops his child in time; in the past years people would say: he is saving his son from the gallows; now we say that . . . the father saves his son from hard labor and penal settlement, and his daughter from becoming a woman of easy virtue.[32]

Yet it was hardly clear how Kronenberg's disciplinary methods were strengthening the family or the state. The weekly *Nedelia* caught on to this, asking how the Kronenberg case was different from the recent trial of a Moscow artisan, Ivan Fedorov, who had decided to sacrifice his eight-year-old son to God and was caught in the nick of time.[33] More generally, according to the journalist from *Nedelia,* the legal and political prominence of the family as part of the state structure had been important in the past, but now, in the 1870s, the law was based on individual rights and obligations, while the patriarch's arbitrary authority was more appropriate to the age of ancient Rome. Today's state did not need immoral patriarchs like Kronenberg to support its authority. While legally the jurors' verdict was correct, "if the jurors, in their acquittal of Kronenberg, were guided by the principle that the concept of parental authority is inseparable from the concept of family, this means that we have not departed very far from Priest Sylvester's [sixteenth-century] ideals of Domostroi."[34] Today's family was very different because when its authority is maintained through immoral or illegal means, it does not at all contribute to the strength of the state, "which does not need any artificial crutches." Today's family, he continued, had ceased to be a bureaucratic-political institution "amounting, supposedly, to be virtually at the center of gravity of a state's existence" and instead became only a "personal union" occupying a "rather modest position in modern [political] life." Moreover, the journalist concluded, Russians would only become better citizens and the state would only gain if they rooted out the abuses in their most private and intimate relations; this procedure would neither lessen nor denigrate the significance of the family. Family would always have an independent and untouchable role in the state. But the state could not deny itself the right to regulate it.[35] The way Spasovich talked about family seems simply to refer to arbitrary patriarchal authority, although implied in that polemical framework was an assumption that Kronenberg's good objective justified his vile means. (It was above all this idea of expedience that aroused Dostoevsky's ire.)

Like all "great" trials, Kronenberg's did not simply raise important social issues. It also produced competing narratives or at least gave a greater indication of what some existing narratives might mean. At the heart of Kronenberg's case were conflicts about social class and hierarchies of power: he was a wealthy and educated banker, while the people who reported his abuses to the police were lowly servants. The distinction was very clear during the trial in the testimony of the two servants and the two "outside witnesses" (*poniatye*) as opposed to Kronenberg's tutors and governesses, who claimed that they did not see or hear any violence whatsoever, or the esteemed fighter against masturbation, Dr. Suslova. Poor and uneducated Russian servants appeared in the trial as more humane and cultured than rich and educated foreigners, thus overturning the stereotype persisting in scholarly literature to this day that the mass of Russia's peasants held back the nation's legal and other development, in opposition to the beneficial but misunderstood influence of more the humane "Western" values of the upper classes. *Nedelia* concluded that "in general the intelligentsia has shown itself in a most pathetic way in the case of Mr. Kronenberg."[36]

Another set of responses on the question of Kronenberg's status was both confused and confusing. An observer from *Sudebnyi vestnik,* a specialized legal newspaper, mechanistically repeated the trope of the allegedly backward and violent Russian merchants who were supposedly ignorant of humane Western values: "This case is also characteristic as a depiction of the mores that to this day exist among our 'men of business' (*del'tsov*) who claim to be advanced and educated." Kronenberg's transgression, in this view, was mainly his "lack of development and of a sense of dignity," neither of which could be instilled by putting him in prison but could be created only by "schooling and better life conditions."[37] A similar interpretation was offered by Russia's great satirist,

Mikhail Saltykov-Shchedrin, who claimed that Kronenberg's social milieu knew only one pedagogical method—slapping and whipping (he strangely considered Kronenberg to occupy the same social milieu as the jurors).[38] Given Kronenberg's education all the way to his doctorate from the Sorbonne, however, a lack of living conditions or schooling in Western values could hardly have been his problem.

A subset of this narrative was offered by Spasovich with the value sign reversed. He claimed that Maria's early upbringing among Swiss peasants and the later influence of Russian domestic servants had caused her alleged bad behavior: "That taint that assaulted the girl, must be attributed to the people surrounding her."[39] Looking at this rhetoric more closely, we may surmise that Spasovich was right in his own way, that the social conflict at the heart of the case resulted from Kronenberg's attempt to literally beat peasant habits out of his daughter, to eradicate such customs as freely helping herself to prunes and other treats and freely interacting with peasants (which she had no trouble doing despite the fact that they only spoke Russian, while she only spoke French). Instead, she was to be subjected to round-the-clock supervision designed as a crash course in upper-class, respectable manners.

The Kronenberg case reverberated throughout Russian society and the legal system to the end of the imperial period.[40] It was much more difficult for children to get away from an abuser without outside help compared to victims of spousal abuse, which was already hard enough. The limits to parental violence would never be officially defined in legislation or by the Senate, but many similar cases from the post-reform era showed that limits did exist in practice.

An earlier case in fact showed that it was possible to impose effective legal boundaries on patriarchal parental authority; it took place in the very beginning of Russia's age of jury trials, in September 1867. Although it attracted strong public attention, it did not enjoy the services of Russia's top lawyers and publicists, and while a top defense attorney, Prince Urusov, took part, this was still the beginning of his long career, and no one yet knew that he would prove to be an equal to Plevako or Spasovich. On trial in the small town of Kashira to the south of Moscow was a family of landowning gentry: fifteen-year-old Olga Umetskaia and her parents.[41] Olga was accused of setting her parents' estate on fire three times, and her elderly parents were prosecuted for inducing their daughter to commit that crime (ironically, against their own property). Olga was suspected because she often complained of being beaten by her parents and was the first to discover each fire. During one of the fires, she had even moved as if she wanted to jump into the flames but was pulled away by the estate's laborers. She claimed that her parents often punished her, fed her badly, and took absolutely no care of her education, aside from an early attempt to teach her to play the piano, during which her mother broke one of her fingers.

Witnesses claimed that despite the family's wealth, Umetskii kept his children very badly, out of miserliness. His income derived from his going to Moscow twice a year to bid on foreclosed estates being sold at an auction; he did this not to buy anything but to get a payout from the real buyers to get him to go away; otherwise he was so wealthy that he did not even need to sell the grain produced in abundance on his estate. He had served at the local District Court (*uezdnyi sud*) since 1830 and had married into the very prominent and aristocratic Bakhmetiev family. When Umetskii claimed that he himself lived very simply, a witness, a local official, responded that his house indeed looked simple but that he had very nice rooms for himself with real furniture, while his children lived in a special room with an earthen floor; the children were ordered to serve the official like lackeys and were clearly embarrassed to do it. The official also witnessed the children doing the peasants' work on the estate and had for a long time assumed that Olga was one of Umetskii's servants because she was dressed like a chambermaid. The witness had also been acquainted with the governess whom the Umetskiis hired for their older, privileged daughter, Aleksandra; the governess spent almost all of her wages to buy food for the younger children.

Their neighbor, Prince Meshcherskii, testified of the Umetskiis: "[They] lead a most miserly of life and force their children to perform such work that is appropriate only in an extremely impoverished condition of life, which is very far from being the Umetskiis' situation."[42] As many as nine neighboring nobles testified that the Umetskiis lived a life inappropriate for nobles and that the children would sometimes go to the peasants' huts to beg for food. Aside from the material deprivations, the children were completely lacking in any religious or moral instruction and never went to church. Umetskii regarded his children as free labor and punished them as "moral freaks" anytime they failed to perform as expected. In contrast, Olga's elder sister, Aleksandra, the only child who was given an education and treated well, was married to a local nobleman (named Voronin) and was the only witness who (together with her husband) claimed without a shadow of shame that there was no abuse or anything inappropriate whatsoever happening at her parents' estate. The local priest confirmed that the Umetskii children never went to church but testified that he had no knowledge of abuse.

The wife of the inspector of the local prison testified, however, that when Olga was first arrested she took her to bathe and was so horrified to see the bruises and scars that covered her entire body that she fainted. Similarly,

Umetskii's estate manager testified that the father often beat Olga "without any mercy and kept her, because of his miserliness, extremely badly and in hunger. . . . Although she is indeed a very lively girl, she is not so rude and bad to her father to deserve such inhumane treatment, and if she has any bad inclinations, it's only because her mother abandoned her completely, and the father treats her cruelly without any regard for her upbringing."[43]

Another local nobleman, Polivanov, who had been long acquainted with the Umetskiis, said that he had always felt sorry about the miserable condition of their children. The mother's custom was to go to their southern steppe estate to give birth and only later bring the children to Kashira. It turned out during the trial that she had borne more than twenty children, all but five of whom died at an early age. The witness said that when the two boys who were still living at the time of the trial were brought to the Kashira estate, they were seven years old and still did not even know how to talk. When the Umetskii parents were away, they asked Polivanov to look after them. He was horrified to see that the children slept with the farm animals in the barn on the earthen floor covered in straw and some rags. They were fed stale bread and milk. One must add that neither Polivanov nor any of the other neighbors did anything about this situation, but at least they had the courage to speak the truth at the trial. Under serfdom, in legal cases involving serf abuse that in part followed a similar dynamic, local nobles who were called to testify against their sadistic neighbors almost invariably claimed that they were unaware of anything excessive or inappropriate.

After witness testimony, the prosecutor gave an unimpressive speech: "This case is a family drama that touches upon the untouchable sacredness of family relations that are respected even among savage peoples. It is important to have something strong and unusual to cause family relations in all of their nakedness, with all of their details, to be subjected to public legal proceedings."[44] Thankfully, the prosecutor was in effect assisted by Prince Urusov, who represented Olga. Urusov claimed that this was the "most remarkable case that has been seen in Russia since the trial by jury was introduced." He raised the issue of the Umetskii children who had died young and implied that this happened because of neglect. He said that they were "invisible witnesses to the parents' neglect of their children and their abuse of their power" (this part caused a "movement" among the public, who generally sympathized with the parents). "Here, in front of your eyes, there was a moment when two sisters were standing next to each other, one dressed like a lady and the other one looking like a chambermaid. Despite this obvious difference, the lady insisted that all the children [in the family] were treated equally."[45]

The jury's verdict was that Olga was legally innocent of arson, even though she admitted setting fire to the buildings. With a twist of reasoning, the verdict established that while Olga was not "guilty" of setting the fire, her parents were guilty of inducing her to do so. After a round of appeals, the father was sentenced to three months in the workhouse, and the mother to four months. Their lawyer argued that "the Umetskiis' treatment of their daughter could have been influenced by an unclear understanding of those patriarchal customs that made the parents' power nearly limitless. These customs were supported by our legislation that prohibited the children to complain against insults from their parents. Their religious education went in the same direction, so that what is now, in the new courts, treated as a crime, in the old ones perhaps would not even have been accepted for an examination." This is unconvincing, however, because these laws had been in existence since well before the new courts.[46]

Several other examples of limits the law placed on patriarchs' discretion are found in the (unsurprisingly) unpublished writings and personal papers of judge Anatolii Koni. One example, which Koni explicitly compared to the Kronenberg case, was the 1889 story of the Zolotnitskii family from Warsaw, compared to which Kronenberg looked positively humanitarian (incidentally, in Russian Zolotnitskii is a near-homophone of the word for Cinderella).[47] Fourteen-year-old Nina had wealthy parents who abused her in extremely vicious and graphically described ways until she attempted to commit suicide by jumping out of a window. The parents went on trial under Article 1476 (inducing someone to commit suicide) at the Warsaw District court, without a jury, which did not exist in the Russian-ruled part of Poland. While the parents and their two elder children all testified against Nina, the girl was supported by approximately a dozen of the Zolotnitskiis' neighbors, former servants, and military orderlies. Still, the judges ruled that there was no evidence of abuse or a suicide attempt. Since this very patently went against the evidence, the prosecutor appealed the case to the higher-up Warsaw Judicial Chamber, which overruled the decision and sentenced both parents to several months in prison.

Perhaps the most truly horrifying case from Koni's notes is the tragedy of seven-year-old Marfa Kushchinskaia-Domantovich from a minor gentry family in Poltava province in Ukraine.[48] She died on 17 April 1887, and her body was examined by the police after a rumor immediately appeared that her twenty-six-year-old stepmother, Maria, had caused her death through beatings and starvation. Marfa's body entirely lacked a layer of fat under her skin, her face and entire body were a "mass" of fresh and healed wounds, scars, and bruises. Her clothing and hair were thickly covered in lice. The medical report noted that "her anal opening was surrounded by an ulcerous sore that penetrated the skin into the sphincter muscle." Marfa's stomach was completely empty, her intestines were so thin they were translucent, and the feces in her intestines consisted of clay mixed with coal. The wounds appear to have been inflicted by shoe heels, a stick, and lashes. The last time she had eaten was a day and a half before her death. The witnesses, a lower-middle-class Jewish family (illiterate according to the police report) who were renting an apartment in the same house that was owned by her father, testified that Marfa was treated cruelly and inhumanely (*ne po-chelovecheski*). Her clothing was never changed, and she was never washed. She also "for some reason" was defecating on herself and smelled bad; "her feet and her shift were always covered in feces." She slept on the bare floor, and her stepmother often kicked her out into the cold foyer (*seni*) even in winter. Marfa's father worked as manager of a large agricultural estate (*ekonomia*) and only came home on Sundays. He would supposedly order Marfa to be fed when he visited, but his wife would not do it. Otherwise he watched Marfa being mistreated but never intervened. He claimed that his daughter never complained. The stepmother said that Marfa had to sleep on the floor because since November 1886 she had begun to defecate on herself. She liked to eat chalk and coal for some reason that no one bothered to investigate. And no one could understand why she had been infested with lice since 1885. To deal with that affliction, her father administered a mercury-based gray Neapolitan ointment (*politan'*), of all things. On 13 April, the day before her death, Marfa told her neighbors that she did not even want to eat any more.

The parents were charged with torture (Article 1489, same as Kronenberg) and related offenses and tried by a jury in Poltava. In sum, it is not surprising that the trial took place given the brutality of the facts, but it is rather startling, as in the cases described earlier, that several families lived under the same roof as Marfa's parents, visited their home for months, later reported having seen these horrors over a very long time, and yet reported the matter to police only after she died.

Another case from Koni's personal archive that occurred in 1889 also involved Russo-Polish elites, but it did not end with even partial justice.[49] The seventeen-year-old noblewoman Liza Tychinskaia was working at a clerical job at a railroad when she killed herself with rat poison because of persistent sexual harassment by her dissolute and formerly wealthy father, Konrad Tychinskii. The man was prosecuted, but the outcome of the case is not clear. It is striking, however, that the tragedy happened not on some isolated country estate but in the center of Kiev and in full view of a large and prosperous professionalized gentry family that included Liza's grandmother, mother, cousins, and uncles, all of whom had for years been aware of Konrad's behavior and had even taken concrete and partly effective steps to help Liza, yet were ultimately still unable to save her.

It is well known to this day that cases of sexual abuse, due to their nonpublic nature, are typically difficult to prove, and the following story shows how even an episode that could have resulted in a true trial of the century was extremely easy to hush up. In his published memoirs Koni briefly discusses a striking incident from the early 1870s involving the family of a civil servant named Kostevich from St. Petersburg.[50] He had two beautiful daughters: the elder was married to Klimov, also a civil servant, but did not live with her husband. The younger, Nadezhda, was nineteen and in love with an officer of the Life Guards Cossack Regiment, Ilovaiskii. The father ran into financial difficulties and became acquainted with a wealthy banker named Rosenthal, whose special interest was to deflower young virgins in exchange for "large sums" of money. The Kostevich family decided to swindle him, to sell him their elder daughter only pretending to be a virgin, and, Koni reported, they were likely paid an advance. Rosenthal discovered the ruse, however, and demanded that the Kosteviches hold up their end of the deal. The family then decided to sacrifice the younger Nadezhda and deliver her to the banker, with the elder sister serving as the go-between making the arrangements with Rosenthal. After much "psychological coercion" Nadezhda agreed to the arrangement, but on the eve of the day she wrote a note to the young officer Ilovaiskii asking him to have supper with her in one of the restaurants just outside the city (commonly used for illicit romantic meetings). But he never showed up. She went to see him at the barracks, but he was not there. She was not seen again until early the next morning, when she came home in a cab, untidy and staggering. The family did not understand what was going on until they heard a shot. Nadezhda was still alive, but her spinal cord was fatally damaged. The parents did not call the police, however, instead inviting in their elder daughter's boyfriend, Dr. Dediulin, a professor at the Imperial Medical-Surgical Academy, who according to the elder sister had been engaged to assist her in faking her virginity for Rosenthal's benefit. Only after Nadezhda could no longer speak or move her hands was a police doctor called. When he examined Nadezhda, it turned out that she had recently been "deflowered and possessed" multiple times, likely by several men. There were no signs of violence on her body. Nadezhda died several days later from her gunshot wound and acute uremia. The investigation focused on the role of Nadezhda's sister but failed to uncover exactly what had happened or to build a case. Koni wrote that a few months later Dediulin came to his chambers and said that he no longer wanted to be the surety for the elder sister because they had broken up. Koni told him about the direction of the case, and Dediulin laughingly said that all of these were false leads, and that Nadezhda, if she were still alive, could tell something "quite unexpected." She had told everything to him before she lost her speech, Dediulin continued, but he would share some of that information with Koni only if he gave his word that he would never reveal or otherwise use that information. Koni would not agree, and Dediulin left. "The case was closed by the Judicial Chamber." Koni reported that at the end of their conversation Dediulin laughingly rejected Koni's moralizing appeals to his better instincts, replying that "whatever is expedient is also moral," quite in line with Spasovich's argument in the Kronenberg case.

Taken together, cases of extreme abuse of patriarchal authority exposed the fault lines within a social system that assumed goodwill from those holding the power, while showcasing the difficulties, both legal and rhetorical, in satisfying any sense of justice without inherently questioning a hierarchy that was meant to remain inviolable. Stories of extreme transgression can serve to reinforce narratives of "proper" behavior, but the discussion of these cases shows Russian observers and jurists of the time lacking direction about how to achieve this balancing act.

THE PATRIARCH IN THE SUITCASE: WHO WAS TO BLAME?

In the cases discussed above, patriarchs (or a matriarch temporarily taking the place of patriarch, as in the case of Marfa's abusive stepmother) were directly prosecuted for harming their dependents, but there were other equally revealing cases that were about different offenses entirely but still pulled the trial narrative back to a transgressing patriarch, debating his power and responsibilities and the tension between genuine relationships and external proprieties, attesting to how much this concern underlay a variety of conflicts and unresolvable questions in the period. This applies not only to the Nepenins' case, which I revisit later in this chapter, or to the von Zon murder trial of 1873 (the scandalous "suitcase" murder, so called because the victim's body was shipped out of Petersburg in a suitcase) but also to the still-famous trials of the radical revolutionary Sergei Nechaev in 1873 and of his followers two years before. Since Nechaev's name is familiar to anyone interested in the origins of modern terrorism, his appearance in this chapter requires some elucidation that will produce a richer understanding of this influential and perhaps underestimated figure. Finally, the chapter concludes with a closer look at the travails of Mademoiselle Jujean and the dark underbelly of middle-class family life exposed by her case.

I earlier discussed the case of Nikolai Nepenin and his wife, Evgenia, who were tried for stabbing Evgenia's former lover, Petr Chikhachev, in the context of gendered ideas about honor as well as the rage and possibly greed that drove this married couple to pursue Judge Chikhachev to his death. The case revealed both men to be failed patriarchs, but it also focused on their relationship to Yevgenia Nepenina and on her reaction to the two men's rage and cowardice. The didactic objective was thick in the air of the courtroom. A journalist overheard a gentleman softly noting to his wife: "You see, my heart, how bad it is to cheat on your husband."[51]

In the beginning of the trial both Nepenin and Chikhachev were presented, in a somewhat abstract way, as ordinary men. Only gradually over the course of the proceedings were their images transformed from autonomous agents free to pursue or not pursue their appetites and instincts into patriarchs in their community who were subject to certain expectations of behavior. Both served as justices of the peace; these were elected judgeships, requiring each judge to operate in a particular district (urban or rural) and be closely involved in the life of their community, dealing with small-scale civil disputes and petty crime. Chikhachev, as the wealthier of the two (who in any event was more interested in painting than the law) held an "honorary" judgeship, which meant that he was not required to physically reside in his district but would be called in to hear particular cases. Chikhachev's ancestors had been living in that part of Pskov province for centuries, and even after the emancipation he acted as a benefactor to his community. He set up a special pension fund for his former "household serfs" (*dvorovye*)—those serfs who did not have land of their own and who mostly acted as domestic servants and laborers to the master. After the emancipation their lives obviously took a turn for the worse unless their master was willing to help. In addition, Chikhachev set aside a large sum of money—ten thousand rubles—to fund a local school and pay the teacher's salary. He also set up a local mutual aid society—a community bank that was intended to resist the influence of local "usurers" (rural usury was one of the key problems for rural development after the emancipation). Nepenin also held a succession of public offices that at the time were crucial in holding post-emancipation society together. First he was a "peace mediator," an official designated to negotiate emancipation settlements between peasant communities and their masters. Then he headed the local self-government office (*uprava*) before being elected as a judge.

Both men had their flaws: Nepenin, his bad temper and tendency to speak evil about others, as well as his tendency to neglect the more boring aspects of his job like keeping accurate accounts; Chikhachev, a certain lack of financial acumen, which would have been helpful for running a bank. But these faults, carefully noted in the case record, did not reduce their effectiveness as community leaders as far as locals were concerned. Both men had reputations for honesty, generosity, and the intelligence provided by education, all of which they were known to have put at the disposal of their township.

Their failure as social actors came from the way they treated women. Chikhachev saw women only as sexual objects. The trial portrayed him as a man who craved a genuine relationship with his wife but was unable to gain her affection. Failing to find another "respectable" woman, he ultimately turned to prostitutes. He could not act decisively, could not fight, could not resolve conflicts. In other words, he lacked masculinity in every way other than his sexual voraciousness, which seems to have been explained as its own kind of failure.

By contrast, Nepenin appears throughout the trial record as a man of pure rage, embodying violence, emotion, and physical force, and unable to calculate or to plan. Only gradually did the trial reveal how shrewd he actually was in setting up the face-to-face meeting between his wife and Chikhachev and watching it in the capacity of an amused spectator. At the end of the trial transcript, a letter from Chikhachev's friend was read in which he alleged—long before the murder—that Nepenin would make his wife the tool of his revenge, hoping that either she would be acquitted by the jury or he would be rid of her. As it happened, Nepenin handed her the revolver at the entrance to Chikhachev's apartment. The final failure of Nepenin as a man and as a patriarch with other people in his care was his inability to combine his uncontrollable temper with cold calculation: as the journalist from *Nedelia* noted, "Doubtlessly, he conducted the entire affair as a prudent man of business (*del'tsom*), who aims at every opportunity to unload all the risk on the others, and to himself only keep pure profits."[52]

As noted earlier, Evgenia Nepenina's personality and earlier life were examined during the trial in excruciating detail. The trial "unfold[ed] the entire secret tale of her life, penetrate[d] the innermost chambers of her girlhood bedroom and marital bed, turn[ed] out the inner side that a man is afraid to whisper even to his best friend, sometimes is afraid even to think about in the privacy of his own self." The shame of this procedure caused red spots to break out on her pale and prematurely aging face and head (although the way this scene was presented makes it likely that the observer was hinting that Nepenina had contracted consumption).

As to Nepenina's psychological portrait, the two defense attorneys claimed she was of course ambitious above all for a happy domestic life, as was appropriate for a gentlewoman, but that she was unprepared for any authentic social life and that even her healthy desire for a family was somehow defective, since her only child died in infancy and she allegedly did not create much of a home for her husband, given his appearance in the trial record as singularly undomesticated. Koni, the prosecutor in the case, for all of his well-known claims to objectivity, worked hard in his speech to paint a favorable picture of Nepenina, but at the same time he described her as being completely under her husband's influence, to the point that she had no will of her own: "[S]he belongs among such persons, who are common mostly among women, who can cry, pine, suffer, regret what was done and especially what was said, but they cannot and sometimes do not wish to decide for themselves what to do and how to find a way out of a false and difficult situation. They need someone else's willpower and example. . . . Her letter shows that even her expressions and her style, her manners are completely identical to those used by her husband."[53]

The trial record does note evidence that is contradictory to this picture of Evgenia, though mentioned so briefly that the public seem not to have noticed it. When she still hoped for a long and harmonious family life with her husband, Evgenia had begun to help him in his legal work and essentially served as his assistant, which required more education than she was said to have acquired at the Smolny Institute and, moreover, she needed concentration, diligence, and common sense, otherwise she would have made mistakes that would have ruined her husband's career. In other words, Evgenia must have possessed a fully developed adult mind, but during the trial she was presented as equivalent to a child or a person with reduced intellectual capacity, who could not function until and unless she was educated by an older and experienced man.

The three available men in her life—her brother (we only know that he was striving for a judiciary position), Chikhachev, and her husband—apparently failed utterly in this task. Chikhachev's duties to not treat Evgenia as a mere object of his desire or, failing that, not to disclose their relationship, were quite simple. Nepenin's spousal obligations were more complicated, but aside from their joint legal work, the case mentions only one pedagogical effort on his part. He testified that the objective of arranging the initial confrontation between his wife and Chikhachev at a tavern—and, by implication, the point of the entire manhunt that resulted from that meeting—were "a kind of pedagogical exercise, conducted in order to open his wife's eyes." He was apparently convinced that she thought that Chikhachev was in love with her, and that Chikhachev thought the same about her, and that a personal meeting would clear up any misunderstanding, as well as help Nepenin discover the truth.

Evgenia seemingly thought at first that it was her duty to play up and placate her husband's anger: she demanded, to Nepenin's amusement, that Chikhachev commit suicide (claiming that only Chikhachev's death would save her from dishonor). But even several months after that meeting, her independent personality and her melodramatic writing style show through (despite Koni's claims to the contrary) in her letters to Chikhachev, in which she understandably cursed him for ruining her life. But already at this point Nepenin was no longer interested in a further partnership with his wife.

Evgenia Nepenina's diary is clear evidence of that. It began on 2 November 1873, less than a month before the murder of Chikhachev:

> O, what a terrible day it was! How I was beaten! I think I will remember it for a long time. But for what? O! How I curse that horrible day! How I suffer! When will it end? How pathetic I am! I don't have anyone to turn to, no one will be sorry for me! I think we are through. . . . How strong is my rage! How happy I was when nothing had been yet revealed; it is sad to convey all of this and it's even sadder to leave a man whom I love so strongly. Where will I go now? I am penniless and covered in shame, everyone has nothing but contempt for me. . . . I of course want to correct the evil but how—it is something I cannot do by myself.

In the subsequent three weeks Evgenia continued to narrate how her husband beat her (although she almost never wrote, "he beat me" instead using the passive, "I was beaten") and dragged her around "painfully" by her hair. And yet days of beatings were followed by "good" days when she would write "What a wonderful day it was! . . . How much love and passion was expressed! O! How strongly I love him! My dear husband! What wouldn't I do so that such days would be, if not constant, at least without those terrible stains that ruined our life so much." A few days later "there was another attempt to beat me up but [he] held himself back. Then I sang; we made peace." A few days later Nepenin's sister visited them, and "in her presence he called me a liar and inflicted all kinds of unpleasantness." She passed a sleepless night. Then: "In a fit of rage he bit me on my nose. I screamed and for that was called a vile one (*podlaia*). I know that I must submit and never dare to scream. But I could not take it anymore and smacked him (*dala pliukhu*) and called him a scoundrel. By sunrise we made peace and fell asleep." On 12 November she wrote that "of course I must perish. . . . But I agree to everything, as long as it would make him happy. But I doubt it will make him happy. At least I had five years of a good life and this means I really do love him, if all the humiliations and insults I forget instantly whenever he is kind to me, and he poor thing (*bedniazhka*) has no rest and it's all my fault. I will gladly do anything to make him happy. It is only sad that he, through such treatment of me, brought me to such horrible fear of him." On a particular day she would praise Nepenin's "exalted, deep soul" and claim "how much that is good I adopt from him!" But at the same time she would say, "I become more and more convinced that I will depart from him." One day she left the house at night and lay on the snow for three hours hoping to catch a cough (she seems to have succeeded in contracting tuberculosis). On 14 November she noticed that he was in a bad mood and "came up to him to talk . . . I don't know what was it that I said but he hit me very hard with the pipe he was smoking. . . . It is terribly hard to stop his anger. . . . The torture of the interrogation began again." During the questioning Nepenin thought that she smiled at his words, "and then he gave me such a slap that blood streamed out of my nose. I could not even open my eyes—he has never beaten me so painfully. He said N. [his sister] is always right about you. Last time she said that everyone beats such women as yourself."[54]

The journalist from the weekly *Nedelia* interpreted Evgenia's behavior as that of a child: "Weak and oblivious people always resemble a child who, having hurt himself against something, begins to beat the object against which he hurt himself." Therefore, the journalist reasoned that prior to the final incident she lashed out at what she thought was the cause of her misery, Chikhachev and his seduction, "instead of accepting the consequences of her actions to understand what she did as opposed to what other people did"—meaning that the true cause of her misery was her husband. *Nedelia*'s writer concluded that by shooting at Chikhachev Evgenia was also symbolically shooting at her husband and thus finally rebelling against an abusive, failed patriarch (or, from a present-day perspective, against men and patriarchy in general). This narrative resembles the way Vera Zasulich was presented at her trial as having shot General Trepov in 1877 to aim symbolically at prior arbitrary abuses of the regime (which is why the public, including senior officials observing the trial, applauded the verdict of acquittal), although this was not why she herself believed she fired the shot and almost certainly not why the jurors actually acquitted her.

While the abusive authority figures discussed so far in this chapter were vested with legitimate authority over their victims, several important criminal cases focused on the figure of a male patriarch whose authority was false, even though it was originally enacted in a sphere which the tsar's laws could not easily control, and thus it was challenged only after tragedy had struck. The antiheroes here were therefore not technically patriarchs at all, yet they were discussed in the same terms as Nepenin and Chikhachev.

The first of these trials took place in Petersburg on 24 March 1870 and attracted much of the capital's highest society. The main defendant was a pimp: twenty-six-year-old Maksim Ivanov, who kept a mini brothel in an apartment with three women; one was his mistress and the other two—eighteen-year-old Aleksandra Avdeeva and nineteen-year-old Daria Turbina—were prostitutes.[55] Also prosecuted were two other men who lived in the apartment. One day Ivanov and his two prostitutes went to the "dancing establishment" called El Dorado, and met his habitual customer Aulic Councilor von Zon (Sohn). Ivanov told the bureaucrat that he had an innocent young girl staying in his apartment and offered him the opportunity to take her virginity for thirty rubles, to which the man agreed. Once in the apartment, the group gave him a poisoned drink, strangled him with a belt, and then hit him with a clothing iron. Throughout these violent proceedings Avdeeva was tasked with masking noise, which she did by randomly striking keys on a piano, singing, and stomping her feet. Afterward von Zon's body was stuffed into a large suitcase and sent by railroad mail to Moscow to be opened by horrified postmen there, hence its infamy as the "suitcase murder." This murder was thus as "aggravated" as possible, combining as it did robbery, torture, poison, strangling, and "beating with a clothing iron." Of further note is the disturbing fact that aside from Ivanov all the participants were minors at the time of the crime.

The central social and legal issue that captured so much attention in the trial was the existence of organized child prostitution within the fabric of respectable Petersburg society. Its greater significance, however, lies in the fact that the story presented a picture of an alternative, perverse version of domesticity. The women of this household were exploited in every sense, yet at the same time the curiously domestic arrangement of Ivanov's operation performed certain services to its victim. These prostitutes, unlike most occupying any large city, lived in relative comfort, and since Ivanov was using these women primarily to rob his victims, he was apparently allowing them to avoid the physical exploitation of their bodies at least some of the time.

The success of the scheme depended on maintaining social hierarchies and proprieties, such that a mid-ranking official could pay a visit to an apparently respectable domestic space without comment, unlike a bathhouse or other venue of ill-repute. Von Zon went there expecting to pay for the opportunity to transgress every rule of polite society by deflowering a respectable virgin without consequence. In other words, the proprieties were supposed to be real, to provide the thrill for von Zon's transgression. Instead all the trappings of respectability were a thin facade, and von Zon became the dupe in a mundanely brutal, clumsy crime worthy of the lowest-caliber back alley.

Spasovich defended Avdeeva, and his strategy was to push all the blame on Ivanov, in effect serving as a second (and far more talented) prosecutor.[56] Daughter of a tailor, Avdeeva was seduced and abandoned by a military officer at fourteen and went to Petersburg, where she joined a brothel owned by one Rybakova or Rybakovskaia on Nevsky Prospect. In a place of amusement similar to the El Dorado—this one called Elysium—she met Maksim Ivanov, who enticed her to move in with him at the end of July 1869. Enjoying this relative improvement in her condition, she continued to live there and to sell her body for Ivanov's benefit. Spasovich presented Adveeva very similarly to the narratives in the Nepenina and Kronenberg cases, as not fully human because her handler, Ivanov, "treated her like some merchandise":

> If you discard this El Dorado–style polish, this woman is shown to be a savage in the full sense of this word . . . she has no education, she can only read large printed letters and very poorly at that; she never learned anything. I tried to find out whether she can play piano—it turns out that she had no idea—she hits the keys with her fists and stamps her feet when asked to play . . . at all times she acts like a trained little dog . . . this woman has no attachments, she never loved anyone, . . . one can say that straight out of her childhood she moved into a brothel . . . her entire life does not leave the bounds of the most crude cynicism . . . one cannot say that she lacks any feeling: she is not a stone, she has nerves, she cried in my presence, but she only cried about herself and not about others . . . a creature barely resembling an underdeveloped human, who can only be treated as a mindless animal.

Spasovich concluded that the defendants aside from Ivanov were "completely ordinary persons, so that they should rather induce pity" than blame—and that any verdict for Avdeeva would be an improvement over her life with Maksim Ivanov.[57] In the event, Ivanov was sentenced to twelve years of hard labor in Siberia, the other two men who had also participated in the murder received four years each, and Avdeeva got only exile to Siberia, with no hard labor.

THE NEGLIGENT PATRIARCH AND MADEMOISELLE JUJEAN

The case of Marguerite Jujean mentioned at the opening of this chapter is exceptionally rich in detail, made up of a polyphonic narrative by a large number of witnesses. Compared to open violence, poisoning is difficult to prosecute (unless poisoners make the obvious mistake of feeding their victims enough arsenic to kill an elephant). It was seen as a crime of the weak, a "women's crime."[58] This particular poisoning trial turned into a powerful exposé of respectable middle-class life, showing every fear, tension, and conflict of post-reform society resulting from sex, the upbringing of a younger generation that did not remember serfdom, science, political subversion, hierarchies, and family relations. Jujean's character and actions were scrutinized at the trial, but the characters of Colonel Poznanskii and his sixteen-year-old son were scrutinized at much greater length. Criticized every bit as harshly as the banker child beater Kronenberg, Poznanskii failed in all the opposite ways, accused by journalists of negligence—failing to properly bring up his son—rather than of violence and harsh mistreatment. Poznanskii thus exposed to the Russian public a completely different and more complicated—and more modern—form of abuse within the supposedly respectable family. The story that is recounted below came out only gradually over the course of several days during the trial, so that to the people who heard it in person it would have sounded far less cogent.[59]

Ignatii Nikolaevich Poznanskii was a senior officer (and later a general) of the Corps of Gendarmes, whose officers also staffed Russia's political police known as the Third Section. He headed the capital's railroad gendarmes, however, rather than the regular ones who served in the political police. Railroads of course were vital to the empire's daily operations, hence the special body to oversee it—and yet among the gendarmes railroad assignments went to second-best officers.[60] Gendarmes could not be Catholic (and so Poznanskii, despite his and his wife's Polish names, appears to have been Russified) and they rarely came from aristocratic families, but the job paid well and never lacked eager recruits. Poznanskii started out as a career soldier, graduating from the prestigious and demanding General Staff Academy, and transferred to the Corps of Gendarmes in 1871. His wife, Aleksandra Frantsevna, was originally an actress from Kiev. His son Kolya (Nikolai) was not yet seventeen, his daughter Nadia (Nadezhda) was eleven, and his younger son Misha (Mikhail) was only six. Their social network was limited, aside from their family members, servants, and their nanny, Rudneva, to about half a dozen friends, mostly Kolya's classmates.

And then there was Marguerite Jujean, her name Russified as Margarita or even the diminutive Margosha. Born in Bordeaux, she came to Russia in 1863 when she was twenty-five, making her about thirty-eight at the time of the trial. Her origins and her earlier life were shrouded in mystery: her education was said to be much better than one could see from her papers. She was an excellent calligrapher and at one point had enjoyed an independent, respectable life, with her own household and a maid. Her fortunes then declined, but she had no trouble finding a job as a governess in the households of aristocrats and high officials, like that of the general's wife Popova, who recommended her highly to Poznanskii when Kolya was about ten. Everyone who knew her gave a glowing account: she was very kind to the children, spent her own money to buy them sweets and presents, had been employed by very good families and lived very modestly.

After Kolya grew up and even the younger Nadia had begun her formal schooling, Jujean did not want to leave her position with the family. Her official duties at this point were merely to walk Nadia to school and help with her French in exchange for eating with the family (but living in her own apartment). Her status in the household was unclear: neither a friend nor hired help but a strange mixture of both. The prosecutor tried to explain this strangeness as an artifact of the Poznanskiis' provincial background:

> These simple and frank Russian people began to lead a life that was not that of high-society (*otkrytuiu*), but one they could afford and at the same time was hospitable and welcoming. Their circle of acquaintance was defined by the needs of their children's upbringing and meeting their old acquaintances from the province. They did not give receptions to maintain connections or pursue some other objectives. Rather, they led an entirely introspective family life with a shade of good old times. Anyone who ended up at the Poznanskiis, even accidentally, could have a place at their table and if necessary even a corner to sleep in ... the Poznanskiis lived exceedingly rationally and hospitably. Moreover, in their home one could always find young people. People gathered there, and whenever there are young people it is loud, merry, and free.[61]

This merry life ended on 18 April 1878 (less than three weeks after Vera Zasulich's acquittal), when Kolya failed to wake up. The maid said that he went to bed the night before at just before midnight and seemed perfectly cheerful. He was standing in the doorway to his room and chatting in French with Jujean, who was about to go home. In the end he said in Russian as he always did when he was in a good mood: "See you later Mariusha" (another diminutive). The maid came into Kolya's room the next morning to wake him up and found him lying in his bed with his feet at the head on the pillows, his lips swollen and black, his mouth half open and drooling, his tongue dark.

Several doctors immediately rushed to the apartment. The police doctor thought Kolya had had a stroke, but other doctors dissected Kolya's body and put his organs in jars for further analysis. His mother pointed out a bottle of medicine on the shelf in Kolya's room, which was supposed to be a potassium iodide prescription. At the doctor's suggestion, the father tasted the medicine and he said it was bitter like morphine. The organs turned out to contain morphine as well. But the testimony by various witnesses was so confusing that it remains unclear exactly how much was in the bottle and how much of the medicine Kolya had taken. In any event, morphine's effectiveness depended on how used he was to taking it, which is also unknown. Had Kolya taken that morphine-laced medicine at bedtime, he would have had spasms and nausea within the hour, but his body was still warm in the morning when the doctors arrived.

The Poznanskiis' medical history was complicated, given that they were among the most privileged inhabitants of Petersburg, known for its exceedingly unpleasant climate. Misha, the youngest boy, had typhus, Nadia had rubella, which she gave to Kolya, who also had swollen lymph nodes (for which he took iodized iron) and an eye disease, with the suspicion of a scrofula-like condition. Everyone had coughs, rashes, and other such illnesses. And all the members of the family, including the two youngest children, were taking morphine. When after Kolya's death Ignatii was transferred to Nizhny Novgorod to head the gendarmes there, he was infamous for his addiction.[62] He was something of an authority on morphine and kept a large jar in his room, testifying that he "himself had been many times poisoned by morphine, and this is the feeling he experienced: one feels a sort of tickling in the brain (*kakoe-to shchekotanie v mozgu*), a heaviness in the limbs, and finally one loses consciousness; a person rushes about, does not know what to do with [his] arms and legs." Kolya was prescribed morphine two days before his death for his rubella. It came out during the trial, however, that he also smoked cigarettes laced with morphine, but—because he was obsessed with his health—he limited himself to four per day and used a cottonwool filter, apparently to prevent an overdose.

It does not seem particularly surprising that in an apartment full of morphine taken by everyone in the family, a sixteen-year-old boy would eventually suffer from an overdose. At first everyone assumed it was an accident, that he took too much of his nighttime medicine. But he had started taking it two days previously and would likely have felt the effects then. Could it have been suicide? Everyone said that he was the least inclined toward suicide of anyone they knew: he was "extremely suspicious, took great care of his health, was interested in all the hygienic rules and tried to always follow them." For example, when he read that it was unhealthy to eat before bed, he stopped eating supper. Because smoking was bad, he limited his intake. His relations to his parents were of "extreme friendliness and limitless mutual [life]." He never used force, never had arguments. Moreover, his expensive educational chemistry kit included strong poisons that he could easily have taken but did not.

At the parents' suggestion, the police then turned to Jujean. The parents said that they were surprised by how she reacted to Kolya's death: when Ignatii ran into her on the street, she did not become hysterical but only said "I already know about it. Akh, what a pity! And I was bringing him barbaris candy." At the same time, she visited the family daily from the day of Kolya's death until his funeral and, as her lawyer, Khartulari, later noted, she would have had to be a super-criminal not to look suspicious day after day. There were several other arguments about her possible involvement included in the indictment, most of which make little sense. She did spend Kolya's last evening in their apartment, with everyone mostly sitting in Ignatii's room, reading and talking, and theoretically she could have poisoned Kolya, except that Jujean was never alone in any of the rooms and one may reason that Ignatii, like all drug addicts, would have kept a careful watch on his jar of morphine.

While no one mentioned it at the trial, Kolya's mother had had a longstanding conflict with Jujean, as we know from Jujean's letters to the investigator and the prosecutor in her case that she wrote before the trial, as she did to Judge Koni, who managed to get hold of these letters and to preserve them in his personal archive. The prosecutor asked to read the letters, but Jujean did not give permission, so they stayed out of the trial. In these letters, Jujean in turn accused Madame Poznanskii of intentionally poisoning Kolya because he threatened to expose her extramarital affairs.[63]

The most important reason everyone's attention turned to Jujean is that she and Kolya allegedly had had a sexual relationship. Friends and relatives had noticed it, the parents said that they suspected it, and the servants knew about it but said nothing (his room was completely private; servants entered it only when called). Even one of Poznanskii's officers, who once had to housesit his apartment and watch over the children, noticed it but thought it was not his place to get involved. Their relations had initially been the ordinary ones of a governess and a pupil, but they became "special" (*osobye*) after Kolya turned

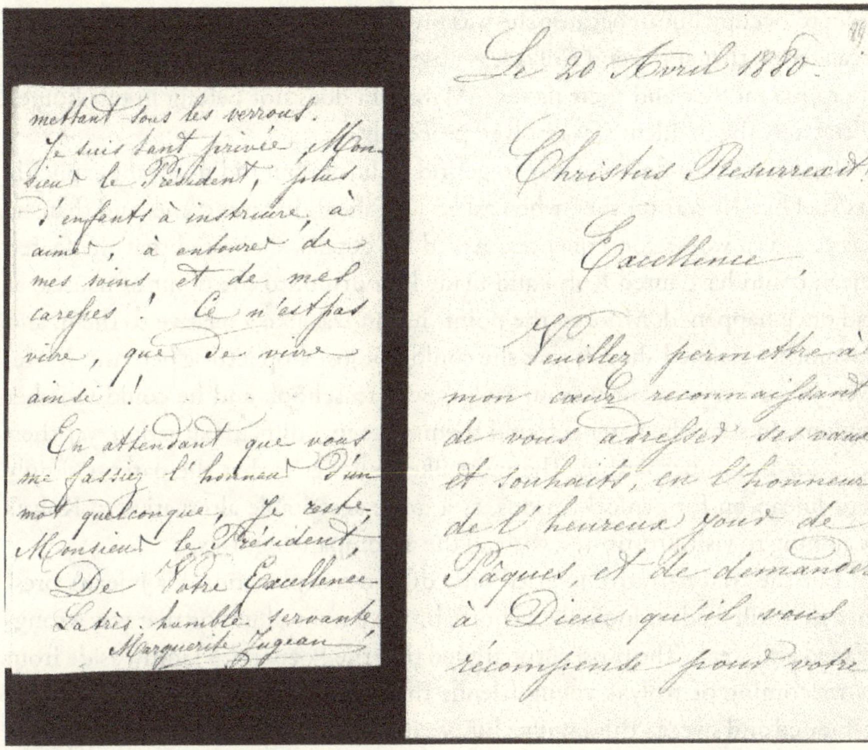
mettant sous les verrous.
Je suis tant privée, Monsieur le Président, plus d'enfants à instruire, à aimer, à entourer de mes soins et de mes caresses! Ce n'est pas vivre, que de vivre ainsi!
En attendant que vous me fassiez l'honneur d'un mot quelconque, je reste, Monsieur le Président, De Votre Excellence
La très humble servante
Marguerite Jujean

89
Le 20 Avril 1880.
Christus Resurrexit!
Excellence
Veuillez permettre à mon cœur reconnaissant de vous adresser ses vœux et souhaits, en l'honneur de l'heureux jour de Pâques, et de demander à Dieu qu'il vous récompense pour votre

Figure 17. One of Marguerite Jujean's letters to Anatoly Koni, dated 20 April 1880. IRLI 134.4.250, l. 89.

fourteen. They kissed and sought to be alone with each other. The father testified that in 1876 he accidentally walked into a room and saw Kolya lying on a sofa and Jujean sitting nearby, making a suspicious noise (the room was dark). It looked as though a woman's dress or a blanket was perhaps pulled up. Ignatii had a stern talk with Kolya, who gave evasive answers. Their family physician, Dr. Nikolaev, was then called to examine the boy but did not find any "premature development of the sexual organs." Jujean continued to stay late with Kolya, often until two or three in the morning.

When Kolya turned fifteen, he grew into a tall, handsome youth who began to pay attention to schoolwork and to be interested in reading, music, and chemistry. He was becoming healthier and more energetic. His relations with Jujean also changed: they began to quarrel more and more, and Jujean sometimes became so hysterical that a doctor had to be called. One day the younger children, Nadia and Misha, walked into their brother's room, and he asked them to occupy Jujean because she was preventing him from reading. The scene escalated so that at the end Kolya was waving his small dagger in the air and saying to his mother and their nanny, "Margarita does not belong in our home." Ultimately the incident was resolved peaceably.

Ignatii tried to find of a way to get rid of Jujean but did not want explicitly to expel her. Kolya's mother, when asked why she didn't intervene, said that she was afraid of worse consequences. Asked for details, she stated that she feared Jujean could have lured Kolya and made him drunk to the point of nausea, as had once happened. More to the point, Jujean was like a relative to them, and the mother claimed she felt that she could not just stop letting her visit. Moreover, Jujean's apartment was on Kolya's way to school, and he could visit her anytime. In sum, the parents found themselves in a difficult situation, yet their behavior is also perplexing. The most likely answer is that the parents simply kept Jujean on for cynical reasons, as a more acceptable alternative to Kolya's beginning to visit prostitutes, with all the accompanying risks.

But the trial narrative focused on a different explanation for Jujean's presence that still made it look like a choice by the parents, but one that was wrongheaded and weak. The prosecutor argued that the Poznanskii family, aside from its welcoming of Kolya's young friends that the prosecutor thought was old-fashioned and sweet, "this family's life . . . also had something new. This new element, I believe, resulted from rethinking the old principles of upbringing *(vospitaniia)*. Children here have, so to speak, autonomy. They have a considerable measure of freedom, they are treated mildly, and the house does not use strong punitive measures."[64] Kolya's uncle testified that his brother's disciplinary system did not utilize repression or punishment, only "good advice": Kolya had complete freedom to choose his acquaintances, readings, and activities. When one parent did not like something he did, he or she would try to prove to him the harm or uselessness of his actions.[65] Judge Koni later described this upbringing as "anarchic."[66]

The father testified that he did not want to expel Jujean and hurt Kolya's feelings, but he calculated that Kolya would simply grow out of her and become interested in other things. Ignatii therefore bought his son an expensive set for chemical experiments and a photo camera, and also allowed him to invite friends to his apartment, to visit them, and to have parties. For example, in December 1877, Kolya and twelve of his friends celebrated the fall of the Ottoman fortress of Plevna to the Russian army with a party, during which they drank four bottles of alcohol, including one of cognac, one of port, and two of red wine. Kolya also started visiting homes that included young ladies of his own age. Toward the end of 1877 and beginning of 1878 Kolya began to visit the family of Pliushchinskii, who had a sixteen-year-old daughter, Vera, who went to the same school as his sister. Kolya began to pass notes with her, and there was some talk of an amateur play, a common pastime for upper-middle-class youth. Their friendship did not end well, however, which made some observers wonder if Kolya had killed himself out of depression over their breakup. Vera's note to Kolya was read in the courtroom:

> [W]hat is the point of this constant demand to love you? You know it's impossible to force someone to love you and the heart knows no fatherland. I told you once and for all that I love you as a kind and good young man, but will never love you in any other way; why am I to blame if this does not satisfy you? And if you will bother me with fake compliments, with nonexistent feelings, or with requests for love that I cannot give you—I will stop liking you. Be a good boy (*pain'ka*), and if you want me to like you, then be always what you were that time at our place: do you remember how you came by on a Saturday, no one else was home and the two of us chatted over our math and geography, please be like you were then, and I will always love you.[67]

After this confrontation Kolya wrote in his diary: "One young lady has acquired a bad opinion about me, considering me a fop (*fat*) . . . and I indeed thought a lot about myself, caring after my health and mental development . . . as far as possible I try not to create idols for myself, but one idol did come about. My idol is myself, I love myself, care about myself so much that God give any mother to take care of her children this diligently."

Kolya wanted to eventually work for a living and help his family financially, but he was frustrated that he had "so long left to grind the books (*tianut' liamku*): two and a half years of *gimnazia,* then five years in the academy, whereas I only have about ten or so years left to live. . . . All of my hope is for medicine and for music. They will help me to become famous." Kolya also wrote about some "F.I." who was getting in his way with Vera. The end of the diary was scratched out, but Jujean's defense lawyer, Khartulari, said that it was possible to make out the phrase "one of us will have to move to a better world."[68]

Journalists interpreted this language as evidence of moral bankruptcy: the weekly *Nedelia*'s columnist thought that

> The defendant in this case was actually not Madame Jujean but rather some kind of worn-out form of life, some kind of 'thing,' some kind of 'x' that

> creates moral corpses out of living people in their seventeen years of age, creating dead bodies unneeded in the world of the living. And if life creates only tens of thousands of such Kolyas, then the atmosphere in which they form should give some thought to the society. . . . N. Poznanskii . . . has neither a burning heart, nor passion, nor noble pursuits. You see a cold calculation that is only seventeen years of age, and a reason directed only at egotistical cares and dreams about personal happiness. He is discontented with everything, tired of everything, disappointed with everything.[69]

But others were not convinced: no one who actually knew Kolya had noticed any alarming signs in his behavior. His uncle said that Kolya was phlegmatic, reserved, maybe not completely sincere, since he positively refused to discuss with him his relations with Jujean. But he was often merry, he joked around, played the piano, and sang songs. Even Kolya's diary does not look particularly unusual for any sixteen-year-old boy; the entries do not show him to be morally decadent or suicidal. He was reported to be looking better than ever before, healthier than before, and having more fun than before.

But he did not seem to have cut off his connection with Jujean. Some testimony suggested that after Kolya acquired an outside social life with other youths of his age, Jujean became involved in these activities as well. She took part in some of their parties and according to one of Kolya's friends "held herself rather liberally: she allowed us to take off our coats in her presence and to treat her freely . . . we would drink to *bruderschaft* . . . there were also some other indecencies!" Another friend said that "because she had a good, merry personality and knew how to engage a company, it really was boring without her." But at these parties she "did not conduct herself as is proper for a woman. . . . For example, instead of laughing she constantly shrieked and allowed herself other such things." These stories show the way middle-class respectability was carefully constructed, and that Jujean was toeing a fine line between being a friend of the family and behaving essentially like a fallen woman. Kolya freely admitted to his friends that he had had sexual relations with Jujean, and to one of the friends he even used a word that he considered indecent to refer to her. The youth would not repeat the word in the courtroom, and Judge Koni did not want to clear the court just for that one piece of information, so he famously had the boy write the word on a sheet of paper, which he later tore up (only to find a high-ranking official embarrassing himself after the trial by picking up the scraps and trying to put the word together). In response to the boy's revelation, Koni only asked: "Do you understand this verb in its indecent sense?"[70]

In addition to her frequent emotional outbursts, Jujean seems to have developed the habit of writing anonymous letters.[71] First, she sent one to Kolya stating that Jujean intended to poison herself but that he could prevent it because "it is known that you take an interest in Margarita Jujean." Even more important, in early April, shortly before Kolya's death, the Third Section received an anonymous letter stating that Kolya and as many as six of his friends had formed a political conspiracy and set up a chemical laboratory in his room for the purpose of preparing poisons to kill the city's governor and members of the imperial family. The letter also said that these plotters met under the excuse of rehearsing a play. It added that Nikolai Poznanskii had too much freedom for his age, came home late and drunk, and had three lovers although he was only seventeen, one of whom was a Pole and an extreme nihilist. The Third Section hinted to Ignatii that something was going on, and it appears that one of the officers even informally searched Kolya's room on the pretext of visiting his father. But the chief of the Third Section, General Mezentsov, showed the letter to Ignatii only after Kolya's death, when he thought that it could help to clear up a murder. All of this was of course very serious, given that a series of terrorist attacks against the tsar and his officials were taking place—these attacks would culminate in the regicide of 1881, and Mezentsov would himself be assassinated only a few months after Kolya's death. Many radicals came from privileged backgrounds, and even the Third Section was not impervious to penetration by anarchist agents. According to one account Ignatii immediately recognized Jujean's handwriting, and according to another he did not but said that the manner of writing was hers and that only she would have known all the facts mentioned in the letter. Ignatii later testified that he became convinced of Jujean's guilt after he was given this letter.

Three handwriting experts confirmed that it was her handwriting. Two teachers of French who also looked at the letter said that the style was incorrect but also included "completely" French expressions, and the mistakes appear to have been made intentionally because difficult words were written correctly and ordinary ones had serious mistakes that no one who could write in French like that would ever make. Some letters were written in a form that natural Frenchmen write letters.

The trial included a session closed to the public. Jujean and Kolya's father could choose three persons each to stay inside. The newspaper reporter could not reveal "even in a general way" what went on, "but you can figure it out from the speeches given by the parties and from the Chairman's summation."[72] Jujean's position, from which she did not deviate, was to deny all charges and insinuations, including writing the anonymous letter to the Third Section. She said that she treated Kolya as a mother would. The Poznanskii family was kind, but the children were neglected. "The wife was at the club, the husband was in the service, and the children were left by themselves." Khartulari, Jujean's capable lawyer, argued that she must be either an archcriminal or innocent. She was with the family and around the body from the day of Kolya's death and until his funeral and had not once shown any suspicious behavior. Khartulari also suggested that some of the witnesses and accusers, especially Kolya's parents, were not all that they purported to be: "And indeed, do you not consider to be puzzling and problematic such facts that, for example, into a family that is completely respectable and patriarchal, a woman enters who virtually with the parents' permission engages in debauching their fourteen-year-old son, surrounding him, according to the parents, not with a mother's care or a sister's concern, but by the tenderness of a passionate woman, and despite that, the parents not only [fail to?] expel her from their home, but allow her to continue her criminal activity with impunity."[73] With Koni's summation also clearly sympathetic to Jujean, the jury acquitted her, and "the public met the jury's verdict at first with applause and then with a general hissing, which accompanied Jujean on her way from the dock. Behind closed doors her hysterical weeping could be heard. Later in his memoirs Koni more or less admitted that he had manipulated the jury: his account of the case transitions smoothly into a general discussion of the extent judges can or should influence juries' verdicts, comparing the practice in France, where a judge could say directly that he believed a defendant should be convicted or acquitted, and Russia, where this was not seen as appropriate but, as Koni proved time and again, was not particularly difficult to accomplish indirectly.[74]

In sum, Kolya probably overdosed on morphine, but the interest of the case is in how the Poznanskiis' "patriarchal" (according to the prosecutor) provincial lifestyle with a fashionable French governess danced so lightly on the edge of Russian modernity, allowing Kolya a life with all the drugs, sex, money, and freedom desired by any postmodern teenager. Kolya was a victim of Jujean's passion and anger to some degree (almost certainly short of murder), but society concluded that he was above all the victim of his father's unbounded permissiveness, the opposite, but equally defective, transgression from the other antipatriarchs' unbridled violence.

A Russian public that had never before been privy to the entertaining but deeply unsettling minutiae of violent crime, police investigations, and the competing narratives of an adversarial trial had much to take in over the course of only a few years in the 1870s. These trials could not resolve the untenable social conflicts at issue, despite the efforts of a large bureaucracy and a newly professionalized class of lawyers and jurists. Instead, the trials put these unresolvable conflicts into the spotlight, forcing the public to make sense of a world in which horrific crimes happened inexplicably to (sometimes) innocent people and justice did not always have a means of bringing their world back to at least a perception of order. More specifically, the public was drawn to trials involving elites, the people who enjoyed extraordinary privileges, who were insulated from ordinary realities by titles, uniforms, or wealth, yet who, as the newspapers revealed to the public, nonetheless were capable of and susceptible to the basest motives, or who despite their elegant homes and assertions of independence and privacy were as subject to sudden, inexplicable violence as any denizen of the street, or so it seemed. Crimes involving elites were very much less common than "ordinary" violence, yet the prominence of these trials placed such incidents on a stage, giving them a place in the consciousness of the population that subsequently informed the ways most people looked at the world's arrangements and possibilities. If the first, most striking lesson of the legal theater of the 1870s was the ever-present role of money and property as a driver of seemingly inhuman acts and the second lesson was the persistence of honor as a core value when crimes of "passion" overrode all other factors, then the third lesson was that the logic of patriarchy that structured all of Russian society depended on characteristics like adherence to duty and honesty that suddenly seemed all too easy to fake or subvert.

PART THREE

Deception

Figure 18. Cartoon of the Jacks of Hearts from Russia's leading satirical weekly, *Budil'nik,* 1877, no. 9, back cover. The captions read: "All of Moscow is reading the cards. . . . For itself . . . for its heart. . . . Wondering how it will all end."

For almost a month in 1877, the Russian public was engrossed in one of the largest nonpolitical trials in the history of Russian law. An alleged criminal organization dubbed the Jacks of Hearts Club (*Klub chervonnykh valetov*) involved forty-eight defendants in addition to several who had died or managed to escape, as well as more than three hundred witnesses.[1] The charges included dozens of episodes of fraud and forgery committed between 1866 and 1875, one murder, and one count of sacrilege. Each of these episodes could have merited a separate trial, but instead they were united in one huge and uniquely complex proceeding.[2] Equally sensational was the fact that the defendants belonged to respectable society, among them wealthy merchants, landowning nobles, and even a member of the aristocratic Dolgorukov family. In the Russian popular lexicon, a Jack of Hearts became enduring shorthand for a personable young swindler of upper-class origins. Over the years, the story grew in the telling, with some of the legends traveling from author to author, such as the story of Pavel Karlovich Speier, the alleged leader of the group, who supposedly tricked a naive English tourist into "buying" the official residence of the Moscow governor-general on Tverskaia Street.[3]

The case record reads as a veritable encyclopedia of life in post-emancipation Moscow with all its iniquities, anxieties, and opportunities. Even before the Great Reforms Moscow had been a major center of manufacturing, trade, and finance, attracting not only peasants and laborers but also men and women of the respectable classes looking for white-collar jobs, marriage prospects, education, or money. The reforms intensified this trend, liberalizing the financial and legal framework and also encouraging the belief that quick wealth was within reach, as long as one invested shrewdly or successfully played the stock market.[4] This social and emotional environment encouraged diverse types of fraud and forgery, which of course were neither new nor unique to Russia, but the old tricks, such as selling nonexistent real estate or pretending to be rich to borrow money, were now joined by new ones, for example stock fraud and railway swindles.[5] A columnist of the *Saint Petersburg Times,* writing in the midst of the Jacks of Hearts' trial in early 1877, commented ironically that while some people thought they were living in the age of iron, or coal, or kerosene, it should be known more appropriately as "the age of the Great Swindle," because "almost every day every newspaper page is filled with news about fraudulent tricks effected everywhere."[6] Also new was public exposure and public attention to these great fraud scandals, which were particularly frequent in the 1870s. The trial of the Jacks of Hearts was widely seen to be part of a series—indeed (in the apt words of court reporter and memoirist Yekaterina Ivanovna Kozlinina) their "apotheosis."[7]

Among the most prominent post-reform legal scandals, these fraud cases stand out both individually and as a group. They featured larger casts of participants and combined more diverse factual circumstances compared to even the most spectacular cases of murder or political crime.[8] Defendants were typically among the leaders in their field of activity, and their prosecution was publicly, socially, and even politically impactful. Large fraud cases debated the most contentious and ambiguous questions of the law that shaped Russia's financial and commercial system. Jurors had to respond to questions that, objectively speaking, did not have yes or no answers. Conceptually, fraud cases differ from the violent ones discussed in part II because they were nonviolent, that is, did not inflict or threaten immediate bodily harm but relied on deception, breaking the victim's trust, manipulating and subverting the all-important notion that documents, institutions, and markers of social status conferred a degree of security upon a transaction or activity. But there were important differences among fraud cases as well, which justify dividing this part of the book into three chapters. Chapter 8 discusses fraud carried out by individual swindlers and con artists, that is, persons who were educated or respectable or at least socially polished but who did not hold any formal or legitimate position of responsibility. Con artists were as ubiquitous in the nineteenth century as they are today, but there were other varieties of financial crime. Chapter 9 discusses prominent trials for forgery of official documents, such as testaments or debt notes, by persons who were not impostors and could easily have been holding these papers legitimately. The chapter explores the tangle of ideas and practices relating to gender, kinship hierarchies, and social status. Finally, chapter 10 examines Russia's first large-scale corporate scandals, perpetuated by bankers, merchants, or other trusted company and institutional officials with control over large sums of money.

CHAPTER 8

The Age of Fraud

Among all the great fraud trials, that of the Jacks of Hearts begins this inquiry because it targeted the most primeval variety of what today is known as white-collar crime; that is, it prosecuted a loose network of con artists or swindlers lacking any legitimate influence in a commercial or governmental organization.[1] Rather, they relied on their looks, manners, and acting ability, with sporadic and unreliable assistance from family and friends to create a veneer of wealth and social respectability. The case presented extensive evidence that in Moscow alone there were hundreds of such criminals and demi-criminals from gentry, merchant, or servitor (state-servant) families who operated in a nebulous and by definition barely identifiable legal and social gray zone.[2] Their arsenal of tricks and schemes mimicked, infiltrated, and thus undermined the entire range of legitimate transactions that defined Russia's regime of private property and commerce. Fraud undermined legitimate structures and practices by revealing their principles to be every bit as contingent and even ephemeral as the swindlers' tricks, thus throwing into doubt the very notion of elite and middle-class respectability as ensuring safety and prosperity.[3]

The legal and social framework of property ownership in Russia had taken centuries to develop, but the principle most visible in the mid-nineteenth century was that of absolute ownership: the notion that an asset, such as a landed estate or a commercial enterprise, was presumed to have only one owner, a person who could control and dispose of it at will. The principle that society and the body politic amounted to a set of such independent property owners is traced, most immediately, to John Locke in the case of England and to Jean Bodin and several other thinkers in early modern France, whereas in Russia it is associated with Catherine II.[4] A series of laws during her reign turned Russia's servitor class into virtually unconditional owners of serf-populated villages and other related assets, with similar protections also extended to Russian merchants and entrepreneurs.[5] The legal and administrative system erected under Catherine ensured that elite and middle-class property was well protected, especially in comparison to limited political rights, and that, for instance, property disputes would not be automatically won by wealthier or more violent participants. The principle of absolute ownership was complicated in practice by the existence of a lively and complex property market and by alternative forms of property ownership and control, including joint ownership, familial properties, leaseholds, commercial partnerships, and other commercial and credit arrangements.[6] My earlier study of pre-reform Russia's property regime suggests that absolute property rights created a higher risk of fraud, since criminals would only need to deceive one individual, but a more diffuse arrangement was also risky, making it easier to falsify some of its more vulnerable elements, thereby endangering the entire structure.[7] During the reforms of the 1860s all of these fundamental structures and risks remained in place, although ways to become wealthy, as well as to lose everything, became far more diverse.

The two strategies used to manage the risk of participating in a Victorian-era property regime were, first, to rely on informal signs of trust and respectability, which criminals could manipulate or imitate, but only to a certain extent. The second strategy was to resort to the law to formalize property transactions and to report fraud, which was punishable with Siberian exile (though not by hard labor, nor—as it was in England—by execution).[8] But fraud trials, and especially the case of the Jacks of Hearts, showed that legal norms and sanctions raised questions of their own. While everyone had some understanding of deception and pretense, it was not easy to fashion a clear rule about what kinds of "information asymmetries" were criminal as opposed to daring or reckless. Nor was it easy to evaluate the criminal responsibility of "uncommon" offenders and the reasons for their choosing to transgress.

In sum, the case of the Jacks of Hearts systematically exposed the fundamental principles of Russia's regimes of property, knowledge, and respectability as highly vulnerable and easily manipulated. It appeared that many Russian property owners had done at least some of the things the Jacks of Hearts were charged with, and the swindlers used the same forms of property transactions and had the same mentalities as their victims and accomplices, who were bewitched by promises of quick enrichment. The world of fraud was largely defined in the breach when swindlers were caught and prosecuted, and this lack of physical and especially mental boundaries arguably made the world of respectable criminals even more subversive than the better known underworlds of violent and political offenders, to which it was compared implicitly and explicitly.[9] The case of the Jacks of Hearts was initiated in the wake of Russia's first public trial for political conspiracy, that of the Nechaev Circle in 1871, and was prepared for trial at the same time as Russia's largest political trial, that of the "193" members of the "going to the people" movement. While the Jacks of Hearts had only one or two links to political sedition, their case similarly alleged the existence of a vast criminal conspiracy and was conceptually and structurally very similar to the great political trials of the late 1870s, even their nonpolitical equivalent seemingly designed to purge Moscow's commercial and propertied society of wayward members.

THE UNCOMMON CRIMINAL

The investigation of the Jacks of Hearts began in 1871, when the wife of a young, wealthy, and deliriously alcoholic merchant, Klavdii Yeremeev, complained to the police that his friends used his drunken state to make him sign numerous debt obligations without giving him any money. The notary public Aleksei Podkovshchikov certified the transactions, even though Yeremeev's wife begged him not to; the corrupt notary claimed that she failed to provide any official evidence that her husband was a habitual drunk. Not long afterward Yeremeev died penniless.[10] Other episodes soon began to surface involving the same men from Moscow's middle classes—Pavel Karlovich Speier, employed at a major bank, noblemen Ivan Davydovskii and Vladimir Anufriev, and honorary citizen (elite merchant) Aleksei Mazurin, soon joined by many others. By the time the case went to trial in early 1877, it had evolved into a comprehensive blueprint of Russia's culture and practices of private property and bourgeois sociability. In the process, the case revealed rather uncomfortably the mutual dependence of cultural and economic forms of capital, typically thought of as each other's antipode.[11] But the relationships reconstructed in the great fraud trials show that the foundations of middle-class culture, such as kinship, honor, and civility, were inextricably merged into property and abstract evaluation. At the same time, material property and value were to a significant extent perceived and evaluated in cultural terms. On a practical level, respectable criminals

Figure 19. The defendants' bench at the trial of the Jacks of Hearts. *Vsemirnaia illustratsia,* 1877, no 13, p. 245. The women are seated separately and wear identical kerchiefs covering their hair fully; one is crying. The men, by contrast, look either bored or tense. The four men in front are defense attorneys, appearing relaxed and even amused. It is unclear where the rest of the forty-eight defendants are. The entire area is surrounded by grills and railings, evoking prison bars.

seem to have spent their time partying, drinking, buying and selling, and exchanging various kinds of tokens of value, such as banknotes, bonds, and stocks. The Jacks of Hearts used authentic relationships and items whenever possible, as well as skillfully imitating them when necessary.

The trial of the Jacks of Hearts for the first time—and surprisingly late—brought to full public attention the figure of a swindler or con artist, abundant in the long nineteenth century, in Russia and elsewhere.[12] The people watching the trial were struck by the defendants' "good looks, youth, strength, self-assurance, gentility, and . . . a sort of intelligent knavery."[13] Good looks were helpful to a con artist, but even more so were the external trappings of success and prosperity—good clothes and respectable manners. These of course came easiest to people with a genuine elite upbringing, which many of the defendants had enjoyed. For example, the key defendants Dmitry Massari and Aleksandr Protopopov came from formerly wealthy landowning families, and three others were former officers of the elite and expensive Pavlograd Life Hussar Regiment.[14] Also notable was the forger Professor Aleksandr Neofitov, who belonged to Dostoevsky's family circle and taught world history at Moscow's private Practical Academy of Commercial Sciences.[15] But the sole actual aristocrat among the defendants was Vsevolod Alekseevich Dolgorukov, from a wealthy senior branch of that large and ancient clan; he was the source of the popular contemporary misconception that all his friends were similarly privileged. Paradoxically, Vsevolod was both an avid swindler and an impostor, occasionally claiming to be the nephew of Moscow's governor-general, Prince Vladimir Andreevich Dolgorukov, and at the same time among the most genuinely respectable members of the group in the sense that he was not bankrupt or even truly déclassé. His life did start with a stigma: it turned out that his father had married bigamously, and Vsedolod was not allowed to use his princely title, although the tsar permitted him to keep his name and noble status. But Dolgorukov was accepted by Russia's elite and even allowed to enroll in the prestigious Naval Cadet Corps, which was reserved for hereditary nobles. In secret police documents he was still referred to as a prince. As an officer candidate (*iunker*) in 1864, he had already attracted negative attention from the Third Section, which received regular anonymous reports from someone close to Dolgorukov. One report noted him singing a prohibited revolutionary song in a restaurant, and soon he became known to the authorities for his "tricks" (*plutni*).[16] By 1869 he had been discharged from the navy without obtaining his commission, convicted of minor fraud, and placed in the debtors' prison in Petersburg, where he married a prostitute in exchange for five thousand rubles.[17] Dolgorukov eventually found his calling in third-rate publishing (specializing in guidebooks) and journalism, and after being convicted in the Jacks of Hearts trial and exiled to Tomsk in Siberia, he spent the rest of his life as an honest citizen (as far as we know) engaged in journalism, publishing, and even legal work.[18]

Nineteenth-century Russia was full of bankrupt merchants and destitute nobles who had lost their landed estates and factories. Even for individuals who legally belonged to Russia's noble estate, life on the streets could never be completely ruled out: according to official government reports on pauperism, several dozen homeless nobles were picked up by the police every year in Moscow alone.[19] The lucky ones could live as hangers-on with better-off friends and relatives. Impoverished nobles at the end of their rope could therefore often count themselves lucky to be picked up by future handlers, like Speier (the illegitimate son of an artillery general), Davydovskii, and the merchant and innkeeper Aleksandr Smirnov, and placed in circumstances that resembled their formerly prosperous lifestyle.[20] The story of Aleksandr Protopopov, the former owner of landed estates in Orel and Tula provinces, was described in the indictment with particular detail because, according to the prosecution, he had started out as a reluctant accomplice but eventually became converted to a life of fraud and began to participate in it voluntarily and even enthusiastically. His was one of the first episodes in the case that the jurors learned about before being subjected to four weeks of testimony. Protopopov had managed to keep an outdated certificate of ownership of one of his former estates, and Speier and Davydovskii set him up in style as a wealthy nobleman, also spreading the rumor that he owned a distillery in Tula province and that he had received a large inheritance from his uncle consisting of cultivated land and a horse-breeding farm.[21] He "drove around in carriages (*karety*), spent large sums on parties [and] received guests."[22] Nearly identical schemes centered on the destitute former landowners Nikolai Dmitriev-Mamonov and Vasily Toporkov. In public, Protopopov, Toporkov, and Dmitriev-Mamonov all affected a stern tone with their "estate managers," who skillfully imitated subservience.[23] Their swindles were recounted in great detail during the trial, teaching the public not to blindly believe anyone who rode in a nice carriage or wore an expensive coat. In retrospect, though, one might wonder whether the expense of imitating wealth—even if much of it was obtained on credit—was worth the comparably slender pickings.

In addition to appearance, manners, and acting ability, an essential requirement for a successful con artist was a social and family network, whether genuine or bogus.[24] The American sociologist Edwin H. Sutherland, who coined the term "white-collar crime," argued that its practices depended on a permissive social environment.[25] Among factors making fraud so ubiquitous in modern society is that it relies on close ties with accomplices, some willing, some unwilling, and some simply negligent. These can be family and friends or simply an organization with lax safeguards or a tacit policy of ignoring malfeasance, even though individual high-status offenders can be treated with exemplary severity.[26] In imperial Russia, propertied classes lived in extensive kinship structures, and an important sign of status was one's circle of relatives, friends, and dependents of all kinds who could support, and vouch for, one's character and past conduct.[27] Therefore, it was obvious and no doubt disturbing to anyone hearing or reading the indictment and testimony about the Jacks of Hearts that they did not operate as an autonomous "underworld" but rather were very much part of Moscow's social and commercial milieu. Not only friends but also wives, mothers, and siblings actively participated in shady activities. Some relatives and friends did so willingly, and others were most likely innocent dupes, but all worked to reassure victims, provide shelter to criminals, and create the impression of long-standing and secure social ties.

Nearly every complex scheme of the Jacks of Hearts involved various assistants and intricate chains of acquaintance. For example, Protopopov's handlers, Speier and Davydovsky, combined his genteel manners and his apparently opulent lifestyle with his bogus social connections, introducing him as a relative of Speier's wife and claiming that Vasily Karlovich Sanftleben, a wealthy moneylender with aristocratic friends, was personally familiar with Protopopov's properties. In a different episode, the penniless nobleman and bogus industrialist Nikolai Dmitriev-Mamonov worked with several friends, their roles strictly divided: one was the general office manager, another was the chief technician and mechanic for his nonexistent factories, yet another was a master distiller who, because of his Jewish ethnicity, was tasked with targeting Jewish victims. The owner of the hotel in which Dmitriev-Mamonov's "office" was located, Smirnov, spread rumors about his wealth and continued to reassure victims after Dmitriev-Mamonov suddenly remembered urgent business elsewhere that prevented him from repaying them.[28] The noble-born forgers Vereshchagin and Golumbievskii used a close woman acquaintance, Alexandra Zmieva, to engage a go-between, the previously convicted Maria Miklashevskaia, who found yet another woman to provide false evidence on behalf of Golumbievskii.[29]

Déclassé members of the elite were particularly visible in the Jacks of Hearts case, but they also appeared in other trials of the post-reform era, which are discussed in more detail in the next chapter. An important 1875 trial in St. Petersburg featured a smaller group almost identical to the Jacks of Hearts, accused of forging the testament of a wealthy moneylender, Captain Mikhail Sedkov. In addition to civil servants and officers of the imperial guard, the group included a former judge of the Odessa District Court who became completely dependent on the leader of the group because of his large family and broken finances.[30] An earlier forgery trial, of the millionaire Miasnikov brothers, included testimony from Lieutenant Nikolai Shevelev, whose activities closely resemble those of the abovementioned Prince Dolgorukov.[31] One of the numerous unpublished embezzlement prosecutions of branch managers and clerks of the Russian State Bank in the 1860s and 1870s took the issue of purchasing and appropriating respectability to its logical limits. The managers of the Kiev office purchased worthless debt paper from local "retired chancery clerks, factory employees and bookkeepers, Jewish factors, the most insignificant and petty traders," who enrolled (completely legally) as licensed merchants and paid the required fees with borrowed money in order to be able to issue (worthless) bills of exchange, which circulated like cash and could be "discounted" (sold) to the bank.[32] Thus, a merchant's honor was manufactured intentionally and out of nothing as a commodity and used to steal cash from the state.

Even the swindler who appeared to be a lone adventurer—a common nineteenth-century cultural image—was in fact deeply embedded in networks of relatives and friends. Sociability was indispensable even in the typical modern-era crime of train or hotel swindling, which in one version involved attractive women who drugged and robbed amorously minded rich passengers or hotel guests.[33] The most famous example from Russia is Sofia Bluvstein (Blyuvshtein), more widely known as Son'ka the Golden Hand. Today she is remembered as among Russia's two or three most famous criminals, although ironically at the time she seems to have mostly enjoyed local fame, and her trial did not attract nearly the same attention as those of the high-born swindlers discussed in this book. Son'ka's story is recounted in several popular late imperial and post-Soviet novels and even a 2007 television series. It appears that any information about Son'ka's life is considered to have high market value by people who control access to archival documents, which are therefore extremely difficult to come by, even for researchers able to pay for access.[34] An abbreviated newspaper transcript shows that Son'ka was a powerful personality with several smaller convictions before 1880 and a complex ethnic background: she was born a middle-class Polish Jew but ended up a Romanian citizen who had lived in Poland, Odessa, Moscow, and even Austria by the time the police began to pursue her in earnest. In her confidence tricks Son'ka was assisted by several husbands and other accomplices, who, in a striking turn of legal fortunes, were all acquitted, whereas Son'ka ended her days in Russia's most remote penal colony, on the island of Sakhalin.[35]

The elite criminal network of sociability also strongly depended on individuals—usually older men—who provided financial and logistical backing but only rarely ended up on trial themselves. Overall, there were at least ten such men mentioned in the Jacks of Hearts case, with one of them, the merchant Kalinin, even being referred to in the published transcript as the case's Rocambole (criminal mastermind). These people appear from the transcripts to have actually been the sinews holding together Moscow's financial heterotopia. They owned the hotels and taverns where the schemes were acted out, they loaned money, and provided notarial or legal services. Some were the swindlers' full-fledged partners: for example, the "gray-haired" Armenian merchant, Erganianz, who "worked" with Massari. Others served as "managers" or handlers:

Andreev, a music teacher and a former police officer with a shady record, provided logistical support to Dolgorukov, while the innkeeper Smirnov did so to Dmitriev-Mamonov.[36] Notaries were particularly important in Russia, as in other civil-law systems, for certifying the bona fide status of property transactions and for identifying any irregularities or potential legal issues. In the service of criminals, a notary could sign off on a transaction even when his accomplice falsely claimed to be over twenty-one (the deal would be void if that fact were discovered), or on a transaction when the victim was incapacitated with drink. One of the defendants in the Jacks of Hearts case was the notary Aleksei Podkovshchikov, who was a witness in another prominent fraud case, that of Mother Superior Mitrofania in 1874, and had previously helped her with documenting illegal loans.[37] In the earlier Sedkov forgery case, the alleged ringleader was a posh Petersburg notary and former guard officer, Lysenkov, who appeared to have been a go-to person for questionable financial deals. In the Jacks of Hearts case the prosecution also alleged that the group had access to legal advice from the lawyer Sergei Slavyshenskii, who was conveniently murdered by his lover in 1871 at the very beginning of the investigation.

But the most important behind-the-scenes group were the moneylenders and capitalists who supported the Jacks of Hearts by lending them money, providing them with information, and putting into circulation forged notes and debt documents. Davydovskii (the key defendant aside from Speier, who fled Moscow before the trial and disappeared forever) and the wayward merchant, Pegov, were said to have been surrounded and exploited by "usurers."[38] Pegov, after being expelled from his father's home for his dissolute behavior, was taken in by the moneylender Sviatoslav Zhardetskii, a former police chief of Chernigov, described as an "old, thin, grey-haired Pole . . . the toughest usurer able to scare a man into committing a crime, to suck out all of his blood, to frighten the father of his [young] victim with a criminal trial and then, when his scheme failed, to pretend to be actually penniless."[39] Another similar character, the merchant Kradovil', took part in the scheme to swindle the horse trader, Popov, and was able to outsmart not only Popov but also Speier, Davydovskii, and Protopopov—that is, the entire group—although Popov died during the investigation and therefore was not among the defendants.[40] Popov was sharply criticized in absentia during the trial as having no moral right to be counted among the victims, given his specialization in fleecing rich young men by selling them horses at excessive prices.[41] Another elderly victim, described by Muraviev as an honest retiree seeking to invest his modest capital of approximately thirty-five hundred rubles, was most likely a professional moneylender, as he had in his possession debt documents issued by other people and, moreover, on meeting the above-mentioned company of former Hussars, proceeded to get dead drunk with them for four days in a row, until his new aristocratic friends became frustrated with tempting him to purchase a bogus landed estate and decided to simply rob him of his money chest.[42]

Given these scathing descriptions, it is surprising and indeed ironic that most of them were either acquitted outright (Zhardetskii and Smirnov, and Kalinin, the alleged master criminal) or punished mildly (Erganiantz and another moneylender, Chistiakov, and even Andreev, who avoided Siberian exile). Popov, as already mentioned, managed to avoid indictment altogether. In part, this surprising outcome may have occurred because the jurors, perfectly happy to discipline the Jacks of Hearts proper, were reluctant to upset Russia's credit and property system, which could not at that time function without people like Zhardetskii or Kalinin; however, also in part, this mild treatment was likely the result of Muraviev's prosecutorial strategy, which attacked the younger defendants more strongly than their handlers, and which alleged the existence of a vast criminal conspiracy, which if proven would have sent too large a number of Moscow's capitalists to Siberian exile.

WHO WAS TO BLAME?

When the trial of the Jacks of Hearts opened on 8 February 1877, spectators were initially intrigued by the length of the indictment (its printed version was immediately sold out) and by the defendants' respectable appearance and relaxed manners, but they quickly became distressed and even "depressed" by the fact that the men did not act like accused criminals.[43] According to Kozlinina, they joked among themselves and with the younger defense attorneys, demonstrated their skill in forging signatures, and generally were perceived to act as if their schemes and swindles were simply a game. Given the youth of many of the defendants, there appears to have been an element of adolescent imitation in the way they mimicked legitimate businesses and financial transactions. Not surprisingly, commentators of different political persuasions attempted to dampen this spirit of playfulness. The feuilletonist from the leading St. Petersburg paper, *Sankt-Peterburgskie Vedomosti,* noted that most of the schemes were well known but that similar cases had not previously attracted attention.[44] The liberal jurist Grigorii Dzhanshiev later groused that the Jacks of Hearts were "petty" and "mediocre."[45] The conservative journalist Mikhail Katkov argued that the public inaccurately assumed them to be "skillful, resourceful and elusive."[46] The lawyer for Ivan Davydovskii, who was one of the key defendants, argued that the allegedly "brilliant criminals" were in fact "ordinary" and "weak" men "prowling around Moscow in search of sustenance."[47] But accurate claims that the club's activities were not new, or unfair claims that they were boring, only served to highlight the discomfort of the ruling elite at seeing such a large group of criminal defendants from respectable classes. Given that Russia at that time had an insatiable demand for educated people, it was disturbing that the defendants not only were not productive members of society but could not even be good parasites, since as it turned out their schemes were not particularly profitable financially. Since the "great" criminal trials dissected and scrutinized their objects, the trial of the Jacks of Hearts engaged with the tortuous question of the origins and the motivations of such "uncommon" criminals. It was not easy or sufficient to simply condemn greed, and it was impossible to condemn the driving forces behind fraudulent trickeries without at the same time undermining Russia's entire social and economic structure.

The deputy procurator of the Moscow District Court, Nikolai Muraviev, was seen as the rising star of Russia's post-reform judiciary. One account described him as "nimble, scathing, clever, and spirited."[48] Kozlinina claimed that he was "beyond compare" among prosecutors and a "mighty talent" whose only equal was Russia's legendary defense attorney, Fedor Nikiforovich Plevako.[49] Muraviev's didactic rhetoric notably diverged from that in the other landmark fraud trials of the 1870s, which focused on defendants' individual greed and ambition. Instead, Muraviev traced criminality to Russia's serf-owning past, which had allegedly thoroughly corrupted the younger generations. Given Russia's political climate in 1877, at the height of the repressive campaign against revolutionary propagandists and on the eve of the campaign of terror by the People's Will, this move was bold and even risky because any hint of being critical toward Russia's political regime was likely to elicit sharp criticism.[50] Muraviev therefore needed to avoid appearing too subversive and to make sure that his speech explained the Jacks of Hearts and their crimes without criticizing the foundations of Russia's regime of private property. His task was further complicated by the fact that the trial was large and complex, and that—unlike during the smaller fraud trials of the 1870s—many defense lawyers felt free to sharply criticize his arguments. Ultimately, Muraviev was unable to keep his didactic narrative free of contradictions, much less impose it on the jurors or the public. In the narrative presented during the trial, the new capitalist Russia did not look any more morally upstanding than the old one of nobles and serfs, so that it was arguably not clear which of them was actually on trial.

Modern historians have also traced criminality in post-emancipation Russia to the social and cultural conflicts inherited from the age of serfdom, especially to the dislocation caused by mass migration from villages to cities.[51] This narrative was found across the globe in the mid to late nineteenth century; for example, in American advice literature produced to put young country males migrating to rapidly growing cities on their guard against gamblers and other con artists.[52] In the United States with its similarly recent and extensive experience of unfree labor, swindling was also directly linked to slavery, with con artists being compared to slave traders because of the way they were thought to deprive America's youth of their identity and autonomy. In Russia, this analogy was used somewhat differently. Serfdom was thought to accustom young nobles to a parasitical life using free serf labor, whereas the habit of buying, selling, and punishing other humans (as well as indulging appetites at their expense) led them to disregard the moral values they were otherwise being taught at home or at school. After emancipation, nobles' lack of skills left them without any means once they lost their income.

One noteworthy example of blaming crime on Russia's serf-owning past is Konstantin Staniukovich's 1877 short story about the Jacks of Hearts, allegedly based on an interview with one of them.[53] The story's main character, George, is a collective portrait loosely resembling some of the Jacks of Hearts, especially Pavel Speier (known in Moscow for his exceptionally good looks and for the military background of his family).[54] His eventual downfall is traced to a series of illicit love affairs, thefts, and forgeries, and is explained by pre-reform Russia's superficially strict discipline without a system or an inner moral core combined with the nation's alleged lack of family values. Before becoming a criminal, George had learned to love luxury and to evade society's rules and prohibitions, and he became accustomed to getting away with his transgressions because his relatives, lovers, and acquaintances preferred to avoid public shame. Even the Third Section, the tsar's political police, argued in a secret 1878 memo that political criminals were individuals "torn away from their social (*soslovnye*) organisms."[55]

The historical and reform-centered explanation underpinned the other important fraud scandals of the 1870s, but in an indirect and ambiguous way. The trials of Mother Mitrofania in 1874, of the managers and directors of the Moscow Commercial Loan Bank in 1876, and of General Gartung later in 1877 all criticized Russia's recent past and its social elites, but in a very veiled way, mostly limiting themselves to the technical facts. During the trial of the Jacks of Hearts, by contrast, Muraviev's strategy was to make the sociohistorical explanation of crime explicit. Kozlinina recalled that Muraviev had tried it out in a slightly earlier case, that of a Moscow attorney, El'kin, accused of swindling his rich fiancée, when he "with an unusual pathos . . . demolished not so much El'kin himself, as an entire society that rejected the old ideals and failed to create anything in its stead except an insatiable thirst for profit, the product of which condition was El'kin, who knew no other god except for the golden calf."[56] In his concluding speech at the trial of the Jacks of Hearts, Muraviev focused his wrath on the nobles Davydovskii and Massari as "impoverished men who drew from all the [bad] qualities of the old environment of serfdom," and he finished one of his passages with the exclamation that was reported, with slightly different variations, as: "The law of serfdom has fallen, let, then, its offspring fall as well!"[57] He referred to another impoverished noble, Dmitriev-Mamonov, as the "progeny of the fallen gentry," which in its original Russian (*ischadie pavshego barstva*) sounds very offensive and has clear associations with the biblical Fall.[58] Muraviev was less scathing but still critical of the young merchants involved in the case, such as Pegov and even Yeremeev (officially a victim), who were too attached to a life of luxury paid for with their parents' money.[59]

Some defendants and their lawyers went along with this narrative, including the forger Arkadii Vereshchagin and Massari's lawyer, Nikolai Basnin, both of whom blamed lazy habits inherited by Russia's elites from the age of serfdom. But it was equally common, perhaps more so, to connect elite crime to Russia's modern transformation. One of Russia's most prominent defense lawyers, Aleksandr Lokhvitskii, objected to the historical explanation, undoubtedly because it made his client, an impoverished nobleman and (unlike Vereshchagin or Massari) a minor participant in the club, look like a habitual criminal. Instead he argued that serfdom had been abolished when most of the defendants were still children and that in any case many of them could not have been corrupted by serfdom, because their families had some money but never owned serfs. Unpublished pretrial testimony by a typical defendant, the nobleman Vasilii Toporkov, shows that his father was a hired estate manager, whereas Toporkov himself had neither the intelligence nor the discipline to succeed as an office clerk and after his father's death ended up in Moscow without money, a home, or even winter clothing.[60] Dmitriev-Mamonov's lawyer, Durnovo, argued, in a play of words that is difficult to render in English, that his client—only twenty-three years of age when serfdom fell—was not a "progeny" (*ischadie*) of the old noble culture but rather its "baby" (*ditia*).[61]

The "modernist" interpretation was also fairly common among journalists and memoirists reporting on other cases. Vladimir Spasovich in his speech in defense of the child-abusing banker Kronenberg blamed a permissive modern society that did not punish and discipline sternly enough and instead prosecuted those who (like his client) did: "I submit that there is an open and direct road from [stealing] plums to sugar, from sugar to money, from money to bank notes."[62] The prominent scholar, censorship official, and memoirist Aleksandr Nikitenko, who followed the major legal events in the 1870s, noted: "Forging papers, frauds of all kinds, theft of government and public money, huge swindles involving railways, which create enormous capitals out of nothing—in our days all of these became the most commonplace events. And in the meantime only the capital cities enjoy social respect and honor, and their owners occupy high positions."[63] The feuilletonist from *Sankt-Peterburgskie Vedomosti* also connected fraud to the peculiarly modern pursuit of fast riches and the easy acquisition of daily comforts, quoting a folk saying: "You will not acquire a mansion through righteous labor." Just a month later, however, an (apparently) different feuilletonist from the same newspaper came to the more unsettling conclusion that "material need plays a most insignificant role in creating swindlers," and that fraud stems from a special pleasure in deceiving others akin to an addiction to gambling, hunting, or drinking.[64] He and other observers made the puzzling calculation that the club's swindles were—despite all the publicity—not all that profitable. The total loot was less than three hundred thousand rubles, a large amount but slim compared to the damage inflicted by contemporaneous multimillion-ruble bank frauds. Divided among all the defendants (most of whom never saw any of the money), the amount was only 648 rubles per year; that is, equivalent to the wages of a clerk, which could easily be earned legally.[65] Moreover, most of this money consisted of forged notes that were never cashed. This suggested either incompetence (disproved by the inventiveness of the club's schemes) or the unsettling idea that greed was not the sole motivating factor.

Both feuilletonists concluded that the ubiquity of fraud was a significant, even a defining, feature of their age, but in his speech lawyer Lokhvitsky rejected this type of explanation as well, noting that the defendants' "fathers, without even mentioning [what had happened earlier, in] the second half of the eighteenth century, even in the first half of the nineteenth allowed themselves such orgies, in comparison to which a trip to [a] Gypsies' [a restaurant] looks like children's play."[66] Moreover, some of his client's and other defendants' schemes were identical to those of forgers and swindlers in the age of serfdom.[67]

It is therefore not at all evident that the 1860s and 1870s, or, arguably, any other historical ages, were an exceptional "age of fraud," as one journalist put it.[68] The links among the legacy of serfdom, the social dislocation that it caused, and the increased economic and especially financial activity of the post-reform period appear to be less than straightforward. During the trial, neither Muraviev nor any of the defense attorneys were able to craft a single intellectual narrative, much less impose it on the jurors or the public, and therefore it seems that the didactic effect of the historical explanation of the Jacks of Hearts largely foundered. Muraviev criticized the "new" Russia of money and capitalism as strongly as he did the "old" one, allegedly characterized by sloth and arbitrary authority, and it was not clear at all which of the two was on trial.

THE LAW OF DECEIT

Russian Old Believers broke away from the Orthodox Church in the late seventeenth century and split into dozens of movements and denominations. The largest and best organized was the Rogozhskoe settlement on the outskirts of Moscow with its own cathedral, cemetery, almshouse, and numerous other buildings. Moscow Old Believers were commercially minded and wealthy. On 5 September 1865, the gatekeepers of the almshouse opened the gates to three uniformed gendarmes and two civilians—so-called good-faith witnesses who were required to be present when the police searched private homes. Colonel Kuznetsov ordered the gates to be relocked and started the search. Although Old Believers were frequently subject to persecution even in the midst of the liberal reforms, Moscow was generally safe under the benign eye of its governor in 1865–1891, Prince Vladimir Dolgorukov. This visit was not surprising, but it was not expected either. The Old Believers' clerk surrendered all the papers but would not open the moneybox containing sixty thousand rubles, saying that he did not have the key. Kuznetsov wrote up a receipt, took the box, and the police left. Half an hour later, the steward and the clerk had doubts and went to the police station only to find out that the police were not conducting any action against them.

Using secret agents, the police arrested a retired soldier, a coachman, and a bath attendant, all in their early thirties, and a nineteen-year-old townsman (*meshchanin*) with no known occupation. Their trial in January 1867 was one of the first cases to go before a jury in Moscow and belonged to the same series as the celebrated murder cases of Mavra Volokhova and Aleksei Danilov, thus being of utmost importance in setting the trend of the newly reformed court system.[69] The question was whether the jury would be able to evaluate the mass of indirect and conflicting testimony and character claims; moreover, it's not impossible that Moscow's leading police detective, Rebrov, doctored the case by rounding up a few suspicious characters and forcing one of them to confess.

From a legal standpoint the issue was more subtle, however: the group were accused of robbery (*grabezh*), that is, an open taking of property against the victim's will.[70] Karl Richter, one of Moscow's first prominent post-reform defense attorneys, argued that there was no robbery, since the victims had no idea that they were being robbed. The Old Believers testified that they were so frightened of the gendarmes that they did not even think about resisting, but if they had had any doubts about the identity of their visitors they could easily have detained them.[71] But Assistant Procurator Mikhail Gromnitskii argued that the criminals put "moral pressure" on the victims, who felt powerless to resist and thus committed robbery, rather than fraud. Gromnitskii claimed that the criminals entered the Old Believers' compound through fraud, but when they locked the gates and pretended to detain the caretaker it turned into a robbery. It is likely that he wanted the defendants to be convicted of robbery because it entailed a much heavier sentence of hard labor than the other, more applicable provisions for fraud (Article 1665) and fraud committed under the pretense of being state officials (Article 1668). Gromnitskii's arguments were not particularly sensible, but the jury panel was uncommonly strict, composed solely of elite men and headed by the prominent economics professor Ivan Babst; it convicted the defendants. We can only surmise that had the defendants in the Rogozhskoe case been members of the respectable classes, such as one of the later Jacks of Hearts defendants, they would have been charged only with fraud. The main defendant, the former soldier Ivan Semenov, was presented in Gromnitskii's memoir as an exceedingly intelligent man, almost an arch-villain, with a military bearing one would expect in a gendarme officer. This early case shows that even the most basic definitions of white-collar offenses completely depended on the social context. Fraud needed to be separated from robbery or theft, as well as from innocent bragging, whereas forgery was only seemingly easier to define.

It is ironic that Russian law had for centuries defined fraud (*moshennichestvo*) as a nonviolent but mostly open taking of personal property, and originally included a broad range of activities, such as retail fraud and not paying for one's purchases, as well as pickpocketing and even openly snatching someone's personal property, such as a hat.[72] Designed to regulate behavior in the marketplace or other crowded places, Russia's traditional antifraud law was therefore not intended or particularly well suited for suppressing swindlers operating in a diffuse market of credit documents and investment deals. It was only in 1845 that the new penal code reworked the definition of fraud as "any theft (*pokhishchenie*) of another's possessions, money, or other movable property, effected through any kind of deceit."[73] This definition was concise but created loopholes and questions that strongly depended on the factual circumstances and therefore required years of courtroom and Senate practice to clarify, making the Russian law of white-collar crime particularly dynamic and amorphous. Perhaps not surprisingly, Russian lawyers and judges did not come up with clear-cut answers, but thanks to the reforms they were at least able to discuss them in print, as well as in the courtroom.

One of the most important legal questions was what counted as criminally punishable deceit and how to distinguish it from practices that were dishonest and perhaps actionable in civil court but not punishable and even unavoidable in the dynamic and loosely regulated commercial world. For imperial Russia, the leading tome on the law of fraud was a treatise by Professor Ivan Foinitskii, who together with Professor Nikolai Tagantsev would soon cowrite the new draft penal code of 1903. Foinitskii's book came out in 1871, just as the fraud and forgery prosecutions in the post-reform courts were gathering momentum. He argued that simple deceit was not enough to constitute criminal fraud, and that the deceit had to directly result in the misappropriation of another's property.[74] The same reasoning can be found in the treatise by Aleksandr Vladimirovich Lokhvitskii, a former law professor who became one of Russia's most prominent defense attorneys and something of an enfant terrible of the legal profession for taking cases shunned by his colleagues and making arguments generally considered to be morally objectionable.[75] During the trial of the Jacks of Hearts, Lokhvitskii was engaged by one of the lesser defendants, the nobleman Alexander Polivanov (who was acquitted by the jury). In his book, Lokhvitskii described different types of deceit, some of them allegedly essential for conducting commerce, such as when merchants claimed that their goods were the best or the cheapest.[76] But neither Lokhvitskii nor Foinitskii was able to precisely explain the boundary between permissible trickery and fraud, although they suggested that providing any specific details to substantiate one's false claim was likely to be fraudulent. In a similar vein, in Anglo-American common law a finding of fraud requires material representation about existing facts.[77] This helped to exclude some obvious cases but was still problematic: whereas openly claiming to be an aristocrat or a factory owner was clearly illegal, how was this different from dressing above one's station when visiting a moneylender?[78]

As discussed earlier, the Jacks of Hearts used a variety of strategies and thrived in legally questionable situations, and so the debate about the meaning of deceit was very much present during the trial, both in the indictment's descriptions of the club's schemes and in the courtroom speeches. Defendants and their lawyers repeatedly claimed that their activities were perhaps suspect or even immoral but basically amounted to innocent pranks and tricks. The most forceful argument came from lawyer Kharitonov, in what was perhaps the most lucid defense speech of the trial (most speeches in this and in many other trials were either too long and convoluted or too brief and vague).[79] Kharitonov's client, a wealthy citizen of Revel (Tallinn) in Estonia named Nikolai Adamchevskii, may have introduced his friend Vsevolod Dolgorukov as the nephew of Moscow's powerful governor-general, Prince Vladimir Dolgorukov, even though—Kharitonov argued somewhat disingenuously—this relationship by itself should not have determined the question of Vsevolod's financial standing. More important was that Kharitonov interpreted the law to mean that "criminal" fraud involved the use of some "special means," such as forged documents, to convince the victim of one's wealth or other material facts, but that it was not a crime to simply fail to repay a loan, especially when the borrower was not asked for any particular evidence of creditworthiness and did not volunteer to produce it. Noncriminal deceit (*obman*) could be avoided through "regular everyday caution." For example, if a borrower claimed that he owned a nice house and the lender did not check that this was indeed so, it was the lender's fault. Kharitonov concluded that the facts of the case were "rather unsavory, dishonorable, even immoral, but, I repeat, not at all criminal."[80] Kharitonov's interpretation was technically incorrect, because under the penal code the use of "special means" increased the punishment but did not separate criminal fraud from permissible trickery. More to the point was Kharitonov's argument that if the government indicted every person in Moscow who did not repay a debt, it would require a trial with hundreds of defendants that would last for months, "especially given present-day political and financial difficulties."[81] The question of how much pretense constitutes fraud remained open, but the arguments about Dolgorukov's and Adamchevskii's activities raised two additional issues.

First, it was generally agreed in the juridical field in Russia and elsewhere that fraud charges apply only to claims about existing facts and not about future promises, specifically including a promise to repay a debt. A swindler from the early post-reform era, Pavel Kosach, published his entire case file to prove his innocence on these grounds.[82] In 1869, Kosach purchased an expensive carriage, the merchant delivered it to his house and waited in vain for payment in Kosach's apartment until he had to leave. Kosach immediately sold the carriage to his wife, Matilda Bartelson, who pawned it for cash. The criminal prosecution against Kosach eventually failed. As Foinitskii argued in his treatise, the

Senate's appellate decisions on the subject were likewise not consistent. Some held that in this instance a failed promise did not constitute a fraud, but in other situations it did. Separating existing facts from future promises was clearly difficult in a commercial setting where transactions were typically contingent on future events. Perhaps the most celebrated post-reform case when a jury convicted someone for not keeping her promise was that of the aristocratic nun Mother Mitrofania (Rosen), who took money from a rich merchant woman, promising to use her connections to free her from trusteeship (imposed because of the woman's alcoholism) but failing to deliver. The prosecutor claimed that Mitrofania had no intention to fulfill her promise and that she provided false information about her ability to influence the case.[83] This raises the second conceptual distinction brought up by the legal authorities, one between existing facts and mere opinions, and, to me at least, Mitrofania's views of her own political influence seem to have been of the latter kind.

Most fraud cases in some way debated whether the state of mind of the victim mattered, and if yes, what the standard was. Anglo-American common law required the victim to have exercised ordinary precautions. By definition deception requires (at least) two people. Overall, it was difficult to lay down a precise rule about the level of intelligence one can expect in one's counterpart in a transaction. If the other side makes a stupid mistake, does this get me off the hook or should the law guard naive people especially vigilantly? In the context of late imperial Russia, as can be seen throughout this book, the mental state of the defendant and that of the victim were virtually always inquired into during the trial. Prosecutors and lawyers for victims usually tried to show that the victim reasonably relied on the statements by the defendant. For instance, in the Mitrofania trial the prosecutor took pains to show that the nun's victim, Medyntseva, was not particularly intelligent and was "blinded" by the show of Mitrofania's power and influence.

CREATING A SHOW TRIAL

Early newspaper accounts, as well as the official indictment and—subsequently—popular literature portrayed the Jacks of Hearts Club as a sinister mafia-like conspiracy (*prestupnoe obshchestvo*). This image was traced to the popular French Rocambole series of novels by Pierre Alexis Ponson du Terrail (1829–1871) that featured a shadowy adventurer-mastermind long before Fantomas and Professor Moriarty. One of the novels, *Le Club des Valets de Coeur* (1858), featured a powerful gang of swindlers with tight discipline and strict rules of secrecy. According to one account, Rocambole's exploits came to the mind of one of the lawyers who found out about the swindles of Pavel Speier and his friends.[84] The real Russian case, however, brought together criminal episodes that were for the most part completely unrelated, so it can therefore be described as a show trial not simply because of its intended didactic impact of disciplining Russia's property owners and merchants—something that all prominent trials did—but also because its central structure was carefully fabricated, though not entirely fictitious like its later Soviet-era counterparts.

The tales of Rocambole notwithstanding, it appears that the idea of a vast criminal conspiracy was created by Muraviev and by the investigator in the case, Piotr Mikhailovich Globo-Mikhalenko. Kozlinina thought that Muraviev became "dizzy" with his early successes after being appointed deputy prosecutor at the Moscow District Court in 1873, and that he strove to be assigned the most prominent and challenging cases. Globo-Mikhalenko, in turn, specialized in complex and high-profile fraud and embezzlement cases. In 1874, he participated in the investigation of Mother Superior Mitrofania and served as a witness at her trial.[85] Two years later, he made his name as the investigator of the crash of the Moscow Commercial Loan Bank. As some of the defense lawyers pointed out during the trial, he was clearly interested in presenting the Jacks of Hearts as a serious public threat. From a legal perspective, at stake was the rule that treated individuals who formed a "gang" (*shaika*) with intent to commit crimes much more severely than it did individuals acting independently, even when this "gang" never had a chance to do more than plot.[86] For the Jacks of Hearts, this meant that even minor defendants risked Siberian exile instead of the short prison sentence otherwise imposed for petty fraud. From the perspective of post-reform political conflicts, the trial of the Jacks of Hearts took place in the age of large trials for political sedition, which alleged the existence of a single radical political organization dedicated to the overthrow of the tsarist government. Their trial ran simultaneously to that of the twenty-one participants in Russia's first political demonstration on Kazan Square in Petersburg (18–25 January) and to the "Fifty" socialist propagandists (21 February to 14 March). Moreover, as noted above, throughout 1877 the government was preparing what proved to be the largest judicial trial in Russian history, that of the 193 members of the "going to the people" movement, which began in October.[87] These political cases were tried by a special board of the Senate (OPPS), and other than the presence at them of Russia's top defense lawyers were not part of mainstream legal culture. A handful of other political cases were, however, tried within the mainstream judicial system. These were the murder trials of Sergei Nechaev in 1873 and of Vera Zasulich in 1878, and especially Russia's first public political trial, of Nechaev's followers in 1871. The trial of the Jacks of Hearts was not a political case in that it did not target the tsar's political opponents.[88] Its gargantuan size can be explained only by the contemporary fashion for megatrials that was most clearly manifested in the large political cases.

The Nechaev Circle case in particular resembles that of the Jacks of Hearts so much that one wonders whether Muraviev's purpose was consciously or unconsciously to outdo his predecessors, to show himself and his judiciary as able to meet the challenge and to justify the monarch's trust. There are three aspects that must be pointed out. First, Nechaev and his followers were accused of politically motivated murder—that is, a crime that was punishable under Russia's regular penal laws. While the circle's seditious activities were dissected to a considerable extent, the huge trial focused on proving the murder. Second, exactly like the case of the Jacks of Hearts, the Nechaev Circle case was divided into several sub-proceedings according to the severity of the alleged offenses, and it was even tried in sequence, so that the lesser defendants tried last did not attract much public attention and were basically let off, while the killers of Nechaev's rebellious follower Ivanov were sent to hard labor, as was Nechaev himself two years later, after he had been extradited from Switzerland. In the case of the Jacks of Hearts, there was only one proceeding, but, as we shall see, Muraviev distinguished various groups within the club and was similarly lenient toward secondary defendants. Finally, while the trial of the Nechaev Circle took place in his absence, the indictment and courtroom testimony created an image of this important early revolutionary as an arch-swindler, who in turn deceived the exiled anarchist Mikhail Bakunin about the existence of a vast revolutionary party in Russia, and then deceived Bakunin's followers about the backing of a vast international anarchist organization that would allegedly provide assistance to the Russian radicals. To maintain the deception of a vast radical party, Nechaev, just like the bogus industrialists in the Jacks of Hearts case, prepared large amounts of his own stationery, an entire archive of a nonexistent organization, fake messages from abroad, and even membership cards. It is likely that even his famous program known as the Catechism of a Revolutionary was part of the same scheme of deception.

Contemporaries clearly recognized this proclivity of the judiciary to stage large trials that often combined numerous barely related episodes. The jurists Anatolii Koni and Grigorii Dzanshiev made this point explicitly: Koni characterized the political trial of the "Fifty" as "prepared in Moscow and encompassing diverse groups of defendants, rather artificially connected to each other pursuant to Moscow's method to combine similar cases, giving it a loud title, for example, the 'Jacks of Hearts,' etc."[89] Dzhanshiev recalled that period's "mania for grandiose *causes célèbres* with a mass of defendants and with grandiose furnishings. One could think that Count Pahlen's ministry [of Justice], having noted the weakening of the public's attention to court proceedings, attempted to artificially awaken its waning interest." Dzhanshiev specifically referred to the cases of the Moscow Commercial Loan Bank and the Jacks of Hearts.[90] The nobleman Massari's lawyer, Basnin, who in his speech focused on the social and historical origins of fraud, discussed the common origins of fraud and of the "bulk of political crime." He urged the jurors to be "sorry . . . for those young men who became enticed by ideas incompatible with our state order, and wasted their strength in a fight against unachievable chimeras, whereas they could have otherwise caused much good . . . but on the other hand, gentlemen of the jury, let us not treat too severely also those weak-willed persons who gave way . . . to the temptation of luxury—a sensual side of the human organism." While other large fraud trials of the 1870s, such as that of Mother Mitrofania or of the Moscow Commercial Loan Bank, made vague claims about "crowds" or "gangs" of criminals, the case of the Jacks of Hearts was the only one to officially allege the existence of a criminal conspiracy.[91] Other fraud trials also took steps in that direction, however, including the Mitrofania trial, which consisted of three unrelated episodes, with two of them added in order to prove the main case (involving the fortune of the millionaire castrate [*skopets*] Solodovnikov); the bank case likewise consisted of several completely different narratives, as I discuss in a later chapter.

In the case of the Jacks of Hearts, the defendants never actually imitated or called themselves by that or any other name. Although many of them were partners or at least acquainted, their relationships never amounted to more than a loose network that operated together for a few short months in 1871 and then again in 1873. The so-called club had no internal discipline like that found in underground revolutionary cells; indeed, defendants fleeced each other almost as often as they did unconnected victims. Nor was there any structure, organized planning, or common finances. The Jacks of Hearts were typically caught when some number of the members switched sides. In the Popov fraud, the second episode in the investigation, it was Pavel Speier, the alleged master criminal himself, who was the first to go to the police and testify against Protopopov and other participants.[92] The forgers' ring that at one point operated in Moscow's Butyrskaia prison was likewise exposed (after two police informants suffered untimely deaths) when one of the participants, the nobleman Aleksandr

Nikitin, became tired of waiting for his share of the loot and threatened exposure, which in turn stimulated another member, Nikolai Andreev, to go to the police out of fright.[93]

Journalists and jurists quickly noticed all of this and corrected their original sensationalist interpretation. The prominent conservative journalist and a critic of the post-reform courts, Mikhail Katkov, wrote in an editorial in *Moskovskie vedomosti* that the trial gathered "in one enormous proceeding numerous criminal cases with hardly any connection among them."[94] The liberal weekly *Nedelia* compared the case to a "mosaic" that was "not very skillful or subtle" and mocked the prosecution's efforts to stage a supertrial with the popular saying derived from Aesop: "A mountain gave birth to a mouse" (*gora mysh rodila*).[95] Incidentally, one of the more literary-minded political defendants at the later "trial of 193" (sentenced to nine years of hard labor), Sergei Silych Sinegub, used the same saying: "They messed around for almost five years in creating this case, trying to save the fatherland . . . and created a monster-case, created a noise in all of Russia and suddenly [it turned out that] the mountain gave birth to a mouse."[96]

Muraviev realized that he needed to defend his decision to stage one enormous proceeding and argued that as early as 1871, before most of the Jacks of Hearts Club's crimes took place, and even before its members knew each other, they were already "invisibly connected by their common situation[:] lack of money on the one hand, and their riotous epicurean tastes on the other."[97] His explicit practical justification for staging a supertrial was the convenience of everyone involved, given that many of the defendants had already spent years in prison awaiting trial and that it was difficult to assemble so many witnesses.[98] At the same time, Muraviev took pains to distance his case from the overdramatized popular image and claimed that he did not at all want to allege the existence of one single conspiracy.[99] Instead, he decided to allege the existence of three key overlapping groups—approximately a dozen persons in each—which would land the key defendants in Siberia, while the minor defendants were tried solely for individual criminal acts and not for conspiracy.

To strengthen his case, Muraviev also included in the indictment numerous episodes that were not directly related to the club's activities but that suggested a pattern of moral depravity. This included buying expensive items (such as guns or furs) on credit and then disappearing from one's (bogus) address. Also included were swindles that degenerated into simple thefts when the victim could not be persuaded. One of the defendants, Konstantin Golumbievsky, in addition to his main activity as a skillful forger, at one point took a position as a manservant to a rich merchant and stole his valuables.[100] Another prolific forger, a merchant named Vasilii Pegov, also stole from his friends, from his father's customers, and even from his father's elderly cook.[101] A major variety of the club's fraud took advantage of the business practice of the time requiring hired managers and clerks to post money roughly equivalent to their annual salary (a few hundred rubles for a regular clerk and several thousand for a manager) to their employer as security against embezzlement. The "employer" then opened a bogus office that would at first conduct business activity but within weeks or even days disappear with the bond money.[102] Finally, there was the murder of Collegiate Councilor Sergei Slavyshenskii by his lover, townswoman Ekaterina Bashkirova, in December 1871. Born in Russian Alaska, she moved to the mainland after its sale to the United States in 1867, took a succession of military officers and merchants as lovers, made a small fortune running a high-end canteen (*bufet*) in Nikolaevsk (today Komsomolsk-na-Amure), and nearly died in a shipwreck off Japan. At last coming to Moscow, she met Slavyshenskii, who professed passionate love for her but soon became violently jealous. It was likely that her killing of him was premeditated, given that Bashkirova had obtained a gun ahead of time and practiced shooting it, but the jury predictably ruled that it was committed in the heat of passion and acquitted her. This murder was included in the case because Slavyshenskii was a lawyer who had allegedly advised the Jacks of Hearts but had quarreled with them and threatened to go to the police.[103]

At the same time, Muraviev chose not to actively prosecute about a quarter of the defendants, and he sometimes explicitly asked for their acquittal. Most likely, he wanted to reward those who provided helpful testimony, as well as to show fairness and mercy while at the same time highlighting his resolve with respect to key defendants. The lawyers for the minor defendants were not impressed; they argued that if the case against their clients was so weak, there was no point in keeping them in prison for years before the trial. Other lawyers complained that their clients who were accused of minor crimes appeared far less favorably to the jurors when seen next to hardened swindlers whose guilt was obvious.

In the end, Muraviev managed to persuade the jury of the existence of the three alleged gangs. Fifteen of their participants were sentenced to penal settlement in Siberia. Other Jacks of Hearts received much milder sentences, varying from a small fine to a brief prison sentence, including Dolgorukov (surprisingly, given the aggravating factor of his prior criminal conviction for fraud). Nineteen of the defendants were acquitted, mostly those with minor roles or those who, like Toporkov (one of the bogus industrialists), cooperated with authorities.

There is no direct confirmation in Muraviev's surviving papers, but it seems reasonable to propose that this megatrial was intended to demonstrate his ability to stage-manage a huge proceeding, whereas his major competitor, Konstantin Nikolaevich Zhukov, had failed during the recent "trial of the Fifty," and another important conservative jurist, Vladislav Antonovich Zhelekhovskii, would fail only a few months later at the "trial of the 193" (and his predecessors had failed during the trial of Nechaev's followers in 1871). The government clearly noticed that Muraviev's organizational talents complemented his suitably loyalist political credentials and his already outstanding reputation as Russia's leading courtroom speaker: Muraviev would prosecute during Russia's next landmark political trial, that of Alexander II's assassins in 1881, and he would become the minister of justice in 1894.

This link between the trial of the Jacks of Hearts in 1877 and Russia's infamous political trials of the 1870s may come as a surprise to most readers, used to viewing Russia's regular judiciary as more enlightened and liberal than the political proceedings. This disconnect did exist, and as noted earlier it is incorrect to claim that the conduct of political trials was typical of the entire legal system. But similarities and direct links were also significant. This includes the involvement of the same judges, prosecutors, and lawyers, but also the technique of managing dozens and even hundreds of defendants and witnesses in one huge proceeding, which required careful untangling of their complex but usually poorly documented relationships. The trials' overall objectives were not identical but came from the same impetus to police wayward members of Russia's elite classes and to separate prohibited deception and dissent from permissible commercial activity or independent thinking.

•

The trial of the Jacks of Hearts was a major public event in Russia in the late 1870s, competing for front-page newspaper space with the unfolding Balkan crisis and the large-scale political trials. It clearly stood out among other landmark fraud trials because of its size and complexity and, above all, because of its in-depth exposition of Russia's daily culture of credit and commerce: hundreds of defendants, witnesses, victims, their family members and lawyers, and policemen created and reenacted an intricate web of relationships and conflicts. Because of this complexity, none of the competing narratives and explanations of "respectable" crime offered during the trial was able to dominate, least of all the version offered by Muraviev. If Russia was living through an "age of fraud," it was unclear where it came from or how it could be combated. Swindling and forgery appeared during the trial as commonplace, even banal, as ingrained in capitalism, and as almost impossible to distinguish from legitimate practices. But in a larger sense, the trial empowered Russia's elites to continue using the law and especially public trials to address the most important current political and social conflicts and to continue staging supersized political trials. The trial was also moderately successful in disciplining Russia's culture of business and property exchange: although it was clear to any observer or participant at the trial that the problems it identified were too fundamental to be resolved during any one proceeding, the case showed fraud and forgery to be neither glamorous nor even profitable and, in this sense, demystified them, without at the same time undermining the fundamental structures of private property.

CHAPTER 9

The Art of Forgery

One of the earliest post-reform legal scandals began in 1858 when a wealthy merchant died in St. Petersburg of bladder cancer. Kuz'ma Beliaev's wealth came from vodka buyout contracts, a signature pre-reform institution whereby entrepreneurs paid the government for the right to manufacture and sell alcohol in a particular area.[1] Beliaev was childless and left everything to his widow, who soon sold his former business investments to her nephews, who were also grandchildren of Beliaev's former employer and benefactor, Ivan Miasnikov—a much grander, astronomically wealthy vodka tycoon. Ten years later, in 1868, the Miasnikov heirs, Aleksandr and Ivan, were charged with forging Beliaev's will, and in 1872 they were brought to trial in St. Petersburg. The man claiming to be the true heir, Izhboldin, was not related to Beliaev at all but had previously acquired the potential inheritance rights as a gift from Beliaev's long-estranged and forgotten sister, who lived far away in the Urals. The extra twist in this story was the fact that Aleksandr Miasnikov was a gendarme officer and personal adjutant to General Nikolai Mezentsev, the director of the Third Section, Russia's secret political police.[2] Even before the trial, journalists and their readers had divided into two camps, one eager to see a patrician family humiliated and the other disgusted with the group of unscrupulous adventurers who had instigated the prosecution. The twenty-eight-year-old prosecutor, Anatolii Koni, had only recently transferred to Petersburg, and this was his first scandalous and politically sensitive trial, although he had already acquired a reputation for pursuing elite criminals from his earlier work in Kharkov.

Inheritance disputes were very common in the court practice of the time, especially among landowning gentry with their complex property arrangements and large kinship groups.[3] Moreover, elite families often owned property in widely dispersed patterns and moved to remote provinces for service postings. The law of inheritance in Russia was far more flexible and open to dispute than, for example, in England and France, allowing testators freedom to dispose of all property that they themselves acquired during their lifetime.[4] Restrictions applied to bequeathing inherited property, but these were easy to circumvent. In merchant families, however, inheritance lawsuits were "extremely rare" according to a recent study.[5] Nonetheless, several of the most prominent post-reform criminal trials focused on intergenerational property transfer among elite families. The Miasnikov case was followed by the forgery trial of Sofia Sedkova, widow of a noble moneylender, and of the widow of another moneylender, Olga Sanftleben, who stood trial together with Alexander Pushkin's son-in-law, General Leonid Gartung. All three were disputes between young widows and their husbands' relatives. The celebrated trials of the aristocratic nun Mother Mitrofania (Rosen) and of the noblewoman Liudmila Gulak-Artemovskaia illustrate several different developments in post-reform criminal justice, but at the core they were likewise inheritance disputes, although more complicated ones. All these cases began as bitter family feuds following the death of a wealthy and socially prominent man who sought to provide for his wife or partner or make other arrangements at the expense of his expected heirs. Unlike the habitual swindlers discussed in the previous chapter, the defendants in these cases—if they were guilty at all—were occasional or situational criminals who operated in a routine everyday world.

The participants' high status no doubt attracted attention to these cases, but their significance goes much farther. By the mid-nineteenth century Eurocentric legal systems were structured around the rights of private property, which in turn rested heavily on inheritance laws and practices that allowed elite and middle-class families to safely transfer wealth to their descendants.[6] The cases discussed in this chapter threatened these foundations of elite wealth and power, and thus endangered the Russian legal and social regime no less than the Jacks of Hearts or the revolutionary activists.

Threat came from several directions. First, the types of commercial and property transactions featuring in these cases were inherently risky and socially disreputable: not only liquor buyouts but also commercial lobbying and high-risk private moneylending and investing. Second, irregular sexual and nuptial arrangements could easily disrupt property structures and ownership transfer. Third, the defendants in these cases formed social and business connections that were not unheard of but were considered inappropriate, especially the mingling of disparate social groups. Finally, while it was common in imperial Russia for elite women to own and manage property, the cases discussed here attacked their taking more active economic, social, and even political roles, which seemed objectionable even to such liberal post-reform jurists as Koni. Among all the cases discussed in this book, this set showed Russia's post-reform judiciary in a particularly unflattering light, perhaps in part because these cases were relatively fully reported and they exposed especially vicious and nonsensical things uttered by prominent lawyers and judges. Moreover, very few other types of criminal cases invaded elites' private lives to a comparable extent; after all, private property was private not only because it was owned by individuals but also because much of its workings was concealed. The courts' and the public's panoptical gaze thus scrutinized some of the most fundamental aspects of the culture of private property in Russia and some of the most intimate aspects of elite culture, evaluated persons who sought to gain wealth or status, and condemned questionable ways of doing so. This panoptical gaze sharpened over the years, beginning with the heirs to disreputable tycoons and moneylenders and eventually cutting into the very core of financial and political power in post-reform Russia, as well as constructing a sharp legal critique of the growing culture of acquisitive capitalism.

DEAD CAPITALISTS AND FALSE HEIRS

Beliaev was a self-made man. He started out as an office boy to Ivan Miasnikov (1750–1855), by far the largest liquor tax farmer in Russia. His annual payment for the liquor-sale monopoly in several well-populated regions was more than nineteen million rubles, whereas the average was about half a million.[7] This patronage helped of course, but Miasnikov had dozens of clerks, and only Beliaev made it to the top. Eventually he became Miasnikov's most trusted agent, managed the family's fortune after Ivan's death, and lived on the same street.

Beliaev was at once trustworthy, diligent, and creative, and he soon became engaged in numerous enterprises and investments of his own, including the vodka trade, distilling, Astrakhan fisheries, goldmining, timber, and furniture sales, and shortly before his death he was negotiating the purchase of the Baird mechanical plant in St. Petersburg (the first and for a long time the only one of its kind in Russia). Several months before he died he wrote a will leaving everything to his wife, a noblewoman by birth with some property of her own and a sister to the late Ivan Miasnikov's wife. The will was properly witnessed by a well-respected elderly priest and a doctor, and it was duly authenticated by the civil court in St. Petersburg. Two months after Beliaev's death, the widow sold everything to the young Miasnikov brothers who were Ivan's grandsons.[8]

Were it not for this will, Beliaev's heir would have been his sister from the distant town of Sarapul in the Urals. She came to the capital to dispute the inheritance but soon died of cholera, although not before she had bequeathed her legal claim to a Sarapul merchant named Izhboldin, who had no connection whatsoever to anyone else involved. This transaction had the effect of turning a routine legal dispute among relatives, where some respect for the proprieties might be expected, into a fully commercialized enterprise similar to the way rich "capitalists" bought up personal debt claims against people they had never met and then sued them in court. Izhboldin came to St. Petersburg and hired a series of cutthroat lawyers who sued in every court possible and petitioned every authority in the capital to dispute the will, including the Third Section, but every time the complaint was dismissed as baseless, belying the pre-reform courts' subsequent and not always fair reputation for mindless formalistic litigiousness. The Third Section's director officially responded that this was not his business but secretly had the issue investigated.[9]

Only in 1868 did Izhboldin finally strike gold, when he apparently reached an understanding with the officials of the newly opened courts in the capital, which can only be explained by the court officials' eagerness to harm the reputation of their rival, the Third Section, by showing that one of its senior officers was a forger. Several men who were most likely police agents, as well as the assistant procurator of St. Petersburg District Court, found themselves in faraway Voronezh province at a distillery owned by the Miasnikovs, where one of their old employees named Karaganov was living a life of alcoholic delirium. Filling him up with vodka for several weeks, the agents induced him to say that he had forged Beliaev's signature on a blank sheet of paper at the request of the Miasnikov brothers. This was enough for procuracy officials to finally have the brothers indicted and arrested, and the case went to trial in February 1872.[10] Not only was the trial extremely well attended by the general public, but the audience included several members of the imperial family and an agent of the secret police.

Typically, the beginning and the end of an inheritance dispute would be the will document itself. Authenticity disputes were ubiquitous in inheritance, debt, and contract claims, and the courts both before and after the reform of 1864 dealt with them by inviting handwriting experts, usually calligraphy teachers, to analyze signatures. Both nineteenth-century lawyers and today's legal historians have recognized that handwriting analysis is not a reliable procedure. During trials, experts frequently failed to agree among themselves or spouted nonsense, requiring the judges or the juries to interpret their opinions as best they could. This is precisely what happened in the Miasnikov case, which involved no fewer than five evaluations, mostly by the same people but all with different results.[11] In a pre-reform court, this confusion would and did end the inquiry and get the case dismissed, but in a post-1864 jury trial this simply meant that the proceedings focused less on the document and more on Karaganov's testimony and on his moral character and conduct and that of everyone else involved in the case.

Both sides first scrutinized the character, wealth, and intentions of the long-dead Beliaev, debating whether he was likely to bequeath his entire fortune to his wife and whether that fortune was large enough to tempt two young millionaires to risk criminal charges. Prosecutor Koni sought to portray Beliaev as a grand industrialist and thus a tempting target even for a very wealthy criminal. Koni was assisted by Aleksandr Lokhvitskii, a law professor and star defense attorney, who represented Izhboldin as the civil plaintiff. The Miasnikovs, however, hired superlawyers of their own. One of them, Konstantin Arseniev, argued that Beliaev, for all his energy and diligence, lacked investment capital and that by 1858 his finances were shaky and thus not worth the trouble for the much wealthier Miasnikov brothers.[12]

The only issue that Koni, Lokhvitskii, and the defense agreed on was their open disdain for Beliaev and for liquor buyouts as a particularly immoral commercial activity.[13] While Koni ostensibly paid tribute to Beliaev's diligence and loyalty, he also openly mocked him, likening him to an old gruff servant from the bygone age of serfdom, "incorruptible and persistent, with a faithful dedication to his master" (*vernopoddanicheskaia predannost'*, sounding dissonant in this context).[14] He also hinted that Beliaev's fortune came from embezzling from the Miasnikovs and later in his memoirs claimed this explicitly.[15] Arseniev in turn complimented Koni for not denigrating Beliaev, but he sounded as if such treatment would normally be expected. Arseniev described Beliaev as far beneath other, truly rich liquor merchants of his age like Voronin, Kokorev, and Benardaki, whom he referred to as "little tsars of the *otkup*" (*otkupnye tsar'ki*), also a disdainful term suggesting petty self-importance and excessive but localized power.[16] Lokhvitskii was even more explicit, and responding to Arseniev's claim that selling liquor is not a crime, said: "Mr. Arseniev should remember that tax farmers (*otkupshchiki*) never thought it a sin to turn people into drunks . . . millions have been made exclusively through making six or seven provinces completely alcoholic all at once." When Arseniev said that the Miasnikovs were incapable of forgery because of their upbringing, Lokhvitskii responded that liquor buyouts were nothing but "a constant and systematic forgery."[17]

Koni and Lokhvitskii were both highly educated intellectuals from noble, though not very wealthy families, and they also competed in nastiness against Beliaev's noble-born widow. Showing the characteristic misogyny that would show up again and again in future trials, Koni explained that she was not indicted because it was "obvious that she did not herself manufacture the forged testament, and this business is not at all, as the folk saying goes 'a job for a woman's mind' (*ne zhenskogo uma eto delo*)."[18] Beliaeva was a witness, however, and during cross-examination she responded stoically to several hours of insults by Koni and Lokhvitskii. Years earlier she had refused to deal with one of her late husband's less savory partners, and Lokhvitskii held it against her as a "tax farmer's habit" (*otkupshchitskuiu privychku*) to mistreat staff.[19] By contrast, Koni attacked Beliaeva's alleged gentry hauteur, claiming that she was "proud and arrogant" and "could not give up that role" or "diminish her grandeur."[20] Arseniev in her defense responded that noble pride would not explain why she married a merchant. Lokhvitskii had an explanation, though, claiming that Beliaeva's marriage to a lower-status man made her particularly protective of her noble status: "It is known that noblewomen, especially those who marry merchants, like to safeguard their noble dignity." Lokhvitskii continued with the ludicrous allegation that Beliaeva contrived to have her nephews take over her husband's property because she felt partial to the "noble blood [that was] in their veins."[21]

Compared to this withering barrage against the dead merchant and his widow, the actual defendants, the Miasnikov brothers, were left almost unscathed. Only Koni attacked their character, focusing on their choice to abandon commerce and "squeeze their way into 'gentility,'" that is, to become nobles by entering state service.[22] In a similar way, the important "thick" monthly journal, *Notes of the Fatherland,* would later mock Aleksandr Miasnikov for serving in the Third Section, supposedly to obtain "a more or less illustrious position in high society," the implication being that such service was not honorable.[23] As to Koni, he immediately contradicted himself by arguing that the Miasnikovs despite their ennoblement were still fully engaged in business, which was supposedly why despite their wealth they needed every bit of money they could get.

Finally, the civil plaintiff in this case—the merchant Izhboldin who had acquired the inheritance rights from Beliaev's late sister—was also subjected to the elite lawyers' merciless panoptic dissection. Koni dismissed him as an "uncouth provincial" and then focused on his representatives and attorneys, all from the lower strata of the profession, branding them as "new argonauts" who were out in force to strip the Miasnikovs of their golden fleece. Criticizing the crime's alleged victim was not a promising strategy for a prosecutor who wants to win a case, and it is a bit of a puzzle given Koni's already-formidable reputation that he could appear so incompetent.

The trial's outcome rested on the contest of two witnesses whose careers are highly illustrative of Russia's age of capitalist transformation. The prosecution's witness and also the third defendant in the case was the Miasnikovs' office clerk, a failed entrepreneur named Karaganov, who admitted to forging Beliaev's signature on a blank sheet of paper. Supporting this story was the fact that shortly after Beliaev's death, Karaganov married an opera singer (who was Aleksandr Miasnikov's former lover) and left St. Petersburg to settle with a hefty annual allowance of a thousand rubles on one of the Miasnikovs' distilleries in Voronezh province. There he drank and caroused, allegedly breaking windows, shooting his gun in the village, and walking down the street naked.[24] During the trial he also acted as if mentally disturbed: he responded to questions in a halting and incoherent way, added nonsensical phrases, and mumbled so that the stenographer did not hear much of what he said, although the judges did. Despite this obvious problem, Arseniev's request to carry out a mental evaluation was denied. Koni then attempted to argue that Karaganov became disturbed because of a guilty conscience.[25] Karaganov's testimony was clearly deranged, and no one seems to have taken it any more seriously than that of the handwriting experts.[26]

It also turned out that Izhboldin had paid several of the witnesses to testify in his favor. The key defense witness, Lieutenant Shevelev, was himself disreputable, but he testified that he was hired by Izhboldin to write one of the incriminating letters used by the police to reopen the investigation. Unlike the other witnesses, who were taciturn and not particularly cultured, Shevelev was well educated and as eloquent as any of the lawyers, and he was clearly going to sway the jury. Koni and Lokhvitskii did their best to undermine his credibility, aided by his colorful biography. Shevelev had arrived at the court straight from the Peter and Paul Fortress prison, where he had landed after being extradited from France for having fought for the Paris Commune in the Corps des Enfants de Paris. Born into a noble landowning family, Shevelev at first worked as a manager for the Miasnikovs, who fired him when he represented to his fiancée that some of the assets he was managing actually belonged to him. Shevelev had also worked as a government customs agent in Poland and in other similar jobs, some of them under a false name. But he dabbled too in radical politics and was accused of participating in Karakozov's attempt on the tsar in 1866, although in a minor way such that he was able to use Izhboldin's money to flee Russia to Switzerland, where he wrote and published a treatise on the Molokan religious sect, for which he is remembered in Russia to this day as a very minor literary figure.[27] Both Koni and Lokhvitskii tried to impeach Shevelev, but in vain since there were other witnesses with similar testimony.

It is not too surprising that the jury acquitted the Miasnikov brothers and Karaganov. The government vigorously appealed the verdict and was able to get it set aside on a preposterous technicality and have a new trial held in Moscow—with the same result. Koni claimed in his memoirs that he was convinced that the will had indeed been forged but that he was not actually trying to win because he had been so disgusted with Izhboldin and his friends once he saw them in the courtroom. A simple look at the trial record does not support this claim, however, since Koni clearly did his best to get a conviction and readily employed vicious and manipulative tricks to make up for the fact that his case was not supported by the evidence. But whether Koni was genuinely lashing out at everyone involved in the case or trying to sabotage his own position, he displayed exactly the kind of behavior he had a reputation for strongly opposing and the kind of manipulative tactics he would display in several other famous cases, including the trial of Vera Zasulich in 1878. Koni was effective, though, in conveying his contempt, which he shared with Lokhvitskii and Arseniev, for the get-rich-fast culture of self-made millionaires and government contractors, and for Russia's general climate of shady speculation facilitated by a crowd of brokers, agents, and low-level legal practitioners.

The Miasnikov case was not the first time influential persons were prosecuted for white-collar crime. There had been important trials for counterfeiting and official embezzlement in the late 1860s. But this case was the first and therefore the trend-setting example of a publicly scandalous criminal prosecution coming out of the routine and even boring private practices of the wealthy, sending a threatening message to Russia's elites, whether old or new. The theme of confronting the runaway spirit of acquisitiveness continued to develop in other trials, and the list of undesirable activities and participants was gradually extended. In 1875 Koni prosecuted another prominent forgery case (one of the most prominent trials of the mid-1870s along with those of Mother Mitrofania and millionaire arsonist Stepan Ovsiannikov) that involved poor relatives from faraway coming to the capital to dispute the inheritance of a wealthy man. This time, Koni attacked the practice of private moneylending and the character of an enterprising, commercially minded woman.

Mikhail Sedkov came from an old gentry family and was a captain in the prestigious Izmailovsky Regiment of the imperial guard, but his real profession both before and after he left service was moneylending. After he died from tuberculosis in 1874, his widow, Sofia, and several other officers and civil servants were prosecuted for forging his will. Koni's job should have been easy because everyone involved had confessed. Compared to the Miasnikov case, where even the basic facts were in doubt, this trial revolved solely around the character of the defendants. It also helped Koni's case that two of the most ethically questionable members of the Russian bar—Spasovich and Lokhvitskii—worked hard to redirect the blame away from the less important defendants who were their clients.

Koni's prosecutorial zeal was dispersed among the dead Captain Sedkov, his twenty-three-year-old widow, Sofia, and the corrupt thirty-one-year-old notary Lysenkov, who had masterminded the forgery project. Each challenged one of Koni's sensibilities. Sedkov was a moneylender, Sofia was a commercially minded young woman, and Lysenkov was a nobleman who held an important position of public trust. As in the Miasnikov case, Koni went far beyond his obligations as prosecutor and beyond his avowed code to work cleanly and ethically. He argued that the case was

> the product of a large city with a huge and diverse population . . ., which created a certain stratum of people, who are distinguished by respectable manners and external respectability and always contains gentlemen always ready for any unseemly but easy profit. To this stratum belong not only the defendants but also the late Sedkov—this experienced and distinguished usurer, whom we can partially resurrect in front of our eyes . . . and even some of the witnesses. None of them are hungry and cold in the ordinary meaning of the word—all of them have some means and ways to avoid the defendants' bench through honest labors. One of them is a well-known Petersburg notary, from one of the most commercially lively areas of the city, who completed the Military Juridical Academy; the other [Lysenkov's assistant, Borozdin] is a lawyer by education and occupation [who] was, to the regret of the judicial branch, a member of a court; the third one is a young . . . civil servant, the fourth—an officer

> from an honored and prosperous family. And all of them were brought to the dock by the desire for others' money. . . . Some of the witnesses . . . are [from] that little world in which people who have capital munificently distribute money [to] the needy and which returns to their hands having grown two or three times in a short period of time.[28]

In Koni's depiction, Sedkov was "an energetic and active Petersburg usurer," operating like a spider crawling and casting his nets to extend his business.[29] Amazingly, even Sedkov's plan to eventually go out of business and retire showed that he was a "cold and callous man."[30] Koni even attempted to weaponize Sedkov's religious sentiment and mentioned that in his papers there was a notebook with a cross drawn on one page with the words "the way to true life: meekness, truth, purity," noting that on the other side there was a detailed description "of one of those illnesses that are treated with mercury [that is, syphilis]."[31]

In turn, Russia's top legal enfants terribles, Spasovich and Lokhvitskii, sought to describe their clients as Sedkov's victims rather than unscrupulous forgers. Spasovich represented two of the defendants who witnessed the forged will, describing Sedkov's life as a constant "heartless" war "to the death" with his debtors.[32] Given these cruelties, according to Spasovich, even ordinary upstanding people like his clients hated usurers with all their heart and viewed deceiving one as a dashing, clever, and commendable feat.[33] Lokhvitskii represented the notary Lysenkov, who masterminded the forgery, and likewise argued that the true "evil genius" of the case was not his client but the late Sedkov. His wealth, "according to popular understanding," was "cursed, devilish [and] acquired through devastating one's neighbors, by extracting from them their last drop of blood, which is what all usurers do . . . when they take 100% interest per year."[34] In other words, it appears that these elite lawyers were attacking Russia's rapidly changing financial and economic culture already described in the previous chapter, a life full of banknotes, collections, lawsuits, bonds, and discounted debt notes. To Koni, Spasovich, and Lokhvitskii it was a life similar to war. Yet it seems like a poor trial strategy (although one used frequently in post-reform trials) to frame the case to be mainly about the dead Sedkov, to make him sound even worse than the defendants, and especially to attempt, as Koni did, to "partially resurrect" him.[35]

In retrospect, it was also a mistake for Koni to spend so much energy attacking Sedkov's widow, Sofia, as the product of her husband's corruption, to which she fell prey because her earlier life was equally defective. Sofia's story reveals both the opportunities and the iniquities dealt to elite women during the reform era. She came from a wealthy family, but her father gambled his wealth away. After losing her parents she was raised at a boarding school, where according to Koni she received a "meager semi-education," learned to "babble in French," and acquired a taste for "leisure and pleasures."[36] At fifteen she was taken in by her wealthy grandmother, but they did not get along, and Sofia went on to live by herself in the city, where she committed an unspecified but obvious transgression. The grandmother still managed to arrange Sofia's marriage to Sedkov, who was looking for a dowry to expand his lending operations. During the preliminary negotiations he managed to fleece the grandmother and was forced to resign from his regiment. Colonel Vladimir Klevezal of the Izmailovskii Regiment had known Sofia since childhood and recounted much of the story of her commercialized marriage to Sedkov.[37] Sofia herself testified as well.[38] From being a sheltered boarding-school student (*institutka*) and then a fallen woman, Sofia became a bourgeois wife, which did not turn out well, because Sedkov was a miser and also had another "family" on the side. As Koni summarized it, Sofia had to deal with accounts, notebooks, quarrels, complaints, and a petty and humiliating miserliness (*rostovshchichie skopidomstvo*). Koni then viciously attacked Sofia's diary writing, claiming illogically that it revealed "petty jealousy" and a habit of "posing and dramatizing things for some unknown future readers." Koni even ridiculed at length Sofia's attempted suicide, preceded by a self-conscious note in her diary, after which, to be sure, her husband began to treat her better and started to groom her to help with his lending business. Needless to say, Koni could not have approved less of this proceeding. Sofia attracted young officers to their home, where they were eager to borrow money from her husband. She helped her husband with his accounts and even started to loan money herself, "tasting the charms of usury" in Koni's expression. Lest anyone doubt his abysmal view of her character, Koni also claimed that she was at the same time spending money on "fur coats and perfume."[39] Not only Koni but also Spasovich and Lokhvitskii, and even her own attorney, Yazykov, defeminized and even dehumanized Sofia by referring to her in the neutral gender as "it," as a "creature" (*sushchestvo*), or a "personage" (*litso*).[40] According to Spasovich, his wastrel client who borrowed money from Sedkova saw above all a greedy usurer (*zhadnuiu rostovshchitsu*) and an "unattractive creature," not a beautiful woman.[41] Given that Koni reserved the main role in the case for Lysenkov the notary, he claimed that "it is unthinkable that [Sofia] had with her own intelligence masterminded the entire complex machination of forging a testament, that she knew who what and how to write and to sign."[42] At the end, Koni claimed that "Sedkova is not a naive child. . . . Here she shows great resourcefulness and knowledge of life affairs. . . . She looks at people with sober eyes and knows how to get at them on occasion. . . . Only a word of condemnation can make her see reason and start to evaluate her actions differently. It will be difficult but it will be just."[43]

By contrast, Sofia's lawyer, Aleksandr Yazykov—who had previously represented Ivan Miasnikov—had at his disposal only one tactic that tended to work on Russian juries: to appeal to Sofia's youth, since at twenty-three she was barely above the age of legal majority in Russia (twenty-one). It was unfair of Koni to hold Sofia guilty for things she had done at fifteen years of age.[44] Yazykov argued that acquitting Sofia despite her confession would not mean leaving her without retribution because the lengthy investigation, the trial, and all the suffering involved could "on certain occasions be a sufficient retribution for the crime."[45]

While Koni would have sent Sofia to Siberia, the jury acquitted her. Her lending activities no doubt counted against her, but her youth, her confession, and the fact that she brought property into the marriage clearly helped her.

Reading the transcript of the trial, one is struck by the unscrupulousness of Russia's top three jurists Koni, Spasovich, and Lokhvitskii, and by how they went above and beyond (or rather beneath and below) their professional duties, unless they understood those duties as securing the power of the juridical field rather than defending justice and the rule of law. Also notable is that while in the Miasnikov case Koni most likely focused on combating the brothers' status and connections, in the Sedkov case he appears to have fought not so much the young widow but those elements in the old Russian service gentry that were apparently to his disgust successfully adjusting to the new economic and social realities, making loans and investments as eagerly as they had been serving in the guards' regiments only a few years earlier. Behind the private drama of Sedkov and his wife one can see a larger social group that in many ways resembled the behind-the-scenes sponsors of the Jacks of Hearts and were just as difficult to catch in the act. Lysenkov, the corrupt notary, formerly an officer in a posh Hussar regiment of the imperial guard, who changed his occupation to suit the times and could have easily enjoyed a lucrative career, did end up confessing and being convicted. It is unclear why he became involved in the scheme; he did not need money, and one can surmise that he was attracted to Sofia, since they ended up having a brief romantic fling. In addition to Lysenkov, the case involved a group of men who very closely fit the description of the participants in the Jacks of Hearts case or Lieutenant Shevelev from the Miasnikov trial. Their ages and material circumstances varied greatly, but they came from genteel families and were looking for easy money. Their collective testimony suggests that

Lysenkov had no trouble finding men to write the bogus will, to witness it, to forge the signature, and then to record it in the local court. Lysenkov's assistant, Borozdin, attracted the particular attention of the prosecution, since he was formerly a judge in Odessa and left the bench to test himself—and fail—in the world of railway investment, ending up, in the words of his lawyer, Spasovich, a "crackpot (*svikhnuvshiisia*) . . . *un homme déclassé*."[46] In sum, the top lawyers attacked the new commercial milieu as corrupting the private sphere of family, comfort, and domesticity because it turned personal relations into business transactions. The speeches by elite lawyers reveal acute discomfort with the world in which middling landowners, prestigious officers, an *institutka,* a rentier grandmother, and a judge were transformed into a moneylender, a notary, or a déclassé commercial agent. Sedkov was attacked not only as a moneylender who charged high interest but also as a husband who married for money because of his greed, failed to properly care for his wife, and then corrupted her by initiating her into the world of money. But aside from blaming life in a large city, there was no explanation for why this was happening.

ENTERPRISING WOMEN

The Sedkov case was the most direct and aggressive critique of acquisitive capitalism in post-reform courts, but two other, even more famous trials probed far deeper into the conjunction of political, social, and economic power in post-emancipation Russia. The trials of Mother Mitrofania in 1874 and of the Smolny-educated Liudmila Gulak-Artemovskaia began similarly with routine property disputes about testamentary arrangements and wealth transfer; they questioned, as many other cases also had, the limits of individual autonomy in a bourgeois world. Even more sharply than the Sedkova trials, these two cases directly attacked the figure of an independent and entrepreneurial elite woman. But the debates about the boundaries of Russia's revamped capitalist market also publicly exposed the mechanics of influence peddling and informal connections that continued to be informally deployed and even regarded as indispensable.

Mitrofania's public prominence derived from her aristocratic background: her father was a decorated war hero and administrator under Nicholas I. Soon after taking her vows, Mitrofania came to head a prominent convent in the town of Serpukhov and then proceeded to construct a veritable empire of charitable institutions. While both the prosecution and the journalistic accounts of the case claimed that Mitrofania's projects were overambitious and brought her to the verge of bankruptcy—which then induced her to commit forgery—the numbers quoted in the indictment show that her finances were perfectly sound.[47] In her article on the politics of Mitrofania's case Sandra Dahlke makes a Weberian argument that the meaning of the trial lay in the discourse emanating from modern-minded jurists and aimed at suppressing corrupt practices of networking and patronage allegedly associated with an "Old Russia."[48] Dahlke argues that this modernizing effort "probably" failed to convince the general public because the lawyers involved in the case—especially Fedor Plevako, who represented the victims' interests—themselves engaged in rather shady behind-the-scenes maneuvering.[49] Plevako had a financial stake in the trial, but the judge quickly shut down that line of questioning, and Mitrofania's defense attorneys did not persist.[50] Plevako's activities more readily suggest that the Weber-inspired dichotomy of old and new legality was and is itself unconvincing and that actual court practice reveals not so much "competing conceptions of law and justice" as an interplay of far more ambiguous and particularist objectives and interests.

While to most observers the factual circumstances of Mitrofania's activities did not raise many questions, upon a closer look the conventional narrative offered, for instance, by Anatolii Koni and by the popular journalist Nikolai Demert, appears at best questionable and perhaps even contrived, but in any event a far cry from a colorful story of unrestrained corruption and greed.[51] Any top defense lawyer would have sought to present Mitrofania's activities as normal business practices, perhaps actionable in a civil court but not amounting to fraud punishable by Siberian exile.[52] This was not lost on all observers—for example, the memoirist and self-taught lawyer Ekaterina Kozlinina very effectively defended Mitrofania's innocence.[53] It is easy to conceive a different outcome to Mitrofania's case given more robust legal representation and perhaps less manipulation of public opinion by the press.

The case against Mitrofania consisted of three complex episodes, each of which could easily have resulted in a separate full-scale trial.[54] The first episode alleged that Mitrofania obtained money by fraud from a wealthy woman merchant, Praskovia Medyntseva, who owned valuable real estate in Moscow. Medyntseva's husband successfully had her person and property placed under trusteeship because of her alcoholism and dissolute life (cohabitation with a servant, allegedly also a drunk), but Medyntseva managed to escape under the protection of Mitrofania, who promised to facilitate a legal case to have the trusteeship lifted. That lawsuit eventually failed, but while living with Mitrofania, Medyntseva issued a large number of blank bills of exchange (*vekseli*): that

Figure 20. Mother Mitrofania, *Russkaia starina* 109, no. 1 (1902), app. 2.

is, she signed a number of blank sheets of special stamped paper, which Mitrofania later filled out with the amount and name of the lender. As a nun, Mitrofania could not issue *vekseli* in her own name, and all the borrowers in the case were officially her associates and business partners, most of whom also ended up as her codefendants but unlike the men charged in the Sedkova case were treated as completely subordinate to Mitrofania's evil genius.[55] Medyntseva claimed that she signed debt papers thinking they were going to be filled out with the text of legal petitions to be submitted in her name and that she did not mean these to be turned into *vekseli.* Mitrofania, however, said that Medyntseva gave her these blank *vekseli* to pay for her upkeep and for her legal expenses. Medyntseva's testimony was obviously not especially trustworthy, and yet the jury accepted her story against Mitrofania's.

The second episode, which the unpublished records of the case reveal as the most important one for the judicial officials preparing the trial, involved the elderly and wealthy merchant Mikhail Solodovnikov, who was being prosecuted by the government for his membership in the *skoptsy* (castrati) sect and in 1870, about a year before his death, asked Mitrofania to use her influence to improve his treatment by the authorities.[56] After Solodovnikov himself had died, his heirs claimed that the *vekseli* that he supposedly gave Mitrofania for expenses and as payment for her services (as well as a "receipt" [*raspiska*]) promising a large donation to her charity) were forged. Mitrofania had enough sense, however, to have Solodovnikov pay one such *veksel* before his death in order to establish that his *vekseli* were genuine, although the jury did not take this into account either.

The third episode involved the wealthy merchant Dmitrii Lebedev, who claimed that Mitrofania's agents attempted to sell *vekseli* in his name that he claimed were forgeries. Lebedev argued that he never issued *vekseli* except for very short terms and in very narrow situations pertaining to his trade in timber. Given that Medyntseva was an alcoholic and Solodovnikov was a dead heretic, Lebedev became the prosecution's model Russian merchant—an image manufactured in all the other large white-collar trials in the 1870s—who conducted his affairs in the same way as his father and grandfather had done, and who was cautious and ignorant of the latest commercial practices, such as using blank signed *vekseli.* The only problem with that image of modesty and thrift that could not be ignored was that Lebedev was eager to pay Mitrofania to obtain medals and thus elevate his social status.

Conceptually these three sets of charges can be broken into two categories, one being the charge of forgery, that is, that Mitrofania had herself signed Solodovnikov's and Lebedev's *vekseli.*[57] As I have argued elsewhere, the claim of forgery was not unusual in Russia's culture of credit, turning what would otherwise be a civil-law debt-collection proceeding into a criminal case with potentially dire consequences. A criminal investigation in such a setting was largely a risky negotiating tactic. Forgery claims were evaluated by handwriting experts. In the mid-nineteenth century the courts typically used panels of several experts: teachers of calligraphy (*chistopisanie*) or engravers. They gave their opinions in complex and usually cryptic language—for example, that some of the letters in a signature had "some resemblance" to the genuine sample, or "resemblance in certain characters," or "very strong resemblance" or "weak resemblance." As Jennifer Mnookin has pointed out, today handwriting analysis is often treated by the courts with suspicion due to its obvious lack of empirical foundation. But the later nineteenth century was the heyday of handwriting comparison, when it was very difficult to be challenged successfully. Mitrofania's attorney, Shaikevich, found no better solution than to appeal to the earlier practice of handwriting identification used in England in the eighteenth and early nineteenth centuries, which asked witnesses whether they were personally familiar with the handwriting in question instead of asking them to compare different samples.[58] Shaikevich's arguments, though, were too subtle and passive and did not offer an alternative explanation, and they were predictably lost on the jurors.

Handwriting analysis performed in the Mitrofania case was not foolproof even on its own merits, however. First, there had been two different comparisons. One was performed during the preliminary investigation in St. Petersburg, by experts who were not cross-examined during the trial and whose opinions were only extremely briefly summarized in the indictment. The second was conducted during the trial by a set of Moscow calligraphy teachers (and one engraver) who were routinely employed by the courts for this purpose.[59] One might wonder how their continued careers, both as experts and as teachers in prestigious government high schools, would have proceeded if they had not endorsed the indictment. Still, unlike the Petersburg panel, the Moscow experts were far less certain of Mitrofania's guilt: they were sure that Solodovnikov's and Lebedev's signatures were forged but were not at all positive that the forgery was done in Mitrofania's hand. Nor could they agree on whether the forgery was "crude" or "skillful." If Lebedev's signature was forged and the forgery was discovered because it mistakenly used his wife's signature as the model, why, then, did the experts conclude that it had "some resemblance" to the original?[60] When the experts conducted a third, unplanned analysis and compared the disputed signatures on Solodovnikov's and Lebedev's *vekseli*—both allegedly forged by Mitrofania—none of them could confirm that these were made by the same hand.

Moreover, there was one dissenter among those nine experts, who offered detailed opinions (the tenth expert also dissented but offered no details). The only teacher without an apparent connection to government service, the expert Mikhailov appears to have been invited because of his experience teaching "*malogramotnye*" (barely literate) students. He offered a detailed explanation for his views that was later grossly misrepresented in the prosecutor's concluding statement, but that actually offered a strong attack on the very principles of handwriting analysis. He argued that both sets of signatures, the disputed ones as well as those on genuine documents, did in general resemble each other.

After the prosecutor (reasonably) asked whether it was not obvious that a forger would have succeeded in creating some resemblance to the original and that therefore was it not important to look at the details of individual letters, Mikhailov argued that individual characters were written in a variety of different ways even in those documents that were not being disputed. Moreover, it was highly unlikely that a forger would have neglected to copy some rather obvious handwriting peculiarities found in undisputed documents. Attention to small details of individual letters was of little use, Mikhailov suggested, which was presented by the prosecution and by Plevako, Solodovnikov's lawyer, as an evasive tactic on the part of Mikhailov.[61]

Aside from the questionable handwriting analysis, the bulk of the trial transcript is occupied by a mass of circumstantial evidence that detailed Mitrofania's credit operations with all three alleged victims and provided a wealth of detail about the world of money and commerce in post-emancipation Russia. These transactions were used to support the forgery charges, but they also comprised the entirety of the second type of charges against Mitrofania, those concerning her dealings with Medyntseva. Given that Medyntseva's signatures were genuine, there was only one way to prove fraud: by showing that she thought she was signing a different type of document and not a blank bill of exchange. There was no evidence other than Medyntseva's testimony about her state of mind. Also described in-depth were Mitrofania's dealings with her agents, who were defendants as well during the trial and who were attempting to shift the blame onto each other and onto Mitrofania by, for example, claiming that she forged their signatures too and acted in their name.

While such stories did not speak directly to the facts of the case, they cast unfavorable light on Mitrofania's character by simply being associated with her. As Kozlinina noted, the people involved were all essentially scoundrels who would not have carried much weight in a less politicized courtroom.[62] Even if one reads through the details of Mitrofania's operations, this mass of testimony appears so contradictory and so voluminous that to us today it is rather difficult to lift the "fog of war," as is also the case for many other massive trials of the 1870s. For this reason, the reasoning—whether offered by prosecution, civil plaintiffs, or defense lawyers—based on all this testimony by Mitrofania's alleged victims and accomplices appears today to be unreliable. For example, the fact that Medyntseva and Solodovnikov signed debt obligations in excess of their assets violated the early modern convention that one was not supposed to borrow more money than one could immediately repay in cash, and yet doing so was routine and indeed unavoidable in actual commercial practice. The claim that Lebedev and Solodovnikov could not have issued their *vekseli* because they were rather miserly and had plenty of liquid cash is based on the contrary premise—that people borrow money only when they run out of cash—and ignores both men's unusual circumstances of seeking a government medal (requiring a certain status) and attempting to fend off legal prosecution. Nor was there anything illegal or unusual in using blank *vekseli* sheets signed by the borrower; the prosecution grossly misrepresented this practice as a peculiar criminal act practiced by Mitrofania.

In order to create a coherent narrative out of all the conflicting and complex testimony the prosecution relied heavily on misogynistic and anti-Semitic images designed to identify the types of persons who were not welcome in Russia's rapidly developing capitalist marketplace. There was no simple answer to the question of whether Mitrofania herself was old-fashioned or newly capitalistic, whether her alleged greed was old or new. Kozlinina thought that Mitrofania was somewhat naive regarding finances.[63] Solodovnikov's lawyer, Plevako, argued that Mitrofania was greedy but ignorant and not particularly competent—conclusions strongly contradicted by all of her previous activities. A large part of the ideological attack against Mitrofania focused not so much on her personal character as on her association and partnership with Jewish intermediaries, merchants, and bankers—an unsavory factor also found in trial records of other major white-collar cases in the 1870s. Both prosecutors in the Mitrofania case set the theme: Zhukov's opening remarks claimed, "A colorful crowd of witnesses has passed in front of you, beginning with persons in holy orders and ending with small-scale agents, credit brokers and Jews. Over this crowd towers the figure of a woman that is the clearest of them all—wearing a nun's clothing, ruling over everything; she is surrounded by such a staff, such a crowd of minions, who at her smallest sign pounce and commit anything ordered by this woman."[64]

Prosecutor Zhukov then claimed, characteristically, that Mitrofania's witnesses were all clergy or Jewish brokers who only appeared in the courtroom to confirm Mitrofania's testimony (as if she should have invited witnesses who would not testify in her favor).[65] The victims' attorney, Fedor Plevako, amplified this imagery with similar rhetoric that in journalist Nikolai Demert's view was crucial for securing Mitrofania's conviction: "To whom did [she sell] the *vekseli?* Some Jews from Mogilev and Minsk; to some Israelsons, Fridensons, Moiases, Meiers, Epsteins, Rossianskys, all slithered out of their holes . . . these people remind me of worms . . . as if they find any unclean affair by its smell; but you can't find them at any honest and open deal, which could not have come out of Mitrofania's cell."[66]

Plevako's remarks caused at first "shy" and then "general applause," so that the public were expelled from the courtroom for the rest of that session.[67] Demert, who summarized the lengthy trial transcript for the public, amplified the anti-Semitic theme even more, focusing, for instance, on one of Mitrofania's agents, the dentist Trakhtenberg (who was acquitted by the jury), claiming that to his testimony "the public could not listen without roaring laughter, looking at the antics of that little Russified Jew."[68] Demert further added an attack against Germans, which was not raised at the trial but was characteristic of another prominent fraud scandal of 1875 involving the failure of the Moscow Commercial Loan Bank.

This imagery of a greedy but incompetent nun and nefarious Jewish brokers was contrasted to that of an idealized Russian merchant also found in most other large fraud scandals of the 1870s. The merchant Lebedev was described as "very wealthy . . . he leads a quiet, modest life, . . . he is somewhat miserly, has few acquaintances, spends most of his time with his family and at home . . . completely honest and would never permit himself to deny his signature."[69] There were two difficulties, however, with Lebedev's image. One concerned his supposed modesty: Mitrofania claimed that Lebedev gave her the *vekseli* to guarantee a large charitable donation, which would make him eligible for a government decoration (the Order of St. Anna). While Lebedev denied it, there was enough evidence to suggest this narrative was true (and later he obtained another decoration, from a different source). The second issue was Lebedev's obvious familiarity with the world of finance: he served on the board of a bank in Petersburg and could not possibly have been ignorant of the fact that his *vekseli* were being sold ("discounted") to that very same bank. Moreover, if Lebedev was so miserly and suspicious, it is improbable that he would have paid thousands of rubles to clear the one *veksel* that he did accept solely out of respect for Mitrofania. More generally, as Mitrofania's lawyer pointed out and as we also know from the work of George Munro and Alexander Kamenskii, Russian merchants were not nearly as ignorant as has often been presumed and were already routinely using *vekseli* in the eighteenth century.[70]

The case against Mitrofania was reasonably strong but, perhaps inevitably in such a massive proceeding, sufficiently full of weak spots that any skillful lawyer should have been able to exploit them. Yet her lawyers—not first-rate stars of the bar but nevertheless competent and experienced in financial litigation—were unable either to mount an appeal to emotion in Plevako's style or to offer a detailed narrative to attack the substance of the prosecution's case. Instead, Mitrofania's lawyers introduced a jumble of hairsplitting points without a coherent theme. They did identify a few problem spots in the indictment but failed to exploit them. For example, they pointed to the claim that Mitrofania did not derive any financial benefit from her crimes even if she were guilty of them. Judging by the prosecutors' nervous response, this was a serious point. To prove fraud under Russian law, financial benefit was a required element, and in Mitrofania's case there was no benefit to her or, as it turned out, any real financial loss to any of the victims. Attorney Shaikevich, who addressed the forgery charges, could have also done much more to attack the handwriting experts, but instead he began his speech with the immensely harmful statement that the handwriting evidence against Mitrofania was "strong and almost incontrovertible." Mitrofania's own final testimony was rather confusing but made one important argument—which, again, should have been better developed—that her affairs were financially sound and she had no objective need to commit forgery.[71] A good example of what a competent defense speech on Mitrofania's behalf could have looked like can be found in Kozlinina's memoirs.[72]

In sum, the meaning of Mitrofania's case lies not in an elemental struggle by modern lawyers against a corrupt "Old Russia" but rather in a political opportunity to compromise the imperial family and the imperial court that supported Mitrofania's activities. Equally important for the leading lawyer in the case, Plevako, the goal was private vengeance by his clients, Solodovnikov's heirs, who incidentally were the ones who had denounced their late relative to the authorities and were dispossessed by him for that reason. Plevako used criminal law to pursue a property dispute, which he would have likely won in a civil lawsuit. This private opportunistic motive was combined with the shared chauvinistic theme of purging Russia's business culture of the alleged influence of women, sectarians, clergy, and Jews.

The case of Mitrofania, for all of its scandalousness, did not and could not probe further than her own ambition and lack of scruples. It is likely that digging deeper would have caused serious problems even for the autonomous judiciary. The next case was virtually unconstrained by such considerations and poked into the very heart of financial and even political power in post-reform Russia. The forgery trial of the Smolny-educated noblewoman Liudmila Gulak-Artemovskaia represented the culmination of Anatolii Koni's crusade against modernity and was the high point of his misogyny. The case took place only a few months after the trial of Vera Zasulich, and it seems that Koni must have thought that his judgeship was nearly over and he did need to hold anything back.

Initially the case looked like another routine family feud in which a deceased person's legal heirs fought against his spouse (or, in this case, his near-spouse).

Gulak-Artemovskaia found herself in legal trouble in 1877, shortly after the millionaire industrialist Nikolai Pastukhov died in Petersburg of a brain tumor. His brothers, Ivan and Dmitrii, were presented with debt claims for fifty-eight thousand rubles from Liudmila, a twenty-nine-year-old widow and Nikolai's former love interest. The brothers claimed that the debt papers (*vekseli*) were forged, and they launched a criminal investigation. Handwriting experts concluded that the *vekseli* were not written by Nikolai but resembled the handwriting of Liudmila's associate, one Bogdanov. So far this was a simple debt dispute, even though it had to go to a criminal trial because of the doubt regarding the document's authenticity. Ordinarily, the jury could have ruled either way because there was no direct evidence against Liudmila, who also had influential supporters—her bail bond was posted by the important elderly judge and scholar Baron Nikolai Tornau, and her regular counsel was Prince Keikuatov, who had been the judge in the Miasnikov case discussed earlier and had now become a top defense attorney. Bogdanov, whose signature was on the *vekseli*, claimed that he wrote them up at Nikolai's own request. The social context of the case was also ordinary enough: debt documents were routinely exchanged to cement out-of-wedlock relationships, as well as in testamentary arrangements and other forms of wealth transfer that could not be made more directly, because of legal or social constraints. But the case became a celebrity affair and was regarded by the press as one of the high-profile "women's cases" of the 1870s along with the Kovalchukova and Jujean murder trials discussed earlier.[73] This comparison is true but superficial, because Liudmila was accused of forgery, and issues of sexual morality and women's social status were in her case linked very explicitly to property and political power.

No doubt realizing that his evidence was weak, the prosecutor, Prince Aleksandr Urusov, one of Russia's top lawyers, built it around scandalous in-depth exposés of Liudmila and the dead Nikolai Pastukhov.[74] The prosecution was actively assisted by Nikolai's brothers and by his former romantic competitor Petr Polevoi, a minor novelist and literary critic (son of the better known litterateur Nikolai Polevoi), who testified at the trial and imparted to the case a thick overtone of sexual scandal. Equally activist was Chairman Koni, whose interventions during the trial were so forceful that one would think he were a second prosecutor rather than a judge, even taking into account that Russian courts followed the Continental procedural model allowing judges a much more active role than in the Anglo-American system. Koni did more than simply take an active role: he effectively took over the cross-examination of the most important witnesses.[75] Also uncommonly active was the foreman of the jury—as was usually the case, the most educated and high-status member of the panel. Here it was Vasilii Poletika, a notable journalist of anti-government persuasion and co-owner of the influential St. Petersburg newspaper *Birzhevye vedomosti*.[76] While jurors occasionally asked questions during trials, Poletika posed the most delicate questions to the defendant, such as what the precise nature of her relationship with Nikolai was.[77] Given that the prosecutor and the main witness in the case were also people with literary connections and ambitions, and given that influential persons sometimes contrived to get themselves on juries, one gets the impression that the case was rather slanted against Liudmila, who, as we shall see, represented an opposing cultural and political group.[78]

Urusov and his witnesses attempted to create a positive image of Nikolai Pastukhov as "an authentic pure-bred Russian millionaire," presenting him as pure-hearted, almost naive, kind, and soft, and without any experience in higher society, but also honest and proud, and meticulous in his financial dealings.[79] He never borrowed money, or if he did, then only from close friends and family, and he definitely never signed *vekseli*; indeed, he was so wary of fraudulent claims that he avoided giving out samples of his handwriting whenever possible. His finances were in perfect order, and he owned the imposing building at 18 Nevsky Avenue that housed the Wolf and Beranger confectionary (valued at about eight hundred thousand rubles), famous for its customers from the world of letters. He had stopped playing the stock market in 1869 already and drank only in moderation. Even his love life was self-effacing; as a university student he fell in love with a prostitute and bought her out of the brothel, then spent most of his adult life in an informal relationship with a woman "of simple status" (*prostogo zvania*).[80]

Pastukhov's doom came in 1875 when he met Liudmila through his best friend, Polevoi, and was bewitched by the beautiful widow, who shared his passion for music and who supposedly beat him at cards for the astronomical amount of 170,000 rubles, which he paid off in cash. After that Nikolai supposedly became disenchanted and broke off the relationship, falling ill soon afterward. The three main witnesses claimed that Liudmila made a bad impression upon them almost from the start as an adventuress who kept bad company. Polevoi was especially expressive, referring to Liudmila's "company of little Yids" (*zhidki*) ("I thought the three Haimovich brothers to be especially suspicious"). Polevoi also used unspecified expressions that caused Koni to remind him—in an ambivalent way suggesting that he was adding to the insult instead of protesting it—"to restrain himself in his expressions because after all he is talking about a woman, even though she is accused of a certain crime." Polevoi's own business activities were not particularly impressive, since he mostly reprinted other authors' children's books and anthologies in fancy expensive editions. When Liudmila's lawyer asked him when he had determined that she was up to no good, he responded that he "formed this impression because she was put on trial."[81]

The trio of witnesses claimed that Liudmila forged the *vekseli* because she was hoping that her claim would be paid up without much attention, given the Pastukhov brothers' kind and forgiving nature and their preoccupation with their business, which is highly doubtful because Liudmila was obviously aware that the brothers did not trust her, nor did their friend Polevoi. It also came out during the trial that while Nikolai was most likely indeed honest and frugal, he was also secretive and often depressed, and the three witnesses' claims to know his financial affairs or activities were not convincing. Polevoi's testimony was especially questionable because in the courtroom he denied knowing things about Nikolai's circumstances that he had reported during the preliminary investigation. Nikolai was also proud, so that he would most likely not tell his family and friends if he lost money in the stock market after he swore off it. His accounting habits were messy as well, with numerous payments recorded without any notations. Equally weak was the prosecution's claim that Nikolai did not even know Bogdanov, who supposedly forged his *vekseli,* and so could not have asked him to write these out for him. They clearly had known each other for years and even traveled together to Moscow and Yaroslavl', and Bogdanov could draw a detailed plan of Nikolai's apartment from memory. In sum, during cross-examination the perfect merchant turned into an idle young millionaire who had become involved with an adventuress, lost 20 percent of his fortune in a simple game of cards, and engaged in social activism solely to the extent of publishing a book about the game of whist and helping Polevoi publish derivative and overpriced children's books.[82]

Liudmila was defended by Vladimir Zhukovskii, a top-tier attorney and until a few months previously a highly successful assistant prosecutor in the same court. He had refused to prosecute Vera Zasulich and had to leave state service, joining the bar instead. The defense showed that for several years neither Polevoi nor the Pastukhovs thought Liudmila to be an adventuress; rather, they socialized with her extensively, and Polevoi enjoyed her company over wine, to which he was rather partial. Ivan Pastukhov even pushed Nikolai to marry her. Liudmila claimed that Nikolai did not lose to her at cards and that he proposed marriage, which she turned down, after which their relations cooled. They remained friends, however, and he took money from her either to help her invest it or because even millionaires occasionally need quick cash (the trial transcript mentions both explanations). Nikolai himself brought her the three *vekseli*, and she did not know under what circumstances they were written or signed. Although there was some evidence that her finances were not lavish, there is no doubt that if she happened to be in particularly tight financial straits she could have borrowed from some of her numerous friends, and there was no compelling need that we know of to risk a criminal prosecution.

Liudmila also had several character witnesses, some of whom were her women companions, but they were not any more prejudiced than the two Pastukhov brothers and Polevoi. Although none of her high-society patrons showed up at the trial, Baron Tornau submitted a written statement that he had known her well for thirteen or fourteen years and that "neither her convictions, nor character nor way of life fit in the slightest the crime of which she is accused and I cannot allow the thought that she could have forged *vekseli*." Tornau believed, "given all the circumstances known to me, that this case . . . is initiated for the purpose of inciting a scandal against a person from the higher estate with the involvement at least as witnesses, of persons from that same society."[83] Secret police records include a Third Section report from 1875 that Gulak-Artemovskaia and Tornau had a love affair, which if true would have been the real reason he had to retire in disgrace after the trial and not, as Koni claimed, because he vouched for her good character.[84] Liudmila's other character witnesses were the eccentric but respected former governor of St. Petersburg, Prince Suvorov-Rymnikskii (grandson of the legendary general), who had known her for more than twelve years and could not allow the thought that she could have committed a fraud; Privy Councilor Mikhail Mitkov (an important official active in the 1861 reform and a bibliophile); and Lieutenant General Mikhail Annenkov, who enjoyed the lucrative position of running the empire's military railway communications, and who in 1899 would be accused of embezzlement and commit suicide.[85]

As Koni himself would later acknowledge, the prosecution's case was based on unreliable and inconclusive handwriting analysis and on witness testimony that sounded like imaginative fantasy motivated by a personal grudge. Seeing this, Koni stepped in to help the prosecutor and target Liudmila's character. First, he worked to get her emotionally off-balance by appearing to focus on a ludicrous theory that Nikolai may have deliberately issued bad *vekseli*. Liudmila took the bait and started to discuss the possibility that he could have done it out of revenge for her rejection, which sounded equally strange. And then Koni went in for the kill, asking her how she came by the money to loan to Nikolai.

Her best option would have been to act the role of a sympathetic, beautiful noblewoman who did not really understand what was happening—a strategy that worked time and again on Russian jurors. Zhukovskii would later attempt this in his speech, claiming that Liudmila had been careless and allowed bad people to take advantage of her.[86] But it was too late, as Liudmila by then had attempted to respond directly to the question.

As we know, women had more extensive property rights in Russia than they did in most other Eurocentric legal systems, and throughout the nineteenth century it was not unusual to anyone that a noblewoman or a woman merchant owned property and invested money, and she would not have expected trouble unless faced, as in this case, with a group of men who were dead set against capitalism and especially against capitalistic women, as one can see directly from Koni's memoir about the case. Not foreseeing his trap, Liudmila explained that she earned money by facilitating business transactions ("conducted matters," *provodila dela*), for instance, by connecting merchants who wished to set up a joint-stock company with officials who could facilitate the approval of the company charter. Today she would be called a lobbyist, and there is no indication that what she did was illegal. What little we do know about her origins explains her interest in business: her father was Lieutenant General Mikhail Rudnev, whose career involved supply and engineering work, that is, work with private contractors prized for opportunities to make money on the side. This explains why a secret investigation by the Third Section noted that she was friendly with important officers from these agencies, who would be in a position to award contracts to merchants who came to Liudmila for help.[87]

The extent of her activities does not come through the sanitized version of the trial that appeared in newspapers, and Koni's memoir adds such details as Liudmila actually waving a briefcase that supposedly contained documentation of her activities. Upon foreman Poletika's request, she gave some examples of her deals, one of which was to push through a civil case in the Senate. She also had in her possession a copy of the company charter of the Romanov Linen Manufacture, presumably for the purpose of getting it approved by the government. In his memoir Koni wrote that Liudmila connected moneyed provincials with Petersburg influence pushers close to the liberal and powerful Grand Duke Konstantin Nikolaevich. The secret Third Section report mentioned a leather merchant named Kurikov, who, with Liudmila's help, received an eight-hundred-thousand-ruble contract with the military.[88] At the trial Koni asked her whether she acted as a legal representative (*poverennyi*), and Liudmila replied: "I could not be an official attorney because women here are not given that right but I used my acquaintances, connections, and relations to help conduct a certain transaction, as long as it was of the honest variety."[89] It is not, however, surprising that she would not present all her papers or name all the people with whom she had worked, since she no doubt hoped to turn to them in the future, whether or not she was convicted. She did use one name, though: that of Varentsov, an important capitalist from Moscow, whom Koni predictably refused to summon as a witness.

Whatever the extent of Liudmila's activities, Koni was no doubt correct in concluding in his memoir that her fate was sealed when she made that defense and her lawyer either could not or would not stop her. Prosecutor Urusov's final speech sounded as if Liudmila was on trial not for forgery, of which her guilt was not proven, but for engaging in lobbying activities. In one of the most paranoid and panoptically minded speeches in the post-reform courtroom, Urusov envisioned "a field whose existence we could only guess at," one of secret brokerage (*tainye khodataistva*), seeing "some profiles, some silhouettes [that] appeared, crept by, and disappeared again," and that formed a "dark but powerful milieu," seeking "profit at all costs." Urusov ludicrously claimed that there were only two "lawful" forms of *khodataistvo*—legal practice as sworn attorneys or as less strictly regulated (but still male) private attorneys. Urusov alleged that Liudmila's social occupation was to fleece naive provincials who were impressed with her manners and her claimed influence. He noted that even though she had received some education, Liudmila, in his words, "does not understand that [this occupation is] dishonest and that [it is] improper to admit to."

Zhukovskii's speech in Liudmila's defense was equally colorful and even witty, in an unfortunate sense. He very sensibly tried to go back to the only feasible way to win the case, claiming that Liudmila was careless and allowed bad people to exploit her social talents. Zhukovskii mocked Urusov's paranoid style, which he described as treating Liudmila as a *rusalka* (the malicious mermaid of Russian folklore) pulling down the entire edifice of the Russian state.[90] As this case happened about a year and a half after the trial of the Jacks of Hearts, Zhukovskii also ironically referred to his client as the Queen of Hearts, again meaning to mock Urusov's style, which resembled Muraviev's earlier performance, except that it was obviously not a good strategy to suggest any such analogy in juror's heads. Like Urusov, Zhukovskii painted a broad picture and did not sufficiently focus on the forged *vekseli.* The jury convicted both defendants; both unsuccessfully appealed to the tsar's mercy, with Liudmila recalling the special bond Alexander II allegedly formed with Smolny graduates. Bogdanov soon died in Siberian exile. Liudmila found a different solution and married a civil servant who was willing to accompany her to Siberia, where she continued to submit unsuccessful petitions for pardon.

In retrospect, it is difficult to determine whether Gulak-Artemovskaia actually committed forgery. The crime does not fit well with her intelligence and social connections, but she could have made a mistake or changed her habits. It is equally possible that the debt claim came from transactions with Nikolai Pastukhov that were not explained during the trial. The important and very clear conclusion we can draw is that there was some form of collusion or at least a meeting of the minds between Koni, Urusov, Polevoi, Zhukovskii, and even the foreman of the jury that seems to go beyond the common norms of a fair trial. Their objective was to make an impression on society that even well-born and well-connected persons were not above the law when they attempted to subvert the regime of private property, that holy foundation of social and political consensus in imperial Russia.

In doing so, the juridical field raised and debated two questions. One was the larger question of the overall parameters of the Russian culture of private property. What kinds of transactions were not permitted, what was tolerated, what was frowned upon, what would be rigorously prosecuted? Clearly the formal and informal rules of how private property worked as an institution in Russia were changing rapidly. With excessive emotional exaggeration the case of Gulak-Artemovskaia, as well that of Mitrofania, publicized the fact that successful business depended on good relations with the administration and that nonpublic, gray-zone brokerage and influence peddling were indispensable. The second related question was which individuals and organizations were encouraged or at least allowed to participate in this reformed market. Mitrofania had operated a network of charitable institutions that were not financed from the state budget and fully relied on her fundraising abilities, facilitated by her connections with the imperial court. Gulak-Artemovskaia was clearly an insider in several networks, including the top tier of Russian officialdom, among noble-born brokers like her father the general, as well as marginalized participants both in the capital and in the provinces. Liudmila was successful until she made the mistake of demanding payment from people who already despised her and had the necessary legal tools at their disposal, and then she made another mistake in publicizing her activities and compromising a number of influential officials.

CHAPTER 10

Thieving Masters

Imperial Russia was no stranger to large bankruptcies and official corruption, but the crash of the Moscow Commercial Loan Bank (MCLB) in October 1875 was its first modern corporate scandal. It came suddenly and wrecked an important joint-stock company that had enjoyed an unparalleled level of public trust. The crash had a ripple effect, within months ruining a quarter of Russia's private banks and thousands of individual businesses.[1] The root cause was the global slowdown that began in 1873 and severely affected Russia's neighbors and economic partners in Europe.[2] MCLB had invested heavily in worthless French and German securities, but the most damaging cause of the crash was the collusion of its top executives with the German "railroad king" Bethel Henry Strousberg (1823–1884), who managed to loot the bank's assets in less than a year through fraudulent loans.[3] Equally destructive was the negligence of the bank's board of directors, some of whom were experienced Moscow financiers. The two trials that followed were rivaled by only a handful of other cases in terms of public interest and exposure.[4] The public saw that criminal misconduct permeated and in effect took over a major commercial structure. The immediate human impact was also enormous: the crash ruined thousands of middle-class Russians who had sought financial safety in MCLB's reputation. New corporate forms now appeared to be no more secure than the earlier property regime that was based on personal responsibility and personal connections. The case thus exposed and scrutinized the very foundations of the modern corporate capitalism

Figure 21. Vladimir Makovskii, *The Collapse of a Bank* (1881), oil on canvas. The State Tretyakov Gallery, Moscow, Russia/Bridgeman Images. This painting was inspired by the failure of the Moscow Commercial Loan Bank in 1875. The letters on the wall read "The Deposit Section." Bank customers came in to attempt to retrieve their deposits. The group is a mix of social classes. The man in the center wears the red-collared overcoat of an army general and next to him, facing away from the viewer, is a man in a lower-middle-class coat known as a *zipun.* On the right are two police officers and three bank clerks (not wearing outer coats). One is walking off with a dishonest look, tucking away some papers.

that had been rapidly growing in Russia since the 1860s.[5] Minister of Justice Konstantin von Pahlen wrote in a memo to the tsar that the investigation sought to "uncover all the dark sides of Moscow's financial world and to prove that no fraudulent actions in its midst can remain unpunished."[6] Unaware of this memo, the lawyer and legal journalist Nikolai Karabchevskii noted that the case was the first chance for the law to break the seclusion of the "world of money and speculation."[7]

MCLB's failure was neither the first nor the last major white-collar scandal in late imperial Russia. These scandals came in two varieties. The first was simple embezzlement, when the criminals used their legitimate position of trust within an organization to appropriate its assets for their own benefit. Such cases included embezzlement by government officials, bank clerks, and business executives. Embezzlement scandals were routine in post-reform Russia, beginning with the infamous "salt case" of 1867 and ending with the equally scandalous Yukhantsev and Melnitskii trials of 1879 and 1881–1883, respectively. The public was struck by the sheer amount of money easily stolen by modest clerks and cashiers, and also by how ludicrously insufficient were the safety mechanisms within organizations. In the second variety an entire organization was in effect taken over by criminals and turned into a mechanism for cheating the firm's clients and partners.[8] The MCLB case was a prominent example (though it also involved simple embezzlement), as was the trial of the millionaire arsonist Stepan Ovsiannikov in November 1875, only two weeks after the MCLB case began.[9] And as the bank case was unfolding, another even more unscrupulous crime ring was busy advertising itself in all the major newspapers and would continue stealing vast amounts with complete impunity for years to come.

ACES OF EMBEZZLEMENT

Imperial Russia's most brazen embezzlement scandal began on 3 November 1881, when a saintly old man came in tears to Moscow's police headquarters and confessed to losing more than three hundred thousand rubles of government money. Fedor Iliodorovich Melnitskii was the head treasurer of the Imperial Orphanage in Moscow, a vast charitable empire of schools, hospitals, and shelters originally established under Catherine II in 1763. The money lost constituted six months' worth of the orphanage's operating budget. Earlier that afternoon, Melnitskii went to the office of the State Bank to withdraw the money in cash, put it in a leather *sac-voyage* and walked with it to the nearby office of the Moscow Merchant Bank to deposit it into the orphanage's account. He explained that on his way to the bank he had a fainting spell and had to sit down on a pile of logs; when he came to his senses the money had disappeared. Police officers were sympathetic and almost let him go home after recording his statement, but they also notified the orphanage's managing director, A. A. Sheremetievskii, who demanded Melnitskii's arrest and a full investigation.[10]

The two legal cases that followed—that of Melnitskii himself and that of his family members who were accused of being his accessories—caused a stampede in the court building, even though access was limited to the "educated public" (*intelligentnaia publika*). But the Melnitskii scandal was only the latest iteration of a long-established set of legal narratives that predated the Great Reforms. Similar to the trials of swindlers and forgers I discussed earlier in the book, landmark embezzlement and corruption cases questioned Russian elites' notions about individual character, the significance of family ties and hierarchies, and the rather tangled and contradictory ideological narratives of tradition and modernity. Because embezzlement by definition is committed by persons with legitimate access to an organization's resources, its exposure publicized the inner workings of private firms and government agencies. The two themes—that of linking the institutional and the personal, and that of the financial exposé—merged into the larger background discussion underlying this book that went beyond targeting individual wrongdoers to scrutinize the fundamental qualities of Russia's educated and propertied elites and their fitness to rule.

Society and the economy in the second half of the nineteenth century, despite rapid progress in communication technology, still relied on personal connections and trust in daily social and economic dealings. The figure of an intermediary entrusted with managing assets for others' benefit was central and irreplaceable, as has been demonstrated in the scholarship on trusts and trustees in Victorian Britain.[11] In the Anglo-American common law of trusts, the two fundamental "equitable" duties of the trustee are the duty of loyalty and the duty of care, which require trustees to operate solely in their principal's interest with the appropriate degree of attention and competence.[12] In the Russian context, the precise legal categorization of official misconduct, which through Article 1154 of the Penal Code applied also to large private organizations such as banks, was somewhat different, but the two fundamental questions of fin-de-siècle Russia later famously raised during the First World War by the historian and politician Pavel Miliukov—"Was it stupidity or was it treason?"—also loom large in the background of every major embezzlement scandal.[13] Cases of embezzlement and corruption projected the image of the Russian ruling class either as too incompetent to be trusted or as faithless to the state, to the public, to the people, and to its own members . . . or perhaps both.

Historians and the public alike have for a long time believed that Russian government and big business are and have always been exceptionally corrupt, beholden to endemic bribery, embezzlement, and the misuse of personal connections (*blat*). One of Sergei Nechaev's proclamations to his fellow revolutionaries in the early 1870s urged that "before beginning a general popular uprising we will necessarily need to exterminate the entire horde of looters of the treasury."[14] The late imperial government, despite improved professionalism among so-called enlightened bureaucrats was permeated by personal networks of nepotism and patronage.[15] Similar narratives with less detail are typically offered about Russian business culture.[16] But these emotional and ideology-laden narratives must be evaluated in comparison to the extensive literature about pervasive fraud, bribery, and corruption in Victorian Britain and the United States.[17] The large number of corruption prosecutions in late imperial Russia on all levels reveals the problem, but also a determination to combat it. This chapter identifies the competing narratives and scripts that were created during the reign of Alexander II, both by the government and by the public, to make sense of and attempt to draw lines between forgivable gray areas and those that could not be condoned. After all, stealing a bag weighing seventeen pounds filled with cash belonging to orphans is not the same as giving a job to one's former classmate, and taking bribes from a foreign capitalist is a far stretch from building a railroad on the cheap that causes a deadly crash. The embezzlers' individual circumstances varied, but at least those of them who were caught almost always operated under some threat to their status, inviting an invasive discussion of their personal and family lives and of their moral qualities. These discussions expose a wider public dialogue about the boundaries of behavior expected of individuals endowed with responsibility for others.

In the Melnitskii case, the police failed to find the money or any witnesses to his alleged fainting spell. The case against him therefore rested entirely on tenuous arguments derived from the social and cultural context and on testing the jurors' reasoning powers and moral convictions, as well as probing Russia's topography of power and trust to explore whether Melnitskii's past behavior and beliefs justified his position of responsibility.

Initially Fedor Melnitskii seemed an unlikely criminal. Before the emancipation of 1861 his family owned several landed estates in nearby Tver province and then made a largely successful transition, keeping some of these lands, dealing in timber, and becoming active in local politics. Fedor became the head of the local self-government (*zemstvo*) in the small town of Korcheva, while his brother Lev was elected justice of the peace in the nearby Bezhetsk district. Around 1870 Fedor gave up his local influence and moved to Moscow with his six children, and within a few months obtained the prestigious position of treasurer of the orphanage. In addition to the income from his remaining estates, Melnitskii owned a house in Moscow worth more than twenty thousand rubles and received a salary of twelve hundred rubles a year. He was not known for any disreputable habits that could have drained his financial resources, such as gambling, drinking, or womanizing. To the contrary, he struck everyone by his modesty and scrupulous religious observance. His fellow officials at the orphanage initially had only good things to say about him, claiming that he was exceedingly dependable and kind, a "dear old chap" (*milyi dedushka*). One of the trustees, Degai, even said that the board trusted him "more than it did any bank."[18]

More critical opinions about Melnitskii's character soon surfaced, however. To some of his fellow officials the kindly old man appeared as a ruthless capitalist ready to fleece his neighbors. Acting as legal representative for his wife he sued her relative, seizing this woman's entire property of fifteen hundred rubles. When one of Melnitskii's brothers died, leaving behind an illegitimate wife and an infant son, Fedor ensured that the hapless woman was dispossessed and that her baby was transferred to foster care, for which he soon stopped paying. He was not any less cruel to his coworkers, once taking advantage of an accounting mistake to appropriate two thousand rubles and sticking his colleague with the obligation to make up the loss. The narrative of a kindly *dedushka* was thus replaced in the indictment with that of a smooth-talking but cold-hearted "cunning Jesuit."[19] It also turned out that Melnitskii's professional trustworthiness was likewise suspect, since smaller sums of a few thousand rubles had disappeared from the orphanage on several occasions. Even more striking, Melnitskii administered a mutual aid fund for orphanage officials, which he drained by issuing several large and uncollectable loans. Finally, a few years earlier, the orphanage lost a safe box that belonged to Dr. Gugenberg containing valuables worth about fifty thousand rubles. Melnitskii was in charge of that box but claimed that he was absent when the loss was discovered. Although there was an official criminal investigation, the police did not find any evidence to back up its suspicions against Melnitskii.[20] Even his popularity with fellow officials derived largely from a violation of the law, namely, from his willingness to issue their salaries before payday. Finally, Melnitskii ran a robust illegal lending operation using government money and pocketing the interest, charging low rates to orphanage officials and higher ones to outsiders. Even some of the board members of the orphanage, appointed from Russia's most elite circles, had been among his clients.[21]

Armed with this damaging evidence, the investigation constructed a narrative of the tension between Melnitskii's outward pious respectability and inner corruption and avarice. But as in the case of the Jacks of Hearts the sources of this corruption were more difficult to explain. One easy explanation would be to blame the Melnitskiis' serf-owning past. But the trope of an impoverished former serf owner who cannot adjust to new realities and is thus driven to crime was difficult to apply to Melnitskii. Everything in his life showed that he had adjusted very well to capitalist modernization. Alternatively, Melnitskii could have been corrupted by the new mentality of acquisitive capitalism, and the indictment quoted him as allegedly saying to his son Boris: "Money is everything in our age."[22] But this theory was contradicted by Melnitskii's modest lifestyle and his disdain for daring business ventures, playing the stock market, or other typical modern capitalist activities, aside from moneylending, which is as old as civilization itself. Melnitskii's character thus contrasted sharply with Russia's other famous embezzlers, such as General Politkovskii, who was the treasurer of Russia's charitable war veterans' foundation in 1834–1853 and was known for his luxurious habits and high-stakes gambling, or Konstantin Yukhantsev, a bank cashier in St. Petersburg who embezzled largely because he enjoyed a good life in the capital.

Even less helpful but clearly symptomatic of its age was the investigators' attempt to turn Melnitskii and his family into political offenders. This part of the investigation was never made public, but the police from the very beginning considered the possibility that Melnitskii appropriated the money to benefit the radical underground.[23] His daughter Valentina spent four months under arrest by the Third Section based on a denunciation by some of Melnitskii's colleagues.[24] In November 1882, just a few days after her father's trial, Valentina married a young lawyer named Getmanchuk, who was nothing less than an assistant to Mr. Sakharov, the chief investigator in the case.[25] This revelation produced a lively secret correspondence between Moscow and Petersburg, and Procurator Goncharov assured his superiors that Getmanchuk had no access to sensitive information.[26]

When the Melnitskii case went on trial at the end of 1882, the theme of political disloyalty was absent from the indictment, and the opposition between the old and the new Russia was barely perceptible. Instead, the indictment highlighted Melnitskii's personal greed, and, given his modest lifestyle, it appeared rather illogical, especially since all the evidence against him was entirely circumstantial and the cash was still missing. But the jurors seem not to have believed that he would have marched around Moscow on a cold November afternoon carrying seventeen pounds of cash and lose it after a dizzy spell. They convicted Melnitskii with apparent ease, much as in other trials based on circumstantial or otherwise questionable evidence, such as those of Mother Mitrofania and the millionaire arsonist Stepan Ovsiannikov. Melnitskii was sentenced to Siberian exile and began to make travel plans, to be helped by at least some of his children and two servants. But the case soon acquired an additional dimension and a new, unique meaning within Russia's legal culture.

The police waited for almost two months after the trial and on the last day of 1882 raided the apartments of Melnitskii's eldest son, Boris, of his daughter

Valentina, and of Boris's relative and business partner, Albert Dorvoidt. This timing was no doubt meant to allow Melnitskii's children to let down their guard, but it also suggests that the police were not completely sure about where the missing cash was hidden, otherwise there would not have been any need to wait. In Dorvoidt's apartment the detectives found about a hundred thousand rubles in bank notes tossed in a dresser with dirty laundry. At that point Boris broke down and confessed that his father stole the money and forced him to assist him under threat of suicide, claiming to Boris that he was doing it solely to provide for all his children's futures. Boris also said that Dorvoidt had the rest of the money, and after another search the police found another hundred thousand rubles sealed in two plaster plant stands. A sum of roughly thirty thousand rubles was also recovered from various other sources, but the rest of the money was never found.

Boris and his fiancée, Elena, her brother-in-law Dorvoidt, Valentina, Fedor's other daughter, Varvara, Fedor's aunt Vera, and Fedor's brother Lev were all charged as accessories to the embezzlement. The discovery of the money strengthened the institution of the trial by jury, since a case with abundant but entirely indirect evidence was proven to have been judged correctly. Also, the entire case acquired a direct social significance. From an inexplicable incident in which a lone criminal stole money he did not need just because he could (with a hint of criticism of the modern worship of money), the case turned into a sharp scrutiny and even an indictment of the modern Russian family.

Previous chapters have already argued that family ties were intimately involved in the habitus of crime in late imperial Russia. Spouses, siblings, parents, and children all acted as victims, enablers, or beneficiaries of criminals. In embezzlement cases, family members were typically presented as having benefited from the crime. Thus, in the 1850s General Politkovskii bought an expensive house as his daughter's dowry. Other embezzlers were said to have had an early marriage, or a wife accustomed to luxury, or to have had an unhappy family life.[27] The Melnitskii case elaborated on this narrative in recasting the entire family as active participants in the crime, since the most difficult aspect of the case from the state's perspective was finding the missing money, and the family was active and ingenious in hiding it. Ironically, Melnitskii robbed several thousand children who had no parents in order to provide for the future of his own children, thereby consigning them to infamy.

While some of the defense lawyers attempted to argue that Fedor Melnitskii had complete control over his children, especially over Boris, so that they would not dare to contradict his commands, there was no evidence that this was a dysfunctional or even a particularly traditional or patriarchal family. The children were educated: Boris had studied at the prestigious Moscow Technical School, which he dropped out of to make a living as a taxidermist; his brother Mikhail failed to enter a military school and instead enrolled as a volunteer (*volnoopredeliaiushchiisia*), which was a common alternative path to an officer commission, and served in the prestigious Sumy Hussar Regiment stationed in Moscow. Valentina was attending the Moscow Higher Women's Courses, while her fourteen-year-old sister, Varvara, studied in a girls' high school (*gimnazia*). Even Albert Dorvoidt, as a hereditary honorary citizen clearly from an upper-middle-class background, was employed by a successful kerosene merchant. Thus all of the Melnitskii children and their relations were poised to make a comfortable middle-class living for themselves and did not require the head of the family to risk criminal trial and Siberian exile in order to provide for them.

Although for the first few months Boris was careful not to spend more than a few rubles at one time, he quickly began to provide his imprisoned father with fresh linen and ever nicer delicacies to eat; he also gradually confided in the rest of his family, although his uncle Lev persisted implausibly in denying that he knew anything. Gradually, Boris started to spend more, and the family's living conditions began to improve. The indictment went to great lengths to reconstruct the Melnitskiis' financial affairs, in effect crafting a fantasy picture of what an ordinary middle-class Russian would do with a virtually unlimited supply of money, living out the story of a real-life Count of Monte Cristo. Boris was of course aware that he was being watched by the police and instead of spending in his own name went to Dorvoidt and offered him money to start his own business. Previously down on his luck, Dorvoidt agreed and rented a spacious warehouse for a new kerosene retail business, bought horses to make deliveries, and rented a new apartment for his family. Boris was employed as a bookkeeper and had his living quarters in the shop building. But he had absolutely no understanding of accounting, and so Dorvoidt had to retain the clerks from his earlier failed venture. These clerks were graphically described in the trial transcript as essentially drunk doofuses, but they knew enough to immediately offer their services to the police investigator, Sakharov, although he insisted that he kept them on only to distract his targets and that the key incriminating information had come from elsewhere.

Melnitskii's other relatives benefited in smaller ways. Valentina was angry when she first found out that her father did in fact steal the money and at first cut off her relations with him, but she soon changed her mind and used some of the money to rent an apartment for herself and her younger siblings, as well as to purchase some fashionable items. Varvara acquired some spending money, as her job was to pass notes from her father: the guards would not dare to search a teenage noblewoman. Fedor's fifty-year-old Aunt Vera took seven thousand rubles to pay off her four stepsons in a property-division arrangement, the dream of any middle-class widow who also had eight natural children and no unencumbered money of her own.[28] None of these people denied knowingly using the stolen money, aside from Lev Melnitskii, who was independently wealthy but was charged with helping Boris and Fedor to administer the loot, providing advice and serving as the front to retain high-quality counsel. At the second trial, at the end of 1883, however, the jury acquitted everyone.

Judicial officials were predictably livid, given that this was one of those high-profile occasions when juries acquitted defendants who had openly confessed to their crime, similar to the recent acquittal of Vera Zasulich. The officials found enough procedural grounds to appeal the decision and hold another trial, in 1884, when Boris Melnitskii and Albert Dorvoidt were convicted and sentenced to Siberian exile. The rest of the defendants were once again acquitted, however. Given the conservative political climate of the early 1880s, these proceedings were arguably even more threatening to the future of the Russian jury trial than the Zasulich case. The journalist Sergei Keltsev somewhat counterintuitively argued, however, that the acquittal actually "sanctified . . . the belief [in the future of Russian youth], to lose which would be for Russian society tantamount to being sentenced to be buried alive."[29] Keltsev's query was whether the Melnitskii family's activities were a freak exception, "a victim of an outside evil will," or whether they were a "typical modern Russian family," which would mean that for today's youth there were no other principles than that "all happiness lies in money." Keltsev thus convincingly suggested that the jury decided to blame everything on the father's influence. The children participated in theft, but at least they did not rebel. Filial obedience was seen as preferable to preventing or reporting a crime. To Keltsev, at least, the trial vindicated not only the young Russians of his age but also the very principle of family loyalty and of obedience to the family patriarch.

CRIMINAL CAPITALISTS

Within a few weeks in 1875 the Russian public read about two history-making scandals involving leading figures of the country's business community. On 11 October the Moscow Commercial Loan Bank suspended operations, and that same evening the judicial investigator Petr Mikhailovich Globo-Mikhalenko sealed the bank building and seized its papers. Two days later the entire board of directors was arrested and then freed upon submission of staggering bail bonds of hundreds of thousands of rubles per person.[30] And on 25 November the St. Petersburg District Court opened the trial of Stepan Tarasovich Ovsiannikov, a seventy-year-old grain merchant, one of the wealthiest in a country known for its grain production. Ovsiannikov and two of his clerks were accused of burning down an enormous new steam grain mill located on the corner of Izmailovskii Prospect and the Obvodnyi Canal in order to collect the insurance payout.

Superficially the two cases could not have been more different. The bank's directors and managers belonged to Russia's new capitalist elite, leaders of the developing culture of corporations and stock markets. Ovsiannikov had been in the business of government supply contracts since the 1830s and had been both decorated and subjected to criminal investigation several times. With his long beard he looked every bit the traditional Russian merchant, and the act of burning a state-of-the-art steam flour mill evoked the image of traditional forces unable to cope with modernity. Yet fundamentally both cases addressed the same general uncertainty about what it meant to own property in post-emancipation Russia, and what kinds of responsibilities came with ownership rights, in particular the duty to exercise certain standards of care and competence, to disclose certain information to one's clients and partners, and to avoid practices described as fraud, embezzlement, and corruption. Both trials engaged forensic experts, especially bankers and accountants, to reconstruct the defendants' financial affairs, in the bank case producing an accessible and highly informative primer on the operations of a modern business corporation. Ideologically, both cases constructed an image of a foreign-derived innovation destroyed by entrenched networks of power and corruption, with Ovsiannikov destroying his own mill, and the Moscow bank's demise assisted or even caused by the German Strousberg, a foreign adventurer tempted by instant and easy wealth. Ovsiannikov was purely Russian, but a suspected sectarian, and in effect Strousberg's counterpart, suggesting some unpleasant ramifications for supporters of Russia's economic nationalism.[31] Similar to Strousberg and his accomplices, Ovsiannikov was alleged to have advanced from simple fraud, embezzlement, and bribery to creating a vast network of criminal business. Even more ambitious—and also Russian—were the creators of one of the world's first modern Ponzi schemes, which operated from the modest provincial town of Skopin through the 1860s and 1870s but came to trial only in 1884.

Stepan Tarasovich Ovsiannikov acquired his marvelous mill in 1871 in partnership with another top-shelf capitalist, Vasilii Kokorev. Their main

Figure 22. Stepan Ovsiannikov's mill on fire. *Vsemirnaia illustratsia,* 1875, no. 9, p. 160.

customer was the military, which needed huge amounts of flour to feed the troops. The army insisted on using the steam mill located expensively in the city in order to fight corruption and control quality. Ovsiannikov calculated that even with this obstacle the contract was still lucrative, but his relations with Kokorev soon deteriorated into massive civil-law litigation. On 5 February 1875, just days before Ovsiannikov was required to turn the mill over to his former partner, the mill went up in flames. Its sophisticated firefighting system was shut off on Ovsiannikov's orders, ostensibly to prevent the water pipes from freezing while the mill's boilers were not operational. The doorman would not even open the gates to firefighters, who had to break in. The next day it did not take the judicial investigators long to charge Ovsiannikov with arson for the purpose of collecting the hefty insurance payout.

No observers or commentators seem to have ever doubted Ovsiannikov's responsibility for the fire. But the actual evidence against Ovsiannikov "was seen by many as very weak."[32] The case tops the list of post-reform criminal convictions that were based on indirect and conflicted evidence, especially the convictions of Gulak-Artemovskaia and Mother Mitrofania. Ovsiannikov was prosecuted by two of Russia's top jurists. Vladimir Zhukovskii was the star of

Figure 23. The defendants and their lawyers at the arson trial of Stepan Ovsiannikov. *Vsemirnaia illustratsia,* 1875, no. 24, p. 433. This appears to be the same courtroom as the one depicted in figure 4. The man on the bottom right is one of Russia's leading capitalists, Vasily Kokorev, the mill's legal owner, acting as a civil plaintiff against Ovsiannikov. Next to him is lawyer Vladimir Spasovich, representing the company that insured the mill.

the procuracy but would leave it two years later for refusing to prosecute Vera Zasulich. After subsequently joining the bar, he would represent prominent white-collar defendants, such as Gulak-Artemovskaia and Yukhantsev. Zhukovskii was assisted by Vladimir Spasovich himself acting as the lawyer for the defrauded insurance company. They sought to rhetorically shift the burden of proof to the defendants and deployed a small army of expert witnesses to prove, first, that the fire was intentional and, second, that Ovsiannikov had profited financially. The prosecution even built a large clay model of the mill to show how the fire spread throughout the building. Read in isolation, the arguments against Ovsiannikov appear reasonable, but so do those of his own lawyer, Pavel Potekhin. Since there was no reliable science dealing with incinerating large industrial buildings, today their lengthy discussions about the fire seem unconvincing.

Similarly, Ovsiannikov's financial profit appears doubtful because he was still entangled in complex dealings with Kokorev and other commercial tycoons and would be able to stay in business only if he maintained his lucrative military contract. His being at least suspected of arson by the entire public put a permanent end to his commercial endeavors. Kokorev thus stood much more to gain financially because he would get rid of the giant money-losing mill and also of his key competitor. Zhukovsky admitted this predicament in his speech, but both he and Spasovich worked hard to argue the opposite, ultimately claiming that Ovsiannikov set the fire because of his anger and pride at losing his business. This was entirely conjectural, however. Spasovich famously described the case through the metaphor of seeing "strokes and dashes" on a sheet of paper, which on a closer look combine into letters, and the letters become the word "arson." Witty as this was, one can equally readily conclude that the "letters" read "reasonable doubt."[33]

As they did in other factually weak cases, the prosecutors crafted images and arguments about Russia and its troubles that Ovsiannikov, they argued, had exploited. To one journalist he was the "living type" of a "capitalist kulak . . . a soulless, heartless, vain egotist." Spasovich skillfully dehumanized him as "capital incarnate," claiming that of all types of economic exchange the most important one, commerce, is "always full of deceptions and abuses," thus suggesting that it was acquisitive capitalism itself that was actually on trial. This could not go too far, however: it was difficult to attack pure acquisitiveness while representing, as Spasovich did, a major insurance company. Instead Ovsiannikov was portrayed as a habitual criminal simply by being a major government contractor. Middlemen contractors, Zhukovsky argued, were the weak link in the development of Russia's productive social and economic forces. Their interests were always at odds with those of the government, but they could be neither eliminated nor improved: "Neither sudden audits, nor penalties, nor criminal prosecutions, nor official prohibitions have been able to discourage suspect contractors from gravitating towards grain provisioning." More at liberty to speak as a private lawyer, Spasovich added that in addition to fierce market competition, contractors necessarily had to bribe government officials at all levels, establishing a certain "average level of dishonesty."[34]

The implication was that Ovsiannikov personally had exceeded this average level, since he was prosecuted at least seven and maybe fifteen times beginning in the early 1840s, accumulating what Zhukovsky called a "clinical chart of criminality." Spasovich labeled his operations as "the rule of the bashi-bazouk [i.e., poorly disciplined Ottoman cavalry] that leaves behind only piles of rubbish and turn the mill into a ruin as if after an enemy invasion." To be sure, neither Zhukovsky nor Spasovich elaborated on the bribery and other abuses by government officials, which appear in archival records of Ovsiannikov's prior legal difficulties. For example, in 1854 he was engaged in lengthy litigation with the military, which wanted to charge him an exorbitant penalty when his flour deliveries were late due to a cholera epidemic, on the premise that cholera did not legally constitute "pestilence" (*morovaia iazva*), which would have excused the delay. In 1841 Ovsiannikov donated large amounts of good flour to the government but was denied a promotion because of his Old Believer background. Such stories did not come up at the trial, though they would explain Ovsiannikov's likely mentality: formed by cut-throat deals, fleeting alliances, and crushing losses.[35]

The narrative of entire commercial organizations and practices being corrupt and perhaps irredeemably criminal developed in a series of major bank failures, beginning with the Moscow Commercial Loan Bank only a few weeks before the conviction of Stepan Ovsiannikov. The first Russian joint-stock bank—the St. Petersburg Private Commercial Bank—appeared in 1864, followed by the Moscow Merchant Bank two years later and then approximately a dozen others, including MCLB in 1870.[36] The explosion in company formation in Russia included not only banks and mutual credit societies but also railroads, insurance, mining, and shipping companies.[37] Until the end of the tsarist empire the law required government permission for companies to incorporate, but this was not a barrier to larger companies.[38] Other indispensable legal frameworks had existed for decades: Russia had had a bankruptcy statute since 1800 and limited corporate liability since 1805, while a comprehensive corporate-law statute appeared in 1836. The Great Reforms of the 1860s thus did not involve significant formal alterations in the financial and commercial sphere, merely a lessening of government oversight. In sum, it is difficult to accept at face value the observation made by contemporaries during the Strousberg Affair that Moscow's commercial leaders who sat on MCLB's and other banks' boards were in effect punished for their backwardness and ignorance about modern finance.[39]

As with other prominent early joint-stock banks in Russia, MCLB's directors were among the most recognizable individuals in Moscow. Its chairman in 1870–1873 was Daniil Danilovich Schumacher (1819–1908), Dostoevskii's classmate and an experienced financier who had previously worked at the all-important state-owned mortgage bank in Moscow since 1839 and headed it since 1865. In 1873 Schumacher was elected mayor of Moscow and gave up his leadership of the bank, but he remained on its board of directors.[40] During the

Figures 24a and 24b. "The Tale of the Fisherman and the Goldfish." *Budil'nik,* 1876, no. 44. A satirical cartoon alluding to Alexander Pushkin's popular tale and directed against Dr. Strousberg. At the behest of his wife, "Commerce," Strousberg (actually married to an English woman) fishes in the murky waters of the commercial world, using stocks as bait. At first he gets rich, but eventually the ocean is infuriated and Strousberg is cast out, ending up impoverished and under prosecution. Pushkin's tale is about a poor fisherman lucky enough to catch a wish-granting goldfish. At his wife's bidding, he keeps coming back to the fish, asking for more favors, until it refuses to answer his call, and the fisherman finds himself back at his tiny shack.

investigation many shareholders testified that the bank was supervised by persons of "of such high social standing, commercial significance, knowledge and experience, who talked so much about their business success, that the failure of the Bank appeared unthinkable."[41] The directors spared no expense in hiring what they believed were top-notch managers to run the executive board

(*pravlenie*) responsible for the day-to-day operations of the bank. These included a former owner of a private banking house in Warsaw, Gustav Iakovlevich Landau, hired to manage MCLB's investments in foreign securities. The bank's managing director and Schumacher's protégé, Pavel Moiseevich Polianskii, was a municipal deputy and a popular justice of the peace. On the downside, none of the shareholders or directors held enough stock to control or even effectively oversee the bank's operations, which was somewhat unusual at that time. Nor did MCLB employ the common safety mechanism of appointing several directors who were outsiders to the world of finance (that is, academics, journalists, and so on) and thus less vulnerable to unreasonable risk-taking or corruption.

Bad foreign investments and a lack of board oversight combined with a global economic crisis to destroy MCLB. After they were arrested and indicted, the directors maintained that the crash came as a complete shock. I discuss below how much they knew about their bank's condition, but the global slowdown that began in 1873 was not a secret and clearly called for caution. While it was most likely not quite the first full-blown Great Depression, as some historians have maintained, the crisis lowered prices for agricultural products and led to bankruptcies and bank failures in North America and throughout Europe, especially in Germany and Austria-Hungary.[42] Among the casualties of the crisis was a leading German railroad entrepreneur, Dr. Henry Bethel Strousberg (1823–1884). Hannah Davies attributes his fame to skillfully managed publicity, with biographies and newspaper articles making him sound more important than he actually was.[43] It seems that his flamboyance and his reputation as a great "operator [*Macher*]" seduced the German upper classes, and apparently Russian capitalists as well.[44] Strousberg was born into a converted Jewish family in East Prussia and educated in England. After being imprisoned in England for embezzlement, he fled back to Prussia and in the 1860s made a fortune constructing railways in Germany, Russian-ruled Poland, and Hungary.[45] His strategy came to be called the Strousberg system and was designed to evade excessive and archaic legal restrictions on raising capital under Prussian law. He attracted large pools of private investors and hired a general contractor who was paid with the future railroad's shares and could sell them below par to finance the project.[46] While common for major infrastructure projects, this system closely resembled a pyramid scheme, since Strousberg was "undertaking new ventures in order to mend new holes" in his finances.[47] The system was successful in modernizing Germany's railway network in the 1860s. It failed, however, in Romania's province of Transylvania, causing massive losses to Strousberg's well-connected partners and investors, as well as ordinary middle-class Germans.[48] The oncoming depression and the disruptions of the Franco-Prussian War brought Strousberg's business empire to the brink of collapse.

Backed by Russia's own railway kingpin, Samuil Poliakov, Strousberg turned to Russia's growing credit market in a last-ditch hope to revive his fortunes. While he later presented himself as a complete stranger to Russia and its capital markets, we know that German financiers had long been in contact with Russian merchants and even officials, such as the powerful minister Petr Valuev.[49] Strousberg was connected to Russian capitalists by several intermediaries, and in 1874 MCLB's board approved a loan of 1.2 million rubles to Strousberg, allegedly believing it to be secured by solid assets: shipping bills for railway cars manufactured at Strousberg's factory and earmarked for one of Poliakov's new railroads. At that same time, the board did take some precautions: Landau, the bank's manager of investments in foreign securities, was ordered to discontinue risky foreign operations, especially purchases of French and German securities tied to railroads and other assets that had not yet been constructed. Landau's foreign-investment department ceased to be an autonomous unit within the MCLB and was placed under direct supervision of the bank's managing director, Polianskii.[50]

Some directors soon became suspicious about Landau's continuing dealings with Strousberg and took advantage of Polianskii's vacation in Crimea in September 1875. A prominent Moscow merchant of Greek extraction, Dmitrii Millioti, temporarily took over as the managing director and immediately conducted an independent audit, discovering that Polianskii and Landau had given Strousberg more than eight million rubles in unsecured loans. Even the shipping bills (bills of lading) for the railway cars that Strousberg had presented as loan collateral were actually cleverly disguised futures contracts for items to be constructed at a factory that did not yet exist. The full board found out about this on 5 October and at a panicky meeting initially decided to keep this information secret to try to save the bank. For almost a week the board, including the whistleblower Millioti, continued to take deposits from unsuspecting customers, while at the same time paying out themselves, their relatives, and their business partners.[51] In just a few days, the bank's remaining liquid cash of nearly 2.5 million rubles vanished.[52]

The directors also traveled to St. Petersburg to ask the minister of finance for a bailout but were refused. It is conceivable that the government wanted to teach a lesson to irresponsible entrepreneurs.[53] The government was also likely reluctant to pay such a large amount of money to, in effect, sponsor Strousberg, who was by that time widely regarded as a "swindler" (*aferist*). It is reasonable to assume that Strousberg's predations by this point were even greater than eight million rubles and extended to other banks. In addition to approaching Petersburg authorities, the directors went to other Moscow banks for help, and failed again. Finally, on 11 October the bank shut down its operations, and the scene depicted in Vladimir Makovskii's painting ensued: shareholders besieged the building to retrieve their deposits and tried to sell their stock to individuals who had not yet heard the news, while others rushed to file legal complaints against the bank. Acting on these complaints, the police arrested the bank's managers and directors, as well as Strousberg himself.

The investigation and pretrial proceedings revealed the extent to which even the newly reformed judiciary was still embedded in a network of personal and business relations with Moscow's business and professional elites. Secret correspondence between the procurator of the Moscow Judicial Chamber, Nikolai

Manasein, and the minister of justice, Konstantin von Pahlen, shows that several judges had conflicts of interest and were pushing to discontinue the investigation.[54] One of the judges of the district court, Shestakov, argued for closing the case against the bank's directors, under the influence of the directors' prominent attorneys, Kupernik, Plevako, Przhevalskii, and others, with whom he was "on most friendly terms."[55] The judges of the Moscow Judicial Chamber were also inclined to view the directors' activities as not criminal. Two of the judges, Okhliabinin and Pavlov, spread rumors criticizing the investigation, alleging that its strictness was due to the fact that several judicial officials, including the minister's chief secretary, the procurator Manasein, and the investigator Globo-Mikhalenko, all owned the bank's stock and lost large sums of money. Judge Okhliabinin was related to a bank director, while Judge Pavlov owed his lucrative seat on the board of a railroad to Schumacher and was good friends with another director. Another judge, P. G. Izvolskii, was related to one of the directors, Borisovskii, and likewise lobbied for his release. After listening to these rumors, Moscow's governor-general, Prince Vladimir Dolgorukov, also began to lobby in favor of the defendants and criticize the procuracy, and he even retaliated against the city's chief of police for following Manasein's instructions.[56] Manasein had to have informal discussions with all of these jurists to convince them not to hinder the investigation. Moreover, the chairman of the Moscow District Court, Petr Deier, decided that this was a good moment to advance his own professional network by promoting several of his protégés: he refused to try the case until his demands were met.[57] Pahlen also reported to the tsar that Schumacher and other defendants were "slandering" Moscow's judicial officials. Numerous unrelated but influential individuals petitioned authorities on the defendants' behalf, much as they had done in the Mitrofania case. Finally, after the trial had already begun, the district court was informed unofficially that the foreman of the jury, Timofei Bolin, was related to one director and was a business partner to another, while another juror was assistant to Attorney Plevako.[58] While Manasein and Pahlen had the tsar's attention and support, and were able to push the investigation through, the informal influence of the upper classes would still affect the outcome of the case.

The opening day of the trial, 29 May 1876, was among the most impactful episodes in the history of late imperial Russia. The sheer size of the trial actually strained the resources of Moscow's bar, which at the time had fewer than 250 full attorneys and between one hundred and two hundred assistants.[59] As already noted, in Russia crime victims could participate in a trial as civil plaintiffs, and they typically hired their own attorneys, who in effect supported the prosecution. In the MCLB case, there were thousands of victims, and the trial risked becoming wholly unmanageable. Legal officials attempted to address this potential logistical disaster by collecting petitions from the victims, and about six hundred were submitted. The petitions are preserved in the archival file, revealing the identities of investors and the basic circumstances of their investments and losses.[60] But other victims, numbering approximately two thousand, simply showed up at the trial without warning, many of them poorly dressed, whether because they had actually been dispossessed or because they wanted to impress the jury. It became obvious that the mere presence of these people in the courtroom would make the trial superfluous and ensure a guilty verdict. The leading defense attorney in Moscow at that time, Fedor Plevako (defending director Borisovskii), was able to have the trial postponed on the technicality that the jury panel was supposedly selected incorrectly.[61] By the time the trial recommenced on 2 October, the accused board members managed to find enough resources to compensate in full all the smaller-scale victims with deposits under eight thousand rubles, while the larger ones recouped 75 percent, and so the victims' presence in the courtroom was no longer a threat to defendants.[62] While during the first few days of the trial the courtroom was full, the public's attention soon waned.

From a legal standpoint the bank case raised several complex and important issues, some of them at the core of modern corporate law and still contentious.[63] The didactic, public impact of the case would depend in part on how and in what order these issues would be presented during the trial. The case involved three sets of defendants: Strousberg was accused of bribery, as were Polianskii and Landau, who were also accused of embezzlement. The directors were accused of negligence, and several of them were also charged with fraud for selling their stock and withdrawing their deposits after the board had officially learned about its bank's crash. The prosecution could have chosen to blame the disaster on the foreigners Strousberg and Landau, who supposedly deceived inexperienced Russian capitalists.[64] This line of argument can in fact be found in some journalistic accounts of the case. But the prosecution chose instead to focus on the directors, all members of Moscow's business elite, on their negligence and even corruption, which enabled swindlers and embezzlers.

The prosecution's first and therefore most impactful argument was that the bank's daily structure and operations were flawed from the time it was established in 1870. The root cause of the disaster was a lack of transparency and accountability in the operations of a major joint-stock bank.[65] As with any joint-stock company, MCLB's shareholders had the power to elect the board of directors, which then appointed the management that operated the bank. The Russian word for the board's role (*rukovodit'*) was much more forceful than the English "direct" and suggested leadership rather than mere oversight. Shareholders, in turn, were seen as more than passive investors and were viewed rather as actual owners of the bank who had the right to change the board and to receive accurate reports about the bank's affairs.[66] Yet, the indictment alleged, from the very start the board was able to exclude most shareholders from having any say in the bank's affairs by a fictitious distribution of stock to the directors' relatives, friends, and even bank employees, thus obtaining an artificial majority at all general meetings and creating "organized uncontrollability and deliberate irresponsibility."[67] The directors responded to this charge by arguing that this was the only way to have a quorum at the meetings due to lack of interest from the shareholders, and that this was a common practice in other institutions.[68] Commentators such as the memoirist Ekaterina Kozlinina or the lawyer and legal journalist Nikolai Karabchevskii argued that the case was a lesson to Russia's entire propertied classes to be more aware and active about their assets rather than simply handing them over to potentially unreliable agents.[69] What made the board members "savages" in Kozlinina's view was not simply their ignorance about banking but also their selfishness, which led them to ignore the public's interests and to run the bank as their own personal asset. The foreign swindlers took advantage of this greed to teach their Russian counterparts a good lesson.[70]

The board members were charged with negligence in that the managers were able to loan virtually all the bank's assets to Strousberg without the directors' approval, even though as early as 1871 it was known in Russia, as well as in Western Europe, that Strousberg was a "desperate swindler, with whom it was dangerous to have any dealings."[71] The board was also charged with approving inaccurate and even fraudulent annual reports and concealing losses by falsely listing the bank's bad investments as profitably sold.[72] The chief accountant of the foreign-investment division testified that the bank's management purchased unsecured stocks in hopes of making a quick profit, which did not materialize (no doubt due to the global slowdown), and the bank lost money even before it made illegal loans to Strousberg.[73] The managing director, Polianskii, claimed that the entire board and his fellow managers all examined these investments "most thoroughly" and approved all transactions.[74] The directors, predictably, claimed that they knew nothing about their bank's actual state of affairs. On the surface, there were no egregious violations of the accounting practices of that time, but other bankers who acted as expert witnesses testified that in general directors who audited account books were always informed about the most important issues of their company. The fact that Strousberg owed the bank more than eight million rubles would be impossible to miss accidentally.[75] Also, during each audit of MCLB at least one participant understood banking, but the directors each time looked selectively at some falsified accounts and found everything to be in order. It was only during the last audit, on the eve of the crash, that the temporary managing director Millioti, the whistleblower, pointed the audit members to the foreign-investments section, which had previously been left untouched, and the audit immediately discovered glaring violations.[76] Finally, a separate charge accused the board chairman, Schumacher, and two other board members of withdrawing their deposits, and four others of selling their shares shortly before the bank's failure became publicly known.[77] These board members unconvincingly claimed they had no idea they could not remove their own money from a crashed bank.

The second set of charges concerned the bank's loans to Henry Bethel Strousberg and his bribery of the bank's foreign-investment officer, Landau, and its managing director, Polianskii. All three men admitted bribery, but the indictment and the trial proceedings still examined the Strousberg loans in great detail, with the help of prominent expert witnesses. These were the director of the Moscow Merchant Bank, A. E. Voinov, chief accountant of the Industrial Bank, P. M. Dufner, and the assistant chief cashier of the Moscow Merchant Mutual Credit Society, N. I. Lazarev.[78] From the outset the prosecution presented Landau as a priori harmful to the bank and owing his appointment to his personal friendship with one of the directors, Givartovskii, pointing out that both men were "of Jewish origin," like Strousberg himself.[79] Much as in the Mitrofania and Gulak-Artemovskaia cases, the Jewish ethnicity of a participant was presented as a negative factor, but it was not elaborated or discussed. The indictment pointed out that Landau was paid twelve thousand rubles a year.[80] This was equivalent to the salary of a government minister or a senior general. Very little additional information was used to prosecute him other than that he had previously owned a bank in Warsaw but became bankrupt. He did have connections with German bankers, and it appears that he was brought to Moscow specifically to work with promising though risky European securities.

The role of chief villain in the case was assigned to Strousberg, who engaged in acrimonious courtroom debates with Landau about which of them had deceived and abused the other. Strousberg argued that the loans were not fraudulent, in that the securities he used as guarantee were a good investment, but only as long as he remained out of prison to fulfill his contractual obligations to construct railway cars and as yet nonexistent railways in Bohemia. After his arrest Strousberg at first categorically denied having any unofficial financial dealings with Landau and Polianskii.[81] But only a few days later, after the two of them had admitted to receiving bribes, Strousberg also confessed to bribery.[82] He claimed that this was done, in his words, "for the purpose of giving presents to [the bank's] directors and employees, because I learned from [another banker] and from my own experience that in Russia there exists a custom to give presents at the closing of a commercial transaction." Strousberg went as far as to explain the trial's educational value: "The present trial may influence beneficially both those who give and those who take; but of course those who give cannot have a very high view about the moral principles of those who take; as to me, I was not under any obligation to polish local customs." Historian Fritz Redlich has characterized this way of thinking as the philosophy of a "fraudulent bankrupt."[83]

During the investigation Strousberg portrayed himself as the actual victim, claiming that Landau used his financial difficulties not simply to extort large bribes, amounting to more than half a million rubles, but also to force him to take questionable paper as loan payouts.[84] Landau's alleged objective was to keep Strousberg under his control, issuing him loans that were insufficient to fix his affairs but making them even more entangled. While hoping to raise money in Russia, Strousberg reported, he had "to be a hypocrite, to express [his] love and gratitude, where [he] only felt deep disgust and hatred."[85] Just in case the Russians did not fully appreciate his grandeur, Strousberg noted: "If this may seem unclear to persons who are used to small transactions, I will point out [that] I built railroads worth several hundred million thalers," most of which were not guaranteed by any government.[86] According to Strousberg, Landau sought to deal with him because he used to admire his ventures and "had faith in [his] star."[87] This is highly unlikely, given that Strousberg's reputation had by then plummeted, and the only reason any financiers in Europe were still dealing with him was to attempt to recover their investments.

A large number of witnesses testified at the trial or sent written statements, including the major industrialists Ivan (Jan) Bloch, Gerson von Bleichroeder, and Fedor Chizhov, who all explained that Strousberg had for years lost all credit in Europe and that they would not agree to have any dealings with him.[88] Neither Landau nor the board members could have failed to be aware of Strousberg's ongoing downfall, and yet they still gave him a loan of seven million rubles secured by doubtful or completely worthless stock.[89] One might venture a guess that in addition to the bribes he received from Strousberg, Landau had the underlying objective of unloading worthless stock that he had earlier purchased for the bank as part of the pre-1873 speculative mania, hoping it would disappear together with Strousberg's entire business empire. Perhaps Landau also wanted to humiliate the man who used to be so highly placed and so condescending that Landau would have to lobby simply to be introduced to him.[90]

In turn, Landau accused Strousberg of swindling him, especially regarding the six hundred railway cars that Strousberg claimed were already being constructed. Landau also referred to the Lasker inquiry in the German Reichstag, which had accused Strousberg of malfeasance and catalyzed his financial ruin, as well as to a book published in Leipzig by one Frohberg, which attacked Strousberg's ventures as worthless and bringing only suffering to those who invested in them.[91] Landau asserted that had he refused to lend more money, Strousberg threatened to file for bankruptcy, causing MCLB to lose its investment. This opinion was shared by the memoirist Kozlinina, who had witnessed all or almost all of the great trials in post-reform Moscow and unofficially practiced law herself: she thought that Strousberg had intentionally established the bogus German-Bohemian railroad in order to "prey upon the money of Russia's newborn banks," and that he had traveled to Russia specifically for that predatory purpose.[92] Not unlike the Jacks of Hearts who were also active in Moscow in those years, Strousberg affected wealth and high status by driving around in a fancy carriage and staying in the best hotels. But Landau could not have been fooled by these pretenses, and it was clear that he colluded with Strousberg for his own purposes.

The only defendant who was physically punished by the court in any serious way was Polianskii, sentenced to exile in Tomsk in Siberia. Landau was as well, but he fled Russia immediately after the trial. Of the board members, Schumacher and Borisovskii, the most obvious culprits, were convicted of negligence but had their sentences set aside after an appeal to the Senate.[93] Strousberg was convicted of bribery and sentenced to be deported from Russia. It is not widely known, however, that this criminal case was not the only legal proceeding against him. The other, potentially much more effective, case was a bankruptcy proceeding carried out by the many Russian merchants to whom Strousberg owed money; moreover, the guilty verdict in the MCLB criminal trial included an order for him to pay restitution for the losses he had caused.[94] Strousberg was therefore not immediately deported from Russia but remained under house arrest while various judicial officials were trying to decide how to expedite the bankruptcy case. It was clear that a full proceeding against Strousberg would take years. It is indeed possible that detaining Strousberg in Russia was a negotiating tactic, since his prolonged absence from Germany would inevitably ruin his remaining credit and operations. It is also possible, however, that this continued imprisonment was actually in Strousberg's interest, because he could blame his failures on being confined in Russia and could in the meantime wait out any legal troubles he was likely to face in Germany. In June 1877 Strousberg was briefly moved into Moscow's debtors' prison, but it is not clear when he was finally allowed to leave Russia.[95]

The MCLB trial publicly revealed the intricate details of modern capitalist banking, its structure and operations, its risks and opportunities, and the precautions that property owners and investors had to take. Like many other cases discussed in this book, it sought to distinguish legitimate capitalist exchange and reciprocity from the illegal bribery and embezzlement committed by Strousberg, Polianskii, and Landau. The trial also raised a key issue of modern corporate law—the extent of personal liability of company directors who are tasked with the overall supervision of a bank's affairs but who delegate operational control to professional managers. In situations when Russian directors did not participate in any wrongdoing but could have easily found out about it, at what point could their actions be described as "negligence" (*neradenie*), similar to the way railroad executives like Sergei Witte could be held criminally culpable for a deadly train crash?[96] Finally, the trial raised a broader concern about the extent to which participants in Russia's evolving capitalist economy had a moral obligation to be informed about their investments and to be knowledgeable about their financial affairs, as opposed to blindly surrendering control to professionals.

While the bank case and other white-collar criminal scandals of the 1870s were unfolding, a group of capitalists in the small town of Skopin in Riazan' province were running an even more ambitious criminal scheme. To this day Skopin boasts beautiful imperial-era buildings, including a train station, a large cathedral, and a school. This prosperity began in 1857, when its leading citizens established a municipal bank with the modest capital of just over ten thousand rubles. This was part of a much larger movement, with community banks opening in dozens of small and medium-sized towns. At first the bank issued small loans secured by local real estate, merchandise, and commercial paper. But in 1863 its operations were taken over by the town's mayor, the merchant Ivan Rykov, who had a charismatic appeal much like Dr. Strousberg and soon acquired "virtually unlimited influence in Skopin."[97] Rykov extended the bank's operations to all of Russia, offering an unheard-of 7.5 percent interest rate on deposits. It became particularly popular among the more economically vulnerable groups, such as the clergy, charitable and educational institutions, and local government (*zemstvo*) boards. Eventually its deposits neared twelve million rubles, on par with the largest joint-stock banks in Moscow and St. Petersburg,

Figure 25. Ivan Rykov. A. Bauman, ed., *Illustrirovannyi kalendar' na 1869 god* (St. Petersburg, 1869), p. 280.

leaving far behind even the largest community banks in important towns like Kharkov, Saratov, and Nyzhny Novgorod.[98] By comparison, Skopin had fewer than ten thousand inhabitants. By the late 1860s Rykov and his bank were lavishly praised in the press as Russia's economic miracle. One illustrated calendar in 1869 placed his portrait and a hagiographic biography next to the shorter ones of Metropolitan Innokenty of Moscow, the mathematician Fedor Somov, and General Fedor Trepov (later shot by Vera Zasulich).[99] Out of about six thousand of Rykov's clients, however, only two were from Skopin and sixteen from Riazan province.

The problem with Rykov's business model was that he needed to invest these enormous deposits to make enough profit to pay high interest, but there were no comparable investment options in Russia at that time. Regular bank loans required sufficient collateral, which most borrowers did not have: wooden houses and shops in Central Russian regions were worth very little. A more risky option was to purchase commercial debt, that is, bills of exchange that completely depended on the success and personal integrity of the issuing merchant. Finally, the bank could buy stocks and bonds, but these brought a a return of 5 percent at best. The appropriate practice would have been to stop taking more deposits and lower the interest rate. Instead Rykov decided to maintain his ephemeral position as a financial leader. He purchased social power by lending to powerful individuals, including officials and several prominent capitalists from the two capitals. These loans were repaid, if at all, in worthless commercial paper, thus showing fictitious profits in the bank's accounts. In what would later become known as a Ponzi scheme, Rykov paid the interest on the existing deposits by attracting new ones through an aggressive and strikingly modern advertising and publicity campaign. Throughout the 1870s the major newspapers printed catchy full-page ads purporting to be statements of the bank's high profits; the bank hired stock exchange agents who bought and sold its notes to each other to raise their market value, and Rykov engaged in large-scale philanthropy to show stability and civic engagement. Whenever a client became disgruntled, Rykov either paid him off or paid journalists to prevent the leak, and even intercepted denunciations mailed from Skopin.[100]

Despite repeated efforts by whistleblowers, the bank remained afloat until August 1882, when it declared bankruptcy and its entire staff was arrested. The Ministry of Justice's records show that the governor of Riazan province and the minister of finance, Nikolai Bunge, both attempted to save the bank and avoid a major criminal investigation. But by that time legal officials had already begun collecting "unofficial" statements and petitions from informants and victims.[101] The crash likely came, however, not from any purposeful action but because of the general financial crisis of the early 1880s. As agricultural prices plummeted, ordinary Russians no longer had any spare cash to deposit, and those municipal banks that had long been living beyond their means were doomed. Rykov's bank was the first and the largest of these.

The Skopin capitalists went on trial at the end of 1884, charged with fraud and banking-law violations punishable with Siberian exile. Present in the courtroom was the twenty-four-year-old journalist Anton Chekhov, who wrote a series of satirical "miniatures" for which he was then becoming famous. Reporting that the financial experts who testified against Rykov were considered to be very competent, Chekhov admitted that he himself understood absolutely nothing of what they said. Instead he poked fun at the defendants and their lawyers. To be sure, prosecutor Nikolai Muraviev also confessed his complete ignorance of financial matters, which, however, is more difficult to believe because he had prosecuted so many white-collar defendants. But unlike most other cases in this book, the Skopin bank trial produced two autonomous legal narratives. First, financial experts reconstructed the bank's long history of operations and abuses, on which the case was based, but these were only superficially explained in the

Figure 26. The Skopin Municipal Bank trial at the Moscow District Court. *Vsemirnaia illustratsia,* 1884, no. 26, p. 512. This is the same courtroom seen in figures 6 and 19. Unusually for the genre, this drawing is made from the perspective of the raised dais of the judges, seen on the right. At the bottom right corner are several elite spectators and the prosecutor's desk next to his podium. To the right of the judges is the small desk with two court secretaries. In the center is the stand for witness and defendant testimony. Further back is the defendants' bench, with a large table given to the defense attorneys. There is also a separate section for those defendants who are the state's prisoners and guarded by two gendarmes with drawn swords. Those defendants who are out on bail or under house arrest sit behind the lawyers. Note the enormous statue of Alexander II. On the left and bottom left are the spectators, and a gendarme is guarding the evidence table with a heap of the bank's account books. This entire arrangement is distinct from those of ordinary courtrooms because of its multiple partitions and subsections, as well as the circular structure that centers on the witness stand. One inset presents the bedroom in which the defendants slept during the trial. The second inset shows Ivan Rykov during the trial, appearing much more haggard and slouched than fifteen years earlier in figure 25.

published materials. While expert witnesses in the post-reform courtroom were typically questioned and even ridiculed by other participants, and often failed to have much impact, now their authority was secure in a way that the authority of handwriting experts, chemists, or even physicians had never been.

The defendants admitted to most of the charges against them, and as in other similar trials the only way to keep it interesting and meaningful to the public was for Muraviev to investigate the bankers' character and motivations. The second key courtroom narrative therefore was a dramatic tale of the thousands of hard-working Russians from every corner of the empire who brought their money to Rykov's bank and were mercilessly robbed. Muraviev left out the obvious implications of his arguments, however. In an editorial about the case, the conservative journalist Mikhail Katkov attacked the liberal municipal reforms that supposedly removed all government oversight from Rykov's activities. The reality, though, was much more disturbing. Top government officials had been aware of the bank's violations for as long as two decades and had more than enough authority to stop them, yet they chose to do nothing more than informally admonish Rykov.[102]

Muraviev was not in a position to openly criticize the government, which he would later join as the minister of justice. Instead of digging at the roots of the problem, he did exactly the opposite: he rhetorically lifted the Skopin bankers from the concrete world of legitimate social relations, banks, and capitalists and compared them to the outlaw highwaymen who infamously infested early modern Russia. The bank, he said, was nothing but a "gang" (*shaika*) of ordinary robbers. But Muraviev still needed to explain why Rykov, their leader, personally appropriated ten million rubles—the largest criminal bounty of that period, it seems—but lived the relatively modest life of a well-to-do provincial merchant. The answer was that Rykov craved pure power, which to him was available through access to money. To Muraviev, the tale of Rykov and his bank was that of a lone predator, a petty despot (*samodur*), described in the same language as Mitrofania, Ovsiannikov, Strousberg, and Melnitskii.[103] But by the mid-1880s this was no longer a great revelation. Nonetheless, Rykov and most of his accomplices were duly convicted and sent to penal exile. This was an important achievement for the judiciary, then under political attack by Katkov and other conservative figures. The juridical sphere asserted itself against the more powerful Ministries of the Interior and Finance and successfully and publicly prosecuted the entire major (financially speaking) government-owned entity that had for decades operated with impunity. The story of the Skopin bank and its end was the epitome of the speculative financial capitalism erected in Russia during the Great Reforms. But just as legal scandals were becoming ever more outrageous and more newsworthy, they had also become less striking as a group, turning into a standard fixture of late imperial Russian society and culture, rather than the exceptional and almost otherworldly spectacle of the early post-reform era.

Conclusion

Prominent criminal trials continued until the end of the imperial regime in 1917, with murders, forgeries, and bank scandals taking turns in press accounts. Chronologically, the last cases discussed in this book came in 1884, those of the Melnitskii family and of the Skopin Municipal Bank, but it would have been just as instructive—though not feasible in one book—to discuss the murders of Sarah Bekker (1883–1885) and Paulina Boldyreva (1895), or the Kharkov financial crash of 1901–1902, as well as the infamous blood libel trials of the Multan peasants in 1894–1896 and of Mendel Beilis in 1912. Many of the same issues and patterns lingered from the early post-reform era; others were new. Criminal justice and in particular appellate practice became more complex, and it would become routine for high-profile cases to undergo two or three trials. This trend was already clear in the Melnitskii case, and it would continue in the Bekker case and in that of the Multan peasants, where a trial, one of several, became only one element in an elaborate proceeding that included private investigations, press campaigns, and protracted appellate battles. Another clear change was that the social impact of the trials remained extensive, and public debate lively, but the popular sensationalist appeal of the trials strengthened enormously, driven by a growing popular press and an entertainment industry catering to proliferating urban lower-middle classes.[1]

Still, the practice and the institution of a public trial would retain their place as a major instrument of power in Russia. After Alexander II was assassinated on

1 March 1881, the new emperor, Alexander III (1881–1894), and some of his advisers firmly rejected any further moves toward a constitutional government. His rule is remembered as the period of "counterreforms," which strengthened conservative rural elements in society at the expense of liberal and urban ones and expanded the state's ability to suppress dissent. Some modern scholars have concluded that Russia's legal system was also eviscerated in the process.[2] There is very little evidence for such claims, especially as regards ordinary criminal courts, which continued to try major crimes until the end of 1917 in the way described in this book. Political offenses, such as terrorism and sedition, continued to be tried in the military courts or by a special tribunal of the Senate as they were before 1881. The regular courts remained an autonomous site of political, social, and cultural power that coexisted alongside other government agencies and with the semiformal authority of the intelligentsia both before and after the constitutional reform in 1905. The tsar and his officials had no intention, nor sufficient political clout, to dismember the new courts: these were firmly entrenched and useful in counterbalancing the ministerial bureaucracy. There was no question of demolishing the network of power that had emerged in the mid-century and linked high officials, the wealthier nobility, and industrial and commercial elites. The core principles of the Great Reforms survived intact, though the conservative Russia developing under the last two tsars was a new construction socially, economically, and ideologically.[3]

The change that did occur in the legal sphere in the 1880s (and really in the late 1870s) was cultural rather than institutional. The first generation of reform-era jurists, such as Koni and top defense attorneys, are often remembered—perhaps not altogether correctly, my research has suggested—as idealistic, even crusaders for the rule of law. Around 1878–1881 they were sidelined by those who clearly expressed their political loyalty and conservative ideology. Nikolai Muraviev was the most notable example but not the only one.[4] Yet this appearance of a fundamental conservative shift is somewhat misleading: Koni himself, having left his judgeship in 1881 after a bureaucratic intrigue, was appointed four years later as Chief Procurator of the Criminal Cassation Department of the Senate, equivalent to an attorney-general for criminal cases, and remained there until 1900. His influence on the legal system was enormous before 1917 and significant still in the early Soviet period. Even under Bolshevik rule, there was not (and never has been since) the slightest movement to completely abolish the public trial as an institution. Secret tribunals would put countless innocent persons to death in the 1930s, and there were other clearly unfair trials before, during, and after the Great Terror. Juries were abolished by the Bolsheviks and replaced by German-style people's assessors, until the jury was resurrected in a limited way in post-Soviet Russia in 1993. And yet even at the height of Stalinism the main principles of the juridical sphere were not destroyed, even if in practice they often had to struggle. Still, there was no question of officially returning regular Soviet courts to anything similar to the legal system that had existed in Russia before the 1860s, with secret trials based almost entirely on written records.

Regardless of the new courts' institutional and cultural resilience, earlier scholars of the legal reform of 1864 have tended to view the reform as disconnected from the other major and longer-term trends in late-imperial politics and society, such as the autocratic state with its bureaucracy, or traditional peasant society. In my view, the significance of the reformed juridical sphere is the way it illustrates the range of the possible in late imperial Russia. It is common to ask about Russia's alternatives, its missed potential, to ask whether tsarist Russia was doomed (the predominant view) or whether a more liberal alternative was viable.[5] The story of how the particular features of the post-reform legal system were introduced, negotiated, and applied in landmark criminal cases suggests that there was a range of viable options for rearranging political and social power in late imperial Russia. The fact that Russian public and civil society as well as the ministerial bureaucracy, the elites, and even the tsar and his top advisers were able to adjust to the new arrangement of juridical power in the 1860s suggests that further ways to rearrange power through negotiation and consensus building were possible. Several leading reform-era statesmen (Grand Duke Konstantin Nikolaevich, Petr Shuvalov, Mikhail Loris-Melikov, and Nikolai Ignatiev) proposed creating some version of a constitutional regime, clearly understanding that it was feasible and safe, and pushed their projects through the empire's bureaucratic machine, only to be eventually rejected by the emperor.[6] The legal reform thus suggested the possibility of political and social change neither from above nor from below but, so to speak, from the middle.[7]

This book has argued that the courtroom procedures that were introduced in 1866 were not uniquely Russian in design or implementation. The post-reform jury trial is very difficult to distinguish from its French model, other than in very minor details. The question then arises whether anything recounted in this book was distinctly Russian. One possible distinction is in how decisive, even forceful, the reform was, how long it took to prepare and how quickly it was actually drafted, how high the social expectations created in the process were, and how heavy the burden placed on the new judiciary was. As one of my colleagues noted in a personal conversation, the tsars "put all of their eggs in one basket." The didactic impact of the trials and the sheer effort involved to ensure that the wealthy and the powerful would not evade justice seem to have been far more forceful than in other European and Eurocentric states. To be sure, other major states completely rebuilt their courts in the nineteenth century. France is the most powerful example. But there the legal change was somewhat sidelined by the more dramatic (and deadly) political perturbations of the nineteenth century. English criminal justice was thoroughly rebuilt in the 1870s, with centuries-old courts and practices vanishing forever. But in England there was not a sense of a revolutionary break with the past similar to that in the Continental regimes.

Another, perhaps more promising response to the question about Russia's unique legal trajectory borrows from the approach by anthropologist Jack Goody mentioned in the beginning of this book. Goody proposed abandoning larger-than-life dichotomies, such as slavery versus freedom, tradition versus modernity, and authoritarianism versus democracy. Instead, he employed an analytical "grid" mapping the range of characteristics and possibilities across cultures and societies.[8] Accordingly, my book has charted a range of Russian courtroom practices and criminal narratives, many of which were also found in other legal systems, and quite a few of which were found in different historical periods before and after the Great Reforms. Russian criminal courts were distinct venues for public debate, given that few other venues were available until after 1905. The courts' complex role as a technology of surveillance was therefore perhaps more pronounced in Russia. But the points of tension, such as the courts' interaction with other loci of power and definitions of who would participate and in what ways, were far from unique.

The same applies to the vision of Russia that emerged during the great trials of the post-reform era. Like people anywhere, Russians killed in the heat of passion and to become rich quickly; they forged documents and plundered their companies; they abused their children and bravely denounced their abusers. The web of transgression revealed in the courtroom connected human love, hatred, greed, and guilt with understandings about rank, value, authority, and autonomy. Trials articulated, questioned, debated, and reaffirmed the fundamental principles of a nineteenth-century European polity: a society of adult male property owners with a variety of subordinate actors: women, children, servants, foreigners, ethnic and religious groups. "Old" and "new" Russia were thoroughly mixed together in a process of constant evolution. It is this very complexity that to this day makes the imperial Russia of Dostoevsky, Alexander II, Vera Zasulich—but also of Liudmila Gulak-Artemovskaia, Stepan Ovsiannikov, Evgenia Nepenina, of Tazetdin Khisamutdinov and Aleksandra Avdeeva—so fascinating.

Notes

ABBREVIATIONS

Berkeley	Berkeley: University of California Press
Cambridge	Cambridge: Cambridge University Press
Chicago	Chicago: University of Chicago Press
Code	*Ulozhenie o nakazaniiakh ugolovnykh i ispravitel'nykh* (the code of capital and correctional punishments), 1845 ed. (unless a later edition is specified)
Cornell	Ithaca, NY: Cornell University Press
Delo Mitrofanii	E. P. Zabelina, ed., *Delo igumen'i Mitrofanii* (Moscow, 1874)
GARF	Gosudarstvennyi arkhiv Rossiiskoi federatsii (the State Archive of the Russian Federation)
Harvard	Cambridge, MA: Harvard University Press
Illinois	DeKalb: Northern Illinois University Press
Indiana	Bloomington: Indiana University Press
Instruction	*The Instruction of Catherine II to the Legislative Commission of 1767*
IRLI	Institut russkoi literatury (Pushkinskii Dom) Rossiiskoi akademii nauk
JMH	*The Journal of Modern History*
Klub	K.N.Z., ed., *Klub chervonnykh valetov: Ugolovnyi protsess* (Moscow, 1877)
Koni	A. F. Koni, *Sobranie sochinenii v vos'mi tomakh* (Moscow: Iuridicheskaia literatura, 1958–1966)
Kritika	*Kritika: Explorations in Russian and Eurasian History*
LHR	*Law and History Review*

Liutetskii	A. Liutestkii, ed., *Zamechatel'nye ugolovnye protsessy, razreshennye v Moskovskom okruzhnom sude s uchastiem prisiazhnykh zasedatelei* (Moscow, 1867)
Macmillan	London: Palgrave Macmillan
Materialy	*Materialy po sudebnoi reforme v Rossii 1864 g.*, vols. 1–74 (St. Petersburg, 1857–1866)
MV	*Moskovskie vedomosti*
Nos	A. E. Nos, ed., *Zamechatelnye sudebnye dela, kn. 1* (Moscow, 1869)
OZ	*Otechestvennye zapiski*
Oxford	Oxford: Oxford University Press
Princeton	Princeton: Princeton University Press
PSZ-1, -2, or -3	*Polnoe sobranie zakonov Rossiiskoi imperii* (the Complete Collection of the Laws of the Russian Empire), 1st, 2nd, or 3rd series
RGIA	*Rossiiskii godudarstvennyi istoricheskii arkhiv* (the Russian State Historical Archive)
RM	*Russkaia mysl'*
Routledge	London: Routledge
RR	*The Russian Review*
RS	*Russkaia starina*
RSO	*Russkie sudebnye oratory v uzvestnykh ugolovnykh protsessakh*, 7 vols. (Moscow, 1895–1903)
RUP	A. Liubavskii, *Novye russkie ugolovnye protsessy*, 4 vols. (St. Petersburg, 1867–1868)
SpbV	*Sanktpeterburgskie vedomosti*
SR	*The Slavic Review*
SV	*Sudebnyi vestnik*
SZ	*Svod zakonov Rossiiskoi imperii* (the Digest of the laws of the Russian Empire)
TsGIA Spb	Tsentralnyi gosudarstvennyi istoricheskii arkhiv Sankt-Peterburga
TsIAM	Tsentralnyi istoricheskii arkhiv Moskvy (current name: Tsentralnyi gosudarstvennyi arkhiv goroda Moskvy, otdel khranenia dokumentov do 1917 goda)
Ustav	*Ustav ugolovnogo sudoproizvodstva*, 1864 (the code of criminal procedure)
VE	*Vestnik Evropy*
Yale	New Haven: Yale University Press
ZhMIu	*Zhurnal ministerstva iustitsii*

INTRODUCTION

1. Sergei Witte, *Iz arkhiva S. Iu. Witte. Vospominaniia*, vol. 1 (St. Petersburg: Dmitrii Bulanin, 2003): 95–99; *"Vnutrennee obozrenie,"* OZ 224, no. 2 (Feb. 1876): 292–299; RGIA 1405.74.625, esp. l. 2 ob. (determining that the crash took place in the Podolia province). Perhaps the real reason for moving the case was that Witte's brother Boris was serving in Odessa as an assistant procurator, creating a conflict of interest.

2. On the 1864 reform, see Richard Wortman, *The Development of a Russian Legal Consciousness* (Chicago, 1976); Jörg Baberowski, *Autokratie und Justiz: Zum Verhältnis von Rechtsstaatlichkeit und Rückständigkeit im ausgehenden Zarenreich 1864–1914* (Frankfurt am Main, 1996); and Mikhail Korotkikh, *Samoderzhavie i sudebnaia reforma 1864 goda v Rossii* (Voronezh, 1994).
3. The total number of criminal cases tried in the first-tier (district) courts varied from ca. forty-five thousand in 1874 to ca. seventy-three thousand in 1880; of these, jury trials totaled between fifteen thousand and twenty thousand, including ca. three thousand to four thousand murder cases. Murder convictions were between thirteen hundred and fourteen hundred. There were slightly fewer fraud cases and approximately three times as many theft cases. Evgenii Tarnovskii, *Itogi russkoi ugolovnoi statistiki za 20 let (1874–1894 gg.)* (St. Petersburg, 1899): 234–235, 286–289. Of this number, only one or two cases a year would be reflected in memoir and fiction literature, and approximately twenty cases would have detailed transcripts published in major newspapers or as separate editions.
4. Dawn L. Rothe and David Kauzlarich, *Crimes of the Powerful: White-Collar Crime and Beyond* (Routledge, 2022). For an introduction to the many elite theories, see Tom Bottomore, *Elites and Society*, 2nd ed. (Routledge, 1993); Richard Lachmann, *Capitalists in Spite of Themselves: Elite Conflict and Economic Transitions in Early Modern Europe* (Oxford, 2000).
5. Existing works discussing Russian criminal trials include Louise McReynolds, *Murder Most Russian: True Crime and Punishment in Late Imperial Russia* (Cornell, 2012); Sandra Dahlke, "Old Russia in the Dock: The Trial against Mother Superior Mitrofaniia before the Moscow District Court (1874)," *Cahiers du Monde russe* 53 (2012): 95–120; Tatiana Borisova, "Public Meaning of the Zasulich Trial 1878: Law, Politics and Gender," *Russian History* 43 (2016): 221–244; Gary Rosenshield, *Western Law, Russian Justice* (Madison: University of Wisconsin Press, 2005); Anna Schur, *The Letters and the Law: Legal and Literary Culture in Late Imperial Russia* (Evanston, IL: Northwestern University Press, 2022); Harriet Murav, *Russia's Legal Fictions: Law, Meaning, and Violence* (University of Michigan Press, 1998); Ronald LeBlanc, "Dostoevsky and the Trial of Nastasia Kairova: Carnal Love, Crimes of Passion, and Spiritual Redemption," *Russian Review* 71, no. 4 (Oct. 2012): 630–654; Girish Bhat, "Trial by Jury in the Reign of Alexander II: A Study in the Legal Culture of Late Imperial Russia, 1864–1881," Ph.D. dissertation, University of California at Berkeley (1995). Stephen Lovell, *How Russia Learned to Talk: A History of Public Speaking in the Stenographic Age, 1860–1930* (Oxford, 2020): 55–61, 77–89. See also Jonathan Daly, *Crime and Punishment in Russia: A Comparative History from Peter the Great to Vladimir Putin* (London: Bloomsbury, 2018), and Frances Nethercott, *Russian Legal Culture before and after Communism: Criminal Justice, Politics, and the Public Sphere* (Routledge, 2007).
6. Alexander Afanasiev, "Jurors and Jury Trials in Imperial Russia, 1866–1885," in Ben Eklof, John Bushnell, and Larissa Zakharova, eds., *Russia's Great Reforms* (Indiana, 1994): 217, 220; A. A. Demichev, *Istoria suda prisiazhnykh v dorevoliutsionnoi Rossii (1864–1917 gg.)* (Moscow, 2007). On the peasants' legal culture, see Stephen Frank, *Crime, Cultural Conflict, and Justice in Rural Russia, 1856–1914* (Berkeley, 1999), and

Jane Burbank, *Russian Peasants Go to Court: Legal Culture in the Countryside, 1905–1917* (Indiana, 2004); Cathy A. Frierson, "'I Must Always Answer to the Law . . .': Rules and Responses in the Reformed *Volost'* Court," *Slavonic and East European Review* 75 (Apr. 1997): 308–334.

7. Holly Case, *The Age of Questions* (Princeton, 2018); Laura Engelstein, *The Keys to Happiness* (Cornell, 1992); Siobhan Hearne, *Policing Prostitution* (Oxford, 2021); E. P. Thompson, *Whigs and Hunters: The Origin of the Black Act* (London: Penguin, 1975): 258–269. On the Great Reforms as a traumatic experience: Semen Ekshtut, *Rossiia pered golgofoi: Epokha Velikikh reform* (Moscow, 2010).
8. Eklof et al., *Russia's Great Reforms;* W. Bruce Lincoln, *The Great Reforms: Autocracy, Bureaucracy, and the Politics of Change in Imperial Russia* (Bloomington, 1990); A. N. Tsamutali et al., eds., *Vlast,' obshchestvo i reformy v Rossii v XIX–nachale XX veka* (St. Petersburg, 2009); I. E. Barykina, *Aleksandr II: Propushchennyi povorot* (Moscow, 2017); Boris Litvak, *Perevorot 1861 goda v Rossii: Pochemu ne realizovalas' reformatorskaia alternativa* (Moscow, 1991); Valentina Chernukha, *Vnutrenniaia politika tsarisma s serediny 50-kh do nachala 80-kh gg. XIX v.* (Leningrad, 1978); V. V. Shekokhaev, I. A. Khristoforov, et al., eds., *Reformy v Rossii: S drevneishikh vremen do kontsa XX v.,* 4 vols. (Moscow, 2016): vol. 3.
9. Zakharova, "Autocracy and the Reforms of 1861–1874 in Russia," in *Russia's Great Reforms,* 19–39; Chernukha, *Vnutrenniaia politika;* Khristoforov, "Velikie reformy," in *Reformy v Rossii,* vol. 3, 14–183.
10. On the politics of the abolition of serfdom, see P. A. Zaionchkovskii, *Otmena krepostnogo prava v Rossii* (Moscow, 1968); David Moon, *The Abolition of Serfdom in Russia: 1762–1907* (New York: Longman, 2001); Daniel Field, *The End of Serfdom: Nobility and Bureaucracy in Russia, 1855–1861* (Harvard, 1976); Terence Emmons, *The Russian Landed Gentry and the Peasant Emancipation of 1861* (Cambridge, 1968); L. G. Zakharova, *Samoderzhavie i otmena krepostnogo prava v Rossii (1856–1861)* (Moscow, 1984); Peter Kolchin, *Emancipation: The Abolition and Aftermath of American Slavery and Russian Serfdom* (Yale, 2024).
11. On post-emancipation elites, see Seymour Becker, *Nobility and Privilege in Late Imperial Russia* (Illinois, 1986); Roberta Thompson Manning, *The Crisis of the Old Order in Russia: Gentry and Government* (Princeton, 1983); Dominic Lieven, *Russia's Rulers under the Old Regime* (Yale, 1991); A. P. Korelin, *Dvorianstvo v poreformennoi Rossii, 1861–1904* (Moscow, 1979).
12. Charles A. Ruud, *Fighting Words: Imperial Censorship and the Russian Press, 1804–1906* (Toronto: University of Toronto Press, 1982, 2009): esp. 97–166; Lincoln, *The Great Reforms,* 121–133; Samuel D. Kassow, "The University Statute of 1863," in *Russia's Great Reforms,* 247–263; V. G. Chernukha, *Pasport v Rossii, 1719–1917* (St. Petersburg, 2007); Eric Lohr, *Russian Citizenship from Empire to Soviet Union* (Harvard, 2012): esp. 43.
13. Peter Gatrell, "The Meaning of the Great Reforms in Russian Economic History," in *Russia's Great Reforms,* 84–101, 85 ("growth accelerated during the final third of the nineteenth century on foundations already laid in the prereform era"). On commerce and the commercial classes in late imperial Russia, see Alfred Rieber, *Merchants and*

Entrepreneurs in Imperial Russia (Chapel Hill: University of North Carolina Press, 1991); Galina Ulianova, *Female Entrepreneurs in Nineteenth-Century Russia* (Routledge, 2009); Thomas Owen, *Capitalism and Politics in Russia: A Social History of the Moscow Merchants, 1855–1905* (Cambridge, 1981).

14. Elise Kimerling Wirtschafter, *Social Identity in Imperial Russia* (Illinois, 1997); Alison Smith, *For the Common Good and Their Own Well-Being: Social Estates in Imperial Russia* (Oxford, 2014); Gregory L. Freeze, "The Soslovie (Estate) Paradigm and Russian Social History," *American Historical Review* 91 (1986): 11–36.
15. *Statisticheskii vremennik rossiiskoi imperii* (St. Petersburg, 1866): 40–47 (one million hereditary and personal nobles, 611,000 clergy, more than 900,000 "various ranks," and 4.8 million registered "urban" inhabitants [merchants and townspeople]).
16. Mikhail Davydov, *Tsena utopii: Istoriia rossiiskoi* modernizatsii (Moscow, 2022): 12–13.
17. I use the term "Eurocentric" to refer to institutions that originated in Europe but are found throughout the world. I avoid the standard term "Western" or "Westernized," to remove the associated valuation and to emphasize that I simply refer to the provenance of particular rules and institutions rather than their quality compared to those of other systems. For a somewhat different use of the term, see Jan Pieterse, "Many Renaissances, Many Modernities? Review of Jack Goody, *Renaissances: The One or the Many?*" *Theory, Culture and Society* 28 (May 2011): 149–160.
18. N. A. Demert, "*Matushka Mitrofania,*" OZ 217, no. 11 (1874): 256–273, 271; George Robb, *White-Collar Crime in Modern England: Financial Fraud and Business Morality, 1845–1929* (Cambridge, 1992); James Taylor, *Boardroom Scandal: The Criminalization of Company Fraud in Nineteenth-Century Britain* (Oxford, 2013); Ian Klaus, *Forging Capitalism: Rogues, Swindlers, Frauds, and the Rise of Modern Finance* (Yale, 2014); Edward J. Balleisen, *Fraud: An American History from Barnum to Madoff* (Princeton, 2017); Susanna L. Blumenthal, *Law and the Modern Mind: Consciousness and Responsibility in American Legal Culture* (Harvard, 2016): 166–195; Christopher J. Berry, *The Idea of Commercial Society in the Scottish Enlightenment* (Edinburgh: Edinburgh University Press, 2013): 150–193.
19. Korotkikh, *Samoderzhavie,* 177–178.
20. I. A. Khristoforov, *"Aristokraticheskaia" oppozitsiia Velikim reformam* (Moscow, 2002), and Alfred Rieber, *The Politics of Autocracy: Letters of Alexander II to Prince A. I. Bariatinskii, 1857–1864* (Paris: Mouton, 1966). Works rethinking the reign of Nicholas I (1825–1855) include Susan Smith-Peter, *Imagining Russian Regions: Subnational Identity and Civil Society in Nineteenth-century Russia* (Leiden: Brill, 2017) (Nicholas I's Smithianism unleashing regionalism in the provinces); Paul Werth, *1837: Russia's Quiet Revolution* (Oxford, 2021); and Sergei Antonov, *Bankrupts and Usurers of Imperial Russia: Debt, Property, and the Law in the Age of Dostoevsky and Tolstoy* (Harvard, 2016) (rethinking pre-1864 courts). See also the earlier studies: Wortman, *Legal Consciousness,* and W. Bruce Lincoln, *In the Vanguard of Reform: Russia's Enlightened Bureacrats, 1825–1861* (Illinois, 1986).
21. V. E. Shkerin, *"Poedinok na shpionakh." Delo petrashevtsev i politicheskaia provokatsiia v Rossii* (Moscow, 2019).

22. Ekaterina Pravilova, *The Ruble: A Political History* (Oxford, 2023): 20, 6–7, 77, 101–103, 140.
23. I. F. Gindin, *Banki i ekonomicheskaia politika v Rossii (xix–nachalo xx v.)* (Moscow, 1997): 468; Antonov, *Bankrupts,* 87.
24. Lieven, *Russia's Rulers;* A. V. Remnev, *Samoderzhavnoe pravitel'stvo: Komitet ministrov v sisteme vysshego upravleniia Rossiiskoi imperii, vtoraia polovina XIX–nachalo XX veka* (Moscow, 2010); R. I. Sementkovskii, *Mikhail Katkov: Ego zhizn' i literaturnaia deiatelnostl* (2015); Martin Katz, *Mikhail N. Katkov: A Political Biography, 1818–1887* (Berlin: De Gruyter Mouton, 1966).
25. A. G. Chukarev, *Tainaia politsiia Rossii, 1825–1855* (Moscow, 2005); Charles A. Ruud and Sergei A. Stepanov, *Fontanka 16: The Tsars' Secret Police* (Montreal: McGill-Queen's University Press, 1999); Jonathan W. Daly, *Autocracy under Siege: Security Police and Opposition in Russia, 1866–1905* (Illinois, 1998); Sidney Monas, *The Third Section: Police and Society in Russia under Nicholas I* (Harvard, 1961); P. S. Squire, *The Third Department: The Political Police in the Russia of Nicholas I* (Cambridge, 1968). On the Third Section's nonpolitical functions, see Antonov, *Bankrupts,* 22–23, 35–73.
26. On the ministerial system: N. P. Yeroshkin, *Istoriia gosudarstvennykh uchrezhdenii dorevoliutsionnoi Rossii* (Moscow, 1983); George L. Yaney, *The Systematization of Russian Government: Social Evolution of the Domestic Administration of Imperial Russia, 1705–1905* (Urbana: University of Illinois Press, 1973).
27. Wortman, *Legal Consciousness.*
28. Wortman, *Legal Consciousness,* 3; Baberowski, *Autokratie und Justiz* and esp. "Law, the Judicial System and the Legal Profession," in Dominic Lieven, ed., *The Cambridge History of Russia,* vol. 2 (Cambridge, 2006): 351; Engelstein, *Keys to Happiness,* 24.
29. Richard Pipes, "The Trial of Vera Z," *Russian History* 37, no. 1 (2010): 6.
30. Richard Wortman, "Russian Monarchy and the Rule of Law: New Considerations of the Court Reform of 1864," *Kritika* 6, no. 1 (2005): 145–170, 147.
31. On the post-reform bar, see William E. Pomeranz, "The Emergence and Development of the Russian 'Advokatura': 1864–1905," Ph.D. dissertation, University of London (1990); Samuel Kucherov, *Courts, Lawyers, and Trials under the Last Three Tsars* (New York: Praeger, 1953).
32. Pierre Bourdieu, "The Force of Law: Toward a Sociology of the Juridical Field," *Hastings Law Journal* 38 (1987): 814–853, 816, 823, 851; Mathieu Hilgers and Eric Mangez, *Bourdieu's Theory of Social Fields: Concepts and Applications* (Routledge, 2015). Also helpful is Paul W. Kahn's *The Cultural Study of Law: Reconstructing Legal Scholarship* (Chicago, 1999).
33. Bruce F. Adams, *The Politics of Punishment: Prison Reform in Russia, 1863–1917* (Cornell, 1996); for the pre-reform era, see Abby Schrader, *Languages of the Lash: Corporal Punishment and Identity in Imperial Russia* (Illinois, 2003); Andrew A. Gentes, *Exile, Murder and Madness in Siberia, 1823–1861* (Macmillan, 2010).
34. Mikhail Grecheskii, *V sem'ie ne bez uroda: biografia velikogo kniazia Nikolaia Konstantinovicha* (Moscow, 2002); see also GARF 109.3a.2618; RGIA 1261.3.156; on Boldarev, see RGIA 1405.73.575; Zaionchkovskii, ed., *Dnevnik P. A. Valueva, ministra vnutrennikh del,* vol. 2 (Moscow, 1961): 357, 521 n. 445; surviving case records of

Senate prosecutions of high officials are in RGIA 1363, op. 10; see also E. A. Pravilova, *Zakonnost' i prava lichnosti: Administrativnaia iustitsiia v Rossii (vtoraia polovina XIX v.–oktiabr' 1917g.* (St. Petersburg, 2000).

35. On (partially) protected courtroom speech, see Louise McReynolds, *The News under Russia's Old Regime: The Development of a Mass-Circulation Press.* (Princeton, 1991); Lovell, *How Russia Learned to Talk.*

36. Michel Foucault, *Discipline and Punish: The Birth of Prison* (New York: Vintage Books, 1977) ("gaze" is *le regard* in the original French). In 1869 one of Russia's leading defense lawyers, Aleksandr Lokhvitskii, noted how public trials "unveil those evil and shameless passions that hide in educated and wealthy society, and are ordinarily covered by the mask of virtue." SV, no. 103 (15 May 1869) (trial of major general's widow Henrietta Khomutova and Aleksandr Borgesani for fraud).

37. Jeremy Bentham, *The Panoptic Writings*, ed. Miran Božovič (London: Verso, 1995); James C. Scott, *Seeing Like a State: How Certain Schemes to Improve the Human Condition Have Failed* (Yale, 1998).

38. Philip Gorski, *The Disciplinary Revolution: Calvinism and the Rise of the State in Early Modern Europe* (Chicago, 2003); David Garland, *The Culture of Control: Crime and Social Order in Contemporary Society* (Chicago, 2001). On Russia, see Igor Fedyukin, "Towards the Panopticon: School Building and Discipline in Early Modern Russia," *Higher School of Economics Research Paper* WP BRP 123/HUM/2016; Tanja Zimmermann, "Panoptic Gaze and Panoramic View in and of Late 18th and Early 19th Century Imperial Russia," *Apparatus: Film, Media and Digital Cultures of Central and Eastern Europe*, no. 15 (November 2022), https://doi.org/10.17892/app.2022.00015.259; Alexander Martin, *Enlightened Metropolis: Constructing Imperial Moscow, 1762–1855* (Oxford, 2013); Schrader, *The Languages of the Lash;* Elisa M. Becker, *Medicine, Law, and the State in Imperial Russia* (Budapest: Central European University Press, 2011); Daniel Beer, *Renovating Russia: The Human Sciences and the Fate of Liberal Modernity, 1880–1930* (Cornell, 2008). The few discussions of trials as disciplinary practices are Katherine Fischer Taylor, *In the Theater of Criminal Justice: The Palais de Justice in Second Empire Paris* (Princeton, 1993): 5–6; Peter J. Hutchings, "Spectacularizing Crime: Ghostwriting the Law," *Law and Critique* 10 (1999): 27–48; Dahlke, "Old Russia in the Dock," 118.

39. Ernest Zitser, *The Transfigured Kingdom: Sacred Parody and Charismatic Authority at the Court of Peter the Great* (Cornell, 2004), 13.

40. Burbank, *Russian Peasants;* Frank, *Crime, Cultural Conflict;* Ilya Gerasimov, *Plebeian Modernity: Social Practices, Illegality, and the Urban Poor in Russia, 1906–1916* (Rochester: University of Rochester Press, 2018).

41. For a similar critique of Foucault's theory, see Schrader, *Languages of the Lash,* 189.

42. Antony Duff et al., *Trial on Trial: Towards a Normative Theory of the Criminal Trial* (Oxford: Hart, 2007): vol. 3, 265; Gerald J. Postema, *Bentham and the Common Law Tradition,* 2nd ed. (Oxford, 2019): 357; Joseph Jaconelli, *Open Justice: A Critique of the Public Trial* (Oxford, 2002): 36; Jeremy Bentham, "Draught for the Organization of Judicial Establishments . . . ," in *The Works of Jeremy Bentham,* vol. 4 (Edinburgh, 1790): 316.

43. Harold Garfinkel, "Conditions of Successful Degradation Ceremonies," *American Journal of Sociology* 61 (1956): 420–424; Linda Ross Meyer, "Burns v. Received View," *Law and Social Inquiry* 28, no. 2 (Spring, 2003): 533–538, 536; Dahlke, "Old Russia in the Dock," 118–119.
44. James M. Donovan, *Juries and the Transformation of Criminal Justice in France in the Nineteenth and Twentieth Centuries* (Chapel Hill: University of North Caroline Press, 2010); David Bentley, *English Criminal Justice in the 19th Century* (London: Bloomsbury Academic, 2003), xii–xiii; also Duff et al., *Trial on Trial,* vol. 3, 50; John H. Langbein, *The Origins of Adversary Criminal Trial* (Oxford, 2003) and *Torture and the Law of Proof: Europe and England in the* Ancien Régime (Chicago, 1976); David J. A. Cairns, *Advocacy and the Making of the Adversarial Criminal Trial, 1800–1865* (Oxford, 1998); Stephan Landsman, "The Rise of the Contentious Spirit: Adversary Procedure in Eighteenth Century England," *Cornell Law Review* 75, no. 3 (1989–1990): 496–608; A. Esmein, *A History of Continental Criminal Procedure with Special Reference to France* (Boston: Little, Brown, 1913).
45. In Britain and France, summary justice was already common in the nineteenth century for lesser offenses. Bentley, *English Criminal Justice;* Donovan, *Juries,* and *Trial on Trial,* vol. 3, 47.
46. Paula Hyman, "Review: The Dreyfus Affair: The Visual and the Historical," *JMH* 61, no. 1 (Mar. 1989): 88–109; Edward Berenson, *The Trial of Madame Caillaux* (Berkeley, 1992); Aaron Freundschuh, *The Courtesan and the Gigolo: The Murders in the Rue Montaigne and the Dark Side of Empire in Nineteenth-Century Paris* (Stanford: Stanford University Press, 2017); Joseph A. Conforti, *Lizzie Borden on Trial: Murder, Ethnicity, and Gender* (Lawrence: University Press of Kansas, 2015); Charles A. Lofgren, *The Plessy Case: A Legal-Historical Interpretation* (Oxford, 1987); Brian McGinty, *John Brown's Trial* (Harvard, 2009); Anne-Marie Kilday and David Nash, eds., *Law, Crime and Deviance since 1700: Micro-studies in the History of Crime* (London: Bloomsbury, 2017).
47. Dahlke, "Old Russia in the Dock"; Eugene Avrutin, *The Velizh Affair: Blood Libel in a Russian Town* (Oxford, 2017); Robert Weinberg, *Blood Libel in Late Imperial Russia: The Ritual Murder of Mendel Beilis* (Indiana, 2014). Eighteenth-century Russian law was "casuistic and precedent-based." Elena Marasinova, *"Zakon" i "grazhdanin" v Rossii vtoroi poloviny XVIII veka: Ocherki istorii obshchestvennogo soznania* (Moscow, 2017): 313.
48. Richard Pipes, "The Trial of Vera Z," *Russian History* 37, no. 1 (2010): v, vii–x, 1–3, 5–31, 33–49, 51–82; A. F. Koni, *"Vospominaniia o dele Very Zasulich,"* in *Sobranie sochinenii,* vol. 2 (Moscow, 1966); Ana Siljak, *Angel of Vengeance: The "Girl Assassin," the Governor of St. Petersburg, and Russia's Revolutionary World* (New York: St. Martin's Press, 2008); Tatiana Borisova, "Public Meaning of the Zasulich Trial 1878: Law, Politics and Gender," *Russian History* 43 (2016): 221–244.
49. Barbara Engel, *Mothers and Daughters: Women of the Intelligentsia in Nineteenth-Century Russia* (Cambridge, 1983): 107.
50. Pipes, "The Trial," 2.
51. The other two feasible explanations of the Zasulich verdict are that the jurors were afraid of reprisals by the revolutionaries or that they thought it was an honor killing (similar to the Nepenina trial or to the 1914 French case of Madame Caillaux). The

third theory that I do not find plausible is that the jurors were persuaded by Chairman Koni's alleged argument that society had the right to protect itself against state abuses. Koni had indeed written a dissertation on this subject, but I find it hard to imagine how the middle-class jury at the end of an exhausting day could have grasped this doctrine, which is barely comprehensible to legal scholars.

52. Thomas A. Green, *Verdict According to Conscience: Perspectives on the English Criminal Trial Jury, 1200–1800* (Chicago, 1985): 404 (the effect of jury nullification is to "invert the object of judgment from attacker to victim"); Martha Merrill Umphrey, "The Dialogics of Legal Meaning: Spectacular Trials, the Unwritten Law, and Narratives of Criminal Responsibility," *Law and Society Review* 33, no. 2 (1999): 393–423.
53. This was the condition of him being extradited by Switzerland, where he had fled after killing a fellow radical. Both cases were prosecuted as ordinary murder and not under the provisions for crimes against the state. Philip Pomper, *Sergei Nechaev* (New Brunswick, NJ: Rutgers University Press, 1979).
54. After the reform of 1864 crimes against the state were tried by the second-tier Judicial Chambers without juries, but in 1872 in response to the supposedly mild sentences meted out to Nechaev's followers, political cases were removed to the Special Board (*osoboe prisutstvie*) of the Senate, which existed until 1917 but was particularly active in the 1870s and 1880s. Political cases involving violence or terrorism went to military courts, which tried all political cases between 1878 and 1881. After 1881 lesser political offenses were punished through extrajudicial administrative exile. N. A. Troitskii, *Bezumstvo khrabrykh. Russkie revoliutsionery i karatel'naia politika tsarizma, 1866–1882 gg.* (Moscow, 1978) and *Tsarizm pod sudom progressivnoi obshchestvennosti, 1866–1895* (Moscow, 1979); Daly, *Autocracy under Siege.*
55. Kucherov, *Courts and Trials;* Wortman, *Legal Consciousness;* Richard Pipes, *Russia under the Old Regime,* 2nd ed. (London: Penguin Books, 1995); I. V. Arkhipov, *Sistematizatsia ugolovnogo zakonodatelstva v Rossii v 30–70-e gody XIX veka* (Saratov, 1997); Engelstein, *Keys to Happiness;* Bhat, *Trial by Jury,* 21 n. 27 (recognizing that political trials were "aberrations in the normal functioning of the new court system and not at all typical of day-to-day adjudication").
56. McReynolds, *Murder Most Russian.* See also Engelstein, *Keys to Happiness;* Joan Neuberger, *Hooliganism: Crime, Culture, and Power in St. Petersburg, 1900–1914* (Berkeley, 1993); Roshanna Sylvester, *Tales of Old Odessa: Crime and Civility in a City of Thieves* (Illinois, 2005); Mark D. Steinberg, *Petersburg Fin de Siècle* (Yale, 2011).
57. Girish N. Bhat, "The Moralization of Guilt in Late Imperial Russian Trial by Jury: The Early Reform Era," *LHR* 15, no. 1 (1997): 79, 82. His full argument is presented in *Trial by Jury.* On the importance of moral factors in Anglo-American trials, see Robert P. Burns, *A Theory of the Trial* (Princeton, 1999); Mike Redmayne, *Character in the Criminal Trial* (Oxford, 2015).
58. Tracy Dennison, *The Institutional Framework of Russian Serfdom* (Cambridge, 2014).
59. Baberowski, "Law, the Judicial System," 351; see also Daly, *Crime and Punishment,* esp. 54.
60. On jury composition, see Afanasiev, "Jurors and Jury Trials."
61. What these values and practices were is still not very clear. See Tomila Lankina, *The Estate Origins of Democracy in Russia* (Cambridge, 2021).

62. Stefan Kirmse, *The Lawful Empire: Legal Change and Cultural Diversity in Late Imperial Russia* (Cambridge, 2019); see also "*Nashi obshchestvennye dela,*" OZ 201 (Mar. 1872): 74 (discussing the Miasnikov brothers' trial of 1872). For the belief in the Russian juries' excessive mercy, see Pipes, *Russia under the Old Regime,* 296; McReynolds, *Murder Most Russian,* e.g., 3, 13; Bhat, *Trial by Jury.*
63. James Q. Whitman, *The Origins of Reasonable Doubt: Theological Roots of the Criminal Trial* (Yale, 2008).
64. Donovan, *Juries.* Eliza Ferguson estimated that in the Third Republic the acquittal rate for crimes against persons was 28 percent for men and 64 percent for women. See *Gender and Justice: Violence, Intimacy, and Community in Fin-de-Siècle Paris* (Baltimore: Johns Hopkins University Press, 2010): 2.
65. Burns, *A Theory of the Trial.* See also Tyrone Kirchengast, *The Criminal Trial in Law and Discourse* (Macmillan, 2010).
66. Marianne Constable, "Introduction: Symposium on Robert Burns's *A Theory of the Trial,*" *Law and Social Inquiry* 28, no. 2 (Spring 2003): 523.
67. Burns, *A Theory of the Trial,* 3.
68. Meyer, "Burns v. Received View"; Burns, *A Theory of the Trial,* 53, 182, 230; Mikhail Bakhtin, *Problems of Dostoevsky's Poetics,* ed. and tr. Caryl Emerson (Minneapolis: University of Minnesota Press, 1984): 6.
69. Umphrey, "The Dialogics of Legal Meaning," 394–396, 420 (trials don't simply mediate between the two domains but also "partially instantiate the domains of script and consciousness themselves"); Bourdieu, "The Force of Law," 816; Robert Cover, "The Supreme Court, 1982 Term—Foreword: Nomos and Narrative," *Harvard Law Review* 97, no. 1 (1983): 4–69.
70. OZ 201 (1872): 78; VE 7, no. 4 (1872): 807.
71. Mikhail Bakhtin, *Rabelais and His World* (Indiana, 1984) (written in 1940 and published in Russian in 1965) and *Problems,* 122 ff. Also noted in Umphrey, "The Dialogics of Legal Meaning," 398. See also Mike Presdee, *Cultural Criminology and the Carnival of Crime* (Routledge, 2000).
72. On the "bourgeois hysteria and the carnivalesque," see Peter Stallybrass and Allon White, *The Politics and Poetics of Transgression* (Cornell, 1986): 171–190.
73. Garfinkel, "Conditions of Successful Degradation Ceremonies."
74. Meyer, "Burns," 536, citing Malcolm M. Feeley, *The Process Is the Punishment: Handling Cases in a Lower Criminal Court* (New York: Russel Sage Foundation, 1979); Trisha Olson, "Of Enchantment: The Passing of the Ordeals and the Rise of the Jury Trial," *Syracuse Law Review* 50, no. 1 (2000): 109–196; Robert M. Cover, "Violence and the Word," *Yale Law Journal* 95 (1985–1986): 1601–1629.
75. Gorski, *The Disciplinary Revolution,* xvi.
76. Taylor, *In the Theater,* 5–6, 65, 106–107, and 111–112; Kirchengast, *The Criminal Trial.*
77. On the nineteenth-century creation of a "pervasive" spectacle of crime and punishment using theatrical and literary practice, see Peter Hutchings, "Spectacularizing Crime: Ghostwriting the Law," *Law and Critique* 10 (1999): 27–48.
78. Burbank, *Russian Peasants.*

79. Sarah Wilson, "History, Narrative and Attacking Chronocentricism in Understanding Financial Crime: The Significance of Micro-history," in Kilday and Nash, eds., *Law, Crime and Deviance,* 37–60; Jan Nederveen Pieterse, "Many Renaissances, Many Modernities?" *Theory, Culture and Society* 28, no. 3 (2011): 149–160.
80. Schur, *The Letters and the Law;* Murav, *Russia's Legal Fictions.*

PART I. THE JURIDICAL FIELD

1. *Dnevniki velikogo kniazia Konstantina Nikolaevicha, 1858–1864* (Moscow, 2019): 368, 370, 372–374, 400 n. 56.
2. V. E. Voronin, *Pol'skoe vosstanie 1863 goda: Opyt "Primiritelnoi politiki" russkogo pravitelstva* (Moscow, 2008): 103–104, 107 (*"goroi stoial"*).
3. Bourdieu, "The Force of Law."
4. *Materialy,* vol. 7: 110–146, and vol. 17, ch. 13 (Zarudnyi's original position) and ch. 15; Korotkikh, *Samoderzhavie,* 104–129; Pravilova, *The Ruble;* Wortman, *Legal Consciousness,* 2.

CHAPTER 1. JUDICIAL AUTONOMY

1. RGIA 1151.7.344 (*Ob otstavnom poruchike Pavle Sergeeve Gavrilove . . .*).
2. Koni, "*Delo o poddelke serii,*" in *Sobranie sochinenii,* vol. 1 (Moscow, 1966); "*Delo Gavrilova I Beklemisheva . . .,*" in R. A. Markovich, ed., *Plevako F.N.: Izbrannye rechi* (Moscow, 1993): 210–233.
3. These laws are found in SZ, I/1.
4. Wortman, *Development of a Russian Legal Consciousness,* 5, 162, 275. See also Daly, *Crime and Punishment;* Baberowski, "Law, the Judicial System."
5. Barykina, *Mezhdu samoderzhaviem i avtokratiiei (Vnutrenniaia politika Rossiiskoi imperii vtoroi poloviny XIX veka . . .)* (St. Petersburg, 2016), 160–164 and 176–190. The right to pardon had been a key attribute of the monarch's power since the sixteenth century, and together with the practice of presenting the public with official manifestos it constituted a complex system of communications and a discrete mode of governance with extensive policy implications. On discretion and mercy in criminal justice, see Carolyn Strange, *Qualities of Mercy: Justice, Punihsment, and Discretion* (Vancouver: UBC Press, 1996)
6. Barbara Engel, *Breaking the Ties That Bound: The Politics of Marital Strife in Late Imperial Russia* (Cornell, 2013).
7. Koni, "*Vospominania o dele Very Zasulich,*" 71. The key precedent was set in 1867, when upon Petr Valuev's request Alexander II almost fired Senator Liuboshchinskii for giving a liberal speech at the St. Petersburg *zemstvo* meeting. The minister of justice, Dmitrii Zamiatnin, convinced the tsar that this was directly against the law, and Alexander relented, although the minister himself had to resign. The senator continued his long and distinguished career and eventually sat on the Council of State. The main antagonist here was Valuev (the minister of the interior) rather than the tsar. Aleksandr Vereshchagin, "*Kazus senatora Liuboshchinskogo,*" *Rossiiskaia iustitsiia,* no. 4 (2022): 72–80.

8. RGIA 1405.68.3352, esp. l. 8–14 and 43–44; Koni, vol. 1, 89; RGIA 1016.1.179, l. 1. Alexander II was regularly informed about the investigation and maintained contact through Pahlen with the procurator of the Moscow Judicial Chamber, Nikolai Manasein. Also, Pahlen ordered the Moscow Commercial Court (kept over from before 1864) to reverse its initial refusal to open bankruptcy proceedings against the bank. RGIA 1405.73.43, l. 1–6.
9. Robert E. Jones, *Emancipation of Russian Nobility, 1762–1785* (Princeton, 1973).
10. The emperor also had the duty to review and confirm decisions of the Council of State, Russia's official legislative body, which handled appeals involving questions of statutory interpretation. Although the tsar sometimes sided with the minority vote when reviewing actual legislative proposals, I have not seen any instances when he would disagree with the council's recommendation in individual appellate cases.
11. Bentley, *English Criminal Justice*, 284–285.
12. RGIA 1405.74.1473, l. 58–58 ob., 2–2 ob., 81–89, and 116–118. Ovsiannikov was freed on 2 September 1881 and regained his civil rights except for the special privileges previously granted to him as a *kommertsii sovetnik,* an honorary rank awarded to the wealthiest merchants. His two much younger accomplices were also freed from hard labor, but it turned out that both had by then died.
13. RGIA 1405.77.229, l. 4.
14. RGIA 1405.77.561.
15. Deborah Boucoyannis, *Kings as Judges: Power, Justice, and the Origins of Parliaments* (Cambridge, 2021); M. A. Kiselev, "*Pravda i zakon vo vtoroi polovine XVII–pervoi chetverti XVIII veka: Ot monarkha-sud'i k monarkhu-zadonodateliu,*" in A. I. Miller et al., eds., *"Poniatie o Rossii": K istoricheskoi semantike imperskogo perioda,* 2 vols. (Moscow, 2011): vol. 1, 49–65; G. O. Sayles, *The King's Parliament of England* (London: Edward Arnold, 1975): 70–93; S. K. Bogoiavlenskii, *Prikaznye sud'i xvii v.* (Moscow, 1946); Nancy Shields Kollmann, *Crime and Punishment in Early Modern Russia* (Cambridge, 2012); Lauren Benton, *Law and Colonial Cultures: Legal Regimes in World History* (Cambridge, 2002).
16. Petr Kropotkin, *Zapiski revoliutsioner: Polnaia versia* (Moscow, 2023), 323–324; Susanne Schattenberg, *Die korrupte Provinz?* (Campus, 2008); Koni, "*Petr IV,*" in *Sobranie sochinenii*, vol. 5, 278–287; Zaionchkovskii, *Krizis samoderzhavie na rubezhe 1870–1880-kh godov* (Moscow, 1964).
17. GARF 109.3a.2799; GARF 109.3a.476, l. 3, 9; RGIA 1405.534.1350.
18. Koni, *Sobranie sochineniii*, vol. 1, 84–91.
19. The Third Section was administratively part of His Imperial Majesty's Own Chancery; in the late 1850s there was a proposal to use the Chancery to create a "parallel administration that would control the [government] agencies and even direct them." Mamonov, *Nesostoiavshiisia ideolog*, 90.
20. Antonov, *Bankrupts and Usurers.*
21. Some independent courts had existed earlier as well but not as part of a uniform structure. For instance, Moscow retained the early modern Judicial Chancellery (*Sudnyi prikaz*) for much of the eighteenth century.
22. Wortman, *Legal Consciousness.*

23. Korotkikh, *Samoderzhavie,* 112–131; *Materialy,* vols. 6 and 7; Aleksandr Vereshchagin, *Kassatsionnyi senat (1866–1917)* (Moscow, 2022).

24. PSZ-1, vol. 20 (1775–1780), no. 14,392, 236 (ch. 4, art. 85).

25. Schattenberg, *Die korrupte Provinz;* Antonov, *Bankrupts and Usurers.*

26. This thesis is especially advanced in B. V. Vilenskii, *Sudebnaia reforma i kontrreforma v Rossii* (Saratov, 1969). See also Pipes, *Russia under the Old Regime,* challenged in Daly, "On the Significance of Emergency Legislation in Late Imperial Russia," SR 54, no. 3 (1995): 602–629 (arguing that the law of 1881 "was not a turning point on the path toward a modern 'police state' but a sign of . . . uneasy transition from an absolutist to a constitutional order" [602]); Peter Waldron, "States of Emergency: Autocracy and Extraordinary Legislation, 1881–1917," *Revolutionary Russia* 8, no. 1 (1995): 1–25.

27. Hsi-Huey Liang, *The Rise of Modern Police and the European State System from Metternich to the Second World War* (Cambridge, 1992); Clive Emsley, *Crime, Police, and Penal Policy: European Experiences 1750–1940* (Oxford, 2007); John Merriman, *Police Stories: Building the French State, 1815–1851* (Oxford, 2006); Marc Raeff, *The Well-Ordered Police State: Social and Institutional Change through Law in the Germanies and Russia, 1600–1800* (Yale, 1983).

28. Paul O. Carrese, *The Cloaking of Power: Montesquieu, Blackstone, and the Rise of Judicial Activism* (Chicago, 2010); M. J. C. Vile, *Constitutionalism and the Separation of Powers* (Indianapolis: Liberty Fund, 1998).

29. "*Temnye storony novogo suda.*" *Nedelia,* no. 12 (9 March 1869).

30. Dahlke, "Old Russia in the Dock"; Ekaterina Kozlinina, *Za polveka, 1862–1912* (Moscow, 1913): 2–16. See also Gromnitskii, *Iz proshlogo (po lichnym vospominaniiam),* RM 20, no. 6 (1899): 20 (discussing Moscow's police bailiff Rebrov in the Rogozhskoe cemetery robbery case); also Liutetskii, 29; V. L-v, "*Tri ubiistva i odin obvinitelnyi prigovor,*" OZ 171, no. 3–4 (1867): 164–180, 297–324, esp. 315; Nos, part 1: 7 (the Mytishchi murder case). Rebrov was still holding his position as of 1880: RSO, vol. 3, 362 (the Kachka murder case).

31. Bourdieu, "The Force of Law"; Garfinkel, "Conditions."

32. Bentley, *English Criminal Justice,* 43–49.

33. "*Temnye storony novogo suda.*"

34. The first complete treatise on post-reform criminal procedure appeared in 1884. See I. Ya. Foinitskii, *Kurs ugolovnogo sudoproizvodstva,* 2 vols. (St. Petersburg, 1884, 4th ed. 1912): esp. vol. 1, 29–31 and 39 (on the concept of the "mixed" procedure adopted in 1864 on the French model). Unlike France and Russia, other European countries, such as Austria, Germany, Norway, and Hungary adopted the adversarial principle in the preliminary investigation. An earlier treatise, which was considered to be incomplete because it covered the code of procedure but not the code of judicial institutions, was A. P. Chebyshev-Dmitriev, *Russkoe ugolovnoe sudoproizvodstvo po sudebnym ustavam 20 noiabria 1864g.* (St. Petersburg, 1875).

35. Investigators were required to provide free copies of all interrogation records (*Ustav,* art. 476–477); prior to trial, the defendant had to be provided with the text of the indictment and the list of witnesses and had seven days to engage an attorney and summon witnesses (*Ustav,* art. 556–557).

36. In the Kronenberg trial his bail was fifteen thousand rubles (TsGIA SPb 487.1.1654, l. 13 ob.); Gulak-Artemovskaia's bail was fifty thousand rubles, and that of the wayward financiers in the Moscow bank case between two hundred thousand and half a million rubles.
37. Clive Emsley, *Crime and Society in England, 1750–1900,* 3rd ed. (Harlow: Pearson Education, 2005), esp. 197–198.
38. LeBlanc, "Dostoevsky and the Trial of Nastasia Kairova"; McReynolds, *Murder Most Russian,* 69–72.
39. A. I. Veretennikov and A. P. Dobachevskii, eds., *Delo o kollezhskom asessore Nikolae L'vove Bel'skom i krestianine Kazanskogo uezda, der. Nizhnie Aty Tazetdine Khisamutdinove, obviniaemykh v ubiistve i podzhoge* (Kazan, 1873), 7; SV, 1873, no. 33 (11 Feb.); SV, 1879, no. 183 (6 July); S. A. Keltsev, *Delo Mel'nitskikh* (Moscow, 1884), 44–46.
40. M. F. Frolenko, *Zapiski semidesiatnika* (Moscow, 1927), 48–49; Kropotkin, *Zapiski,* 322; L. G. Deich (Deutsch), *16 let v Sibiri,* 2nd ed. (St. Petersburg, 1906), 12.
41. *Delo o . . . Bel'skom;* also the case of Jujean discussed in chapter 7.
42. Vera Figner, *Izbrannye proizvedenia,* 3 vols. (Moscow, 1933): vol. 1, 294; Kropotkin, *Zapiski,* 330–331; N. A. Morozov, *Povesti moei zhizni,* 2 vols. (Moscow, 1965): vol. 2, 19–20; Frolenko, *Zapiski,* 70; Ekaterina Breshko-Breshkovskaia, *Skrytye korni russkoi revoliutsii: Otrechenie velikoi revoliutsionerki, 1873–1920* (Moscow, 2006), 73; Keltsev, *Delo Mel'nitskikh,* 46.
43. Breshko-Breshkovskaia, *Skrytye korni,* 72–97.
44. Breshko-Breshkovskaia, *Skrytye korni,* 91 and 97 (her possessions were returned to her even after her long confinement with the lower-class inmates). A vivid description of Moscow's Butyrskaia prison is found in the picaresque memoirs of the swindler Lieutenant Savin. See S. V. Shumikhin, ed., *Sud'ba avantiurista: Zapiski korneta Savina* (Novosibirsk, 2012): 297–305. Unlike other memoirists, he wrote that in the "Butyrka" the "nobles'" quarters were as dirty as the regular ones; Frolenko, *Zapiski,* 71; Morozov, *Povesti,* 10–13 and 45–47.
45. *Delo Mitrofanii,* I/208, 210.
46. *Delo Mitrofanii,* I/35, 207–210, 304. Koni, vol. 1, 64–73; RGIA 1405.534.1073, l. 15–16 (she had three screens, two sofas, two armchairs, two chairs, tables, two dressers, an icon stand, a washstand, and other items).
47. *Delo Mitrofanii,* I/101; Keltsev, *Delo Mel'nitskikh,* 44–48.
48. Kropotkin, *Zapiski,* 325.
49. *Delo Mitrofanii,* I/35, 58, 60–62, 210; RGIA 1405.534.1073, l. 1 ob., 19 ob.
50. RGIA 1405.534.1350, l. 160; GARF 109.208.90, l. 18.
51. Keltsev, *Delo Mel'nitskikh,* 52; Frolenko, *Zapiski,* 71–72; Breshko-Breshkovskaia, *Skrytye korni,* 91; Morozov, *Povesti,* vol. 2, 19–20; Figner, *Izbrannye proizvedenia,* vol. 1, 288–290.
52. *Delo Mitrofanii,* I/213, 216.
53. *Delo Mitrofanii,* I/8, 11, 263, 270.
54. *Delo Mitrofanii,* I/8, 11, 15, 263, 270; RGIA 1405.534.1073; A. Ia. Lipskerov, ed., *Stenograficheskii otchet po delu generala Gartunga* (Moscow, 1878), 15, 16, 85, 87–88; K.N.Z., ed., *Klub chervonnykh valetov: Ugolovnyi protsess* (Moscow, 1877), 36–37.

55. RGIA 1405.534.1211, l. 22 ob.
56. "*Temnye storony novogo suda,*" 357. In 1845 the "famous detective" Anton Sobolev helped to uncover a massive counterfeiting operation in the Guslitsy district outside Moscow. GARF 109.185.107.
57. *Delo o . . . Bel'skom,* 235–236.
58. SV, 1869, no. 97 (7 May). One of the swindlers was the widow of General Khomutov, who had commanded Nicholas I's favorite military detachment, the Guard Sapper Battalion, and the other was a young Italian-born adventurer, Alexander Borgesiani; Keltsev, *Delo Mel'nitskikh,* 65.
59. *Delo Miasnikovykh: Polnyi stenograficheskii otchet* (St. Petersburg, 1872).
60. Keltsev, *Delo,* 120–136, 56, 67.
61. Keltsev, *Delo,* 134–135.
62. Keltsev, *Delo,* 203, 205.
63. Putilin's own description of the case is in P. A. Fedorov, ed., *I. D. Putilin, znamenityi russkii syshchik* (St. Petersburg, 1908), 67–97; SV, 1873, no. 333 (11 Feb.); Koni, vol. 1, 94–95; V. L-v, "*Tri ubiistva,*" 164–166, 173, 316, 322–323 (on the Danilov and Volokhova cases); see also SV, 1869, no. 18 (Jan 23) (on the Gusev Alley murder).

CHAPTER 2. PUBLIC JUSTICE

1. Grigorii Dzhanshiev, *Epokha velikikh reform,* 6th ed. (Moscow, 1898), 399–403; Katkov, "*Tsel' i smysl publichnogo suda. Kakova dolzhna byt' ego obstanovka,*" MV, 1865, no. 185 (24 Aug.); the transcript is in "*Polevoi voennyi sud nad soldatom Komarovym . . .,*" *Sovremenniaia letopis',* 1865, no. 22.
2. Bentham, *Works,* vol. 4, 316 (quoted in Jaconelli, *Open Justice,* 36); Duff et al., *Trial on Trial,* vol. 3, 281.
3. *ZhMIu,* vol. 26 (1865).
4. Including Siberia, the North, Central Asia; the new courts were introduced late and without juries in Right-Bank Ukraine, Poland, Transcaucasia, and the Baltic provinces. Vilenskii, *Sudebnaia reforma,* 202–219.
5. Corporal punishment was retained in the armed forces, for convicted inmates, and for male peasants convicted of petty crime by local township courts, typically as a substitute for arrest and fine. Regular courts in Russia had not imposed the death penalty since Empress Elizabeth's order in 1742, although military courts were allowed to apply it, as were the special courts that tried violent radicals, such as the killers of Tsar Alexander II in 1881. The radicalized landowner Dmitry Lizogub was executed in 1879 for financing revolutionaries.
6. Duff et al., *Trial on Trial,* vol. 3, 277–278; Jaconelli, *Open Justice.* Sarah Maza, *Private Lives and Public Affairs: The Causes Célèbres of Prerevolutionary France* (Berkeley, 1995).
7. Jeremy Bentham, *Rationale of Judicial Evidence, Specially Applied to English Practice,* ed. by J. S. Mill (London: Hunt and Clarke, 1827 [1812]), 512.
8. Thom Standage, *Victorian Internet* (New York: Walker, 1998); Walter Sperling, *Der Aufbruch der Provinz: Die Eisenbahn und die Neuordnung der Räume im Zarenreich* (Frankfurt: Campus, 2011); Pravilova, *The Ruble,* 116–122 ("increase in the quantity of financial information" available to the public in the 1860s). David Vincent, *I Hope I*

Don't Intrude: Privacy and Its Dilemmas in Nineteenth-Century Britain (Oxford, 2015); Deborah Cohen, *Family Secrets: Shame and Privacy in Modern Britain* (Oxford, 2013).

9. Kozlinina, *Za polveka,* 232.
10. Bentham, *Rationale,* 595–596, 585; Amalia D. Kessler, "Our Inquisitorial Tradition: Equity Procedure, Due Process, and the Search for an Alternative to the Adversarial," *Cornell Law Review* 90 (2004–2005): 1181–1275, 1215–1217 (secrecy was "deemed necessary to avoid error and fraud," citing Michael R. T. MacNair, *The Law of Proof in Early Modern Equity* (Berlin: Duncker und Humblot, 1999), 165–168 ("the key to truthful adjudication was to limit party involvement by promoting secrecy in fact-finding"). Law professor and future leading defense lawyer Aleksandr Lokhvitskii noted that prominent French trials were difficult to attend, it was impossible to see defendants' faces or to hear everything properly, and all trials of offenses against morality were conducted behind closed doors. *"Zasedania parizhskogo ugolovnogo suda v 1857–58 g." Russkii vestnik,* vol. 18 (1858): 301–356.
11. Duff et al., *Trial on Trial,* vol. 3, 265.
12. Cesare Beccaria, *"On Crime and Punishments" and Other Writings,* ed. Richard Bellamy (Cambridge, 1995), 36–37.
13. Bentham, *Rationale,* 523–533, 541–542.
14. Martin, *Enlightened Metropolis;* Smith-Peter, *Imagining Russian Regions.*
15. See, e.g., McReynolds, *Murder Most Russian;* Schur, *The Letters and the Law;* Bhat, *Trial by Jury.*
16. OZ 201, no. 3 (1872): 70 (on the Miasnikov brothers' case).
17. Lovell, *How Russia Learned to Talk.*
18. Judicial proceedings were a common theme in eighteenth-century amateur theater in Russia, according to Liudmila Sofronova, *Rossiiskii Featron: Moskovskii liubitel'skii teatr XVIII v.* (Moscow, 2007), 164–167.
19. Nigel Raab, "A Conservative Public Sphere: Imperial Russian Fire Departments, 1850–1914," Ph.D. dissertation, Columbia University (2002).
20. P. S. Reifman, *Tsenzura v dorevoliutsionnoi, sovetskoi i postsovetskoi Rossii,* vol. 1, part 1 (Moscow, 2015): 80. This prohibition was introduced by administrative degree and was not part of the statute of 1804; also citing A. M. Skabichevskii, *Ocherki istorii russkoi tsenzury (1700–1863)* (St. Petersburg, 1892), 158–159.
21. On the Provisional prison, see Antonov, *Bankrupts and Usurers,* 228–260.
22. S. Ya. Barshev, "*Ob ustnosti i glasnosti ugolovnogo sudoproizvodstva,*" *Russkii vestnik*, vol. 10 (1857): 177–218; n/a, "*O slovesnom deloproizvodstve v Rossii,*" *Russkii vestnik,* vol. 11 (1857): 152–173, 169.
23. K. Ya. Yanevich-Yanevskii, *"O publichnosti i ustnosti ugolovnogo sudoproizvodstva po russkomu polozhitel'nomu pravu," Russkii vestnik*, vol. 11, *Sovremennaia letopis'* (1857): 82–89 (also published in *Morskoi sbornik* and as a separate pamphlet).
24. *Materialy,* vol. 7, 116, 133; vol. 17, chs. 12, 8, and 15; Korotkikh, *Samoderzhavie,* 88–91.
25. MV, 1865, no. 185 (24 Aug.).
26. Afanasiev, "Jurors and Jury Trials," 217.
27. *Nedelia,* 1878, no. 44 (29 Oct.).

28. Engelstein, "Revolution and the Theater of Public Life," in *Slavophile Empire: Imperial Russia's Illiberal Path* (Cornell, 2009), 57.
29. *Nedelia,* 1866, no. 24: 383. On Suvorin, see Ye. A. Dinershtein, *A. S. Suvorin: Chelovek, sdelavshii kar'eru* (Moscow, 1998): esp. 23–28.
30. *Nedelia,* 1870, no. 14; SV, no. 85 (29 Mar. 1870).
31. GARF f. 109, op. 3a, d. 2799, l. 4–5.
32. A. V. Nikitenko, *Dnevnik.,* vol. 3 (Moscow, 1956): 272.
33. Siljak, *Angel of Vengeance,* 223.
34. Keltsev, *Delo Mel'nitskikh,* 153.
35. Keltsev, *Delo Mel'nitskikh,* 86, 153.
36. G. K. Gradovskii, *Itogi (1862–1907)* (Kiev, 1908): 16–17.
37. SV, 1869, no. 95 (4 May); cited in N. I. Biiushkina, "*Poreformennyi okruzhnoi sud: Problemy stanovlenia v Rossii (konets 60-kh–nachalo 70-kh gg. XIX v.,*" *Vestnik Nizhegorodskogo gosudarstvennogo universiteta . . ., Seriia pravo,* no. 1 (2001): 45–54.
38. *Delo,* 1876, no. 157 (8 June).
39. Keltsev, *Delo Mel'nitaskikh,* 153.
40. Roger Williams, *Manners and Murders in the World of Louis-Napoleon* (University of Washington Press, 1975), 10.
41. Bentham, *Rationale,* 521.
42. Peter King, "Decision-Makers and Decision-Making in the English Criminal Law, 1750–1830," *Historical Journal* 27, no. 1 (1984): 25–58.
43. Taylor, *In the Theater of Criminal Justice.* A Russian collection of European cases: *Sbornik ugolovnykh protsessov vsekh stran prezhnego i noveishego vremeni* (St. Petersburg, 1880).
44. J. Stephen, *History of the Criminal Law,* 3 vols. (London: Macmillan, 1883), vol. 1, 516 (cited in Duff et al., *Trial on Trial,* vol. 3, 274); J. M. Beattie, "Sir John Fielding and Public Justice: The Bow Street Magistrates' Court, 1754–1780," *LHR* 25, no. 1 (2007): 61–100.
45. MV, 1865, no. 185 (24 Aug.).
46. *Syn otechestva,* no. 50 (1872), quoted in *Delo Miasnikovykh,* 419.
47. Kozlinina, *Za polveka,* 232; *Golos,* no. 303 (1876); McReynolds, *The News under Russia's Old Regime,* 47.
48. Keltsev, *Delo Mel'nitskikh,* 86.
49. V. M. Doroshevich, "*Mefistofel orkuzhnogo suda.*" *Russkoe Slovo,* 1910 (21 Mar.).
50. Anton Chekhov, *Delo skopinskogo banka* (Moscow, 1926), 5. During the first days of the trial the courtroom was half empty, but the public kept adding up, and at the end the courtroom was so stuffed that two spectators sat on the defendants' bench. Chekhov, *Delo,* 43.
51. *Delo Miasnikovykh,* 275.
52. "*Delo o dukhovnom zaveshchanii Beliaeva,*" VE 7, no. 4 (Apr. 1872): 822.
53. Brian McGinty, *John Brown's Trial* (Harvard, 2009).
54. McReynolds, *The News under Russia's Old Regime,* 39–47.
55. In the early 1870s these were *Novoe vremia, Iskra, Novosti,* and *Peterburgskii listok. Delo Miasnikovykh,* 404–407.

56. The official government newspaper, the *Government Herald* (*Pravitelstvennyi vestnik*) may have had appendices that published case transcripts, but while the paper itself is widely available, including in the Sterling Memorial Library at Yale, I have not been able to find any surviving copies of any such appendices, and the staff at the Newspaper Division of the Russian National Library in St. Petersburg had no idea what I was talking about when I asked about them in 2019. Those modern historians who have worked with Russian case records have used only *Sudebnyi vestnik,* which was not an official court register but a private legal newspaper. It was closed down in 1878 after it published a sympathetic account of the trial of Vera Zasulich.
57. The jurors' names were published for the Miasnikov brothers' case: SpbV, 1872, no. 66 (paraphrased in *Delo Miasnikovykh,* 410).
58. Kirmse, *The Lawful Empire.*
59. VE 7, no. 4 (1872): 803–804.
60. On the Miasnikov brothers' case see VE 7, no. 4 (1872): 803–822; *Nedelia,* no. 9 (5 Mar. 1872): 287; OZ, 1872, no. 3.
61. *Delo igumen'i Mitrofanii,* I/29.
62. RGIA 1363.9.18.
63. RSO, vol. 7, 62.
64. MV, no. 185 (24 Aug. 1865).
65. Bentham, *Rationale,* 594; Jaconelli, *Open Justice.*
66. *Materialy,* vol. 17, 12/4.
67. Taylor, *In the Theater.*
68. Bentley, *English Criminal Justice,* 55–56, 11–13.
69. Taylor, *In the Theater;* Rebekka Habermas, *Thieves in Court: The Making of the German Legal System in the Nineteenth Century* (Cambridge, 2016): 209–214.
70. Yaney, *Systematization;* Yeroshkin, *Istoriia gosudarstvennykh uchrezhdenii;* V. V. Ivanovskii, *Russkoe gosudarstvennoe pravo,* vol. 5 (Kazan, 1895–1898).
71. See, e.g., M. F. Zlotnikov, *Pod'iachie ivanovskoi ploshchadi: K istorii notariata Mosk. Rusi* (Petrograd, 1916).
72. Ivanovskii, *Russkoe;* Katkov's 1865 editorial mentioned the "decorum (*blagochinie*) that is required in front of the *zertsalo.*"
73. Dzhanshiev, *Epokha velikikh reform.*
74. D. D. Ivanov, "*Ocherk istorii zdania sudebnykh ustanovlenii v Moskve 1776–1896.*" ZhMIu 1896, no. 3: 281–331, 315, 311, 330–331.
75. Isser Woloch, *The New Regime* (New York: W. W. Norton, 1994).
76. Taylor, *In the Theater,* 13; Bentley, *English Criminal Justice.*
77. Koni, "*Prisiazhnye zasedateli,*" in *Sobranie sochinenii,* vol. 1, 367.
78. ZhMIu, vol. 27 (1866): 400.
79. Duff et al., *Trial on Trial,* vol. 3, 273; Graham, *Ordering Law: The Architectural and Social History of the English Law Court to 1914* (Routledge, 2003).
80. Bentley, *English Criminal Justice,* 64.
81. *Vsemirnaia illustratsia,* 1869, no. 5, 85.
82. Taylor, *In the Theater.*

83. Taylor, *In the Theater.*
84. Bentley, *English Criminal Justice*; Graham, *Ordering Law.*
85. Keltsev, *Delo Mel'nitskikh*, 153.
86. *Delo Miasnikovykh*, 75, 102, 136–138.
87. *Delo Mitrofanii*, I/139.
88. Siljak, *Angel of Vengeance*, 245–247.
89. Green, *Verdict According to Conscience.*
90. Sofronova, *Rossiiskii Featron*, 36–38, 117, 164–167.
91. Duff et al., *Trial on Trial*, vol. 3, 273.
92. *Delo Miasnikovykh*, 414–415, quoting *Syn otechestva*, no. 50 (1872).
93. These were the Kicheev murder case; the Fokin trigamy case; and the Sobakin counterfeiting case. MV, 1865, nos. 78, 80, 84, 92.
94. SV, 1866, no. 16 (16 July).
95. *Russkaya mysl'*, vol. 30 (June 1899): 4.
96. SV, 1866, no. 27 (24 Aug.).
97. Keltsev, *Delo Mel'nitskikh*, 86.
98. *Delo Miasnikovykh*, 414.
99. Another example is the "suitcase murder" of 1870. *Nedelia*, no. 14 (1870); SV, no. 85 (29 Mar. 1870).
100. Keltsev, *Delo Mel'nitskikh*, 153.
101. V. D. Spasovich, *Sochinenia*, vol. 5 (St. Petersburg, 1893): 267; on the Pal'm case, see RGIA f. 560, op. 19, d. 192.
102. "*Delo Yukhantseva*," in RSO, vol. 7, 1–111, 78.
103. *Delo Mitrofanii*, II/115–116.
104. Keltsev, *Delo Mel'nitskikh.*
105. Keltsev, *Delo Mel'nitskikh*, 112–115, 215, 124.
106. Johan Huizinga, *Homo Ludens: A Study of the Play-Element in Culture* (Routledge, 1949), 10.
107. *Delo Miasnikovykh*, 129, Lipskerov, *Delo Gartunga*, 70.
108. Keltsev, *Delo Mel'nitskikh*, 124.
109. *Delo Miasnikovykh*, 55, 77.
110. *Delo Miasnikovykh*, 124, 127, 283.
111. OZ, 1872, no. 3, 86.
112. SpbV, no. 298 (29 Oct. 1878).
113. *Delo igumen'i Mitrofanii* I/77.
114. Antonov, *Bankrupts and Usurers*, 148–149.
115. The case of Dmitrieva and Kostrubo-Karitskii is discussed in chapter 3.
116. On the Jujean case, see chapter 7.
117. RSO, vol. 7, 40.
118. Keltsev, *Delo Melnitskikh*, 151.
119. SpbV, no. 292 (23 Oct. 1878).
120. *Delo Mitrofanii*, II/195.
121. Keltsev, *Delo Melnitskikh.*

CHAPTER 3. THE ADVERSARIAL TRIAL

1. A well-known fictional example is the trial from Dostoevsky's *Brothers Karamazov* (1881) (part 4, book 12, ch. 1).
2. *Protsess G-zhi Dmitrievoi, Polkovnika Karitskogo . . .*, ed. Ya. F. Bogdanov (Moscow, 1871).
3. I therefore cannot agree with Girish Bhat that this trial reveals a peculiarly collegial or "consensual" Russian style of adjudication. See Bhat, "The Consensual Dimension of Late Imperial Russian Criminal Trial Procedure . . .," in Peter H. Solomon Jr., ed. *Reforming Justice in Russia: Power, Culture, and the Limits of Legal Order* (Armonk, NY: M. E. Sharpe, 1997).
4. P. D. Boborykin, "*Zashchitniki vdov i sirot,*" in *Protsess G-zhi Dmitrievoi,* 184.
5. In addition to Zasulich, young women acquitted of murder included Volokhova, Kornilova, Kairova, Palem, Nepenina, and Kovalchukova. Only the first two were peasants.
6. Langbein, *The Origins of Adversary Criminal Trial.*
7. *Materialy,* vol. 17.
8. Chebyshev-Dmitriev, *Russkoe ugolovnoe sudoproizvodstvo,* esp. 683–735.
9. This complexity balanced out the fact that the jury's verdict was final unless overruled for procedural reasons.
10. I am commenting on the trial technology rather than on the moral aspects of that technology, leaving out the issue of whether the defendant was dehumanized and treated as raw material to be processed.
11. On the French rules, see Donovan, *Juries,* 12.
12. *Delo Mitrofanii,* I/1.
13. Emsley, *Crime and Society,* 75, citing Furneaux Jordan, *Character as Seen in Body and Parentage* (London, 1886).
14. SV, 1869, no. 18 (23 Jan.).
15. Nos, vol. 2, 1.
16. SV, 1867, no. 260 (29 Nov.).
17. Demert, "*Matushka Mitrofania,*" 256.
18. V. L-v. "*Tri ubiistva,*" 172–173.
19. Keltsev, *Delo Melnitskikh,* 87.
20. *Ustav*, art. 550, 656; *Uchrezhdenie, sudebnykh ustanovlenii*, art. 84.
21. In France the indictment was "often long and denunciatory" and could say almost anything. Donovan, *Juries,* 12.
22. *Golos,* 1877, no. 40 (9 Feb.).
23. Keltsev, *Delo,* 111–113, 107.
24. RSO, vol. 7, 16–18.
25. Spasovich, *Sochinenia,* vol. 5, 26; GARF 109.39.15/23.
26. *Delo Miasnikovykh,* 47–52.
27. RSO, vol. 7, 57, 60, 102, 73–75. Other examples: in the Gusev Alley murder, when Daria Sokolova was first arrested, she confessed and said she had had a sudden urge to kill but soon changed her story and claimed that the police detective forced her to confess, and that in reality she was hiding under the couch during the murder. SV, 1869, no.

18 (23 Jan.). During the trial Sokolova's lawyer attempted to attack the way her confession was obtained but was prevented from doing so by the judge. SV, 1869, no. 22. Another example is the Mazurin murder case (1867): his lawyer argued that without his client's confession the suspicion would have fallen on his five male servants who would be arrested, while he could easily avoid suspicion because of his wealth and generally good past behavior. Nos, vol. 2, 31–32.

28. Burns, *A Theory of the Trial.*
29. John P. LeDonne, "Criminal Investigations before the Great Reforms," *Russian History* 1, no. 2 (1974): 101–118; LeDonne, *Ruling Russia: Politics and Administration in the Age of Absolutism, 1762–1796* (Princeton, 1984), 145–202.
30. Burns, *A Theory of the Trial.*
31. In Katherine Fischer Taylor's view, criminal trials in Victorian England were ironically less openly confrontational than the French ones: the English courts were modeled after Protestant meeting houses, and "the social paradigm was collegiality, conversation, consensus—not dramatic confrontation." Taylor, *In the Theater,* 12–13.
32. Bhat, *Trial by Jury,* 41–86.
33. *Delo Gartunga;* Gulak-Artemovskaia is discussed in chapter 6.
34. This observation does not fully resolve the complex question of Mitrofania's actual guilt or innocence.
35. *Delo Mitrofanii; Delo Gartunga,* 25.
36. VE 7, no. 4 (Apr. 1872): 807.
37. *Delo Miasnikovykh,* 131, 142, 148–149, 161–162.
38. SpbV, no. 296 (27 Oct. 1878); no. 294 (25 Oct. 1878).
39. Keltsev, *Delo,* 112, 206, 119.
40. Siljak, *Angel of Vengeance.*
41. Nechaev. B. P. Kozmin, ed., *Nechaev i nechaevtsy: Sbornik dokumentov* (Moscow, 1931); K. K. Arseniev, "*Politicheskii protsess. 1869–1871 gg.*" *Vestnik Evropy* 6, no. 11 (1871): 283–320; F. M. Lurie, *Nechaev: Sozidatel' razrushenia* (Moscow, 2001); Pomper, *Nechaev.*
42. *Delo Miasnikovykh,* 220.
43. The purpose of permitting the participation of civil plaintiffs was to allow them to be compensated for their financial losses from the crime without having to undergo a separate civil lawsuit.
44. RGIA 1363.9.18, l. 3ob.
45. *Delo Miasnikovykh,* 50, 70–71.
46. On France, see Donovan, *Juries.*
47. Langbein, *Torture and the Law of Proof.*
48. *Materialy,* vol. 17; SZ, XV/2, art. 304–315.
49. On probabilism, see Piers Beirne, *Inventing Criminology: Essays on the Rise of "Homo Criminalis"* (Albany: SUNY Press, 1993); Lorraine Daston, *Classical Probability in the Enlightenment* (Princeton, 1988).
50. "Perfect" proofs were only considered as such if they satisfied certain parameters that were within the judges' discretion. A confession had to be voluntary and consistent with the circumstances of the case, and witness testimony counted if the defendant did not challenge (*otvel*) the witnesses, their testimony was completely identical, and the

defendant did not offer sufficient refutation. Testimony by men, nobles, clergy, and educated persons had preference only if it was "equally reliable" to that of women, commoners, laypeople, and uneducated persons. SZ, XV/2, art. 317, 328–335.

51. Pre-reform trials showed that lower courts tended to impose more severe sentences, which the next two tiers usually reduced. Antonov, *Bankrupts and Usurers,* 293. The case of playwright Aleksandr Sukhovo-Kobylin in 1850–1857 was remembered for having all three tiers of the court system produce completely different rulings. V. M. Seleznev and E. O. Selezneva, eds., *Delo Sukhovo-Kobylina* (Moscow, 2002).
52. Theoretically the court could omit the question of imputability (that is, only require the jury to rule whether certain facts had taken place), but that would leave the burden of deciding the case on the judge, which is what the reform was trying to avoid. On the way juries "cloak" and augment the judges' power, see Renee Lettow Lerner, "The Surprising Views of Montesquieu and Tocqueville about Juries: Juries Empower Judges," *Louisiana Law Review* 81, no. 1 (2020), article 6; Paul O. Carrese, *The Cloaking of Power: Montesquieu, Blackstone and the Rise of Judicial Activism* (Chicago, 2003). Russian judges could set aside a guilty verdict when they believed an innocent person had been convicted, but they exercised this right only in very exceptional cases. Doroshevich, "*Mefistofel.*"
53. Green, *Verdict.*
54. Including giving the juries the right to find circumstances extenuating the guilt (and thus reducing the punishment), as well as taking smaller offenses away from jury trial. Similarly, in England the use of summary justice was greatly extended during the nineteenth century.
55. In post-Napoleonic France witnesses "were free to say almost anything they pleased." Donovan, *Juries,* 12–13. By contrast, pre-reform procedure imposed stricter rules about witness testimony that were closer to the Anglo-American evidence law in being restricted to sensory data; *Ustav,* art. 718.
56. *Delo Miasnikovykh,* 75–79, 302–305, 76.
57. In the major 1879 embezzlement trial of Konstantin Yukhantsev all the witnesses fell into two groups: finance and accounting specialists testifying about the details of the banking operations and security precautions, and the witnesses explaining Yukhantsev's personality, previous life, and family situation. "*Delo Yukhantseva,*" 19.
58. There are also other exceptions and complications, but the main rule is well known even to nonspecialists.
59. Bentley, *English Criminal Justice,* 237–241; Emsley, *Crime and Society,* 198; Green, *Verdict,* 281–282; Douglas Hay, "Property, Authority and Criminal Law," in Douglas Hay, Peter Linebaugh et al., *Albion's Fatal Tree: Crime and Society in Eighteenth-Century England* (New York: Pantheon Books, 1975), 42.
60. Donovan, *Juries,* 12–13, 61.
61. Cesare Lombroso, *Criminal Man,* tr. Mary Gibson and Nichole Hahn Rafter (Durham: Duke University Press, 2006); McReynolds, *Murder Most Russian,* esp. 59–69. Ruth Harris, *Murders and Madness: Medicine, Law, and Society in the Fin de Siècle* (Oxford, 1989); Daniel Pick, *Faces of Degeneration: A European Disorder, c. 1848–c. 1918* (Cambridge, 1989); Richard F. Wetzell, *Inventing the Criminal: A History of German Criminology, 1880–1945* (Chapel Hill: University of North Carolina Press, 2000).

62. The dichotomy between positivist criminology popular among academic criminologists and classical theories prevalent among legal practitioners is described in many academic and introductory texts. See Beirne, *Inventing Criminology;* Peter Becker and Richard F. Wetzell, eds., *Criminals and Their Scientists: The History of Criminology in International Perspective* (Cambridge, 2006); see also note 18 to chapter 4 below. Girish N. Bhat's view that in nineteenth-century France "one can discern a conceptual diminution of *moral* responsibility in the assessment of criminality after mid-century" ("Moralization of Guilt," 85) is based on Ruth Harris, *Murders and Madness: Medicine, Law, and Society in the Fin de Siècle* (Oxford: Clarendon Press, 1989), 16–17 (discussing a loose group of reformers at the very end of the century, not mainstream courtroom practice), and on Berenson, *The Trial of Madame Caillaux,* 36–38 (discussing a much later 1914 trial, as well as the often sympathetic social and legal attitudes to the crimes of passion in fin-de-siècle France, which were only one peculiar variety of violent crime and, moreover, cannot be explained solely as a triumph of positivist criminology; other political and social factors were clearly also influential).
63. Bhat, "Moralization of Guilt," 80–81.
64. The murder case tried by a jury in Moscow in October 1866 resulted in an acquittal. SV, 1866, no. 74 (30 Oct.). The Vereitinov trial (discussed in McReynolds, *Murder Most Russian,* 63) was not actually for murder but for aggravated battery. SV, 1866, no. 56 (7 Oct.); *Glasnyi sud,* 1866, no. 11 (15 Oct.), 12 (16 Oct.), 14 (18 Oct.), and 15 (19 Oct.).
65. SV, 1866, nos. 92–93 (23–24 Nov.).
66. Becker, *Medicine, Law, and the State,* 228–235; RUP, vol. 1, 207–294.
67. The court could summon "physicians, apothecaries, professors, teachers, technicians, artists, craftsmen, treasurers and persons who acquired a particular experience through a prolonged occupation in some agency or field." *Ustav,* art. 326.
68. Becker, *Medicine;* Antonov, *Bankrupts and Usurers,* 302–308.
69. SZ, XV/2, art. 328 (the translation is my own). Becker, *Medicine, Law, and the State,* 32–34.
70. Becker, *Medicine, Law, and the State,* 241–242.
71. Foucault, *Discipline and Punish.* The quote is from Becker, *Medicine, Law, and the State,* 379 n. 186.
72. See, e.g., MV, 1866, nos. 78, 80, 84, 92.
73. *Delo Miasnikovykh,* 59–68.
74. OZ, 1872, no. 3, 80.
75. SZ, XV/2, art. 324, 326; X/2, art. 349–350, 354.
76. SpbV, 1872, no. 66; *Delo Miasnikovykh,* 43, 44, 112–116, 411–412.
77. RSO, vol. 3, 33.
78. *Delo Mitrofanii,* I/216.
79. Demert, *"Matushka Mitrofania,"* 266.
80. *Delo Mitrofanii,* I/135–136.
81. Jennifer L. Mnookin, "Scripting Expertise: The History of Handwriting Identification Evidence and the Judicial Construction of Reliability," *Virginia Law Review* 87 (2001): 1723–1845.
82. SpbV, 1872, no. 297 (28 Oct.).

83. Anton Chekhov, *Delo skopinskogo banka* (Moscow, 1926).
84. "*Izvlechenie iz protokolov zasedanii Spb. Obshchestva arkhitektorov.*" *Zodchii,* 1876, no. 1, 14.
85. Speeches published in the Soviet period: Ye. M. Vorozheikin, *Sudebnye rechi izvestnykh russkikh iuristov* (Moscow, 1958).
86. Kucherov, *Courts and Trials.*
87. Burns, *A Theory of Trial.*
88. Langbein, *The Origins of Adversary Criminal Trial,* 10–66.
89. Green, *Verdict According to Conscience.*
90. Bentley, *English Criminal Justice,* 71–72.
91. Case materials in the old courts were prepared by the court secretary, whereas the court procurator only reviewed them for conformance with the statutory laws.
92. *Materialy,* vol. 7, 146; vol. 17, 29.
93. Legal aid was introduced in England in 1949; the Sixth Amendment of the U.S. Constitution extended to states in 1963 (*Gideon v. Wainwright*). The Supreme Court rejected the existence of the right to counsel as late as 1942 (*Betts v. Brady,* 316 U.S. 455).
94. *Materialy,* vol 17.
95. William E. Pomeranz, "Justice from Underground: The History of the Underground Advokatura," *Russian Review* 52, no. 3 (1993): 321–340.
96. V. K. Ivanov, *Vzgliad na delo Miasnikovykh s obshchestvennoi tochki zrenia* (St. Petersburg, 1872), 21–22.
97. Kozlinina, *Za polveka.*, 214–216; Koni, "*O dopushchenii zhenshchin v advokaturu,*" in *Sobranie sochinenii,* vol. 4, 426–442.
98. Schur, *The Letters and the Law,* 11–12.
99. Trials in which courtroom debates heavily involved statutory interpretation included those of the banker Kronenberg (discussed in chapter 7) and of the managers and directors of the Moscow Commercial Loan Bank. In the Moscow bank case the appellate decision by the Senate noted disapprovingly that the prosecutor, the defense, and the civil plaintiffs "in their speeches addressed not only the circumstances of the case, but also the laws." This especially applied to the infamously irreverent attorney Alexander Lokhvitskii, whose speech "focused entirely on the interpretation of the law." RGIA, f. 1405, op. 73, d. 2348, l. 280.
100. Nos, vol. 2, 31.
101. The top attorney Vladimir Zhukovskii noted this disbalance at the forgery trial of Gulak-Artemovskaia. SpbV, 1878, no. 300, 31 Oct.
102. Schur, *The Letters and the Law,* 25–33, 41–44.
103. Technically an appeal reviews the entire case, and a cassation reviews only procedural violations.
104. Foinitskii, *Moshennichestvo po russkomu pravu* (St. Petersburg, 1871), part II.
105. There is some indication that requesting a court-appointed lawyer created prejudice against an elite defendant. The student Danilov in his 1867 murder trial claimed that only an "impoverished or an idiot" person would do so. *Dvoinoe ubiistvo na Kislovke v Moskve* (Moscow, 1899), 98.

106. Dinershtein, *Suvorin,* 56.
107. A. N. Markov, *Pravila advokatskoi professii v Rossii* (Moscow, 1913).
108. This is not unique to Russia or to the nineteenth century. It is certainly true at least on the trial level in the United States today.
109. Grigorii Dzhanshiev, *Vedenie nepravykh del* (Moscow, 1886).
110. Similarly, Koni's memoirs recall several interactions with criminal defendants before trying and sometimes before even initiating their case, including Mother Mitrofania, Stepan Ovsiannikov, and Liudmila Gulak-Artemovskaia. Koni, vol. 1, 38, 70, 139.
111. *Delo Miasnikovykh,* 405.
112. *Nedelia,* 1872, no. 9 (5 Mar.), 287.
113. Keltsev, *Delo Mel'nitksikh,* 203.
114. Regardless of their general reputation, top lawyers defended political cases free of charge, and in such trials, for example that of the followers of Sergei Nechaev in 1871, of the participants in the Kazan Square demonstration, and the seditious conspiracy "trial of the 50," both in 1877, the scrupulous Arseniev and Gerard worked together with the unscrupulous Lokhvitskii, Plevako, and Spasovich. On defense lawyers in political trials, see N. A. Troitskii, *Advokatura v Rossii i politicheskie protsessy 1866–1904 gg.* (Tula, 2000).
115. Spasovich, *Sochineniia,* vol. 5, 250–251. For the case file, see RGIA 560.19.192.
116. Spasovich, *Sochineniia,* vol. 5, 18.
117. *Delo Mitrofanii,* II/139—apparently during the trial Shaikevich said that he was no longer sure of Mitrofania's innocence. *Delo Mitrofanii,* I/vi.
118. On Shaikevich's reputation, see Kozlinina, *Za polveka,* 116–119.
119. RSO, vol. 7, 74–75.
120. L. A. Bazunov and M. S. Margulies, eds., *Vydaiushchiiesia russkie sudebnye protsessy* (St. Petersburg, 1903), 125.
121. *Delo Mitrofanii,* II/150; Demert, *Matushka Mitrofania,* 268.
122. Trepov was an idiosyncratic figure who left a heavy mark on how St. Petersburg was policed, and he was widely disliked, but perhaps did not deserve to be shot at point-blank range. He illegally ordered the flogging of a political prisoner, but only after consulting the minister of justice and attempting to consult Koni (who somehow was not available). The prisoner did have a mental breakdown and die, Koni suggested, because of the flogging, but this happened years later, and no causal link can be established. Koni, vol. 2, 54, 395; Feliks Kon et al., eds., *Deiateli revoliutsionnogo dvizhenia v Rossii. Bio-bibliografichevskii slovar',* vol. 1 (Moscow, 1929), 395 (claiming that Aleksei Emelianov, a.k.a. Bogoliubov, died after 1885, not in 1880 as per Koni).
123. *Delo Miasnikovykh,* 284.
124. Zhukovsky also referred to a genuine conflict between criminal law, which punished any forgery, and civil law, in which the side that submitted a debt document for collection had a chance to withdraw a claim if it were rejected by the debtor. SpbV, 1878, no. 300 (31 Oct.).
125. SpbV, 1878, nos. 300–302 (31 Oct.–2 Nov.).
126. *Delo Miasnikovykh,* 224. ("I believe that in England and in America the majority of witnesses in trials in which the government does not have a stake, are engaged in

precisely this fashion. This does not mean that they are bribed to give false testimony; what is purchased is their labor, their time . . . the same happened in this case.")

127. Keltsev, *Delo Melnitskikh,* 211.
128. Schur, *The Letters and the Law,* 28, 44ff.
129. SpbV, 1878, no. 297 (28 Oct.).
130. *Delo Mitrofanii,* x. It appears that this introduction to the transcript was prepared by the Slavophile journalist Nikita Giliarov-Platonov.
131. *Delo Miasnikovykh,* 224.
132. VE, 1872, no. 4, 813 ("The prosecutor was proving the Miasnikovs' guilt mostly the same way it is argued that the Varangians came to rule [Russia] from Sweden, that is, that they could not have come from anywhere else without breaking the established chain of facts").
133. OZ, 1872, no. 3: 83, 86.
134. Schur, *The Letters and the Law;* SpbV, 1878, no. 301 (1 Nov.) and 302 (2 Nov.).
135. *Delo Yukhantseva,* 46: Urusov said that it was not enough to look at the form, that is, to see whether Yukhantsev had confessed, convict him, and move on. Instead it is necessary to ensure "that a careful examination of every individual case would bring benefit in the future, the society must be explained the conditions under which such crimes emerge."
136. "*Delo o . . . Bel'skom,*" 233. The prosecutor could not explain what that inner side was.
137. SV, 1873, no. 53 (10 Mar.); Bazunov and Margulies, *Vydaiushchiiesia,* 305.
138. Spasovich, *Sochineniia,* vol. 5, 262. Pal'm himself took the stand and asked the jury to uncover "not only the formal, external circumstances of [his] relations and actions, but also [to] uncover a man's entire inner life." Spasovich, *Sochineniia,* vol. 5, 268. The Pal'm case file is in RGIA 560.19.192. At the trial of the Polish nobleman Schomberg-Kollontai (accused of counterfeiting), Spasovich urged the jury to go beyond examining the criminal act and look at the "live human, a soul, into whose depths you must gaze and study its twists." Spasovich, *Sochineniia,* vol. 5, 18. On this topic, see also Schur, *The Letters and the Law.*
139. Pal'm's minor literary fame must explain Spasovich's involvement.
140. *Klub,* 183.
141. Langbein, *The Origins of Adversary Criminal Trial;* Bentley, *English Criminal Justice.*
142. Demert, *Matushka Mitrofania,* 256.
143. *Delo Mitrofanii,* I/65. Another example of Deier's meddling was when he asked Mitrofania whether it was acceptable for her to socialize with someone under investigation for belonging to an illegal religious sect. *Delo Mitrofanii,* I/94.
144. Doroshevich, "*Mefistofel okrushnogo suda.*"
145. Kozlinina, *Za polveka,* 277.
146. Keltsev, *Delo Melnitskikh,* 213–215.
147. "You will not miss the fact that [Yukhantsev's] spending on his wife was nothing compared to what he spent after he left her, when in one year he spent over 550,000 rubles; and that then his yearning for his tenderly loved wife was expressed, according to Yukhantsev's own confession in orgies with coquettes and in several relationships, and finally in emptying out the bank, which he committed 'without knowing how he did

it,' and in which one can see according to the experts, a clear and thought out system." RSO, vol. 7, 103–104.

148. Baberowski, "Law, Judicial System."
149. Afanasiev, "Jurors and Jury Trials."
150. On the shared culture of gentility, see Catriona Kelly, *Refining Russia: Advice Literature, Polite Culture, and Gender from Catherine to Yeltsin* (Oxford, 2001).
151. *Delo Mitrofanii*, I/117.
152. On Poletika's questions, see SpbV, 1878, no. 296 (27 Oct.).

CHAPTER 4. TEXTS OF TRANSGRESSION

1. Engelstein, *Keys to Happiness*, 18, 22. This conclusion is traceable to the critical remarks in N. S. Tagantsev, *Russkoe ugolovnoe pravo*, 2nd ed. (St. Petersburg, 1902): vol. 1, 222 (published while the new penal code—of which Tagantsev was a principal author—was under review in the State Council). Tagantsev referred to Spasovich's remarks in his *Uchebnik ugolovnogo prava* (St. Petersburg, 1863): 326. In Spasovich's time there was still a hope that the new procedural law would be followed by a new substantive penal code. Other views that the Code of 1845 was antiquated are in Arkhipov, *Sistematizatsiia*, e.g., 5; Nethercott, *Russian Legal Culture*, 25.
2. Engelstein, *Keys to Happiness*, 39–40.
3. Pipes, *Russia under the Old Regime*, 293–294. Arkhipov pointed out that the Code actually reduced arbitrariness by providing clear definitions of the crimes against the state as compared to the prior law. *Sistematizatsia*, 100. Pipes also argued that attempts by Peter I and Catherine II to establish a separate judiciary "ran into unsurmountable difficulties of all sorts, not the least of which was the absence of a law code." *Russia under the Old Regime*, 288.
4. Arkhipov, *Sistematizatsiia*: 5, 83–84; N. V. Strunnikova et al., eds., *Zakonodatelstvo pervoi poloviny XIX veka*, in *Rossiiskoe zakonodatelstvo X–XX vekov*, 9 vols. (Moscow, 1988): vol. 6, 170.
5. Marc Raeff, *Michael Speransky, Statesman of Imperial Russia, 1772–1839* (The Hague: Martinus Nijhoff, 1957); S. A. Chibiriaev, *Velikii russkii reformator: Zhizn,' deiatel'nost,' politicheskie vzgliady M. M. Speranskogo* (Moscow, 1989).
6. Borisova, "Russian National Legal Tradition: Svod versus Ulozhenie in Nineteenth-Century Russia," *Review of Central and East European Law* 33, no. 3 (2008): 295–341; Borisova, "The Digest of the Laws of the Russian Empire: The Phenomenon of Autocratic Legality," *LHR* 30, no. 3 (2012): 901–925.
7. Nicholas Riasanovsky, *Nicholas I and Official Nationality in Russia, 1825–1855* (Berkeley, 1959); Cynthia Whittaker, *Count S. S. Uvarov: Conservatism and National Enlightenment in Pre-reform Russia* (Ann Arbor: University of Michigan Press, 1981); Lesley Chamberlain, *Ministry of Darkness: How Sergei Uvarov Created Conservative Modern Russia* (Bloomsbury, 2020).
8. Imperial-era works showing that the code of civil law in volume 10 of the SZ was a new production rather than a compilation of old laws were German Barats, "*O chuzhezemnom proiskhozhdenii bol'shinstva russkikh grazhdanskikh zakonov,*" ZhGiUP 14, no. 10 (1884): 109–146; 15, no. 5 (1885): 81–112, no. 6 (1885): 67–81; and no. 9 (1885):

45–80; and Maksim Vinaver, *K voprosu ob istochnikakh X toma* (St. Petersburg, 1895). Works arguing that the SZ merely systematized existing legislation are I. A. Solodkin, *Russkoe ugolovnoe pravo v kontse XVIII–pervoi treti XIX v.* (Leningrad, 1966); V. A. Balybin, "*Osnovnye tendentsii razvitia ugolovnogo zakonodatelstva Rossii v 1861–1881 gg.*," in *Izvestia vysshikh uchebnykh vadedenii. Pravovedenie,* 1977, no. 3: 55–63, 55 (the code "hastily revised and combined" earlier legislation). Works showing that the Penal Code of 1845 was a code rather than a compilation include Yeroshkin, *Krepostnicheskoe samoderzhavie i ego politicheskie instituty* (Moscow, 1981), 157 (concluding that the Code of 1845 was a "genuine" codification but incorrectly claiming that it was the only "genuine" codification effort ever completed by the Second Section); Arkhipov, *Sistematizatsiia,* 80–82 (the dichotomy of codification versus systematization does not make much sense; new legislation as a matter of course was influenced by and included elements of older material); and Borisova, "Russian National Legal Tradition," 314–322 (the presentation of the SZ as a compilation of existing material was an "outward stylization," a rhetorical facade of Speransky's codification project); see also Strunnikova et al., *Zakonodatelstvo,* 19.

9. Arkhipov, *Sistematizatsiia,* 58–64. Arkhipov contradicts himself on whether the State Council left the draft code untouched or heavily modified it. Arkhipov, *Sistematizatsiia,* 76 and 79.

10. Cf. Alfred Rieber's view of imperial Russia. Rieber, "The Sedimentary Society," *Russian History,* vol. 16, nos. 2–4 (1989): 353–376.

11. Borisova, "Russian National Legal Tradition," esp. 310, 332–333; for the information about the training of Russian lawyers by Savigny in the 1820s, I am indebted to Nicholas Moore, "The Rectors of the *Raznochintsy:* Mikhail Speransky and the Second Section's Role in the Development of Russian Jurisprudence under Nicholas I," B.A. thesis, Yale University (2022).

12. Mathias Reimann, "Historical Jurisprudence," in Markus D. Dubber and Christopher Tomlins, eds., *The Oxford Handbook of Legal History* (Oxford, 2018), 397–418.

13. Emotional and personal bonds connecting imperial-era officials are discussed in Mikhail Dolbilov, "Loyalty and Emotion in Nineteenth-Century Russian Imperial Politics," in Martin Schulze Wessel and Jana Osterkamp, eds., *Exploring Loyalty* (Göttingen: Vandenhoeck und Ruprecht, 2017): 17–43; Wortman, *The Development of a Russian Legal Consciousness;* Kirill Soloviev, *Khoziain zemli Russkoi? Samoderzhavie i biurokratia v epokhu moderna* (Moscow, 2017).

14. Sergei Barshev, *Obshchie nachala teorii i zakonodatelstva o prestupleniiakh i nakazaniiakh* (Moscow, 1841): esp. ii; Iakov Barshev, *O vliianii obychaia, praktiki, zakonodatelstva i nauki na razvitie ugolovnogo, v osobennosti russkogo, prava* (St. Petersburg, 1846).

15. Horst Lücke, "The European Natural Law Codes: The Age of Reason and the Powers of Government," *University of Queensland Law Journal* 31, no. 1 (2012): 7–38. Henry Strakosch, *State Absolutism and the Rule of Law: The Struggle for the Codification of Civil Law in Austria 1755–1811* (Sydney University Press, 1963).

16. Thomas S. Kuhn, *The Structure of Scientific Revolutions* (Chicago, 1962).

17. Schrader, *The Languages of the Lash;* M. V. Klochkov, "*Nakaz imperatritsy Ekateriny II-i v sudebnoi praktike,*" *Sbornik statei v chest' M. K. Liubavskogo* (Petrograd, 1917): 1–18.

18. Becker, *Criminals and Their Scientists;* Bierne, *Inventing Criminology;* Paul Knepper and Anja Johansen, eds., *The Oxford Handbook of the History of Crime and Criminal Justice* (Oxford, 2016). David B. Young, "Property and Punishment in the Eighteenth Century: Beccaria and His Critics," *American Journal of Jurisprudence* 31 (1986), 121–136. There are many helpful introductory texts on criminology. See, e.g., George B. Vold, Thomas J. Bernard, and Jeffrey B. Snipes, *Theoretical Criminology,* 4th ed. (Oxford, 1998); Piers Beirne and James Messerschmidt, *Criminology: A Sociological Approach* (Oxford, 2015); Tim Newburn, *Criminology,* 3rd ed. (Routledge, 2017); Hugh Barlow and David Kauzlarich, *Explaining Crime: A Primer in Criminological Theory* (Lanham, MD: Rowman and Littlefield, 2010). On the contemporary theories of crime, see David Garland, *Punishment and Modern Society: A Study in Social Theory* (Chicago, 1990).
19. On the penal calculus in early modern Russia, see Kollmann, *Crime and Punishment;* Evgenii Anisimov, *Dyba i knut: politicheskii sysk i rossiiskoe obshchestvo v XVIII v.* (Moscow, 1999); Evgenii Akeliev, *Povsednevnaia zhizn' vorovskogo mira Moskvy vo vremena Van'ki Kaina* (Moscow, 2012).
20. Cesare Beccaria, *"On Crimes and Punishments" and Other Writings,* tr. Richard Davies, ed. Richard Bellamy (Cambridge, 2012).
21. Foucault, *Discipline and Punish,* 82.
22. Beirne, *Inventing Criminology.* Mark Goldie and Robert Wokler, *The Cambridge History of Eighteenth-Century Political Thought* (Cambridge, 2006).
23. Beccaria, *On Crimes.*
24. Beccaria, *On Crimes,* 104; on Locke, see C. B. MacPherson, *The Political Theory of Possessive Individualism, Hobbes to Locke,* 231–238 (cited in Vold et al., *Theoretical Criminology,* 23).
25. Beccaria, *On Crimes,* 103–104, 49–53, 28.
26. Kollmann, *Crime and Punishment.*
27. John Bessler, *The Birth of American Law: An Italian Philosopher and the American Revolution* (Durham: Carolina Academic Press, 2014); Kollmann, *Crime and Punishment,* 10–11, esp. n. 20 (the Military Statute was not used in civilian trials); see also L. Belogrits-Kotliarevskii, *O vorovstve-krazhe po russkomu pravu* (Kiev, 1880); esp. 118–120 (the Military Statute did have influence in the eighteenth century).
28. Beccaria, *On Crimes,* 67; Marasinova, *"Zakon" i "grazhdanin,"* 67–119; Anisimov, *Elizaveta Petrovna,* 3rd ed. (Moscow, 2002); Marian Lipinsky, "*K istorii russkogo ugolovnogo prava 18 v.,*" ZhGiUP, vol. 15, no. 12 (Dec. 1885), 1–54; Omelchenko, *Zakonnaia monarkhia,* 297; PSZ-1, vol. 19, no. 13,516 (16 Oct. 1770) and no. 13,578 (13 Feb. 1772).
29. Omelchenko, *Zakonnaia monarkhia,* 76–79. On the *Nakaz* and Catherine's legislation generally, see also Omelchenko, *Vlast' i zakon;* G. S. Feldshtein, *Glavnye techenia v istorii nauki ugolovnogo prava v Rossii* (Yaroslavl', 1909); V. Vitt, *Ekaterina II kak kriminalistka* (St. Petersburg, 1910); S. Zarudnyi, *Beccaria o prestupleniakh i nakazaniiakh v sravnenii s glavoiu X-iu nakaza Ekateriny II i s sovremennymi russkimi zakonami* (St. Petersburg, 1879); Isabel de Madariaga, "Penal Policy in the Age of Catherine II," in *Politics and Culture in Eighteenth-Century Russia* (Routledge, 1998), 97–123. For the

complete text of the *Instruction,* including the early drafts, see N. D. Chechulin, ed., *Nakaz imperatritsy Ekateriny II . . .* (St. Petersburg, 1907).

30. Taranovsky, "*Politicheskaia doktrina v nakaze imperatritsy Ekateriny II,*" in M. N. Iasinsky, ed., *Sbornik statei po istorii prava posviaschennyi Mikhailu Flegontovichu Vladimirskomu-Budanovu* (Kiev, 1904), 44–86; *Instruction,* art. 67–79, 85–93, 32, 34, 35; Omelchenko, *Zakonnaia monarkhia,* 297; Omelchenko, "*Ugolovnaia politika prosveshchennogo absoliutizma: Razvitie rusksogo ugolovnogo prava vo vtoroi polovine XVIII v.,*" *Vlast' i zakon v Rossii XVIII veka* (Moscow, 2004): 162.
31. Ekaterina Pravilova, *A Public Empire: Property and the Quest for the Common Good in Imperial Russia* (Princeton: Princeton University Press, 2014).
32. Omelchenko, *Zakonnaia monarkhia,* 83; Omelchenko, "*Ugolovnaia politika,*" 175–179.
33. Klochkov, *Nakaz imperatritsy Ekateriny II,* 3–4; the degrees were issued on 13 November 1767 and 9 November 1774. V. M. Kleandrov et al., *Zakonodatelstvo Ekateriny II,* 2 vols. (Moscow, 2001): vol. 2, 914.
34. *Code,* arts. 213, 229, 230, 329, 310 (also 180 of the *Instruction*).
35. Anisimov, *Dyba i knut;* V. Ikonnikov, "*Stranitsa iz istorii ekaterininskogo nakaza (ob otmene pytki v Rossii),*" in *Chtenia v istoricheskom obshchestve Nestora-Letopistsa,* vol. 5 (Kiev, 1891): 11–35.
36. Klochkov, *Nakaz;* A. F. Kistiakovskii (Gorodisskii), "Vliianie Bekkaria na russkoe ugolovnoe pravo," ZhMIu, vol. 21, no. 9 (Sept. 1864), 459–470; Vitt, *Ekaterina II kak kriminalistka,* 55–66; Omelchenko, *Zakonnaia monarkhia,* 295.
37. Arkhipov, *Sistematizatsiia,* 31, Klochkov, *Nakaz;* PSZ-1, vol. 26, no. 19904 (5 June 1801), 8; PSZ-1, vol. 28, no. 21177 (28 Feb. 1804).
38. Bob Roshier, *Controlling Crime: The Classical Perspective in Criminology* (Chicago: Lyceum Books, 1989); Vold et al., *Theoretical Criminology,* esp. 22–25; Philip Schofield, "'The first steps rightly directed in the track of legislation": Jeremy Bentham on Cesare Beccaria's *Essay on Crimes and Punishments,*" *Diciottesimo Secolo* 4 (2019): 65–74; Schofield, "Jeremy Bentham and Nineteenth-Century English Jurisprudence," *JLH* 12, no. 1 (1991): 58–88. Reassessing Beccaria and Enlightenment criminology: Philip Jenkins, "Varieties of Enlightenment Criminology," *British Journal of Criminology* 24, no. 2 (1984): 112–130; Bentham, *An Introduction to the Principles of Morals and Legislation,* ed. J. H. Burns and H. L. A. Hart (Oxford: Clarendon Press, 1996) (first printed in 1780 and published in 1789).
39. Section references in the text follow Bentham, *An Introduction.*
40. H. L. A. Hart, *Essays on Bentham: Studies in Jurisprudence and Political Theory* (Oxford, 1982).
41. A. N. Pypin "*Russkie otnoshenia Bentama,*" in *Issledovania i stat'i po epokhe Aleksandra I,* vols. 1–3 (Petrograd, 1916–1918; originally published in VE 4, nos. 2 and 4): 108.
42. Borisova, "Publication as a Source of Law in Late Imperial Russia," in George Martyn, Anthony Musson, and Heikki Pihlajamaki, eds., *From the Judge's Arbitrium to the Legality Principle: Legislation as a Source of Law in Criminal Trials.* Comparative Studies in Continental and Anglo-American Legal History 31 (Berlin: Duncker und Humblot, 2013): 295–315.

43. Roger Bartlett, *The Bentham Brothers and Russia: The Imperial Russian Constitution and the St. Petersburg Panopticon* (London: University College London Press, 2022): 54; Pypin "*Russkie otnoshenia Bentama,*" 103, 28–29. See also Isaac Nakhimovsky, *Holy Alliance: The Liberal Idea of a Federal Europe after 1815* (Princeton, 2024).
44. A. G. Bezverkhov and V. S. Korosteliov, *Proekt ugolovnogo ulozhenia Rossiiskoi imperii 1813 goda* (Samara, 2013), 7 (the Bavarian code was consulted in Russia when preparing the 1813 draft); Tatjana Hörnle, "PJA von Feuerbach and his *Textbook of the Common Penal Law,*" in Markus D. Dubber, ed., *Foundational Texts in Modern Criminal Law* (Oxford, 2014): 119–140; Nethercott, *Russian Legal Culture,* 43; Paul Johann Anselm Feuerbach, *Lehrbuch des gemeinen in Deutschland geltenden Peinlichen Rechts* (Giessen: Heyer, 1801). The Russian translation: Pavel Ansel'm Feierbach, *Ugolovnoe pravo,* vol. 1 (St. Petersburg, 1810 [vol.1), 1811 [vol. 2), 1827 [vol. 3]); Feldshtein, *Glavnye techenia v istorii nauki ugolovnogo prava v Rossii,* 369–371.
45. Woloch, *The New Regime;* Peter Mandler, ed., *Liberty and Authority in Victorina Britain* (Oxford, 2006).
46. The first public political trial in imperial Russia was of Sergei Nechaev's followers in 1871. See Arseniev, "*Politicheskii protsess.*"
47. Engelstein, "Combined Underdevelopment," Arkhipov, *Sistematizatsia,* 124.
48. Beccaria, *On Crimes,* 24.
49. Stephen Lovell, Alena Ledeneva, and Andrei Rogachevskii, eds., *Bribery and Blat in Russia: Negotiating Reciprocity from the Middle Ages to the 1990s* (New York: St. Martin's Press, 2000); Pravilova, *Zakonnost' i prava lichnosti.*
50. Raeff, *The Well-Ordered Police State;* W. L. Burn, *The Age of Equipoise: A Study of the Mid-Victorian Generation* (New York: W. W. Norton, 1964), 132–231; Philip Harling, "The Powers of the Victorian State," in Mandler, ed., *Liberty and Authority,* 25–50, and Peter Baldwin, "The Victorian State in Comparative Perspective," in Mandler, ed., *Liberty and Authority,* 51–70; Joan Neuberger, "Popular Legal Cultures: The St. Petersburg *Mirovoi Sud,*" in Eklof et al., *Russia's Great Reforms:* 231–246; I. A. Popp, *Mirovoi sud v Permskoi gubernii* (Ekaterinburg, 2011); *Izbrannye stseny u mirovykh sudei v Peterburge i Moskve* (St. Petersburg, 1867); N. A. Petrovskii, ed., *Sbornik grazhdanskikh i ugolovnykh del, proizvodivshikhsia v S.-Peterburgskikh stolichnykh mirovykh uchrezhdeniiakh s 1868 po 1874 god* (St. Petersburg, 1874); A. E. Nos, *Mirovoi sud v Moskve: Ocherki razbiratelstva u mirovykh sudei,* vols. 1–2 (Moscow, 1869); S. V. Lonskaia, *Mirovaia iustitsia v Rossii* (Kaliningrad, 2000).
51. Martin, *Enlightened Metropolis;* PSZ-1, vol. 21, no. 15147 (3 Apr. 1781); Arkhipov, *Sistematizatsia,* 84; SZ (1857), XV/1, art. 2000.
52. Suzanne Desan, *The Family on Trial in Revolutionary France* (Berkeley: University of California Press, 2004): esp. 283–310; Rafe Blaufarb, *The Great Demarcation: The French Revolution and the Invention of Modern Property* (Oxford, 2016).
53. Wortman, *Scenarios of Power: Myth and Ceremony in Russian Monarchy, vol. 1: From Peter the Great to the Death of Nicholas I* (Princeton, 1995).
54. Pravilova, *A Public Empire.*
55. Murder: PSZ-2, vol. 46, no. 49395 (23 Mar. 1871); illegal groups: PSZ-2, vol. 49, no. 53,606 (1 June 1874); death penalty: PSZ-3, vol. 1, no. 198 (26 May 1881); minors:

PSZ-3, vol. 1, no. 483 (27 Oct. 1881); burglary: PSZ-3, vol. 2, no. 890 (18 May 1882), Arkhipov, *Sistematizatsia,* esp. 122; Balybin, "*Osnovnye tendentsii,*" 61–62.

56. *Materialy dlia peresmotra nashego ugolovnogo zakonodatelstva,* vols. 1–4 (St. Petersburg, 1880–1888). Torben Spaak and Patricia Mindus, *The Cambridge Companion to Legal Positivism* (Cambridge, 2021).
57. Zygmunt Bialkowski, "The Transformation of Academic Criminal Jurisprudence into Criminology in Late Imperial Russia", Ph.D. dissertation, University of California, Berkeley (2007).
58. Irina Reyfman, *Ritualized Violence Russian Style: The Duel in Russian Culture and Literature* (Stanford: Stanford University Press, 1999).

PART II. VIOLENCE

1. *Dvoinoe ubiistvo;* V. L-v, "*Tri ubiistva.*"
2. Gromnitskii, "*Iz proshlogo,*" 8.
3. Almost all the early jury trials were for petty theft. The 1866 Vereitinov case mentioned by McReynolds (*Murder Most Russian,* 63) was actually not a murder case. Rebinder did not contest his prosecution.
4. *Dvoinoe ubiistvo,* 103.
5. Norbert Elias, *The Civilizing Process,* 2 vols. (Oxford: Blackwell, 1969 and 1982); J. Carter Wood, *Violence and Crime in Nineteenth-Century England* (Routledge, 2004); Martin J. Wiener, *Men of Blood: Violence, Manliness, and Criminal Justice in Victorian England* (Cambridge, 2004); Eric A. Johnson and Eric H. Monkkonen, eds., *The Civilization of Crime: Violence in Town and Country since the Middle Ages* (Illinois, 1996); Louis Blom-Cooper and Terence Morris, *With Malice Aforethought: A Study of the Crime and Punishment for Homicide* (Oxford: Hart, 2004) (focusing on England); Tony Waters, *When Killing Is a Crime* (Boulder: Lynne Rienner, 2007).
6. Frank, *Crime, Cultural Conflict;* Gerasimov, *Plebeian Modernity;* Tsuyoshi Hasegawa, *Crime and Punishment in the Russian Revolution: Mob Justice and Police in Petrograd* (Cambridge: Belknap Press of Harvard University Press, 2017). See also Neuberger, *Hooliganism;* Reyfman, *Ritualized Violence.*
7. Émile Durkheim, *The Division of Labor in Society* (New York: Free Press, 1997) (originally published 1893); Stephen R. Marks, "Durkheim's Theory of Anomie," *American Journal of Sociology* 80, no. 2 (Sept. 1974): 329–363; Robert K. Merton, "Social Structure and Anomie," *American Sociological Review* 3, no. 5 (Oct. 1938), 672–682. Relying on the concept of *anomie:* Gerasimov, *Plebeian Modernity;* Hasegawa, *Crime and Punishment.*
8. Taranovskii, *Itogi.* His data are presented and discussed in English in Richard Sutton, "Crime and Social Change in Russia after the Great Reforms: Law, Courts, and Criminals, 1874–1894," Ph.D. dissertation, Indiana University (1984). The Russian government in the 1870s recorded between three thousand and four thousand cases of homicide (*ubiistvo*) per year, with only half of them going to trial, as well as a comparable number of violent robberies and assaults. *Itogi,* 286–287. Only a handful of them, like Danilov's case, attracted public attention and were reported in newspapers.

9. B. N. Mironov, *Sotsialnaia istoria Rossii perioda imperii (XVIII–nachalo XX v.)* (St. Petersburg, 2003): vol. 2, 78–96.
10. One possible cause of increasing conviction rates is improvement in police work, which earlier scholars have inaccurately dismissed out of hand (Sutton). But it's not simply a question of better or worse detection rates. We must consider such questions as how we define various offenses, whether prosecutors dismiss cases or bring lesser charges (cf. England), and any impact of long pretrial detentions.
11. Engelstein's *Keys to Happiness* analyzes Russian legal scholarship and fin-de-siècle popular literature on sexual crime but does not look at individual cases. McReynolds's *Murder Most Russian* is about elite reactions to murder cases (as revealed in the press, legal scholarship, and popular literature) rather than an analysis of the cases themselves.

CHAPTER 5. KILLING FOR PROPERTY

1. The significance of wealth and property is absent in McReynolds and Engelstein.
2. Pravilova, *A Public Empire.*
3. Highway robbery is another type.
4. Rebecca Friedman, *Masculinity, Autocracy, and the Russian University, 1804–1863* (Macmillan, 2005); Reyfman, *Ritualized Violence;* A. V. Katsura, *Duel v istorii Rossii* (Moscow, 2006); Marianna Muravyeva and Raisa Maria Toivo, eds., *Parricide and Violence against Parents Throughout History* (Macmillan, 2018); Muravyeva, "Between Law and Morality: Violence against Women in Nineteenth-Century Russia," in Wendy Rosslyn and Alessandra Tosi, eds., *Women in Nineteenth-Century Russia: Lives and Culture* (Cambridge: Open Book, 2012), 209–238.
5. Frank, *Crime, Cultural Conflict;* Gerasimov, *Plebeian Modernity.*
6. Enserfed peasants regularly murdered or attacked their masters as well. This is not to claim that serfdom provided a safer environment for the upper classes; quite the contrary: I am only claiming that the ideology of the superiority of free labor did not conform to the fact that the post-emancipation elite's daily existence was routinely exposed to deadly physical violence.
7. Although Sukhovo-Kobylin's case ended differently, it can be seen as Russia's equivalent to England's 1760 trial of Laurence Shirley, 4th Earl Ferrers, the last peer to be hanged.
8. *Dvoinoe ubiistvo,* 72.
9. *Dvoinoe ubiistvo,* 50.
10. *Dvoinoe ubiistvo,* 83.
11. "*Tri ubiistva,*" 321.
12. *Dvoinoe ubiistvo,* 83, and "*Tri ubiistva.*"
13. Antonov, *Bankrupts and Usurers,* 148–149.
14. Gromnitskii, *Iz proshlogo,* 15–16; "*Tri ubiistva.*"
15. SV, no. 252 (1867).
16. Gromnitskii, *Iz proshlogo.*
17. *Dvoinoe ubiistvo,* 80.
18. When criminal prosecution involved someone under the jurisdiction of a state agency (an army regiment, a university, a government office), this agency sent a representative to observe the investigation; *Dvoinoe ubiistvo,* 59.

19. *Dvoinoe ubiistvo,* 51. The fake address that he gave to Popov was so close to Danilov's real address that the police officers could have found him easily had they possessed better analytical skills.
20. SPbV, no. 183, 184, 190 (1879) (other issues missing); *Nedelia,* nos. 14, 15, 20 (1879); MV, no. 177 (1879); Koni, vol. 1, 148–166.
21. MV, no. 177 (1879) (Katkov criticizing this lenient sentence).
22. "ростовщику собачья смерть, он меня разорыл, нехай нене буде сыт чортов бис окаянный, нехай на том свити ему жарко буде" (*rostovshchiku sobachia smert', on menia razoryl, nekhai nene bude syt chortov bis okaiannyi, nekhai na tom sviti iemu zharko bude*). *Nedelia,* no. 45 (1878).
23. SV, no. 260 (29 Nov. 1867) and Nos, vol. 2, 4–5.
24. SV, no. 260 (29 Nov. 1867).
25. Nos, vol. 2, 16.
26. Zhdanov liquid consisted of *Ferii sulfurici crudi, aq. ferv., aceti pyrolig. crud., ol. Lavandalae. Entsiklopedicheskii slovar' Brokgauza i Efrona,* vol. 11(a) (St. Petersburg, 1894): 737.
27. *Ubiistvo devitsy Niny Erastovny Andreevskoi 22-go iiulia 1876 golda, v Tiflise* (Tiflis, 1878); "*Smert' G-zhi Andreevskoi*" *Tiflisskii vestnik,* nos. 166 and 171 (1876).
28. Igor Obolensky, ed., *Memuary freiliny imperatritsy* (Moscow, 2015) (memoirs of Baroness Natalia Nikolaevna Meiendorf).
29. Kozlinina, *Za polveka.* Such games are not surprising for a modern attorney, but in the 1870s personal integrity was considered of crucial importance, and one exceptionally talented lawyer and law professor, Lokhvitskii, was even driven out of Moscow because of the devious way he argued his cases.
30. *Sudebnye rechi izvestnykh russkikh iuristov,* vol. 3 (Moscow, 2009): 9–103.
31. *Nedelia,* no. 20 (1870); RGIA, f. 1405, op. 68, d. 3352; *Vsemirnaia illiustratsia,* no. 72 (1870), 357–358; Horace Humbold, *Recollections of a Diplomatist* (London: Edward Arnold, 1902).
32. RGIA f. 1405, op. 68, d. 3352.
33. Koni, vol. 3, 269–279.
34. MV, nos. 96–99 (5 and 7–9 May 1868), no. 100 (11 May 1868); Nikitenko, *Dnevnik,* v. 3, 125; GARF f. 109, op. 208, d. 90.
35. Although Zhemarin legally belonged to the merchant estate usually caricatured as backward and non-European, his lifestyle was typical of the way various propertied groups merged in the mid-nineteenth century into a "common culture of gentility." Kelly, *Refining Russia.* Aside from Zhemarin's shop, nothing in his family's life appears to be different from the family of a civil servant or a landowner away from his or her estate; his wife was referred to as "*barynia,*" the term supposedly reserved for noblewomen.
36. GARF f. 109, op. 208, d. 90, l. 17.
37. GARF f. 109, op. 208, d. 90, l. 37.
38. GARF f. 109, op. 208, d. 90, l. 37.
39. On evaluating the Poles' political loyalty, see Mikhail Dolbilov, "'*Poliak' v imperskom politicheskom leksikone,*" in Aleksei Miller, Denis Sdvizhkov, and Ingrid Schierle, eds., "*Poniatiia o Rossii": K istoricheskoi semantike imperskogo perioda,* in 2 vols. (Moscow, 2012): vol. 2: 292–339, esp. 316–321.

40. There are several errors in McReynolds' brief description of the case, including the claim that he was hanged. *Murder Most Russian,* 74.
41. GARF f. 109, op. 208, d. 90, l. 24.
42. GARF f. 109, op. 208, d. 90, l. 26.
43. GARF f. 109, op. 208, d. 90, l. 44.
44. The trial was on 19–22 December 1872.
45. SV, nos. 7–8 (11–12 Jan. 1873).
46. SV, nos. 7–8 (11–12 Jan. 1873).
47. SV, nos. 18–23 (1869); D. Lutkov, ed., *Sbornik svedenii, raz'iasniaiushchikh primenenie na praktike Ulozhenia o Nakazaniiakh* (Moscow, 1872), 13.
48. The Gusev Alley was later renamed after Uliana Gromova.
49. McReynolds, *Murder Most Russian,* 2, argues that the Gusev Alley was "a test case for exploring how Russians would adapt to the reform of their legal system in 1864." It is not possible to agree with McReynolds that Sokolova's lawyer was "incorrect." *Murder Most Russian,* 6. Rather, the court and then the Senate stretched the statute to make sure Sokolova was punished. Thus, if this was a "test" of the jury system, in the courts' eyes it had clearly failed.
50. Lutkov, ed., *Sbornik svedenii,* 13.
51. Gerasimov, *Plebeian Modernity.* The point of Turgenev's story is of course that his Gerasim did *not* choose violence.

CHAPTER 6. STRIKING FOR HONOR

1. Berenson, *The Trial of Madame Caillaux.*
2. SV, nos. 47–53 (1874); Bazunov and Margulies, *Vydaiushchiiesia,* 124–153; Koni, vol. 3, 279–306; "*Neobyknovennaia istoriia obyknovennykh liudei (Nepeninskoe delo),*" *Nedelia,* no. 10 (1874).
3. William Reddy, *The Invisible Code: Honor and Sentiment in Postrevolutionary France, 1814–1848* (Berkeley, 1997), 24; Robert A. Nye, *Masculinity and Male Codes of Honor in Modern France* (Berkeley, 1993); Bertram Wyatt-Brown, *Southern Honor: Ethics and Behavior in the Old South* (Oxford, 1982); Friedman, *Masculinity, Autocracy.*
4. Umphrey, "The Dialogics of Legal Meaning."
5. Frank, *Crime, Cultural Conflict;* Burbank, *Russian Peasants.*
6. Elite notions and practices are particularly well studied by historians of nineteenth-century Europe. Honor was also central to subordinated groups, however, whether merchants or, in the Russian context, enserfed peasants, who were very much willing to defend their honor even against their masters, whether through violence or through the law. Kollmann, *Crime and Punishment.*
7. By contrast, in the French Caillaux case, Madame Caillaux avenged the libel of her husband by the victim, that is, an offense that was not directly related to her own honor.
8. V. P. Bykova, *Zapiski staroi smolianki* (St. Petersburg, 1898).
9. Katherine Pickering Antonova, *An Ordinary Marriage: The World of a Gentry Family in Provincial Russia* (Oxford, 2013); Michelle Lamarche Marrese, *A Woman's Kingdom: Noblewomen and the Control of Property in Russia, 1700–1861* (Cornell, 2002); John Randolph, *The House in the Garden: The Bakunin Family and the Romance of Russian*

Idealism (Cornell, 2007). The victim Chikhachev was only a distant relation to the Chikhachevs who are the focus of Antonova's study.

10. Reyfman, *Ritualized Violence.*
11. A notable early case was the drunken tavern fight in Petersburg that left the Riga citizen Vagond dead. SV, no. 86 (15 Sept. 1865).
12. Letter from witness Tsereshkevich. SV, no. 52 (9 Mar. 1874).
13. Yulia Safronova, *Ekaterina Yurievskaia: Roman v pismakh* (St. Petersburg, 2017): 57–65.
14. "*Neobyknovennaia istoriia.*"
15. Olga Makarova, "*'Sud'ba kakim-to rokovym obrazom stavit menia poperek Vashei dorogi . . .': 'Delo Kairovoi' i ego sled v biografii A.S. Suvorina . . .,*" *Novoe literaturnoe obozrenie,* 2005, no. 5.
16. McReynolds, *Murder Most Russian,* 72; RSO, vol. 3, 354–394.
17. Crimes against the state at that time were to be tried by a special tribunal of senators, known as the Osoboe prisutstvie Pravitelstvuiushchego Senata. The proceedings could be public or closed, and there were not juries; but defendants were allowed full representation by counsel.
18. The fact that the jury took very little time to acquit (from ten to thirty minutes in different accounts) suggests that it did not fully engage with the facts of the case. Among the reasons for acquittal all other scholars note the way Koni conducted the trial: he admitted witnesses who exposed Trepov's arbitrariness and explicitly suggested to the jurors that they could acquit Zasulich. But had this been the key factor, one would have expected the jury to spend more time deliberating, since they would need to discuss somewhat subtle hints and doctrines. It is also possible—indeed, likely—that the jurors were fully aware of the political nature of the case and of the large crowd of protesters gathered outside the court building and were simply in fear for their safety. In this case, they may have used the popular perceptions of women's honor killings then current as a sort of convenient cover story for their quick verdict, hence the rumors of a relationship between Zasulich and Trepov. On Zasulich, see note 48 in the Introduction.
19. Aleksandrovich's revolver did not go off because she forgot to remove the stopper out of the barrel. For other examples of complicated or subverted gender norms and practices in Russia, see Antonova, *An Ordinary Marriage;* Engel, *Breaking the Ties;* Jessica Tovrov, *The Russian Noble Family: Structure and Change* (New York: Garland, 1987).
20. Soloviev, *Khoziain zemli russkoi.*
21. On the forensic examination of Protopopov, see Becker, *Medicine,* 325–337.
22. RUP/1, 207–294; SV, no. 68 (1866); SPbV, esp. no. 85 (1867).
23. See, e.g., Lieutenant-General Belograskii in the 1840s: RGIA f. 1405, op. 534, d. 373; Senate personnel in the 1880s.
24. RUP/1, 208.
25. The conflict in this case was not between a willful crime of honor and involuntary affect (as per McReynolds, *Murder Most Russian,* 59), but between two types of circumstances that took away one's volition to abstain from violence: one was the strictures of honor and the other—emotions and affect.

26. Which is not the same as a "consensual jurisprudence" hypothesized by Girish N. Bhat in "The Consensual Dimension."
27. RUP/1, 237.
28. RUP/1, 240–242.
29. RUP/I, 243–246.
30. ZhGiUP 1873, no. 2, 209–236; *Nedelia,* 1873, no. 8 (25 Feb.); SV, 1873, no. 32; RSO, vol. 4, 150–200.
31. RSO, vol. 4, 151 and 166.
32. RSO, vol. 4, 153.
33. P. A. Shveikovskii, ed., *Sud obshchestva ofitserov i duel' v voiskakh rossiiskoi armii* (St. Petersburg, 1898).
34. RSO, vol. 4, 152.
35. RSO, vol. 4, 188.
36. RSO, vol. 4, 200.

CHAPTER 7. FALSE PATRIARCHS

1. Nye, *Masculinity;* Jerrold Seigel, *Modernity and Bourgeois Life: Society, Politics, and Culture in England, France, and Germany since 1750* (Cambridge, 2012).
2. Richard Stites, *The Women's Liberation Movement in Russia: Feminism, Nihilism, and Bolshevism, 1860–1930* (Princeton, 1978), 29; see also Engel, *Mothers and Daughters.*
3. Case, *The Age of Questions.*
4. Engel, *Mothers and Daughters;* Engelstein, *Keys to Happiness;* Stites, *The Women's Liberation.*
5. Engelstein, *Keys to Happiness,* 11; Engel, *Mothers and Daughters,* McReynolds, *Murder Most Russian.*
6. Friedman, *Masculinity,* Engelstein, *Keys to Happiness,* Engel, *Mothers and Daughters.*
7. Jack Goody, *The Theft of History* (Cambridge, 2007).
8. Engel, *Women in Russia, 1700–2000* (Cambridge, 2004).
9. SZ, X/1; N. S. Nizhnik, *Pravovoe regulirovanie semeino-brachnykh otnoshenii v russkoi istorii* (St. Petersburg, 2006); Engel, *Breaking the Ties.*
10. Desan, *Family on Trial;* David I. Kertzer and Marzio Barbagli, eds., *Family Life in the Long Nineteenth Century, 1789–1913* (Yale, 2002).
11. Margot Finn, "Women, Consumption and Coverture in England, c. 1760–1860," *Historical Journal* 39, no. 3 (Sept. 1996): 703–722.
12. Marrese, *A Woman's Kingdom;* Antonova, *An Ordinary Marriage;* Ulianova, *Female Entrepreneurs.*
13. Marrese, *A Woman's Kingdom.*
14. Engel, *Breaking the Ties.*
15. Kozlinina, *Za polveka,* 215–216.
16. Schrader, *The Languages of the Lash.*
17. Completing the first four grades of school conferred the privilege of being exempt from any more beatings.
18. SPbV, no. 24 (24 Jan. 1876).
19. *Pokazania i zapiski o pol'skom vosstanii 1863 goda* (Moscow, 1961), 415, 530, 561.

20. GARF f. 109, op. 3a, d. 2898.
21. Murav, *Russia's Legal Fictions.*
22. SPbV, no. 24.
23. F. M. Dostoevskii, *Polnoe sobranie sochinenii,* 30 vols. (Leningrad, 1976): vol. 22, 50–73.
24. SpbV, no. 24 (Jan. 24, 1876).
25. SpbV, no. 25 (1876).
26. She had been trained in Switzerland and was married to a Swiss physician. Her sister was Appolinaria Suslova, Dostoevsky's lover who was the prototype for the heroine in his novella *The Gambler.*
27. SpbV, no. 25 (1876).
28. SpbV, no. 24 (24 Jan. 1876).
29. *Nedelia,* 1876, nos. 3–5 (1876): 146.
30. Schur, *The Letters and the Law.*
31. Art. 138 of the code referred to domestic punishment, but only in the context of punishing underage offenders; domestic punishment was not defined; there are more provisions on parental authority in volume X/1 of SZ, but it was civil law and thus did not include penal sanctions.
32. SpbV, no. 28 (1876).
33. *Nedelia,* nos. 3–5 (1876).
34. The Domostroi was a manual of household management and advice.
35. This is what Laura Engelstein writes about in *The Keys to Happiness,* but she places the emergence of all this discussion at a much later period.
36. *Nedelia,* nos. 3–5 (1876).
37. SV, 1876, no. 20 (25 Jan.).
38. "*Otrezannyi lomot,*'" OZ 225, no. 3 (1876): 154–170.
39. SpbV, no. 28 (1876).
40. I. V. Gessen, *Istoria russkoi advokatury,* vol. 1 (Moscow, 1914): 200–206; Schur, *The Letters and the Law;* Murav, *Russia's Legal Fictions;* Rosenshield, *Dostoevsky and the Law.*
41. Nos, vol. 2, 58–100.
42. Nos, vol. 2, 61.
43. Nos, vol. 2, 76–77.
44. Nos, vol. 2, 83.
45. Nos, vol. 2, 86.
46. Another important and controversial case of extreme domestic abuse was that of Natalia Bulach, accused of tormenting the teenage merchant heiress Anna Mazurina (first cousin of the Vasilii Mazurin discussed in chapter 5). See transcript in MV, nos. 137–142 (1884). See the excellent study criticizing Bulach's conviction by Andrei Novozhilov and Nina Belozherova, *Delo Mazurinoi—Bulach. Apologia.* https://novbelgen.net/article_11_Gamonova (last accessed 15 Nov. 2025).
47. IRLI f. 134, op. 4, d. 218.
48. IRLI f. 135, op. 4, d. 227.
49. IRLI f. 134, op. 4, d. 264.

50. The published version does not provide last names of the persons involved. Koni, vol. 1, 106–109 (orig. *RS* 1908 no. 11: 299–302). The names are given, however, in Koni's unpublished draft. IRLI f. 134 (A. F. Koni), op. 1, d. 5, l. 71–74 ob.
51. *Nedelia,* no. 10 (1874).
52. *Nedelia,* no. 11 (1874).
53. Koni, vol. 3, 281.
54. SV, no. 52, 9 Mar.
55. *Nedelia,* no. 14 (1870); SV, no. 85 (29 Mar. 1870) (subsequent issues were not available); Spasovich, *Sochinenia,* vol. 5, 122–134; Vladimir Spasovich, *Za mnogo let, 1859–1871* (St. Petersburg, 1872): 378–385; Bhat, *Trial by Jury,* 170–177.
56. Spasovich, *Za mnogo let,* 378.
57. Spasovich, *Za mnogo let,* 385.
58. Koni, *Sobranie,* vol. 3, 412.
59. SpbV, nos. 306–312 and 315 (1878).
60. B. N. Grigoriev and B. G. Kolokolov, *Povsednevnaia zhizn' rossiiskikh zhandarmov* (Moscow, 2007); Z. I. Peregudova, ed., *"Okhranka." Vospominania rukovoditelei politicheskogo syska,* 2 vols. (Moscow, 2004).
61. SpbV, no. 315 (1878).
62. In a moment of lucidity Poznanskii would free Aleksei Peshkov from arrest in 1889 and urge that he pursue a writer's career rather than a revolutionary's. Peshkov, later known as Maksim Gorky, followed this advice, but did not thereby do any favors to the regime. Maksim Gorky, "Vremia Korolenko," *Sobranie sochinenii,* vol. 15 (Moscow, 1951), 9–10.
63. Koni preserved Jujean's letters in his personal archive. IRLI, f. 134, op. 4, d. 250.
64. SpbV, no. 315 (15 Nov. 1878).
65. SpbV, no. 307 (7 Nov. 1878).
66. Koni, vol. 1, 171.
67. SpbV, no. 310 (10 Nov. 1878)
68. SpbV, no. 311 (11 Nov. 1878).
69. *Nedelia,* 1878, no. 47.
70. Koni, vol. 1, 176; SpbV, no. 311 (1878).
71. Koni, vol. 1, 174; SpbV, no. 308 (1878).
72. SpbV, no. 309 (1878).
73. SPV, no. 316 (16 Nov. 1878).
74. Koni, vol. 1, 167–191 (esp. 178–181, discussing the French model of the trial summation that was familiar to Jujean), and vol. 3, 412–427.

PART III. DECEPTION

1. *Klub chervonnykh valetov.* Another version of the transcript is RSO, vol. 3, 114–353; see also Kozlinina, *Za polveka,* 250–276.
2. The charge of criminal conspiracy meant that even minor defendants faced harsh punishment.
3. The most detailed version of this legend is found in V. A. Giliarovsky, *Moskva i moskvichi* (Moscow, 1989).

4. S. Z. Moshenskii, *Rynok tsennykh bumag Rossiiskoi imperii* (Moscow: Ekonomika, 2014).
5. William M. Meier, "Aristocrats of Crime: Confidence Men in the Interwar Years," in *Property Crime in London, 1850–Present* (Macmillan, 2011), 85–108; Sarah Wilson, "Law, Morality and Regulation: Victorian Experiences of Financial Crime," *British Journal of Criminology* 46 (2006): 1073–90.
6. SpbV, no. 28 (1877).
7. Kozlinina, *Za polveka,* 249.
8. Murders tended to be committed quickly and in only one episode. Political cases had many defendants but not many witnesses, and their factual circumstances were not very complex.

CHAPTER 8. THE AGE OF FRAUD

1. Some material from this chapter appeared in Sergei Antonov, "Russian Capitalism on Trial: The Case of the Jacks of Hearts," *LHR* 36 (2018): 35–76, reproduced here with permission.
2. The case was reported to the public in a way that evokes Foucault's idea of heterotopia, that is, a discrete cultural practice that may or may not be socially subversive, but that functions spatially alongside or within the mainstream order. Christopher Ely has used heterotopia to investigate the culture of Russia's revolutionary underground in his *Underground Petersburg: Radical Populism, Urban Space, and the Tactics of Subversion in Reform-Era Russia* (Illinois, 2016): 23–28.
3. Signs and performances of respectability in Victorian England could be viewed with suspicion as having "hidden affinities" with fraud. Martin Wiener, *Reconstructing the Criminal: Culture, Law, and Policy in England, 1830–1914* (Cambridge, 1990): 244–256.
4. Blaufarb, *The Great Demarcation;* Omelchenko, *"Zakonnaia monarkhia."*
5. This does not mean, as some scholars have argued, that Russia did not have private property rights before Catherine; rather, the notion of absolute rights as a practical development was still new even in the mid-nineteenth century. On limited property rights, see Pipes, *Russia,* and Lee A. Farrow, *Between Clan and Crown: The Struggle to Define Noble Property Rights in Imperial Russia* (Newark: University of Delaware Press, 2004). The opposite view is in Pravilova, *A Public Empire,* and Antonov, *Bankrupts and Usurers.* On property rights in early modern Russia, see George G. Weickhardt, "The Pre-Petrine Law of Property," *Slavic Review* 52 (1993): 663–679, and Weickhardt, "Due Process and Equal Justice in the Muscovite Codes," *Russian Review* 51 (1992): 463–480.
6. William G. Wagner, *Marriage, Property, and Law in Late Imperial Russia* (Oxford, 1994); Marrese, *A Woman's Kingdom;* Farrow, *Between Clan and Crown;* Dennison, *The Institutional Framework.*
7. Antonov, *Bankrupts and Usurers,* 133–158.
8. Sally Simpson and David Weisburd, eds., *The Criminology of White-Collar Crime* (New York: Springer, 2009); Robb, *White-Collar Crime;* Phil Handler, "Forgery and the End of the 'Bloody Code' in Early Nineteenth-Century England," *Historical Journal* 48 (2005): 683–702.

9. On Russia's radical heterotopia, see Ely, *Underground Petersburg.* Political activists occupied the same physical spaces as the legitimate world but stood out by their social connections and (at least in the earlier period) by their manners and dress. Violent criminals were conceptualized as members of the lower classes and were distinguished by manners, language, and physical location. This is not to forget that respectable persons (men especially) routinely used violence, including sexual violence, on their family, servants, and peasants, and it is misleading to conceive of the upper-class world as more polite or less violent. As to nonviolent crime, we must remember that the emancipation of the serfs centered on a division of land allotment that on balance benefited the nobles at the expense of their peasants and can be seen as one of the largest frauds in Russian history.
10. *Klub,* 1–5.
11. Bourdieu, *The State Nobility,* esp. 261–339.
12. On the famous Anglo-Russian swindler of the Napoleonic era, see E. A. Stogov, "*Roman Medoks,*" *RS* 28 (1880): 791–793; A. Zisserman, "*Samozvanets Medoks,*" *RS* 35 (1882): 620–624.
13. *Klub,* 164.
14. Dmitrii Zasetskii, Nikolai Kalustov, and Nikolai Dmitriev-Mamonov. All three were passing worthless debt paper. *Klub,* 19–21, 48.
15. Valentina Borisova, "'*Chervonnyi valet' A. T. Neofitov iz okruzhenia F.M. Dostoevskogo.*" *Neizvestnyi Dostoevsky,* no. 1 (2020): 156–167.
16. GARF, f. 109, op. 3a, d. 377.
17. GARF 109.3a.2886 (mentioning other high-ranking generals and officials who took money in exchange for officially marrying a former sex worker); see also M. O. Meltsin, "*Avtor odnogo iz pervykh putevoditelei po Novgorodu,*" in *Novgorodika-2006: Materialy nauchnoi konferentsii* (Novgorod, 2007), 257–64 (I am grateful to Maksim Olegovich Meltsin for providing me with a copy of his article); and *Klub,* 39–40.
18. V. M. Kostin et al., eds., *Vsevolod Alekseevich Dolgorukov: Sbornik materialov* (Tomsk, 2013).
19. GARF, f. 123, op. 2, d. 606, ll. 3 ob. and 12. There were fifty-five nobles among 2,704 individuals detained for begging in Moscow in 1850, long before many nobles lost their income as a result of the 1861 serf emancipation.
20. Discussing the culture of fraud in the United States, Edward Balleisen also mentions the importance of "the marketing power of location" and "[m]ore subtle techniques of emulation [and] the trappings of commercial success" in addition to acting ability. Balleisen, *Fraud,* 26–27.
21. *Klub,* 207.
22. *Klub,* 6–10.
23. *Klub,* 46, 141.
24. For an earlier discussion (pertaining mostly to the pre-reform period) of the social and family networks that enabled retail and credit fraud, see Antonov, *Bankrupts and Usurers,* 149–157.
25. Edwin Sutherland, *White Collar Crime* (New York: Dryden Press, 1949).
26. Ostensibly lenient treatment—for instance, firing offenders or otherwise dealing with them informally instead of prosecuting them—could be in fact every bit as punitive.

J. P. Locker, "'Quiet Thieves, Quiet Punishment': Private Responses to the 'Respectable' Offender, c. 1850–1930," *Crime, histoire et sociétés* 9 (2005): 9–31.

27. On sociability in imperial Russia, see Martin, *Enlightened Metropolis;* Antonova, *An Ordinary Marriage;* Catherine Evtuhov, *Portrait of a Russian Province: Economy, Society, and Civilization in Nineteenth-Century Nizhnii Novgorod* (Pittsburgh: University of Pittsburgh Press, 2011; David Ransel, *A Russian Merchant's Tale: The Life and Adventures of Ivan Alekseevich Tolchënov, Based on His Diary* (Indiana, 2008); and Mary Cavender, *Nests of the Gentry: Family, Estate, and Local Loyalties in Provincial Russia* (Newark: University of Delaware Press, 2007).
28. *Klub,* 145.
29. *Klub,* 71.
30. RSO, vol. 5, 457.
31. *Delo Miasnikovykh,* 117. See chapter 3 above.
32. RGIA f. 560, op. 19, d. 200. The quote is from l. 95 ob.
33. Frithjof Benjamin Schenk, *Russlands Fahrt in die Moderne: Mobilität und sozialer Raum im Eisenbahnzeitalter* (Stuttgart: Franz Steiner, 2014); Wolfgang Schivelbusch, *The Railway Journey: The Industrialization of Time and Space in the Nineteenth Century* (Berkeley, 2014).
34. There are popular-culture publications that quote from archival sources and even show photos of some document pages and of Son'ka herself, but they do not provide citations. The full transcript of Son'ka's 1880s trial was published at the time, but the only copy potentially accessible to the public was listed in the catalogue of St. Petersburg's Public Library, whose employees unconvincingly claimed in 2019 that it had been lost.
35. Nikolai Nadezhdin, *Son'ka zolotaia ruchka—koroleva vorov* (Rostov-na-Donu, 2012).
36. *Klub,* 36, 48, 206.
37. *Delo Mitrofanii,* II/2 and 98.
38. *Klub,* 214, 227–228, 343.
39. *Klub,* 58–59, 228.
40. *Klub,* 8–12.
41. *Klub,* 246, 261–262, 341.
42. *Klub,* 335.
43. Kozlinina, *Za polveka,* 262–263.
44. SpbV, no. 44 (1877).
45. Grigorii Dzhanshiev, *Osnovy sudebnoi reformy (k 25ti-letiu novogo suda)* (Moscow, 1891), 209.
46. MV, no. 60 (1877).
47. *Klub,* 245.
48. *Klub,* 161.
49. Kozlinina, *Za polveka,* 180.
50. See, e.g., Koni, *"Vospominaniia o dele V. N. Zasulich";* Troitskii, *Tsarizm pod sudom.*
51. Frank, *Crime, Cultural Conflict;* for interpretations of crime as an aspect of Russia's modernity, see McReynolds, *Murder Most Russian;* and Neuberger, *Hooliganism.*
52. Karen Halttunen, *Confidence Men and Painted Women: A Study of Middle-Class America, 1830–1870* (Yale, 1986).

53. K. M. Staniukovich, "*Chervonnyi valet,*" in *Sobraniie sochinenii v 10 tomakh,* vol. 1 (Moscow, 1977): 44–78.
54. On Speier, see Kozlinina, *Za polveka,* 250–53.
55. Nikolai A. Troitskii, *Tsarskie sudy protiv revoliutsionnoi Rossii: Politicheskie protsessy 1871–1880 gg* (Saratov, 1976), 60. On social and ideological impacts of political radicalism and terrorism in the 1870s see also, e.g., Yulia Safronova, *Russkoe obshchestvo v zerkale revoliutsionnogo terrora: 1879–1881 gody* (Moscow: NLO, 2014); Ely, *Underground Petersburg;* and Oleg Budnitskii, *Terrorizm v rossiiskom osvoboditel'nom dvizhenii: Ideologia, etika, psikhologia (vtoraia polovia XIX–nachalo XX v.)* (Moscow: ROSSPEN, 2000).
56. Kozlinina, *Za polveka,* 240–241.
57. *Klub,* 201 and 232.
58. SpbV, no. 67 (1877). "*Ischadie*" was and is more commonly used in the phrase "*ischadie ada*" (the progeny of hell).
59. *Klub,* 249.
60. TsIAM, f. 142, op. 3, d. 242 (*Predvaritel'noe sledstvie* . . .).
61. *Klub,* 402.
62. SPbV, no. 28 (28 Jan. 1876).
63. Nikitenko, *Dnevnik,* vol. 3, 336.
64. SpbV, no. 44 (1877).
65. *Klub,* 174.
66. *Klub,* 434–435.
67. Antonov, *Bankrupts and Usurers.*
68. SpbV, nos. 13 and 44 (1877).
69. Gromnitskii, *Iz proshlogo.*
70. Code, art. 1637; could have threats and violence but without danger to life or health.
71. Liutetskii, 45–47.
72. SZ, XV/1, art. 702 (limited to "market or any other crowded place").
73. Code, art. 1665 (1866 ed.).
74. Foinitskii, *Moshennichestvo,* part 2, 2–5.
75. Kozlinina, *Za Polveka,* 146–149.
76. A. V. Lokhvitskii, *Kurs ugolovnogo prava* (St. Petersburg, 1871), 679.
77. Balleisen, *Fraud.*
78. Prominent trials problematizing the concept of fraud included that of the general's widow Henrietta Khomutova and Yanina and Wenceslaus Kossow (SV, no. 97, 7 May 1869); and that of the Shishkin spouses, whose attorney, Spasovich, unsuccessfully tried to promote the idea that fraud (*moshennichestvo*) is applicable only in a commercial or at least transactional setting. Spasovich, *Sochinenia,* vol. 5, 35–64.
79. *Klub,* 406–409.
80. *Klub,* 406–408.
81. *Klub,* 411.
82. Pavel Kosach's publication was entitled *Koliaska ili Blagodariu, ne ozhidal! Na pamiat' vesem sluchaino popavshim pod ugolovnoe presledovanie za neistpolenie slovesnykh dogovorov kupli-prodazhi, izdanie kandidata prav Kosacha* (St. Petersburg, 1872)

(A carriage or thank you, I did not expect this! For good memory to all who accidentally end up under criminal prosecution for failing to perform a verbal agreement of purchase and sale, a publication by candidate of the laws, Kosach).

83. *Delo Mitrofanii,* II/43.
84. *Klub,* 1, 173.
85. *Delo Mitrofanii,* 270.
86. Code, arts. 922–931 (1866 ed.).
87. The Decembrists' trial by the Supreme Criminal Court in 1826 was larger, but it was a bureaucratic tribunal and not a trial in its ordinary meaning.
88. Despite some later misinformed rumors to the contrary. Also, one of the defendants, Davydovskii, was married to an important revolutionary, Elizaveta Dmitrieva, who may have been duped by him, as were many others.
89. Koni, *Sobranie,* vol. 2, 33.
90. Dzhanshiev, *Osnovy,* 209.
91. *Delo Mitrofanii,* II/179; Karabchevskii, *Okolo pravosudia,* 154; *Delo Gartunga,* 238, 306.
92. *Klub,* 216.
93. *Klub,* 122.
94. MV, no. 60 (1877); Koni, *Sobranie,* vol. 2, 33; Kozlinina, *Za polveka.,* 242; Dzhanshiev, *Osnovy,* 209.
95. "*Shaika chervonnykh valetov,*" *Nedelia,* no. 9 (1877): 300.
96. Quoted in Troitskii, *Tsarskie sudy,* 197.
97. *Klub,* 201.
98. *Klub,* 192ff.
99. *Klub,* 183–184.
100. *Klub,* 180.
101. *Klub,* 56–59.
102. *Klub,* 15–16, 37–39, 45, 107–110. See also Antonov, "Russian Capitalism on Trial," 47.
103. *Klub,* 26–36, 223.

CHAPTER 9. THE ART OF FORGERY

1. John LeDonne, "Indirect Taxes in Catherine's Russia II: The Liquor Monopoly," *Jahrbücher für Geschichte Osteuropas,* new series, 24, no. 2 (1976): 173–207; David Christian, "A Neglected Great Reform: The Abolition of Tax Farming in Russia," in *Russia's Great Reforms,* 102–114.
2. *Delo Miasnikovykh,* 41.
3. Marrese, *A Woman's Kingdom*; Farrow, *Between Clan and Crown.*
4. K. A. Nevolin, *Polnoe sobranie sochinenii* (St. Petersburg, 1858): vol. 5, 319.
5. Olga Pavlenko, "Overcoming Uncertainty: Moscow Merchants' Wealth and Inheritance in the Second Half of the Nineteenth Century," Ph.D. dissertation, European University Institute (2020): 243.
6. Jon Stobart and Alastair Owens, *Urban Fortunes: Property and Inheritance in the Town, 1700–1900* (Routledge, 2000); John Habakkuk, *Marriage, Debt, and the Estate System: English Landownership, 1650–1950* (Oxford: Clarendon Press, 1994).

7. M. L. Gavlin, "*Rol' vinnykh otkupov v formirovanii krupnykh kapitalov v Rossii. Konets XVIII–XIX v.*" *Ekonomicheskaia istoria. Obozrenie,* ed. L. I. Borodkin, no. 6 (Moscow, 2001): 98–102; V. A. Grigorkin, "*Rol' vinnykh otkupov v formirovanii nachalnogo kapitala rossiiskogo predprinimatelstva XIX v.: na primere D.E. Benardaki,*" *Ekonomicheskaia istoria* 17, no. 4 (2021): 342–348.
8. It is clear that the actual death of a wealthy person was only one step in the process of property transfer, and it would not be surprising that some documentation would end up being backdated in the manner of a legal fiction.
9. Delo Miasnikovykh, 106. GARF f. 109.3a.2784, esp. l. 4 (Izhboldin's lawyer was an "infamous scoundrel, for whom fraudulent tricks were his sole way to earn a living").
10. *Delo Miasnikovykh,* 108–109 (disgraced former employees Kempe and Krasilnikov were among the sources of the rumors on which the indictment was based).
11. *Delo Miasnikovykh,* 300, 321–322, 411–412 (Arseniev arguing that handwriting analysis is not reliable in principle). He also argued that if Karaganov could in fact imitate handwriting, the Miasnikovs would not have him anywhere near their business. *Delo Miasnikovykh,* 42, 300.
12. *Delo Miasnikovykh,* 336–349.
13. Cf. OZ, 1872, no. 3, 81.
14. *Delo Miasnikovykh,* 227.
15. Koni, "*Priemy i zadachi prokuratury,*" in *Sobranie,* vol. 4, 121–200, 165–170.
16. *Delo Miasnikovykh,* 336.
17. OZ, 1872, no. 3, 83 (the final phrase is not found in the published transcript).
18. *Delo Miasnikovykh,* 264.
19. *Delo Miasnikovykh,* 149.
20. *Delo Miasnikovykh,* 263–264.
21. *Delo Miasnikovykh,* 287.
22. *Delo Miasnikovykh,* 227.
23. OZ, 1872, no. 3, 78.
24. *Delo Miasnikovykh,* 82–84.
25. *Delo Miasnikovykh,* 256–257.
26. OZ, 1872, no. 3, 80.
27. *Delo Miasnikovykh,* 117ff.; Ark. Korovin, "*Parizhskii kommunar v Turinske,*" *Uralskii sledopyt,* 1973, no. 3, 43.
28. RSO, vol. 5, 394–483, 410–411.
29. RSO, vol. 5, 402, 423.
30. RSO, vol. 5, 413.
31. RSO, vol. 5, 413.
32. RSO, vol. 5, 468.
33. RSO, vol. 5, 469.
34. RSO, vol. 5, 481–482.
35. RSO, vol. 5, 411.
36. RSO, vol. 5, 413.
37. Klevezal later commanded a regiment during the Russo-Turkish War of 1877–1878 and was infamously captured by the enemy with many of his soldiers.

38. RSO, vol. 5, 409–410.
39. RSO, vol. 5, 413–416.
40. RSO, vol. 5, 447, 468, 477.
41. RSO, vol. 5, 468.
42. RSO, vol. 5, 424.
43. RSO, vol. 5, 441.
44. RSO, vol. 5, 447.
45. RSO, vol. 5, 444.
46. RSO, vol. 5, 457.
47. She managed buildings and properties worth 536,000 rubles and had confirmed donations for 275,000, while her debts amounted to 301,000. See *Delo Mitrofanii,* I/62.
48. "The practice of *khod[a]taistvo,* ambivalent but customary in the first half of the nineteenth century, was criminalized before the court, and became reinterpreted as bribery (*podkup*)." Dahlke, "Old Russia in the Dock," 111. This statement would accurately describe the meaning of another prominent trial—that of the Moscow Commercial Loan Bank in 1876 (discussed in the next chapter), but the Mitrofania case focused on the related but different crimes of fraud and forgery.
49. Dahlke, "Old Russia in the Dock," 110–111.
50. *Delo Mitrofanii,* I/112–113.
51. Koni, vol. 1, 64–73; Demert, *Matushka Mitrofania;* Dahlke, "Old Russia in the Dock," 112 (found evidence against Mitrofania "overwhelming").
52. As noted in chapter 3, the best defense lawyers had turned her down.
53. Kozlinina, *Za polveka,* 184–206.
54. Originally the Ministry of Justice wanted to include five episodes but dropped two of them (with merchant Makarov and "Jew Sangursky" as the victims). RGIA, 1405.534.1073, l. 3.
55. *Delo Mitrofanii,* I/3.
56. RGIA, 1405.69.2100 and 1405.70.4803; Engelstein, *Castration and the Heavenly Kingdom: A Russian Folktale* (Cornell, 1999); A. Ia. Lipskerov, ed., *Skopcheskoe delo: Protsess Kudrinykh i drugikh 24 lits* (Moscow, 1871).
57. *Delo Mitrofanii,* I/12.
58. *Delo Mitrofanii,* II/135–136.
59. For instance, teacher Skino. *Delo Mitrofanii,* I/126, and Antonov, *Bankrupts and Usurers,* 306–307.
60. *Delo Mitrofanii,* II/137.
61. *Delo Mitrofanii,* I, 88, 126, 139–142, 157, 221–222, 250, 280–281.
62. Kozlinina, *Za polveka,* 202.
63. Kozlinina, *Za polveka,* 199.
64. *Delo Mitrofanii,* I/3. "пестрая толпа свидетелей прошла перед вами, начиная с монашествующих лиц и кончая мелкими факторами, дисконтерами и евреями. Над этой толпой царит фигура женщины, ярче всех обрисованной, в монашеском одеянии, заправляющей всем; она окружена таким штатом, такой толпой клевретов, которые при малейшем ее знаке бросаются и совершают все, что укажет эта женщина."

65. *Delo Mitrofanii,* I/10–11. See also Smirnov's speech referring to a "bunch of Jews" (*kompania evreev*). *Delo Mitrofanii,* I/68.
66. *Delo Mitrofanii,* II/106–107; 102, 105. "Кому сбыты векселя? Какие-то могилевские и минские евреи; какие-то Израильсоны, Фриденсоны, Моясы, Мейеры, Эпштейны, Россиянские, выползли из своих нор . . . Эти люди напоминают мне червей . . . как по чутью бегут они на нечистое дело; но их нет там, где идет честная и открытая сделка, а такой сделки не могло выдти из кельи Митрофании."
67. *Delo Mitrofanii.* II/115.
68. Demert, *Matushka Mitrofania,* 260. "показания которого на суде публика не могла слушать без хохота, глядя на ужимки этого обруселого еврейчика."
69. *Delo Mitrofanii,* II/16.
70. George Munro, "The Role of the Veksel' in Russian Capital Formation: A Preliminary Inquiry," in Roger Bartlett, ed., *Russia and the World of the Eighteenth Century* (Slavica, 1988); A. B. Kamenskii, *Rossia v XVIII stoletii: Obshchestvo i pamiat'* (St. Petersburg, 2017); *Delo Mitrofanii,* II/137.
71. *Delo Mitrofanii,* 180–181.
72. Kozlinina, *Za polveka,* 184ff.
73. SpbV, 1878, no. 307 (7 Nov.).
74. Urusov was required to leave the bar and serve as a judge in 1875–1881 to earn the government's forgiveness for his earlier politics (he urged the Swiss government not to extradite Sergei Nechaev to Russia).
75. SbpV, no. 296 (27 Oct.).
76. SbpV, no. 295 (26 Oct.).
77. SbpV, no. 297 (28 Oct.).
78. Dzhanshiev, *"Kak my sudili (Iz vospominanii prisiazhnogo zasedatelia)," Sbornik statei* (Moscow, 1914), 437–456.
79. SpbV, 1878, no. 298 (29 Oct.).
80. SbpV, no. 294 (25 Oct.) and no. 298 (29 Oct.).
81. SbpV, no. 293 (24 Oct.), no. 294 (26 Oct.), and no. 298 (29 Oct.).
82. SbpV, no. 297 (28 Oct.) and no. 300 (31 Oct.).
83. SbpV, no. 297 (28 Oct.).
84. GARF 109.3a.476; Koni, vol. 1, 143.
85. A. F. Rediger, *Istoria moiei zhizni,* 2 vols. (Moscow, 1999): vol. 1, 285–286.
86. SpbV, 1878, no. 302 (2 Nov.).
87. RGIA 1405.77.229, l. 4–4 ob.; GARF 109.3a.476; A. A. Polovtsov, *Russkii biograficheskii slovar',* vol. 17.
88. GARF 109.3a.476.
89. SpbV, 1878, no. 296 (27 Oct.).
90. SpbV, no. 302 (2 Nov.).

CHAPTER 10. THIEVING MASTERS

1. Moshenskii, *Rynok tsennykh bumag,* 75; N. P. Karabchevskii, "*Itogi strusbergskogo protsessa,*" in Karabchevskii, *Okolo pravosudia: Stat'i, soobshchenia i sudebnyc rechi* (St. Petersburg, 1908): 207–246.

2. Hannah Catherine Davies, *Transatlantic Speculations: Globalization and the Panics of 1873* (New York: Columbia University Press, 2018). Davies mentions Strousberg but not his raids on the Russian banks.
3. On Strousberg, see Joachim Borchart, *Der europäische Eisenbahnkönig Bethel Henry Strousberg* (Munich: C. H. Beck, 1991); Manfred Ohlsen, *Der Eisenbahnkönig Bethel Henry Strousberg: Eine preussische Gründerkarriere* (Berlin: Verlag der Nation, 1987); and his own *Strousberg und sein Wirken: Von ihm selbst geschildert* (Berlin: J. Guttentag, 1876); Ralf Roth, "Difficulties of International Railway Investments in Germany: The Example of the 'Railway King' Bethel Henry Strousberg, 1855–1875," in Ralf Roth and Guenter Dinhobl, eds., *Across the Borders: Financing the World's Railways in the Nineteenth and Twentieth Centuries* (Routledge, 2008): 33–48; Fritz Redlich, "Two Nineteenth-Century Financiers and Autobiographers: A Comparative Study in Creative Destructiveness and Business Failure," *Economy and History* 10 (1967): 37–128.
4. While the figure of Strousberg is well known to historians, his dealings with Russia and especially his trial are not.
5. Thomas C. Owen, *Russian Corporate Capitalism from Peter the Great to Perestroika* (Oxford, 1995); Owen, *The Corporation under Russian Law, 1800–1917: A Study in Tsarist Economic Policy* (Cambridge, 1991); B. V. Ananich, *Bankirskie doma v Rossii, 1860–1914 gg* (Leningrad, 1991); Ananich et al., *Kredit i banki v Rossii do nachala XX veka: Sankt-Peterburg i Moskva* (St. Petersburg, 2005); S. A. Salomatina, *Kommercheskie banki v Rossii: Dinamika i struktura operatsii, 1864–1917* (Moscow, 2004).
6. RGIA 1016.1.179.
7. Karabchevskii, *"Itogi,"* 208–209.
8. The case of Mother Mitrofania partially fits this definition, except that her motives and the charges against her more closely fit the factual situations analyzed in the previous chapter.
9. Contemporaries referred to the MCLB case as "the Bank case" or "the Strousberg case." See, e.g., RGIA 1405.73.43, l. 56 (Moscow merchants petitioning the minister of justice).
10. Keltsev, *Delo Melnitskikh;* the Ministry of Justice correspondence and Procuracy reports are in RGIA 1405.534.1350.
11. Chantal Stebbings, *The Private Trustee in Victorian England* (Cambridge, 2001).
12. Philip H. Pettit, *Equity and the Law of Trusts,* 12th ed. (Oxford, 2012): 396–414.
13. Miliukov's speech is found in *Russkoe slovo,* 12 Dec. 1916. He was charging top government officials with high treason, rather than ordinary crime.
14. "До начала всеобщего народного восстания нам необходимо придется истребить целую орду грабителей казны." B. Bazilevskii, *Gosudarstvennye prestupleniia v Rossii v XIX veke* (St. Petersburg, 1906): vol. 1, 177.
15. On influence networks in imperial Russia, see Alfred Rieber, *The Imperial Russian Project: Autocratic Politics, Economic Development, and Social Fragmentation* (Toronto: University of Toronto Press, 2017), esp. 272–298; Lovell, *Bribery and Blat;* Francis W. Wcislo, *Tales of Imperial Russia: The Life and Times of Sergei Witte, 1849–1915* (Oxford, 2011).
16. Owen, *Russian Corporate Capitalism;* Rieber, *Merchants and Entrepreneurs.*

17. Robb, *White-Collar Crime;* Taylor, *Boardroom Scandal;* Klaus, *Forging Capitalism;* Balleisen, *Fraud.* Any quantitative comparison is severely limited by our ability to access and interpret the required data. Simpson and Weisburd, *The Criminology of White-Collar Crime.*
18. Keltsev, *Delo Melnitskikh,* 148.
19. Keltsev, *Delo Melnitskikh.,* 24; RGIA 1405.534.1350, l. 31 ob.
20. RGIA 1405.534.1350, l. 10 ob.
21. RGIA 1405.534.1350, l. 38. Such practices were not unique at the time. One of the important early post-reform scandals involved Privy Councilor Ivan Semenovich Gaevskii, son of a prominent physician and medical administrator. Ivan Gaevsky directed all the educational establishments supervised by the Holy Synod, and he illegally lent out its money to private individuals. RGIA 1363.10.35.
22. Keltsev, *Delo Melnitskikh,* 101, 103, 108.
23. *Nedelia* 1882, no. 46 (14 Nov.), 1479 (mentioned Valentina's arrest in a single sentence).
24. RGIA, 1405.534.1350.
25. Keltsev, *Delo Melnitskikh,* 143 (at first Getmanchuk worked as a teacher, but when a false rumor spread that he was involved in the crime he had to leave this position and joined the judiciary).
26. RGIA, 1405.534.1350, l. 160–164. This episode seems to have had no detrimental effect on Sakharov's career, given that he remained Moscow's top investigator "for the most important cases" and retained Muraviev's most enthusiastic support into the 1880s. N. V. Muraviev, *Iz proshloi deiatelnosti,* 2 vols. (St. Petersburg, 1900): vol. 2, 256–262.
27. RUP, vol. 4, 128, and GARF 109.3a.71 (Politkovskii); Antonov, *Bankrupts and Usurers,* 148–149 (Saltykov); RSO, vol. 7, 38–41, 52–53 (Yukhantsev).
28. Keltsev, *Delo Melnitskikh,* 114.
29. Keltsev, *Delo Melnitskikh,* 211.
30. Kozlinina, *Za polveka,* 228.
31. When Ovsiannikov was awarded the rank of commercial counselor, the Ministry of the Interior inquired whether he was an Old Believer and officially determined that he was not, while "unofficially" informed that he was. RGIA 1287.2.824, l. 6, 10, 20.
32. *Nedelia* 50 (1875): 1665–1668.
33. RSO vol. 2, 559–560; *Sudebnye rechi* 3, 138–139.
34. *Nedelia* 50 (1875): 1665–1668, RSO 2, 544–545; *Sudebnye rechi* 3, 140.
35. RSO 2, 543, 560; *Sudebnye rechi* 3, 143; RGIA 1151.5.7; RGIA 1287.2.824.
36. Ananich, *Kredit i banki,* 268, 305. Other large banks established in 1870 were the Volga-Kama Commercial Bank, Warsaw Commercial Bank, and Merchant Banks in Odessa and Nizhnii Novgorod. Karabchevskii, "*Itogi,*" 212.
37. In 1859, on the eve of the Russian economic liberalization, there were ninety-four joint-stock companies in Russia, 131 in France, and 415 in Germany. Moshenskii, *Rynok tsennykh bumag,* 31.
38. Owen, *The Corporation under Russian Law* (emphasizing the obstacles to incorporation in late imperial Russia).

39. Kozlinina, *Za polveka;* Karabchevskii, *"Itogi."*
40. The state-owned mortgage bank in Moscow (*Moskovskaia sokhrannaia kazna*) by the 1870s no longer issued new loans and was a minor player, but until 1859 it had been the linchpin of Russia's credit system. Schumacher was Moscow's mayor in 1873–1876.
41. For the bill of indictment, see *Obvinitel'nyi akt, sostavlennyi tovarishchem prokurora Moskovskogo okruzhnogo suda Obninskim po delu o raznogo roda zloupotrebleniiakh, obnaruzhennykh v Moskovskom kommercheskom ssudnom banke* (Moscow, 1876); for the documents of the pretrial investigation, see *Kopii s postanovlenii i protokolov po delu o zloupotrebleniiakh v Moskovskom kommercheskom ssudnom banke,* vols. 1–2 (Moscow, 1875–1876). See *Obvinitelnyi akt,* 13; *Kopii,* III/440, 454, 472, 482, 495, I/234.
42. S. B. Saul, *The Myth of the Great Depression, 1873–1896* (Macmillan, 1969); Niek Koning, *The Failure of Agrarian Capitalism: Agrarian Politics in the UK, Germany, the Netherlands and the USA, 1846–1919* (Routledge, 1994); Davies, *Transatlantic Speculations.*
43. Davies, *Transatlantic Speculations,* 17–18.
44. Quoted in Fritz Stern, *Gold and Iron: Bismarck, Bleichröder, and the Building of the German Empire* (New York: Vintage Books, 1977): 360. "From the royal princes and the first aristocratic names down to the smallest capitalists, everybody participated in Strousberg's promotions." On his princely appearance, see Sir Edward Malet, *Shifting Scenes: Or Memories of Many Men in Many Lands* (London: John Murray, 1901): 166–167 (quoted in Stern, *Gold and Iron,* 307–308). But cf. Roth, *Across the Borders,* 37: Strousberg was successful because his early journalistic experience prepared him for public relations work, which was central to project organization and management. Also, his public appearance secured investors' trust, which too was required. Roth, *Across the Borders,* 42.
45. Roth, *Across the Borders,* 34.
46. Roth, *Across the Borders,* 38.
47. Bleichröder's words, quoted in Stern, *Gold and Iron,* 358–359.
48. Stern, *Gold and Iron,* 351–394 (this was the other "Strousberg Affair"). Bismarck wrote: "One fine day, two dukes, one general who is an aide-de-camp, a half-dozen ladies-in-waiting, twice that many chamberlains, a hundred coffeehouse owners and all the cab-men of Berlin found themselves totally ruined." Quoted in Fritz Stern, "Money, Morals, and the Pillars of Bismarck's Society," *Central European History* 3, nos. 1–2 (1970): 49–72, 55.
49. Stern, *Gold and Iron,* 344–348.
50. *Obvinitel'nyi akt,* 86.
51. RGIA 1405.73.43, l. 85 ob.–86 (Borisovskii, Givartovskii, Roeder, and Grabbe sold their stock; Schumacher, Lenivov, Vishniakov, and Millioti withdrew their deposits).
52. *Obvinitel'nyi akt,* 129.
53. Karabchevskii, *"Itogi"*; Kozlinina, *Za polveka.*
54. This discussion is from Pahlen's personal papers, RGIA 1016.1.179.
55. RGIA 1016.1.179, l. 23 ob.
56. RGIA 1016.1.179, l. 24–26 ob.
57. RGIA 1016.1.179, l. 20–21 ob.

58. RGIA 1405.73.2348, l. 301–301 ob.
59. Kozlinina, *Za polveka,* 229. Landau hired Keikuatov and Kupernik; Schumacher hired Spasovich and Shaikevich; directors Givartovskii and Krestovnikov hired Lokhvitskii. RGIA 1363.9.19, l. 189. Borisovskii hired Plevako. RGIA 1363.9.19, l. 99–111.
60. RGIA 1363.9.19–23.
61. Kozlinina, *Za polveka,* 233. She calls the lawyers' tricks (*forteli*) shameless (*bezzastenchivyi*). She reproduces the satirical poem by Petr Kicheev (who had himself been convicted of forgery and manslaughter), "Strusbergiada."
62. The commission that made payments to clients and shareholders was chaired by Plevako's former assistant, Kleist. RGIA 1405.73.2348, l. 300–301.
63. The charges are in *Obvinitelnyi akt,* 129–137.
64. On Russian economic nationalism, see Thomas C. Owen, *Dilemmas of Russian Capitalism: Fedor Chizhov and Corporate Enterprise in the Railroad Age* (Harvard, 2005); Inna Simonova, *Fedor Chizhov* (Moscow, 2002).
65. Karabchevskii, "*Itogi,*" 208.
66. At least one shareholder somehow found out about the bank's losses and sold his shares before the crash. *Obvinitel'nyi akt,* 23, and *Kopii,* III/483.
67. At the 1872 annual meeting, out of 179 votes, 107 were insiders; at the 1873 meeting—55 out of 70; at the 1874 meeting—65 out of 86, and at the last, 1875, meeting—71 out of 87. *Obvinitsl'nyi akt,* 3, 7–11. If there was any threat that outside shareholders could control the meeting, the directors would take the shares kept at the bank and temporarily distribute them to inside persons. Information about shareholder meetings was made as difficult to access as possible. Seven clerks and accountants testified at the trial that they voted at shareholder meetings even though they did not own any stock.
68. *Obvinitel'nyi akt,* 12.
69. Kozlinina, *Za polveka,* 221–240.
70. *Za polveka,* 221–222.
71. *Obvinitelnyi akt,* 4.
72. *Kopii,* III/647.
73. *Obvinitel'nyi akt,* 18–19.
74. *Obvinitel'nyi akt,* 20–21.
75. *Obvinitel'nyi akt,* 34.
76. *Obvinitel'nyi akt,* 26–32.
77. *Obvinitel'nyi akt,* 5.
78. *Obvinitelnyi akt,* 49.
79. On Landau, see *Kopii,* II/314, I/214–215, I/306, II/304, I/305.
80. *Obvinitelnyi akt,* 3.
81. *Obvinitelnyi akt,* 21.
82. *Kopii,* II/373–375, II/146.
83. Redlich, "Two Nineteenth-Century Financiers," 99.
84. *Kopii,* II/150–158.
85. *Kopii,* II/155.
86. That is, the government did not guarantee the payment of a dividend in the event the company did not bring a profit. Raising money for such unsecured ventures was more difficult.

87. *Kopii,* II/156.
88. *Obvinitelnyi akt,* 69–70.
89. *Obvinitel'nyi akt,* 71.
90. *Kopii,* II/156; *Obvinitelnyi akt,* 59–62.
91. *Obvinitel'nyi akt,* 63–64; *Kopii,* II/308–309, III/684.
92. Kozlinina, *Za polveka,* 222–223.
93. Senate's decision: RGIA 1363.9.24.
94. Strousberg's bankruptcy: RGIA 1405.75.5669.
95. RGIA 1405.75.5669. The people who suffered losses from Strousberg's activities petitioned the authorities to keep him in Russia, since he would be unreachable once he left. See, e.g., RGIA 1405.75.5669, l. 71–72 ob.
96. The Tilitgul crash and the trial of Witte: *Golos,* nos. 44, 47, 49, 50, 52 (1877); RGIA 1405.74.625.
97. Muraviev, "*Delo o zloupotrebleniakh v Skopinskom gorodskom obshchestvennom banke,*" in Muraviev, *Iz proshloi deiatelnosti,* vol. 2, 106–209, 107.
98. S. A. Salomatina, "*Bankovskii krizis 1880-kh gg. v Rossiiskoi imperii: novye kolichestvennye dannye i otsenki.*" *Istoricheskii zhurnal: Nauchnye issledovania,* no. 1 (2023): 85–108.
99. A. Bauman, ed., *Illustrirovannyi kalendar' na 1869 god* (St. Petersburg, 1869), 279–281.
100. Rykov also engaged in ordinary company fraud: he set up a well-endowed corporation to exploit nonexistent coal deposits near Skopin and attempted to use its worthless stock to secure government contracts; his agents also tried to sell bogus deposit tickets from nonexistent customers in Moscow, St. Petersburg, and Vitebsk. A. K. Khrostsitskii, "*Grandioznyi zamysel Rykova . . .,*" *RS* 140, no. 11 (1909): 343–346; RSO, vol. 2, 165–170.
101. RGIA 1405.534.1275.
102. Muraviev, *Delo.* Katkov.
103. Muraviev, *Delo,* esp. 195.

CONCLUSION

1. McReynolds, *Murder Most Russian* and *The News under Russia's Old Regime;* Stephen Frank and Mark Steinberg, eds., *Cultures in Flux: Lower-Class Values, Practices, and Resistance in Late Imperial Russia* (Princeton, 1994); Weinberg, *Blood Libel;* Robert Geraci, "Ethnic Minorities, Anthropology, and Russian National Identity on Trial: The Multan Case, 1892–96," RR 59, no. 4 (2000): 530–554.
2. Vilenskii, *Sudebnaia reforma;* Nethercott, *Russian Legal Culture,* 2, 50.
3. Wortman, *Scenarios of Power;* Wcislo, *Tales of Imperial Russia;* Pravilova, *The Ruble.*
4. Kozlinina, *Za polveka.*
5. Eric Lohr, "Tsarism, Tsarist Autocracy, and the Russian *Sonderweg,*" JMH 95, no. 1 (2023): 78–110; Christopher Read, "In Search of Liberal Tsarism: The Historiography of Autocratic Decline," *Historical Journal* 45, no. 1 (2002): 195–210.
6. Chernukha, *Vnutrenniaia politika.*
7. Soloviev, *Soiuz osvobozhdenia. Liberalnaia oppozitsia v Rossii nachala XX veka* (Moscow, 2021).
8. Goody, *The Theft of History.*

Acknowledgments

This book would never have been written without my brilliant partner and colleague, Katherine Pickering Antonova, who has read and edited the manuscript several times and supported my scholarship in myriad ways big and small. Thanks to Kate, my intellectual life has become intertwined with personal happiness.

Nothing that may be creative or interesting in this book would have emerged without mentorship from my brilliant childhood teacher, Olga S., who tragically passed away just as this manuscript was being copyedited. Olga's lifelong academic and personal passion was to awaken aesthetic and creative sensibility in her students, believing that kindness and beauty are practical and can be taught, and are indeed central to being fully human, no matter one's adult occupation.

I am also exceedingly grateful to Paul Bushkovitch for his steadfast support of my scholarship, his model collegiality, and his deep, generously shared wealth of insight, ever since I first met him while interviewing at Yale in 2016. In addition to Paul, several colleagues from Yale and other institutions have commented on the full draft or large portions of it, including Lauren Benton, Rohit De, Mikhail Dolbilov, Nancy Shields Kollmann, Dominic Lieven, Samuel Moyn, Ekaterina Pravilova, Timothy Snyder, and James Whitman, as well as three anonymous readers from Yale University Press. To Sam and Rohit I am especially grateful for their brilliant conversation, for sharing their talents as legal historians, and for understanding and supporting this project from its inception. Many others suffered through the earlier versions of the book and welcomed me at their workshops and conference panels, including Tatiana Borisova, Marijeta Bozovic, Molly Brunson, Jane Burbank, Jonathan Daly, Carolyn Dean, David Engerman, Catherine Evtuhov, Victoria Frede, Eleanor Gilburd, Kathryn Hendley, Faith Hillis, Andrey Ivanov, Yanni Kotsonis, Anne Lounsbery, Kimberly Marten, Alexander Martin, Constantin Muravnik, Victor Muskin, Steven Nafziger, Anne O'Donnell, Vanessa Ogle, Kirill Ospovat, Anatoly Pinsky, William Pomeranz, Douglas Rogers, Nari Shelekpayev, my doctoral adviser Richard Wortman, and Taisu Zhang, as well as many colleagues, friends, and archivists in Russia. Zhenya Sakal, Azat Bilalutdinov, Liudmila Sharaya, Paulina Halley, Alex O'Neill, and Alexia Dochnal saved me much time by copying archival and printed materials and editing the manuscript.

Financial support for my research came primarily from several grants from Yale's MacMillan Center and Griswold Faculty Research Fund. My archival research in Russia was supported in part by the Title VIII Research Scholar Program, which is funded by the U.S. State Department's Program for Research and Training on Eastern Europe and the Independent States of the Former Soviet Union (Title VIII) and administered by American Councils for International Education. The initial stages of this research were supported by faculty research grants from the Harriman Institute at Columbia University.

Last but not least, my mental and emotional stability during these years has been assured by two amazing gnomes who grew in stature and ability alongside the manuscript and are now incredibly kind, talented, and funny young people somewhat interested in history and much more so—in Russia and its culture.

Index